RACE CAPITAL?

RACE CAPITAL?

HARLEM AS SETTING AND SYMBOL

ANDREW M. FEARNLEY
DANIEL MATLIN, EDITORS

Columbia University Press / *New York*

Columbia University Press
Publishers Since 1893
New York   Chichester, West Sussex
cup.columbia.edu
Copyright © 2019 Columbia University Press
Paperback edition, 2021
All rights reserved

Library of Congress Cataloging-in-Publication Data

Names: Fearnley, Andrew M., editor. | Matlin, Daniel, editor.
Title: Race capital? : Harlem as setting and symbol / edited by Andrew M. Fearnley and Daniel Matlin.
Other titles: Harlem as setting and symbol
Description: New York : Columbia University Press, [2018] | Includes bibliographical references and index.
Identifiers: LCCN 2018014962 (print) | LCCN 2018041029 (ebook) | ISBN 9780231183222 (cloth) | ISBN 9780231183239 (pbk.) | ISBN 9780231544801 (electronic)
Subjects: LCSH: Harlem (New York, N.Y.)—Civilization. | Harlem (New York, N.Y.)—Intellectual life. | Harlem (New York, N.Y.)—Race relations. | New York (N.Y.)—Civilization. | New York (N.Y.)—Intellectual life. | New York (N.Y.)—Race relations. | African Americans—New York (State)—New York—History. | African Americans—New York (State)—New York—Intellectual life.
Classification: LCC F128.68.H3 (ebook) | LCC F128.68.H3 R33 2018 (print) | DDC 305.8009747/1—dc23
LC record available at https://lccn.loc.gov/2018014962

Cover design: Lisa Hamm
Cover photograph: *Three Women at a Parade, Harlem NY*, 1978. © Dawoud Bey. Courtesy of Stephen Daiter Gallery

CONTENTS

List of Figures   vii

Acknowledgments   ix

Introduction   1
ANDREW M. FEARNLEY AND DANIEL MATLIN

PART I: MYTHOLOGIES

1. From Prophecy to Preservation: Harlem as Temporal Vector   27
   ANDREW M. FEARNLEY

2. Class, Gender, and Community in *Harlem Sketches*: Representing Black Urban Modernity in Interwar African American Newspapers   47
   CLARE CORBOULD

3. Harlem: The Making of a Ghetto Discourse   71
   DANIEL MATLIN

4. What's the Matter with *Baby Sister*?: Chester Himes's Struggles to Film Harlem   91
   PAULA J. MASSOOD

PART II: MODELS

5. Harlem's Difference   111
   WINSTON JAMES

6. Black Women's Intellectual Labor and the Social Spaces
   of Black Radical Thought in Harlem   143
   MINKAH MAKALANI

7. Harlem as Culture Capital in 1920s African American Fiction   165
   CHERYL A. WALL

8. City of Numbers: Rethinking Harlem's Place in Black
   Business History   183
   SHANE WHITE

9. Harlem, USA: Capital of the Black Freedom Movement   201
   BRIAN PURNELL

10. Richard Bruce Nugent and the Queer Memory of Harlem   221
    DOROTHEA LÖBBERMANN

PART III: BLACK NO MORE?

11. Race, Class, and Gentrification in Harlem Since 1980   243
    THEMIS CHRONOPOULOS

12. When Harlem Was in *Vogue* Magazine   267
    JOHN L. JACKSON JR.

Harlem: An Afterword   285
FARAH JASMINE GRIFFIN

Contributors   289

Index   293

FIGURES

2.1 E. Simms Campbell, *A Night-Club Map of Harlem*, 1932   52
2.2 E. Simms Campbell, "Harlem Sketches," *New York Amsterdam News*, June 8, 1935   54
2.3 E. Simms Campbell, "Harlem Sketches," *Pittsburgh Courier*, January 29, 1938   57
2.4 E. Simms Campbell, "Sketches," *Pittsburgh Courier*, September 26, 1942   62
2.5 E. Simms Campbell, "Harlem Sketches," *Pittsburgh Courier*, July 9, 1938   64
6.1 Map of selected social spaces of Harlem's radical interwar intellectual life   152
11.1 Population in Central Harlem, 1950–2016   245
11.2 Occupied housing units in Central Harlem, and rentals, 1970–2016   246
11.3 Occupations of Central Harlem residents, in percentages, 1970–2016   249
11.4 Race and ethnicity in Central Harlem, 1980–2016   253
11.5 Median household income by race and ethnicity in Central Harlem, 2000–2016   255
11.6 Median household income in Central Harlem, 1980–2016   258

11.7 Median gross rent in Central Harlem, 1980–2016   260

11.8 Percentage of household income spent on housing in Central Harlem, 2000–2016   261

12.1 "Fall's Brightest, Boldest Prints Take a Trip to Harlem," *Vogue* (November 2014)   278

ACKNOWLEDGMENTS

This book had its beginnings in a colloquium hosted at Columbia University's Institute for Research in African-American Studies, July 29–30, 2015. We thank Samuel K. Roberts, Sharon Harris, and Shawn Mendoza for the generosity and warm welcome they extended to us at the institute. A grant from the Manchester Urban Institute provided essential funding during the early phase of the project, and we thank Kevin Ward for his role in facilitating this. We are grateful to all who participated in the colloquium and to all of the contributors to the book for their ideas, commitment, hard work, and patience. We also wish to thank the anonymous reviewers of the manuscript for their close and insightful readings, Christian Winting of Columbia University Press for his expertise and assistance, and Todd Manza for his valuable contribution at the copyediting stage. We owe a huge debt of gratitude to our editor, Bridget Flannery-McCoy, for her dedication to this project and all the advice and support she has given to us. Finally, our deepest thanks, as always, go to Jen and Samantha, and to Heather.

Andrew Fearnley and Daniel Matlin
Manchester and London

RACE CAPITAL?

INTRODUCTION

ANDREW M. FEARNLEY AND DANIEL MATLIN

Obituaries for black Harlem have appeared with notable regularity over the past few years. For close to a century, the name "Harlem" has been loaded with symbolic meanings that have made this narrow stretch of upper Manhattan perhaps second only to "Africa" as a spatial signifier of blackness. But a stream of recent commentary across the United States and around the world has now made Harlem almost a byword for gentrification. By the turn of the twenty-first century, shifting demographics, rising investment, a combination of renovation and new construction, and a proliferation of boutiques and fashionable restaurants were prompting palpable excitement about Harlem in some quarters of the media. After decades of disinvestment, declining population, high crime rates, and physical decay, during which Harlem had been a "no-go zone" in the eyes of many New Yorkers, a "new Harlem Renaissance" was said to be at hand, recalling the glamour of the neighborhood's fabled 1920s "heyday" and, relatedly, marking its revival as a site of recreation, consumption, and exotic spectatorship for whites. Increasingly, however, celebratory stories about Harlem's revival and rediscovery have been overtaken by anguished pronouncements that its eclipse as a black neighborhood is imminent. Commentators have pored over data showing the increase in Harlem's white and Hispanic populations for signs that a point of no return has been reached.[1]

Harlem has scarcely been alone, of course, in undergoing a rapid demographic transition and the broader processes of urban change known as gentrification. Across much of the world, a renewed vogue for city living has combined with deregulation of housing markets and urban "regeneration" policies to help usher an influx of affluent residents and consumers into neighborhoods long home to working-class, low-income, and (often) minority communities, whose hold on these neighborhoods then becomes financially precarious.[2] In Harlem's case, though, both the celebration and the anguish accompanying neighborhood change have been especially intense and voluble. Almost from its inception, black Harlem's preeminence as a site of African American and black diasporic life and consciousness has been asserted, redefined, and rehearsed so widely and frequently that the prospect of its demise assumes an importance radically out of proportion to the neighborhood's slender dimensions.

As the potency of Harlem's iconic blackness has been challenged by the quickening pace of demographic and material changes on the ground, recent work in African American and black diasporic studies has simultaneously mounted a second kind of challenge to the neighborhood's standing, through a variety of disavowals of the "Harlem-centrism" of previous scholarship. Even the idea of a "*Harlem* Renaissance" has increasingly been called into question. As the transnational turn in the humanities has opened up, and drawn new connections across, the geographic terrain of black social, political, cultural, and intellectual life, Harlem, long feted as the "capital of black America" and even as the "capital of the black world," has found itself downgraded, recast as one "province" among many scattered throughout a variegated, interconnected, and multipolar black world.[3] Enjoined to "escape from New York," how do today's scholars of Harlem respond?[4]

MAKING (AND UNMAKING) EXCEPTIONS

Underlying the long history of Harlem-centrism has been a discourse of Harlem exceptionalism that emerged during the 1920s and that would prove remarkably ingrained, and also highly adaptive, over the course of the twentieth century.[5] Its first expression lay in claims to a vanguard status for Harlem, as the neighborhood and community said to embody, more than any other, black progress and potential. And prominent among those claims was an idea—or sometimes a rhetorical device—that would resound through decades of commentary and eventually imbue black Harlem's anticipated passing with deeply ominous significance. This was the trope of Harlem as black "capital," introduced in 1925 by the philosopher and prolific author and editor Alain Locke.

In the special issue of the *Survey Graphic* that he guest-edited that year, which carried the title "Harlem: Mecca of the New Negro," Locke enthused that Harlem had become "the greatest Negro community the world has known—without counterpart in the South or in Africa." Harlem, he proclaimed, "is—or promises at least to be—a race capital. Europe seething in a dozen centers with emergent nationalities, Palestine full of a renascent Judaism—these are no more alive with the spirit of a racial awakening than Harlem; culturally and spiritually it focuses a people."[6] Like the image of the "New Negro" with which it was closely entwined, the image of Harlem was, for Locke, a vital tool to be wielded in "rehabilitating the race in world esteem from that loss of prestige for which the fate and conditions of slavery have so largely been responsible."[7] Having burst rapidly into being in the first decades of the twentieth century, black Harlem offered a fresh, seemingly attractive grounding for the portrayal of New Negro strivings and accomplishments. Harlem, Locke wrote, would serve as both "setting and symbol" in the portrayal of "our contemporary race development."[8]

For Locke and a number of other New Negro strategists and publicists, Harlem's advantages as "setting and symbol" were many. New York was by now a global icon of urban modernity and American cosmopolitanism.[9] Where better to locate the newness of New Negroes and to sunder their image from rural backwardness and agricultural peonage? New York had long since overtaken Boston to become the center of U.S. publishing, entertainment, and artistic life, and its pull was considerable for intellectuals such as Locke, who, despite his employment at Howard University in Washington, DC, would spend extensive periods in Harlem throughout the 1920s. What he and collaborators such as James Weldon Johnson, Jessie Fauset, and Charles S. Johnson were after was a "renaissance": an effusion of black arts and letters that would capture and catalyze "the spirit of a racial awakening."[10] Washington, Locke would write in 1929, might be "the capital of the nation's body," but it was "not the capital of its mind or soul." The "same forces that [had] made New York the culture-capital of America" had also "made Harlem the mecca of the New Negro and the first creative center of the Negro Renaissance."[11] It was important, too, that New York, unlike many U.S. cities, had avoided a major outbreak of racial violence in the aftermath of World War I.[12] And then there was Harlem's physical distinction among black urban neighborhoods: amid its blocks of tenements were elegant streets of town houses and apartment buildings designed for white, bourgeois occupation, where the New Negro elite of professionals and civic leaders could now live visibly dignified lives of accomplishment and service.[13]

Of greatest importance to Locke's conception of Harlem as a "race capital," however, were the size and diversity of its black population, which increased from 50,000 in 1914 to almost 165,000 in 1930.[14] "Here in Manhattan," he wrote, "is not merely the largest Negro community in the world, but the first concentration in history of so many diverse elements of Negro life."[15] Harlem was indeed an extraordinarily cosmopolitan black urban community, forged not only by black New Yorkers who relocated uptown in the wake of the white supremacist violence of the 1900 Tenderloin riot, and by black southerners who streamed into New York in the 1910s and 1920s, but also by tens of thousands of people of African descent from beyond U.S. shores. Indeed, around one in four black Harlemites during the 1920s was foreign born, with the largest contingent hailing from Britain's Caribbean colonies but significant numbers also originating from Spanish-, French-, Danish-, and Dutch-speaking Caribbean islands and from West Africa.[16] For Locke, Harlem had become "the laboratory of a great race-welding" that thrust together Africans and West Indians with "the Negro of the North and the Negro of the South."[17] As the hill towns of Italy had once yielded ambitious youths "first to Florence and then to Rome," so Harlem now drew a "quota of talent" from many black "provinces." And like other storied capitals, Harlem, in Locke's telling, was the seat of an intelligentsia, a crucible of a cultural and artistic "renaissance."[18]

More muted in Locke's writings, but of signal importance to Harlem's enduring reputation as a "capital," was its interwar emergence as a major black political center. As the headquarters of the world's largest mass black political movement, Marcus Garvey's Universal Negro Improvement Association, Harlem took on a certain aura as a locus of racial militancy, even as Garvey spoke not of the bright future in Harlem but of a necessity to "return" to the African "motherland." Prominent black socialists such as A. Philip Randolph, Chandler Owen, and Grace Campbell had their bases in Harlem, while New York also hosted the headquarters of the National Association for the Advancement of Colored People and the National Urban League. These major institutions and a flourishing black press coexisted with the street corner convocations, stepladder oratory, and grassroots activism that were hallmarks of Harlem's distinctive local political culture.[19] Women and men in interwar Harlem engaged in labor strikes, rent strikes, commercial boycotts, and other neighborhood-based protests, helping to engender a politics of "community rights" that would take root across black urban America over successive decades.[20] In 1943, the African American journalist Roi Ottley would enshrine Harlem as "the nerve center of advancing Black America. It is the fountainhead of mass movements. From it flows the progressive vitality of Negro life."[21]

A succession of black voices took up and amplified the motifs of this vanguard exceptionalism, characterizing Harlem as an outlier that carved out the path of progress for black America in its totality. In *Black Manhattan* (1930), James Weldon Johnson reiterated that "Throughout coloured America Harlem is the recognized Negro capital. Indeed, it is the Mecca for the sightseer, the pleasure-seeker, the curious, the adventurous, the enterprising, the ambitious, and the talented of the entire Negro world."[22] Jamaican-born Claude McKay, who made his name as a poet and novelist with *Harlem Shadows* (1922) and *Home to Harlem* (1928), respectively, described the neighborhood in 1940 as "the queen of black belts" and "the Negro capital of the world."[23]

Harlem exceptionalism and its "race capital" motif spread far and wide. In Britain, the *Manchester Guardian* lauded the *Survey Graphic*, in 1925, for its "amazing picture of the cultural meaning of this new capital of an oppressed race."[24] In *La Revue de Paris*, the French academic and League of Nations official Franck Schoell extolled Harlem in 1929, on the basis of his own visits, as "la seule capitale de toute une Race que je connaisse au monde" (the only capital of an entire race that I know of in the world).[25] The South African author and activist Peter Abrahams recounted in 1960 that, as a student during the late 1930s, "I dreamed of Harlem as the center of all my cultural, spiritual and racial needs. And I was one of many in South Africa, in Africa."[26]

As Harlem changed dramatically, the discourse of Harlem exceptionalism modulated and sometimes contracted. The severity of the Depression's impact during the 1930s, uprisings in the neighborhood in 1935, 1943, and 1964, and the departure of much of Harlem's famed professional and artistic elite during the decades of "urban crisis" following World War II all dented Harlem's reputation as the vanguard of black progress and achievement. The dramatic postwar growth of central Brooklyn's black population, which outnumbered Harlem's by the 1960s, and the expansion of the black community in Jamaica, Queens, also led to a decentering of black metropolitan New York.[27] Yet such was the mystique that had adhered to Harlem, and such was the investment in *place*—this place, above all—as the symbolic embodiment of black America's fate and fortunes, that claims of Harlem's preeminence, exceptionalism, and even "capital" status endured, though often in new forms.

Vanguardism increasingly gave way to other variants of exceptionalism, usually of a more tragic hue. Harlem's preeminence came to rest, for many, less on its present greatness or objective difference from other black urban communities than on its exceptional *symbolic* significance, in ways that relied on canonized notions of its past. That Harlem, of all places, had sunk into the stagnation and decay of other "ghettos" only heightened its poignancy as "setting and symbol" of black life, not least for authors such as Ann Petry, Ralph Ellison, James Baldwin, and Chester Himes, who would mine the neighborhood in celebrated postwar novels. "Harlem is a ruin," wrote Ellison in an essay of 1948, and, as such, "Harlem is the scene and symbol of the Negro's perpetual alienation in the land of his birth."[28] For Langston Hughes, famously, Harlem was not quite (or not yet) a ruin, but "a dream deferred."[29] Harlem, opined Michael Harrington a decade later, in 1961, was "much the same as any other Negro ghetto," and yet "Harlem is a Negro capital, much as New York is an unofficial American capital."[30] The word "capital" no longer denoted power and possibility so much as "hypertypicality"—Harlem as the most notorious, most visible of America's "dark ghettos."[31]

As successive immigration restrictions diminished Harlem's cosmopolitanism, and as the climate of the early Cold War suppressed black internationalism, the terms "race capital" and "capital of the black world" became less common than "capital of black America" and "Harlem, USA."[32] Even so, Harlem's "capital" designation retained echoes of its earlier meanings, not least as Malcolm X's national and international prominence in the early 1960s rekindled a sense of Harlem's political import. So, when concerned commentators began to contemplate the "loss" of black Harlem in the late twentieth century, it was not just the blackness of a neighborhood that was seen to be at stake but also the survival of "the symbolic capital of black America."[33]

Yet critiques of Harlem-centrism and Harlem exceptionalism had appeared almost from the outset. In 1928, a review in the *Greater Fisk Herald*, likely written by its literary editor, Eulace Shamberger, could already welcome W. E. B. Du Bois's novel *Dark Princess* as "refreshingly different in that it wanders from the 'inevitable Harlem,' " and urge other authors to "let Harlem rest a season."[34] A year earlier, the black educator and polymath Kelly Miller had glossed Harlem as merely "the largest case of segregation in the U.S."[35] The Washingtonian poet and Howard University professor Sterling Brown mocked the contemporary enchantment with Harlem in "Mecca" and other poems in his collection *Southern Road* (1932).[36] When the term "Harlem Renaissance" entered common usage after World War II, Brown scorned the notion. In words cited approvingly in recent scholarship that often favors the term "New Negro Renaissance," Brown posited that Harlem had been no more than the "show-window, the cashier's till" of a much wider New Negro phenomenon. "Most of the writers were not Harlemites; much of the best writing was not about Harlem," insisted Brown.[37]

Such objections notwithstanding, "Harlem Renaissance" became one of the commanding categories in the periodization and organization of twentieth-century African American literature and history, as a surge of scholarship focusing on interwar black arts, culture, and politics, much of it focused on Harlem's activists and intellectuals, met the demand for black studies programs on American campuses from the late 1960s onward and aided the incorporation of African American subject matter into increasingly multicultural college courses.[38] By the 1990s, hundreds of journal articles and book-length studies featured "Harlem Renaissance" in their titles, giving Harlem a prominence within American pedagogy that surely exceeded that of any other urban neighborhood and, indeed, of almost all American cities.[39]

The call to "let Harlem rest" now reverberated, and a reaction against Harlem-centrism steadily gathered force. Often this has involved scholars traversing a broader U.S. terrain to recover the roles of cities and locales beyond New York in fostering New Negro arts, politics, and consciousness. Important studies have explored the ways in which black intellectual life, consumer culture, entrepreneurship, popular entertainment, and political organizing all flourished in northern and western cities that were destinations of the Great

Migration, such as Chicago, and, indeed, in the cities and black campuses of the South.[40] Sometimes the phrase "Harlem Renaissance" is retained in these studies, perhaps incongruously, as when the editors of *The Harlem Renaissance in the American West* (2012) assert that "the Harlem Renaissance was a truly national phenomenon."[41]

Meanwhile, the rising popularity of transnational approaches across the humanities—in which the publication of Paul Gilroy's *The Black Atlantic: Modernity and Double Consciousness* (1993) played an influential part—has seen the critique of Harlem exceptionalism carried further by scholars who rightly stress "the international exchanges and global reach of black cultural production in the early decades of the twentieth century."[42] Harlem has increasingly served as a foil for scholars wishing to redirect attention to the wider panorama of "the transnational black world of which Renaissance-era Harlem was part."[43] In a series of moves that have elevated Paris, London, Havana, Port of Spain, and numerous other sites to new prominence as hubs of black internationalist thought and activism, the field of black diasporic studies has for the most part dispensed with the notion of a "race capital," instead foregrounding a "global New Negro context" and "provincializing Harlem."[44]

LET HARLEM REST?

How are scholars of Harlem responding to these challenges? What standing does Harlem warrant in future work in African American and black diasporic studies? This volume reappraises the neighborhood's pertinence and power in light of recent scholarship and of Harlem's ongoing transformation, offering fresh accounts of its historical and cultural significance. It recognizes that the recent interventions with regard to Harlem exceptionalism have been highly productive and invigorating, widening the scope of African American, American, and black diasporic studies. It welcomes these moves as a prompt to scrutinize anew the legions of forthright yet often casual and inchoate assertions that have accreted around this neighborhood, and to dispense with reductive claims that "throughout the world, and throughout this century, Harlem has *been* Afro-American life and culture."[45] The volume's contributors take no single position as to how the neighborhood and its symbolism should be rethought and understood. All, however, see the challenges to Harlem exceptionalism as a spur to thinking about Harlem better, not less.[46]

To this end, *Race Capital?* seeks to provide the most sustained consideration of Harlem's career as a "setting and symbol" of black life. In doing so, it builds on the foundational works of Gilbert Osofsky, Nathan Irvin Huggins, David Levering Lewis, and Houston A. Baker Jr., who established the field of Harlem scholarship, and on the works of their many successors, who have brought to this field increased attention to gender, sexuality, class, and ethnicity and to a multitude of Harlem's artistic, intellectual, political, and social formations.[47] Many of these studies have probed the disjuncture between the "sublime" imagery of interwar Harlem and the often more prosaic and embattled character of its denizens' lived experiences.[48]

Yet scholarship on Harlem remains heavily concentrated on the interwar or "renaissance" years, and, most crucially, never have the distinct and successive traditions of Harlem's exceptionalism been scrutinized in the round.[49] The twelve essays gathered in the present volume collectively range across the twentieth century and into the twenty-first, drawing together conversations that often have been fragmented by chronological and disciplinary demarcations, and reaching beyond the few intense points of focus—particularly within the interwar period—that have dominated Harlem scholarship. From vanguardism to claims of hypertypicality to recent responses to gentrification, assertions of Harlem's preeminence, exceptionalism, and capital status have endured and mutated for almost a century.

Even before the veracity of those claims is tested, the sheer persistence and pervasiveness of notions of Harlem's special character needs to be recognized as, in itself, one of the most pronounced features of modern cultural and political discourse by and about African Americans.[50] The first section of this book, "Mythologies," therefore approaches the discourse of Harlem exceptionalism as a key element of modern black life that requires explanation. How and why has Harlem been imagined and reimagined as a distinctive, divergent, indeed dominant site of black being? While these questions relate to Harlem's function as a "symbol," the book's second section, "Models," confronts more directly the question of Harlem's significance as a "setting" of black life. Mindful of recent critiques of Harlem exceptionalism, contributors here offer models for rethinking the neighborhood's location within, and contributions to, broader African American and diasporic social, political, economic, and cultural formations. By adopting comparative and connective frames, or by illuminating hidden aspects of the neighborhood's past, these scholars fashion new ways of thinking about Harlem, and demonstrate new reasons for doing so, without recourse to casual assertions of its preeminence. Finally, the section titled "Black No More?" addresses the upheavals in Harlem's real estate markets, demography, commerce, and iconography that have simultaneously reanimated the discourse of Harlem as black "capital" and placed the present and future of that status further in doubt.

In rethinking Harlem within multiple discursive, comparative, and transnational contexts, *Race Capital?* also makes a broader, methodological intervention through the various ways in which its authors attend, implicitly or explicitly, to *place*. Three currents within the volume are especially salient. The first serves to qualify the argot of, and enthusiasm for, circuits, networks, webs, and flows that has characterized much recent work in transnational studies by underscoring how such dynamic metaphors should make us more, not less, mindful of the specificities of locality and location.[51] If the need to theorize the entanglement of the local and the global calls for understandings of place that are "less bounded, more open-ended," and for recognition of the relations between metropoles and peripheries as multidirectional, it is equally important to stress how the global, transnational, and indeed national all operate through, and are inflected by, site-specific and local institutions, consciousness, and culture.[52]

Winston James's chapter both situates and differentiates Harlem among the "black contact zones" of the early twentieth-century diaspora, attending to the particular ways in which the environments of Harlem and New York City shaped, and were shaped by, black cosmopolitan intermixture and exchange. Minkah Makalani illuminates the "social spaces" of black radical thought in Harlem, revealing the intensely local nexus within which transnational actors moved and internationalist visions germinated. With geographical exceptionalisms under attack within and beyond African American studies, *Race Capital?* offers tools for non-exceptionalist reaffirmations of the indispensability of place and, more specifically, of the local.[53]

Second, the volume underscores the significance of place as a factor in the production and institutionalization of racial categories, symbolism, and social relations. Paul Kellogg, the white editor of the *Survey Graphic*, who commissioned its special Harlem number, wished to spotlight the neighborhood "in order to visualize" the "epic" of the transformation of black life through migration and urbanization.[54] As a number of essays in this volume demonstrate, Harlem's ubiquity as a symbol of black urban modernity testifies to the magnitude of the investment in place-making, both material and discursive, as a means to signify and substantiate black progress and accomplishment or to bear witness to racialized injustice and suffering.[55] As the protagonist of Warren Miller's novel *The Siege of Harlem* (1964) reflects, African Americans "had this secret space in us and now we have located it geographically and made it public for all the world to see."[56] Contributors describe how, during the late twentieth century, the meanings that had accumulated around "Harlem" informed decisions about public policy, service provision, investment, advertising, and tourism, and, crucially, how such decisions not only reinforced those meanings but also gave them a material quality in the built landscape and in social relations.[57]

And third, *Race Capital?* deepens our understanding of the symbolic functions of place that exceed, and sometimes become untethered from, spatial coordinates and the physical and social realms they demarcate. In 1966, members of the Kamoinge Workshop, a black photographic collective, presented images of urban New York, New Jersey, Virginia, Mississippi, and Bermuda under the rubric of "A Photographic Report on Harlem," explaining that they regarded Harlem "as a state of mind, whether it exists in Watts in California, the south side of Chicago, Alabama, or New York."[58] Focusing on the black press in the 1930s and 1940s, Clare Corbould's essay in the present volume attests to a longer history of "Harlem" as a sign that could oscillate between a geographic marker and a more universal embodiment of black urban modernity.

Relatedly, *Race Capital?* probes the dialectic between Harlem's discursive formations and its material conditions by foregrounding the complex interplay between "setting and symbol," as signaled by the work's subtitle. Though it forms part of the historical discourse, this phrase is nonetheless useful as a prompt for contemporary scholars to recognize the distinctions among and intersections of descriptions of Harlem "as an actual place" and Harlem's "central mythologies," thereby avoiding the temptation to read, for example, literary depictions of the neighborhood as factual, "sociological-realist" accounts.[59] Studies of Harlem must be attentive not only to conflations of symbolism and social reality but also to the disciplinary rivalries—especially between the arts and social sciences—that stoked contestations over who could speak of or for Harlem.[60] This is a crucial dimension of the discourses of Harlem exceptionalism, as is evident from Locke's insistence that "formulae" were "out of joint with fact in Harlem," and from later black writers' rejections of "the clichés of sociology."[61] The present volume draws together contributors from several scholarly disciplines—history, urban studies, anthropology, literary studies, and visual studies—with the intention of recognizing the disciplinary conflations and conflicts that produced the storehouse of imagery which has played its part in constituting the place that is Harlem.

WHAT FOLLOWS

"Let me explain this to you," said J. L. Chestnut Jr., who had worked as a lawyer in Selma, Alabama, during the peak years of the southern civil rights campaigns of the 1960s. "If you were black and of my generation, Harlem was almost a mythical place." Harlem, he told an interviewer, was where black people hoped to find "freedom and rest and peace and dignity" and where "all of the black heroes" were.[62] The first section of this book, "Mythologies," confronts an album of images that together suggest the variety, complexity, and persistence of claims about Harlem's special character and explores the roles these mythologies have played within black thought, culture, and politics. While ideas of promised lands, or what Richard Wright called acts of "imagining a place where everything was possible," had long given form to the African American cultural and political imaginations, no other location during the twentieth century became such an intense focus of black hopes—and disappointments—as Harlem.[63]

The four chapters in this section address how such mythologies emerged and were entrenched, adapted, and contested. They describe how Harlem's complex symbolism often gave shape and definition to larger cultural and political propositions, as the anthropologist Arjun Appadurai suggests images of place more generally can do.[64] While four case studies cannot furnish a complete portrait, they work toward a more precise and systematic delineation and exploration of the master tropes of Harlem discourse than past studies have offered, and they clarify the contexts in which, and mechanisms by which, this constellation of images came into being. Together they reveal the roles of different aesthetic tendencies, representational techniques, and media in the formation of Harlem's mythologies and their elevation into metonyms for broader ideas and ideals.

The longevity and protean quality of claims about Harlem's special character are captured in Andrew M. Fearnley's chapter. Over the course of the twentieth century, Fearnley argues, Harlem's key symbolic frameworks were the products of attempts to ground visions of black life not only in place but also in time. If Walter Benjamin would take Paris to be the "capital of the nineteenth century," Harlem, for Alain Locke, was to be a capital for "African peoples in their contact with Twentieth-Century civilization."[65] Yet, in the writings of Locke and other Harlem publicists during the 1920s, the neighborhood's claim on such a status was frequently qualified by being displaced into the near future. Later, when Harlem's image darkened, accounts of its exceptionalism were recalibrated through an alternative temporal framework, with the neighborhood frequently celebrated as the "historic" black capital. Exploring this shift in temporal declensions, from futurity to a "wasness" that was rhetorically and materially embedded by institutions such as the Schomburg Center for Research in Black Culture in the late twentieth century, Fearnley shows how the modulating discourses of Harlem exceptionalism have been tied to, and structured by, successive orders of time, and how Harlem has functioned symbolically, in part, as a means of confronting or projecting the historical trajectory of black people in the modern world.[66]

The question of how far black people's engagement with Harlem's symbolic discourses extended—geographically and socially—is at the heart of Clare Corbould's chapter. Corbould examines the circulation of Harlem imagery through the cartoons of E. Simms Campbell, which were widely syndicated in African American newspapers as *Harlem Sketches* during the late 1930s and early 1940s. In doing so, she looks beyond elite discourse to trace the role of the black press in reflecting, shaping, and disseminating images of Harlem within the spheres of popular black thought and culture. Only occasionally did Campbell's cartoons evoke scenes unique to, or even visually located within, Harlem. Yet the printing of these images under the title of *Harlem Sketches*, by newspapers with hundreds of thousands of black readers throughout the United

States and the Caribbean, was an important means by which Harlem became widely established as a symbol of black urban modernity.[67] Diverging from the idealizations favored by some New Negro strategists, Campbell's often wry cartoons conjured Harlem as a capital of a different kind: a concentrated manifestation of the tensions of class, gender, ethnicity, and sexuality, as well as of the bonds of blood and affection, that constituted community and defined black urban experience. It was this idea that Campbell's fellow newspaperman Roi Ottley likely had in mind when he suggested that "to grasp the inner meanings of life in Black America, one must put his finger on the pulse of Harlem."[68]

Harlem's changing iconography over the course of the twentieth century typically has been characterized as a linear shift from celebrated "capital" to lamented "ghetto." However, Daniel Matlin's chapter demonstrates that these two dominant tropes of Harlem developed not sequentially but simultaneously. That we might think otherwise, Matlin argues, owes much to the efforts of certain New Negro publicists to suppress Harlem's incipient ghetto discourse, which exposed the hard realities of segregation on which their optimistic, exceptionalist forecasts for the neighborhood would soon run aground. In the tension between "race capital" and "ghetto," Matlin sees Harlem's symbolism as structured by competing strategies for racial advancement and by the intrinsic ambiguities of "congregation," the principal mode of African American place-making that sought to turn segregated spaces into vibrant settings and symbols of collective black flourishing.[69]

If Harlem's ghetto discourse emerged fitfully in the 1920s, in the decades after World War II Harlem became "the universal symbol for the Negro ghetto."[70] Film and photography were integral to this process, just as visual culture had magnified Harlem as symbolic of black urban life during the interwar period.[71] In her contribution to this volume, Paula J. Massood considers how questions of aesthetics figured in debates about Harlem's representation during the 1960s. Massood focuses on the frustrated efforts of Chester Himes, the African American author celebrated for his ludic approach to form, to bring his little-known script *Baby Sister* to the cinema screen. Exploring the reasons for Himes's failure, Massood conveys the resistance certain representations of Harlem met with as they shifted across media, from publishing houses to film studios, as well as the profound investment that sections of the black elite maintained, as late as the 1960s, in the mythologies of Harlem as an emblem of racial uplift. Resistance to *Baby Sister* stemmed not only from the script's extravagant portraits of Harlem's criminality, female sexuality, juvenile delinquency, and abject poverty, which by now were pervasive tropes, but also from Himes's attempt to portray what he called "the *absurd* racism of which blacks in the ghettos have been victims," and to capture "the kind of reality that you find in Harlem" by presenting "a rather jumbled and confused picture."[72] As Massood demonstrates, *Baby Sister*'s willful jumbling of the conventions of urban aesthetics proved as consequential as its rattling of the National Association for the Advancement of Colored People, which persistently sought to quash "sensationalized" portrayals of Harlem.[73]

In the volume's second section, "Models," contributors offer a series of new approaches to comprehending Harlem's significance and distinctiveness by reconsidering the neighborhood's specificity and its location and lines of interconnection within broader national and diasporic configurations. These six chapters point to diverse, sometimes divergent pathways for future scholarship but share a conviction that the study of this neighborhood is far from exhausted. Each offers bold ways of theorizing Harlem anew, and together they establish foundations and agendas that should galvanize further discussion and research.

The first three chapters of "Models" manifest the varied positions Harlem scholars are staking out in the wake of recent critiques of Harlem exceptionalism. Winston James mounts a forthright reassertion of "Harlem's difference," furnishing new evidence to argue that in the first half of the twentieth century this neighborhood stood apart from all other sites with which it is now compared, within and outside the United States. In the most panoramic and determinedly comparative analysis of interwar Harlem undertaken for many years, James examines the structural factors that shaped the community's formation and development and argues that black Harlem's singularity and preeminence were rooted in the rapidity of its emergence, the diversity and cosmopolitanism of its residents, the density and "propinquity" of their living conditions, and the community's sheer size. These conditions, and Harlem's situation within New York City, underlay the vibrant and churning social, political, intellectual, and artistic life that gave Harlem its renown, and, James insists, scholars who imply an equivalence with other black settlements commit a category error, so great was Harlem's difference. Harlem may have been a "node" within the circuitry of black internationalism that joined New York with Chicago, Paris, London, Puerto Limón, and myriad other sites, but, he argues, it was *primus inter non-pares*.

Minkah Makalani, meanwhile, takes a finely wrought, granular approach to locality in reappraising the flourishing interwar intellectual life that has been a cornerstone of Harlem's "race capital" reputation. Focusing on the "social spaces of black radical thought"—the dense tapestry of political groupings, informal meetings, lyceums, and street corner lectures that overlay Harlem's landscape—Makalani shows that the entrenched image of Harlem intellectuals as a pantheon of male autodidacts has obscured the social and institutional foundations of Harlem's intellectual life and, crucially, the intellectual labor of the black women who laid many of those foundations. Grace Campbell, Williana Jones Burroughs, Elizabeth Hendrickson, and other female activist intellectuals not only instigated and sustained organizations and forums that gave Harlem radicalism energy and form but also, in doing so, broadened the scope of black left politics beyond the male worker to encompass the Harlem community itself—women and men, consumers and tenants, workers and the unemployed—as an agent of social change. Makalani demonstrates that even internationalist discourse and activism take place *somewhere*, in particular neighborhoods, along certain avenues, and in specific buildings and rooms. Every locality has its distinctiveness and, for Makalani, Harlem's constellation of sites and groupings did not make the neighborhood "*the* center" of black radical thought. Rather, they indicate how Harlem's particular modes of interaction and interconnection textured its political and social fabric—and how histories that ignore the social and spatial dimensions of intellectual life are bound to reinforce the masculinist imagery that Harlem's "race capital" discourse has inscribed.

Turning a fresh eye to African American fiction, Cheryl A. Wall also moves against Lockean conceptions of Harlem as "race capital." Such formulations are perniciously hierarchical, Wall argues, figuring the Great Migration as "a victory march from the feudal to the modern" and embodying "U.S. black exceptionalism at its worst."[74] Yet Wall maintains that for black literary authors in the 1920s, Harlem "exerted an imaginative pull" that no other U.S. locale did. In James Weldon Johnson's alternative notion of Harlem as a "culture capital," Wall finds a means of theorizing how black fiction writers both responded to and extended a conception of Harlem as the most cosmopolitan, dynamic, and generative site of a vernacular, proletarian, and egalitarian black urban culture. Far from portraying Harlem as modernity's triumphant offspring, authors such as Rudolph Fisher, Claude McKay, Zora Neale Hurston, and Wallace Thurman located Harlem's significance in the vernacular cultural forms that were precipitating there under conditions of heightened density, multiplicity, and pressure. These emerged as much from the constraints and frictions of class, gender, region, ethnicity, and sexuality as from the freedoms and commonalities that life in Harlem entailed. The new urban idioms they heard among Harlem's hipsters, musicians, and street corner orators spurred these authors' literary experimentation through the bending of form and genre.[75] Though Wall focuses on fiction writers—and while Harlem's music is one of several important subjects to which this volume is, regrettably, unable to do justice—her chapter helps explain the expansive appeal Harlem held for other artists and creative figures and why, in the mid-1930s, the zoot suit was sometimes called the "Harlem Drape" and the Kansas-born trumpeter Buck Clayton's band, formed in Los Angeles, appeared as the Harlem Gentlemen while in China.[76]

The remaining three chapters of "Models" each underscore the need for new accounts of Harlem by revealing previously ignored or underappreciated aspects of the neighborhood's past that have potential to reshape African American business history, civil rights historiography, and queer studies, respectively. Shane White's chapter on Harlem's gambling phenomenon, numbers, imbues the phrase "race capital" with an alternative, financial meaning. For White, Harlem's significance during the first half of the twentieth century rests not only on the political, cultural, and artistic innovations it engendered but also on the wealth—the racial *capital*—that accrued from Harlemites' business acumen and, in significant part, from the neighborhood's underground economy. Numbers, White argues, was "a signal contribution to the New Negro phenomenon," one that "grew out of, marked the rhythms of, and altered the daily course of life in Harlem," generating much of the "capital" that flowed through the neighborhood and underwrote more widely discussed aspects of its renown. Attending to numbers and the broader underground economy not only elevates Harlem's standing within African American business history but also forces scholars to rethink business history's parameters.

Along related lines, Brian Purnell argues that scholarship on the black freedom struggle has never adequately recognized the nature and magnitude of Harlem's role—notwithstanding critiques of Harlem-centrism, and despite much recent attention to the urban North. For much of the twentieth century, Purnell insists, the neighborhood served as a key organizational hub—an incubator of labor activism and protest strategies and a training ground for nationally and internationally significant activists. Venturing beyond the interwar period with which Harlem's political importance is often associated, Purnell argues that the neighborhood occupied a pivotal position within the organizational and communications networks that launched and sustained the major civil rights and black power mobilizations from the 1940s through the late 1960s. Harlem, he suggests, functioned as a "return address" for the long black freedom struggle, a site at which nationally prominent activists and thinkers convened and from which they carried ideas and tactics to a multitude of theaters of struggle. In doing so, Purnell shows that movement leaders A. Philip Randolph, Adam Clayton Powell Jr., and Ella Baker were just as anchored in Harlem's political culture as were Marcus Garvey and Malcolm X and that Harlem was crucial not only to Garvey's Universal Negro Improvement Association but also to the March on Washington mobilizations, and even influenced the Montgomery Bus Boycott. For all of these reasons and more, Purnell argues, Harlem warrants recognition as the "capital of America's black freedom movement."

Harlem has certainly not been neglected by scholars of sexuality and queer studies; indeed, these fields have produced some of the most innovative perspectives on Harlem in recent years.[77] Yet, as Dorothea Löbbermann's chapter shows, recent moves within African American studies to downgrade Harlem's significance threaten to obscure its crucial role as a "setting and symbol" of queer life, literature, and culture. Building on new geographic models within queer studies, which have critiqued the conflation of gay liberation and the urban, Löbbermann reasserts the importance of place, and of Harlem, to studies of black and queer life and, in doing so, poses new questions about the intersections of temporalities and genres. Focusing on the bohemian writer, visual artist, and actor Richard Bruce Nugent, Löbbermann demonstrates how Nugent functioned both as a historical agent, present during Harlem's toniest years, and as a contributor to the period's historiography, helping to shape the memory of "Queer Harlem," particularly in the 1970s and 1980s. Löbbermann conveys the complex and intricate nature of Nugent's work and shows how the deliberate ambiguities of his corpus often run counter to the various attempts to appropriate him within linear and teleological narratives, including those of gay liberation. Nugent's influence on both sides of history, as actor and chronicler, was seldom straightforward. As Löbbermann's chapter indicates, there remains much to discover about the complexities, fluidities, and ambiguities of Harlem's queer space and memory.

The two chapters composing the volume's final section address the late twentieth- and early twenty-first-century transformations that have led residents and commentators to pose the question "Will Harlem soon be black no more?"[78] Themis Chronopoulos offers a wide-ranging exploration of the demographic, socioeconomic, and policy trends that underlie this question. Tracking Harlem's population shifts since the 1980s, Chronopoulos portrays an increasingly multiethnic, multiracial Harlem. As part of what some scholars have termed the "Latinization of New York," Latinxs, who had long been a dominant presence in neighboring East Harlem, now settled across Fifth Avenue in rising numbers to become Central Harlem's fastest growing population group in the 1980s and 1990s—a phenomenon that, in January 2017, contributed to the Dominican American Adriano D. Espaillat succeeding the African American politicians who had, since 1945, continuously represented in the United States Congress the district that includes Harlem.[79]

Middle-class African Americans, who had departed Harlem in large numbers for New York's outer boroughs and suburbs in the decades following World War II, also have been conspicuous as newcomers to the neighborhood since the 1980s. But it is the presence of significant numbers of white residents, for the first time in generations, alongside the displacement of poorer African Americans, that has stoked anxieties that black Harlem faces eclipse. Harlem's accelerating gentrification, Chronopoulos argues, must be understood as a consequence of New York City's neoliberal municipal governance and housing policies over several decades, which have brought about dramatic instances of displacement, replacement, and exclusion. Yet, as the period of David Dinkins's mayoralty indicated in the early 1990s, there are alternatives, and it is within the power of those responsible for contemporary New York's housing policy to curtail the pressures that have placed Harlem out of reach of many who once considered it their home.

John L. Jackson Jr. brings a different set of questions to bear on Harlem's recent transformations, seeking to understand how the meanings invested in the neighborhood have been shifting in their midst. Jackson explores "two competing conceptions of what we might call *racial capital*, in an economic or quasi-economic sense, both of which circulate in and around black inner-city areas in general and Harlem, the mythologized 'race capital,' in particular." The first is a vernacular African American economic discourse that views black urban places as a form of communal property, essential for collective empowerment and racial identity. From this vantage point, black displacement from Harlem signifies a broader, existential threat. The second form of "racial capital" is the valuable currency that is extracted from constructions of historic Harlem by agents of gentrification, including those commentators and media platforms that have heralded a "new Harlem Renaissance." Paying particular attention to fashion magazines, Jackson shows how a selective, manicured view of Harlem's racial past is packaged for consumption, and "sells" Harlem's "multiracial present."

What would it mean, Farah Jasmine Griffin wonders in her afterword, if Harlem is now reaching the time that James Weldon Johnson imagined, in 1925, was "still very far in the future," when black people would no longer "be able to hold Harlem"?[80] Griffin reminds us that if change has been Harlem's constant, the struggle to define that change has always been a hallmark of its community. Even in the present, she finds a sense of, if not optimism, then certainly of hope among residents. If "Harlem" did not exist, then people of color would once again need to invent such a place, Griffin suggests—to fortify themselves against the ravages of racial violence and to nourish a sense of place in the world.

As early as 1978, one group of urban developers recognized that "although the name 'Harlem' has become tarnished in recent years, it is a highly marketable name" with "an extremely high recognition factor no matter where one is on the globe."[81] They foresaw well how Harlem's extraordinary career as a symbol of blackness could provide a means of circumventing the connotations the neighborhood had acquired in the postwar era of urban uprisings, hypersegregation, and disinvestment. Four decades later, at a moment when the neighborhood's historic blackness features in the names of its main boulevards and its multimillion-dollar condominiums, Harlem's past and present continue to be deeply entangled and contested. It is at these conjunctions, where conflicting uses of space and accounts of history meet, that Harlem—as setting and symbol—will be reconfigured.

NOTES

1. The *New York Times* reported in 2010 that the black population of Central Harlem—the historic heart of black settlement north of Central Park—had fallen to its lowest level since the 1920s, at 77,000, which was 60 percent of Central Harlem's total population. See Sam Roberts, "No Longer Majority Black, Harlem Is in Transition," *New York Times*, January 5, 2010, http://www.nytimes.com/2010/01/06/nyregion/06harlem.html. Claims of

black Harlem's demise, or imminent demise, include Michael Henry Adams, "The End of Black Harlem," *New York Times*, May 27, 2016, http://www.nytimes.com/2016/05/29/opinion/sunday/the-end-of-black-harlem.html; Rose Hackman, "What Will Happen When Harlem Becomes White?," *Guardian*, May 13, 2015, https://www.theguardian.com/us-news/2015/may/13/harlem-gentrification-new-york-race-black-white; Bill Maxwell, "As Black Capital of America Harlem Will Soon Be a Memory," *Korea Times*, April 6, 2010, https://www.koreatimes.co.kr/www/news/opinon/2016/11/160_63718.html; Leslie Gordon Goffe, "The Harlem Gentrification: From Black to White," *New African*, June 25, 2014, http://newafricanmagazine.com/harlem-gentrification-black-white. For enthusiastic coverage of Harlem's transformation, see "Harlem Renaissance," *Vanity Fair* (September 2001), 192–93; "The Everything Guide to Harlem," *New York Magazine* (February 6, 2011), http://nymag.com/guides/everything/harlem.

2. Sharon Zukin, *Naked City: The Death and Life of Authentic Urban Places* (New York: Oxford University Press, 2010); Loretta Lees, Hyun Bang Shin, and Ernesto López-Morales, eds., *Global Gentrifications: Uneven Development and Displacement* (Bristol: Policy, 2015).

3. Lara Putnam, "Provincializing Harlem: The 'Negro Metropolis' as Northern Frontier of a Connected Caribbean," *Modernism/Modernity* 20 (September 2013): 469–84.

4. Davarian L. Baldwin and Minkah Makalani, eds., *Escape from New York: The New Negro Renaissance Beyond Harlem* (Minneapolis: University of Minnesota Press, 2013).

5. Harlem exceptionalism is identified and critiqued in James Edward Smethurst, *The Black Arts Movement: Literary Nationalism in the 1960s and 1970s* (Chapel Hill: University of North Carolina Press, 2005), 114; Shannon King, *Whose Harlem Is This, Anyway?: Community Politics and Grassroots Activism During the New Negro Era* (New York: New York University Press, 2015), 3–4.

6. Alain Locke, "Harlem," *Survey Graphic* 6 (March 1925): 629.

7. Alain Locke, "Enter the New Negro," *Survey Graphic* 6 (March 1925): 633.

8. Alain Locke, draft letter, October 25, 1924, box 164-88, folder 5, Alain Locke Papers, Moorland-Spingarn Research Center, Howard University, Washington, DC.

9. Thomas Bender, *The Unfinished City: New York and the Metropolitan Idea* (New York: New Press, 2002).

10. See especially David Levering Lewis, *When Harlem Was in Vogue* (New York: Alfred A. Knopf, 1981).

11. Alain Locke, "Beauty and the Provinces," *Stylus* (June 1929), reprinted in *The Works of Alain Locke*, ed. Charles Molesworth (New York: Oxford University Press, 2012), 221–22.

12. Kevin McGruder has argued that white opposition to African Americans' moves into Harlem had a qualitatively different character than that found in other U.S. cities. McGruder, *Race and Real Estate: Conflict and Cooperation in Harlem, 1890–1920* (New York: Columbia University Press, 2015).

13. James Weldon Johnson, "The Making of Harlem," *Survey Graphic* 6 (March 1925): 635. See also Gilbert Osofsky, *Harlem: The Making of a Ghetto—Negro New York, 1890–1930* (New York: Harper and Row, 1966), 89–90, 111–12, 119–20.

14. Osofsky, *Harlem*, 105, 130.

15. Locke, "Harlem," 630.

16. Osofsky, *Harlem*, 46–50, 131; Winston James, "Harlem's Difference," present volume.

17. Locke, "Harlem," 630.

18. Locke, "Beauty and the Provinces," 221. See also Jeffrey C. Stewart, *The New Negro: The Life of Alain Locke* (New York: Oxford University Press, 2018), 450–51.

19. Clare Corbould, *Becoming African Americans: Black Public Life in Harlem, 1919–1939* (Cambridge, MA: Harvard University Press, 2009), 18–56; Winston James, *Holding Aloft*

the Banner of Ethiopia: Caribbean Radicalism in Early Twentieth-Century America (New York: Verso, 1998); Minkah Makalani, *In the Cause of Freedom: Radical Black Internationalism from Harlem to London, 1917–1939* (Chapel Hill: University of North Carolina Press, 2011), 23–69; Irma Watkins-Owens, *Blood Relations: Caribbean Immigrants and the Harlem Community, 1900–1930* (Bloomington: Indiana University Press, 1996), 92–111.

20. King, *Whose Harlem Is This, Anyway?*
21. Roi Ottley, *New World A-Coming: Inside Black America* (Boston: Houghton Mifflin, 1943), 1.
22. James Weldon Johnson, *Black Manhattan* (New York: Alfred A. Knopf, 1930), 3.
23. Claude McKay, *Harlem: Negro Metropolis* (New York: E. P. Dutton, 1940), 16.
24. "Harlem," *Manchester Guardian* (April 23, 1925), 18.
25. Franck L. Schoell, "La 'Renaissance Nègre' aux Etats-Unis," *La Revue de Paris* (January 1, 1929), 131.
26. Peter Abrahams, "The Meaning of Harlem," *Holiday* (June 1960), 137.
27. Brian Purnell, *Fighting Jim Crow in the County of Kings: The Congress of Racial Equality in Brooklyn* (Lawrence: University of Kentucky Press, 2013).
28. Ralph Ellison, "Harlem Is Nowhere" (1948), in *The Collected Essays of Ralph Ellison*, ed. John F. Callahan (New York: Modern Library, 2003), 321. Alain Locke's characterization of Harlem as "setting and symbol" even reverberated in the 1965 Moynihan Report on the black urban family, which pronounced Harlem "the center and symbol of the urban life of the Negro American." United States Department of Labor, Office of Policy Planning and Research, *The Negro Family: The Case for National Action* (Washington, DC: U.S. Government Printing Office, 1965), 19.
29. Langston Hughes, *Montage of a Dream Deferred* (1951), reprinted in *The Collected Poems of Langston Hughes*, ed. Arnold Rampersad and David Roessel (New York: Vintage Classics, 1995), 387–429, esp. 426.
30. Michael Harrington, "Harlem Today," *Dissent* 8 (Summer 1961): 371.
31. Kenneth B. Clark, *Dark Ghetto: Dilemmas of Social Power* (New York: Harper and Row, 1965). On Harlem's hypertypicality, see Smethurst, *Black Arts Movement*, 110.
32. Still, John Henrik Clarke averred that "Harlem has been called, and may well be, the cultural and intellectual capital of the black race in the Western world." Clarke, ed., *Harlem, USA* (Berlin: Seven Seas, 1964), 12.
33. Elliott D. Lee, "Will We Lose Harlem? The Symbolic Capital of Black America is Threatened by Gentrification," *Black Enterprise* (June 1981): 191–200.
34. Book review, *Greater Fisk Herald* 3 (June 1928): 27. We thank our fellow contributor Clare Corbould for sharing this quotation.
35. Kelly Miller, quoted in King, *Whose Harlem Is This, Anyway?*, 187.
36. James de Jongh, *Vicious Modernism: Black Harlem and the Literary Imagination* (Cambridge: Cambridge University Press, 1990), 20.
37. Sterling Brown, quoted in Davarian L. Baldwin, "Introduction: New Negroes Forging a New World," in Baldwin and Makalani, *Escape from New York*, 2, and 22, note 4. On the retrospective coining of "Harlem Renaissance" and Brown's opposition to it, see Andrew M. Fearnley, "When the Harlem Renaissance Became Vogue: Periodization and the Organization of Postwar American Historiography," *Modern Intellectual History* 11 (April 2014): 59–87, esp. 72–73.
38. Fearnley, "When the Harlem Renaissance Became Vogue," 78–86.
39. A few landmark works amid this deluge include Nathan Irvin Huggins, *Harlem Renaissance* (New York: Oxford University Press, 1971); Arna Bontemps, ed., *The Harlem Renaissance Remembered: Essays* (New York: Dodd, Mead, 1972); Lewis, *When Harlem Was in*

Vogue; Houston A. Baker Jr., *Modernism and the Harlem Renaissance* (Chicago: University of Chicago Press, 1987); Cheryl A. Wall, *Women of the Harlem Renaissance* (Bloomington: Indiana University Press, 1995); George Hutchinson, *The Harlem Renaissance in Black and White* (Cambridge, MA: Belknap Press of Harvard University Press, 1995).

40. See, especially, Davarian L. Baldwin, *Chicago's New Negroes: Modernity, the Great Migration, and Black Urban Life* (Chapel Hill: University of North Carolina Press, 2007); Darlene Clark Hine and John McCluskey Jr., eds., *The Black Chicago Renaissance* (Urbana: University of Illinois Press, 2012); Emily Lutenski, *West of Harlem: African American Writers and the Borderlands* (Lawrence: University Press of Kansas, 2015); Gabriel A. Briggs, *The New Negro in the Old South* (New Brunswick, NJ: Rutgers University Press, 2015).

41. Cary D. Wintz and Bruce A. Glasrud, "Introduction: The Harlem Renaissance in the West," in *The Harlem Renaissance in the American West: The New Negro's Western Experience*, ed. Bruce A. Glasrud and Cary D. Wintz (New York: Routledge, 2012), 1. See also the series of nine geographically focused entries on U.S. locations outside New York listed in Cary D. Wintz and Paul Finkelman, eds., *Encyclopedia of the Harlem Renaissance* (New York: Routledge, 2004), 1:xv–xvi.

42. Adam McKible and Suzanne W. Churchill, "Introduction: In Conversation—The Harlem Renaissance and the New Modernist Studies," *Modernism/Modernity* 20 (September 2013): 429; Paul Gilroy, *The Black Atlantic: Modernity and Double Consciousness* (London: Verso, 1993).

43. Putnam, "Provincializing Harlem," 471.

44. Baldwin, "Introduction," 21; Putnam, "Provincializing Harlem"; Baldwin and Makalani, *Escape from New York*; Brent Hayes Edwards, *The Practice of Diaspora: Literature, Translation, and the Rise of Black Internationalism* (Cambridge, MA: Harvard University Press, 2003); Makalani, *In the Cause of Freedom*; Marc Matera, *Black London: The Imperial Metropolis and Decolonization in the Twentieth Century* (Berkeley: University of California Press, 2015); Darlene Clark Hine, Trica Danielle Keaton, and Stephen Small, eds., *Black Europe and the African Diaspora* (Urbana: University of Illinois Press, 2009). Among the earliest studies to adopt this expansive geographic approach were Melvin Dixon, "Rivers Remembering Their Source: Comparative Studies in Black Literary History—Langston Hughes, Jacques Roumain, and Negritude," in *Afro-American Literature: The Reconstruction of Instruction*, ed. Dexter Fisher and Robert B. Stepto (New York: Modern Language Association, 1979), 25–43; Michel Fabre, *From Harlem to Paris: Black American Writers in France, 1840–1980* (Urbana: University of Illinois Press, 1991).

45. Nathan Irvin Huggins, "Harlem on My Mind" (1979), in Nathan Irvin Huggins, *Revelations: American History, American Myths*, ed. Brenda Smith Huggins (New York: Oxford University Press, 1995), 21 (emphasis added).

46. The present volume and its authors' other publications join a number of recent studies, often focused on the interwar period, that have opened up important new vistas in Harlem scholarship, including Jacob S. Dorman, *Chosen People: The Rise of American Black Israelite Religions* (New York: Oxford University Press, 2013); LaShawn Harris, *Sex Workers, Psychics, and Numbers Runners: Black Women in New York City's Underground Economy* (Urbana: University of Illinois Press, 2016); Cheryl D. Hicks, *Talk With You Like a Woman: African American Women, Justice, and Reform in New York, 1890–1935* (Chapel Hill: University of North Carolina Press, 2010); King, *Whose Harlem Is This, Anyway?*; McGruder, *Race and Real Estate*; Jeffrey O. G. Ogbar, ed., *The Harlem Renaissance Revisited: Politics, Arts, and Letters* (Baltimore, MD: Johns Hopkins University Press, 2010); Catherine Rottenberg, ed., *Black Harlem and the Jewish Lower East Side: Narratives Out of Time* (Albany: State University of New York Press, 2013).

47. For foundational texts, see especially Osofsky, *Harlem*; Huggins, *Harlem Renaissance*; Lewis, *When Harlem Was in Vogue*; Baker, *Modernism and the Harlem Renaissance*. The subsequent literature is vast, though a few highlights pertaining to the subjects mentioned here are Ann Elizabeth Carroll, *Word, Image, and the New Negro: Representation and Identity in the Harlem Renaissance* (Bloomington: Indiana University Press, 2005); Erin D. Chapman, *Prove It on Me: New Negroes, Sex, and Popular Culture in the 1920s* (New York: Oxford University Press, 2012); George Chauncey, *Gay New York: Gender, Urban Culture, and the Making of the Gay Male World, 1890–1940* (New York: Basic Books, 1994); Barbara Foley, *Spectres of 1919: Class and Nation in the Making of the New Negro* (Urbana: University of Illinois Press, 2003); Cheryl Lynn Greenberg, "Or Does It Explode?": *Black Harlem in the Great Depression* (New York: Oxford University Press, 1991); de Jongh, *Vicious Modernism*; Martha Jane Nadell, *Enter the New Negroes: Images of Race in American Culture* (Cambridge, MA: Harvard University Press, 2004); Watkins-Owens, *Blood Relations*.
48. Henry Louis Gates Jr., "Harlem on Our Minds," *Critical Inquiry* 24 (Autumn 1997): 10.
49. Besides publications by authors of the present volume that are cited elsewhere in its pages, the relatively few studies that give detailed attention to Harlem in the period since World War II include Arnold Rampersad, *The Life of Langston Hughes*, vol. 2, *1941–1967: I Dream a World* (New York: Oxford University Press, 1988); Martha Biondi, *To Stand and Fight: The Struggle for Civil Rights in Postwar New York City* (Cambridge, MA: Harvard University Press, 2003); Peniel E. Joseph, "Malcolm X's Harlem and Black Power Activism," in *Neighborhood Rebels: Black Power at the Local Level*, ed. Peniel E. Joseph (New York: Palgrave Macmillan, 2010), 21–44; Smethurst, *Black Arts Movement*, esp. 100–178; Monique M. Taylor, *Harlem Between Heaven and Hell* (Minneapolis: University of Minnesota Press, 2002); Brian D. Goldstein, *The Roots of Urban Renaissance: Gentrification and the Struggle over Harlem* (Cambridge, MA: Harvard University Press, 2017); David J. Maurrasse, *Listening to Harlem: Gentrification, Community, and Business* (New York: Routledge, 2006).
50. The rhetorical and ideological roles of sibling urban discourses are scrutinized in Robert Beauregard, *Voices of Decline: The Postwar Fate of U.S. Cities* (Oxford: Blackwell, 1993); Carlo Rotella, *October Cities: The Redevelopment of Urban Literature* (Berkeley: University of California Press, 1998).
51. In a similar vein, see Daniel T. Rodgers, "Introduction: Cultures in Motion," in *Cultures in Motion*, ed. Daniel T. Rodgers, Bhavani Ramen, and Helmut Reimitz (Princeton, NJ: Princeton University Press, 2013), 1–19; Michael O'Brien, afterword, in *The Worlds of American Intellectual History*, ed. Joel Isaac, James T. Kloppenberg, Michael O'Brien, and Jennifer Ratner-Rosenhagen (New York: Oxford University Press, 2017), 367.
52. Felix Driver and Raphael Samuel, "Rethinking the Idea of Place," *History Workshop Journal* 39 (Spring 1995): vi. Transnational studies that have adopted such approaches include Tony Ballantyne and Antoinette Burton, eds., *Moving Subjects: Gender, Mobility, and Intimacy in an Age of Global Empire* (Urbana: University of Illinois Press, 2009); Simon J. Potter and Jonathan Saha, "Global History, Imperial History and Connected Histories of Empire," *Journal of Colonialism and Colonial History* 16 (Spring 2015); Andrew Preston and Doug Rossinow, eds., *Outside In: The Transnational Circuitry of U.S. History* (New York: Oxford University Press, 2017); Lara Putnam, "Circum-Atlantic Print Circuits and Internationalism from the Peripheries in the Interwar Era," in *Print Culture Histories Beyond the Metropolis*, ed. James J. Connolly et al. (Toronto: University of Toronto Press, 2016), 215–39; Ian Tyrell, *Transnational Nation: United States History in Global Perspective Since 1789* (Basingstoke: Palgrave Macmillan, 2007).

53. See, for example, Clarence Lang, "Locating the Civil Rights Movement: An Essay on the Deep South, Midwest, and Border South in Black Freedom Studies," *Journal of Social History* 47 (Winter 2013): 371–400; Matthew D. Lassiter and Joseph Crespino, eds., *The Myth of Southern Exceptionalism* (New York: Oxford University Press, 2010); Daniel T. Rodgers, "American Exceptionalism Revisited," *Raritan* 24 (Fall 2004): 21–47.
54. Paul Kellogg to Will Alexander, n.d. [1925], box 164–88, folder 4, Locke Papers.
55. See also Kay J. Anderson, "The Idea of Chinatown: The Power of Place and Institutional Practice in the Making of a Racial Category," *Annals of the Association of American Geographers* 77 (December 1987): 580–98; George Lipsitz, *How Racism Takes Place* (Philadelphia, PA: Temple University Press, 2011).
56. Warren Miller, *The Siege of Harlem* (New York: McGraw-Hill, 1964), 81.
57. On the ways in which systems of racial hierarchy take on a "brick-and-mortar quality" in the making and remaking of places, see N. D. B. Connolly, *A World More Concrete: Real Estate and the Remaking of Jim Crow South Florida* (Chicago: University of Chicago Press, 2014).
58. Erina Duganne, "Transcending the Fixity of Race: The Kamoinge Workshop and the Question of a 'Black Aesthetic' in Photography," in *New Thoughts on the Black Arts Movement*, ed. Lisa Collins and Margo Natalie Crawford (New Brunswick, NJ: Rutgers University Press, 2006), 199.
59. LeRoi Jones (Amiri Baraka), "City of Harlem," in *Home: Social Essays* (New York: William Morrow, 1966), 88; Shane Vogel, *The Scene of Harlem Cabaret: Race, Sexuality, Performance* (Chicago: University of Chicago Press, 2009), 137.
60. Daniel Matlin, *On the Corner: African American Intellectuals and the Urban Crisis* (Cambridge, MA: Harvard University Press, 2013).
61. Alain Locke, "The New Negro," in *The New Negro: Voices of the Harlem Renaissance*, ed. Alain Locke (1925; New York: Touchstone, 1997), 3; Ralph Ellison, "A Very Stern Discipline: An Interview with Ralph Ellison" (1967), in *Conversations with Ralph Ellison*, ed. Maryemma Graham and Amritjit Singh (Oxford: University Press of Mississippi, 1995), 110.
62. J. L. Chestnut Jr., quoted in Carol Polsgrove, *Divided Minds: Intellectuals and the Civil Rights Movement* (New York: W. W. Norton, 2001), 199–200.
63. Richard Wright, *Black Boy: A Record of Youth and Childhood* (1945; London: Vintage, 2000), 169.
64. Arjun Appadurai, "Putting Hierarchy in its Place," *Cultural Anthropology* 3 (February 1988): 45–46.
65. Walter Benjamin, "Paris: Capital of the Nineteenth Century" (1935), reprinted in *Perspecta* 12 (1969): 165–72; Locke, "New Negro," 14.
66. On "wasness," see John L. Jackson Jr., *Harlemworld: Doing Race and Class in Contemporary Black America* (Chicago: University of Chicago Press, 2001).
67. On the symbolic currency Harlem held in interwar Asia, see Fiona Ngô, *Imperial Blues: Geographies of Race and Sex in Jazz Age New York* (Durham, NC: Duke University Press, 2014), 15.
68. Ottley, *New World A-Coming*, 1.
69. On "congregation," see Earl Lewis, *In Their Own Interests: Race, Class, and Power in Twentieth-Century Norfolk, Virginia* (Berkeley: University of California Press, 1991).
70. Jack Newfield, "Robert Kennedy's Bedford-Stuyvesant Legacy," *New York* (December 16, 1968), 26. See also Matlin, *On the Corner*.
71. Paula J. Massood, *Making a Promised Land: Harlem in Twentieth-Century Photography and Film* (New Brunswick, NJ: Rutgers University Press, 2013).

72. Flontina Miller, "Racism Impetus Behind Author's Career" (1973), in *Conversations with Chester Himes*, ed. Michel Fabre and Robert Skinner (Oxford: University Press of Mississippi, 1995), 117 (emphasis added); Michel Fabre, "Interview with Chester Himes" (1970), in Faber and Skinner, *Conversations*, 92.
73. Regarding the National Association for the Advancement of Colored People, see Michael Javen Fortner, *Black Silent Majority: The Rockefeller Drug Laws and the Politics of Punishment* (Cambridge, MA: Harvard University Press, 2015), 30–33.
74. Locke's portrayal of Harlem as a capital for "African peoples in their contact with Twentieth-Century civilization" ("New Negro," 14) may indeed be understood as a continuation of earlier U.S. Pan-Africanist ideas that had privileged African Americans as the agents of civilization within the black world. See, for example, Tunde Adeleke, *UnAfrican Americans: Nineteenth-Century Black Nationalists and the Civilizing Mission* (Lexington: University Press of Kentucky, 1998); Michele Mitchell, *Righteous Propagation: African Americans and the Politics of Racial Destiny After Reconstruction* (Chapel Hill: University of North Carolina Press, 2004).
75. For midcentury popularizations of "Harlemese," see Cab Calloway, *The New Cab Calloway's Hepster Dictionary: Language of Jive* (New York: Cab Calloway, 1944); Dan Burley, *Original Handbook of Harlem Jive* (New York: Dan Burley, 1944).
76. Kathy Peiss, *Zoot Suit: The Enigmatic Career of an Extreme Style* (Philadelphia: University of Pennsylvania Press, 2011), 25; Ngô, *Imperial Blues*, 15. Among the works considering Harlem's significance within black musical history are John Howland, *Ellington Uptown: Duke Ellington, James P. Johnson, and the Birth of Concert Jazz* (Ann Arbor: University of Michigan Press, 2009); Farah Jasmine Griffin, *Harlem Nocturne: Women Artists and Progressive Politics During World War II* (New York: Basic Civitas, 2013), esp. 133–85; Eric Lott, "Double V, Double-Time: Bebop's Politics of Style," *Callaloo* 36 (Summer 1988): 597–605.
77. See, for example, Vogel, *Scene of Harlem Cabaret*; Eric H. Newman, "Ephemeral Utopias: Queer Cruising, Literary Form, and Diasporic Imagination in Claude McKay's *Home to Harlem* and *Banjo*," *Callaloo* 38 (Winter 2015): 167–85.
78. This section's title, "Black No More," alludes to the satirical novel by George S. Schuyler, *Black No More: Being an Account of the Strange and Wonderful Workings of Science in the Land of the Free, A.D. 1933–1940* (New York: Macaulay, 1931).
79. Agustín Laó-Montes and Arlene Dávila, eds., *Mambo Montage: The Latinization of New York* (New York: Columbia University Press, 2001). On Adriano Espaillat's victory, see Brian Purnell, "Harlem, USA: Capital of the Black Freedom Movement," present volume.
80. Johnson, "Making of Harlem," 638.
81. Harlem Urban Development Corporation, with the assistance of the Harlem Commonwealth Council and the Corland Corporation, *125th Street Shopping Mall Complex*, n.d. (c. 1978), box 1, folder 22a, Harlem Development Archive, 1971–2009, City College of the City University of New York.

PART I
MYTHOLOGIES

1.

FROM PROPHECY TO PRESERVATION

Harlem as Temporal Vector

ANDREW M. FEARNLEY

Throughout the twentieth century and into the twenty-first, Harlem has proven to be a durable symbol of black life in part because the idea of Harlem has been used as a temporal vector, a means of charting the historical position and trajectory of black Americans. Artists and writers have frequently imagined Harlem as a metonym for black America and, in doing so, have presented the neighborhood as one of the major epochs of modern black life, investing it with equivalent temporal weight to "Africa," "slavery," or "freedom" in black historical consciousness. Commentators in the early twentieth century referred to this neighborhood, for example, as "a dark symbol upon the skyline of the future," and a 1926 headline in the *Pittsburgh Courier* even suggested that "the enigma of [the black] race's future is hidden in Harlem."[1]

The neighborhood's present setting was seldom enough to support the grandiose visions of those who proclaimed Harlem a "race capital" or the capital of black America. As a consequence, they often pushed their claims to an alternative moment, imagining Harlem's symbolic significance as a future possibility or, in later decades, as a romantic past. This temporal framing of the neighborhood has long underpinned assertions of its exceptionalism. It was evident in the March 1925 special issue of the *Survey Graphic*, "Harlem: Mecca of the New Negro," when Alain Locke declared that Harlem "*is—or promises at least to be*—a race capital" and James Weldon Johnson forecast that it "*will become* the intellectual, the cultural and the financial center for Negroes." To Johnson, Harlem was not just distinctive because "the feeling between the races is so cordial" there. Rather, it was exceptional because, he believed, there was "small probability that Harlem *will ever be* a point of race friction." He thus suggested that Harlem not only differed, but actually diverged from the twenty U.S. cities, particularly Chicago and Washington, DC, that had recently been buffeted by antiblack riots.[2]

Accounts of time have in fact occupied a crucial place in Harlem's symbolism, casting the neighborhood as a temporal vector of black life. On occasion, these have borne some resemblance to what Paul Gilroy has suggested the music of Jimi Hendrix achieved, "reaching for not just the future, but a more philosophically coherent 'not-yet.' " Scholars of Harlem have generally said little about this dimension of its mythology, however, a fact that begins to explain why much of their work has been written within one of its major temporal declensions.[3] The past tense sits proudly in the titles of David Levering Lewis's *When Harlem Was in Vogue* (1981) and Jervis Anderson's *This Was Harlem* (1982), and the nostalgia is amplified further by the comments Ralph Ellison supplied for the latter's dust jacket, which lamented how once Harlem had been "an outpost of American optimism" but "today that Harlem is gone."[4]

While the literary scholar Houston A. Baker Jr. has shrewdly noted that most scholarly accounts of Harlem are "governed by a problematic... that makes certain conclusions and evaluations inevitable," particularly a sense of loss and failure, this orientation needs to be connected to the broader shift in how urban space was imagined in the twentieth century, which led to the replacement of confident forecasts of Harlem's future with wistful reminiscences about its past glamour. It was a shift equally apparent in the contemporaneous rise of "sunshine or noir" depictions of Los Angeles, and it has influenced scholarship on these places as much as it has shaped broader commentary and even material development.[5] Seen from this vantage point, the "failure" that Baker identified as being central to much scholarly work about early twentieth-century black literary production is in fact a symptom of the view that emerged around mid-century, which held Harlem to be exceptional because it had once been so.

In this chapter, I argue that considerations of time have been foundational to Harlem's modern symbolism and explain how and why they were so. The chapter focuses on the two main temporal declensions, futurity and "wasness," both of which served as meta-frameworks to which many claims about Harlem's special character were related. The essay's first section establishes how, in the early twentieth century, those who designated Harlem a "race capital" relied on the projection of that status from the present to the future. When, in later years, such contentions lost their place in cultural commentary, the language of Harlem's special character was recomposed around an alternative mythology of wasness, which took Harlem to be special because of its past profile. By the 1960s, black writers were referring to the neighborhood as "the *historic* black cultural capital," what the poet Amiri Baraka called "the *past* capital of African American people in the US."[6]

The second half of this essay focuses on the campaign to improve what became known as the Schomburg Center for Research in Black Culture, the "chief repository of black history," and describes how, in the late twentieth century, a raft of civic groups strategically used the idea of Harlem's historic significance to shape its redevelopment.[7] Although the nature of the claims about Harlem's significance has changed throughout the twentieth century, one fairly consistent dimension of those claims has been an attempt to place this neighborhood in time. In this way, Harlem has served as a means of thinking about the historical status of black people, drawing temporal contours around "the sheer energy of a culture's mature imagination."[8]

THE PROMISE OF A RACE CAPITAL

From the earliest moment that Harlem figured in black political thought, it invited reflection on the historical trajectory of African Americans. In the early decades of the twentieth century, blacks invested this neighborhood with several different orders of time, in part to disrupt the standard temporality that underwrote America's racial hierarchy—what historian Walter Johnson has referred to as "the grubby real-time politics of colonial domination and exploitation."[9] Both the scientific discourse about evolution and the system of racial hierarchy that propped up Jim Crow relied on the notion that people of color were "backward," possessing "the mind of a savage" and occupying, as Alain Locke wrote in 1924, a "prematurely arrested stage of culture."[10] It was these tenets that he and other black writers hoped to resist with what literary scholar Daylanne K. English terms their "unprecedented sense of presentism."[11]

Locke went about this by presenting Harlem as "ultra-modern," making it representative of an alternative present and future to the one assigned to blacks in the standard temporalities of the country's racial order. Refusing to concede that the African American present was the white American past, Locke presented Harlem as proof that "the culture of the Negro is of a pattern integral with the times" and hoped this would prompt commentators to remove "the dusty spectacles of past controversy." These sentiments registered among those who reviewed *The New Negro* (1925), with the southern writer DuBose Heyward describing Locke's anthology of new black writing as "epoch-making," and V. F. Calverton recognizing it as a "signal contribution to contemporary thought."[12] To grasp why writers like Locke and James Weldon Johnson would set their claims about Harlem within this framework of futurity requires that we first consider the period's regnant discursive setting.

In the aftermath of Reconstruction, one of the key political registers for managing America's racial democracy was to inquire about "the future of the Negro." On the twentieth anniversary of slavery's abolition, the *North American Review*, the country's leading literary periodical, asked ten prominent citizens to provide a prognosis for the social and political prospects of freedmen. Frederick Douglass led the way, dismissing those old heads who entertained theories about racial extinction and declaring that African Americans were a "permanent element of the population of the United States" who "now rise naturally and gradually" and "will not drop from dizziness." Much gloomier visions issued from the literary author Joel Chandler Harris, who suggested that the Fifteenth Amendment was only the first step toward gradual political maturation. By 1900, this had become a familiar trope, enfolded within a resurgent white supremacist culture. The Harvard paleontologist and well-known racist Nathaniel Shaler claimed that the evolution of Anglo-Saxons showed that it had taken "twenty centuries of toil and pain" to "win ... the state of mind of the citizen" and that blacks had been "mocked ... with the gift of the franchise."[13] African Americans reworked this political register in the 1910s and 1920s as part of what Henry Louis Gates Jr. calls a period of sustained "black intellectual reconstruction." Several did so through discussion of, and much dreaming about, Harlem's significance.[14]

The root presumption of America's discourses of racial management held that at some point in the future, but never in the present, blacks might be found worthy of full equality, and it was this that Locke and others were eager to correct. White Americans persisted in "thinking of [blacks] in terms of the Civil War," Locke felt, having "not perceived [the] 'growing up' " that had occurred.[15] It was this antiquated perspective that his cultural projects tried to refute, showing instead that black life had entered a "new dynamic phase," distinct from the "old epoch" that characterized race relations at the turn of the century. His opening essay in the special issue of the *Survey Graphic* related the neighborhood's formation to the mass migration of blacks "from the cotton-field and farm to the heart of the most complex urban civilization," or "from medieval America to modern," as he sharpened the point in the revised version. For Locke and later black writers such as Ralph Ellison, migration to New York was not only a physical journey but also a temporal one, carrying people "two generations in social economy and ... a century and more in civilization." Southern blacks arriving in Harlem "hurdle several generations of experience at a leap," Locke wrote. If Paul Gilroy invites us to think of modernity not as a period but as a region, then these New Negro strategists imagined Harlem as being as much a temporality as a place.[16]

Locke's statements placed Harlem within the same temporality as contemporary American life by adapting two anchors of popular racial logic: an evolutionary language of recapitulation and the stadial theory of social change. These were innovations consistent with a thinker who, since 1916, had been telling students at Howard University that " 'pure race' is a scientific fiction" and who knew that "racial and civic equality" was only possible with what the political scientist Michael Hanchard calls the "annihilation of racialized time."[17] Any lingering sense that Locke harbored of human history being arranged along an upward course was destroyed by the cataclysm of the Great War. That Europe's great powers had gone to war within a century of Napoleon's defeat was proof that "the wheel of progress as well as the clock of time . . . has slipped a cog and turned back," and it made ridiculous any desire "to count each calendar year as so much moral gain."[18]

The moment called for a different philosophy of time, one that conveyed the redemption of older ideas and that was indebted to the cyclical accounts of time sometimes found in late nineteenth-century Afrocentric thought.[19] "Unless history is tragically to repeat itself in terms of other huge struggles for dominance and supremacy," Locke warned, in the context of rising racial consciousness, a "mental revolution" in how race was understood, and how racial groups were organized, was required. Traditional ways of classifying groups—as "superior" or "backward"—were "disruptive," he wrote, indicating the indebtedness of racial hierarchies to theories of time and noting how they worked to thwart the ambitions of racial minorities, not least "the awakened American Negro and the awakening Africa." By the 1930s, he was urging statesmen to "change our false psychology" and to reconcile "racialism with universalism," thereby welcoming people of color into modernity's fold.[20] Locke's attempts to expunge the presumed backwardness of people of African descent, and to fashion a place for them within the modern histories of mankind, would culminate in his work on the philosophy of race. It would commence, though, with his work on Harlem.

When Locke described Harlem as a race capital, he did so by placing the neighborhood in a particular order of time, careful to note that it "*promises at least to be*—a race capital."[21] Harlem's capital status was expressed through the optative mood, a grammatical tense familiar to a classicist like Locke and one that awarded the title wishfully, drawing a distinction between hope and fulfillment, a line commonly found in his work. If such rhetoric made Harlem's status as a race capital tentative, Locke used historical analogy, especially his knowledge of the European Renaissance, to strengthen his prediction. Writing in 1927, he presaged a possible future for African Americans that equated their pedestrian advancement with "Umbrian stiffness" but predicted that "Florentine ease and urbanity looms just ahead." His decision to present Harlem's capital status as a work in progress also derived from the conventions of the *Survey Graphic*, which had characterized other "nascent centers" of cultural nationalism in similar ways, discussing "Irish *anticipations*" and "Mexico—*a promise*," to signal that these were places where nationalist movements had appeared but not yet delivered mature political programs.[22]

For all the comparisons Locke drew between Harlem and these other "centers," he also suggested that much about Harlem was exceptional. It was, he wrote, "the first concentration in history of so many diverse elements of Negro life," having attracted "the African, the West Indian, the Negro American." For this reason, he considered the neighborhood "prophetic," warranting the status of a race capital because it was functioning as "a common area of contact and interaction," an incubator of racial consciousness. It was in Harlem that he detected the emergence of a "new internationalism" and, far from being "obscenely silent" about the popularity of Marcus Garvey's United Negro Improvement Association, as has recently been suggested, Locke enthused about its efforts to bring "contact with the scattered peoples of African derivation."[23] Because Harlem functioned as a place of "great race-welding," its inhabitants represented "the advance-guard of African peoples in their contact with Twentieth Century civilization," a problematic phrase in its echo of Western civilizationist discourse about Africa but one that also constructed the African diaspora as a temporal hierarchy, a rhetorical "elsewhere," and conveyed Harlem's placement within modernity's fold.[24]

Harlem's location in the center of New York City, Locke believed, would also assist in "the reestablishment of contact between the more advanced and representative classes" of black and white Americans, and it was in this regard that he considered Harlem "an *exceptional* seed-bed for the germinating contacts of the enlightened minority." By encouraging interactions between different groups, such communities would "offset some of the unfavorable reaction of the past or at least re-surface race contacts somewhat for the future."[25] For Locke, then, Harlem's exceptionalism lay not straightforwardly in its status as the "capital" of the New Negro nation. Rather, it was exceptional because of the way in which that status ensured that in, and perhaps through, this present-day capital, past and future ideas of the race were adjusted—historical prejudices dissolved, more harmonious future relations developed—and thus the character of time was altered. It was in this precise sense that Locke presented Harlem as classically exceptional, a space that did not fit the existing structure of time.

The notion that Harlem's position as a race capital was unfinished was equally evident in James Weldon Johnson's writings about the neighborhood. The incipience Johnson ascribed to the neighborhood's character in *The New Negro* was repeated five years later in his book *Black Manhattan* (1930), in which he also suggested that the neighborhood was "still in the process of making." By emphasizing the ongoing development of this community, Johnson nurtured the idea that some futures remained "hazy," "unknown," and open to revision.[26]

But uncertainty was just one of the qualities he inscribed on the future, and his related work made clear his complex use of the future tense. In January 1920, Johnson asked readers of the *New York Age* to consider "what the future

Harlem will be." He was not alone in posing the question, for around the same time, the *Chicago Defender* also asked, "What will transpire in Harlem during the next decade?," before declaring that it "will come into its own" if the "school children one sees walking through the streets of Harlem today" grew up to be "fearless, honest and upright." Johnson's answer to his own question was equally forthright, stating that "in the next thirty years the Negro city of Harlem" would geographically expand and would come to "contain a colored population in the neighborhood of a half million."[27] The details of these forecasts matter less than the invitation each offered to contemplate the future of the race through the development of place.

Johnson knew that he could enjoin his readers to see beyond "the circumscribed horizon of the present" by heightening their sense of historical time, and he attempted to do so in his most elaborate account of Harlem.[28] Although *Black Manhattan* dealt extensively with the past, Johnson insisted that it was not "in any strict sense a history," offering instead a more complex meditation on time. The work exposed several layers of historical time, locating "Negro Harlem" as "a development of the past decade," while explaining that "the story behind it goes back a long way." It did this to correct those who presumed that Harlem's development was "a miracle straight out of the skies," "a sudden awakening," "the climax of the incongruous."[29] Such people were prone to explain black cultural achievement as a recent development, a view Johnson called a "historical conspiracy" that "stripped the Negro race of all credit for what it contributed in past ages." *Black Manhattan* therefore pressed its readers to see that recent cultural achievement was of a piece with blacks having "long been a generous giver to America." The "anomaly of the situation," Johnson wrote, "starts to fade out the moment we take account of how far back the story begins."[30] Just as Locke had done in *The New Negro*, Johnson used *Black Manhattan* to show how rewriting the past could also give the future a different shape.

The Puerto Rican–born bibliophile Arturo Schomburg was just as keen as Johnson to "remake" African American history, though few have noticed how he coupled that project to Harlem. Schomburg's contribution to *The New Negro* anthology presented Harlem, complexly, as the site where the future means of correcting the historical record would reside. A recent exhibition of bibliographic materials, Schomburg wrote in 1925, had shown Harlemites that "here is the evidence" by which white supremacist attempts to erase the black past could be refuted. Schomburg's essay also added a more abstract temporal mode to these discussions, noting that the "Negro historian to-day digs under the spot where his predecessor stood and argued." This was a conception of time likely imported from late nineteenth-century debates about the age of the earth, and it reminded readers that present-day Harlem stood atop the political and intellectual strata deposited there by earlier black settlers.[31] The work of all of these scholars and activists not only associated the progress of the race with Harlem's own advancement but also, in a variety of ways, took the neighborhood as a vector by which people of African descent were able to determine their position—not only in the United States but also in the modern world.

The Great Depression was, as Mark Naison has written, "a traumatic experience for Harlem," tearing through its social and economic fabric and, in turn, rearranging how it was positioned in time. The neighborhood endured the worst unemployment rate in one of the most unemployed cities in the nation, as well as rampant poverty, insanitary living conditions, and, according to the city's health department, the highest incidence of every recorded illness in Manhattan. It was these conditions that both caused and were worsened by the riots that erupted in 1935 and 1943.[32]

It was amid discussions of Harlem's deteriorating conditions that a certain view of the neighborhood's past became legible. Once "a scintillating, glamorous place," American commentators now idealized the 1920s as a period when "times were good," and they erected a framework of demise over Harlem's present and future, much as the scholar of urbanism Robert Beauregard has shown many postwar works of urban decline would later do by comparing 1950s cities with dreamy accounts of the "robust cities of the 1920s."[33] Arna Bontemps's essay "The Two Harlems" (1945) popularized this idea, while Robert C. Weaver's *The Negro Ghetto* (1948) carried it into the social sciences, with his work's introduction opening in the "middle twenties" when Harlem "gained its place in the list of famous sections of great cities," before moving to Weaver's present of the mid-1940s, when it had "lost its glamour."[34] While some European journalists continued to report that Harlem remained "in the process of becoming a capital," most U.S. commentators, confronted by its present-day tarnished image, preferred to reminisce about its past. This retrospective orientation became easier when that past had a name, the "Harlem Renaissance," a phrase that entered the American cultural lexicon in the early 1940s.[35]

During the second half of the twentieth century, widespread knowledge of the Harlem Renaissance sustained the idea of the neighborhood as a preeminent locus of black life. The term became a fixture of the postwar academy, while the implicit sense of demise that sat beneath the concept entrenched itself deeply in literary and cultural works. It was evident in Nikki Giovanni's poem "Walking Down Park" (1970) as well as in Melvin Tolson's *Harlem Gallery* (1965), which Tolson called an attempt "to picture the Negro in America before he becomes the giant auk of the melting pot in the dawn of the twenty-second century."[36] The perspective could also be glimpsed in the speeches of politicians and business leaders, many of whom vowed to restore Harlem to its "heyday," what the New York City Planning Commission's *Plan for New York City, 1969* termed its "brightest period." After midcentury, the notion of Harlem's distinctiveness rested on its past. Amiri Baraka's charge that "*promise* is a dying bitch with rotting eyes" came to replace Locke's earlier rhapsody on the theme. Yet even as cities ceased to be what Baraka called "the black man's twentieth century 'Jordan,'" Harlem continued to be perceived as, in some senses, a place apart, said to enjoy "a leg up on some other impoverished neighborhoods" because of its "unique historical heritage," its fading status as a race capital.[37]

A HISTORIC CAPITAL

After midcentury, claims made about Harlem's significance rested overwhelmingly on the neighborhood's position in black historical consciousness. Larry Neal, the poet and self-designated "Harlem nationalist," told a gathering in 1968 that the black arts movement needed to create an institutional presence, and that its "main headquarters should be located in Harlem for *historical reasons*."[38] A decade later, *Ebony Jr.*, a magazine published in Chicago, reassured its young readers that "Harlem will always be an important part of Black history because so much has happened there over the years."[39] Set against the thousands of official reports and television broadcasts that since the early 1960s had made Harlem's squalid housing, crumbling infrastructure, and heroin epidemic a key motif of America's contemporary urban crisis, such statements suggested that to let this neighborhood deteriorate any further would be to accept the loss of a crucial part of black history.

Similar assumptions guided the Harlem Urban Development Corporation (HUDC), which was established in July 1971 and was granted unrivaled powers in reviving the neighborhood. Indeed, the HUDC took the view that Harlem's "historical significance still makes it the capital of Black America." In the agency's first report, it advanced a barrage of projects to rehabilitate the community's building stock, justifying many under the goal of "creat[ing] a new focus for Harlem's historic role as the Black Capital of America."[40] News reports by now alluded to Harlem's exceptional contemporary importance in terms of it being "the archetypal Negro ghetto," and, instructively, an account of its abysmal material conditions by political commentator Michael Harrington appeared under the title "Harlem Today."[41] Yet Harlem also maintained an elevated position because of the perception that it was an extraordinary "historical black community." The evidence for such claims lay, among other factors, in the presence of nationally significant cultural institutions, including The Studio Museum in Harlem and, above all, the Schomburg Center, an "irreplaceable historic reservoir of the black experience."[42]

The bibliographic collection that Arturo Schomburg had compiled in the early twentieth century, and that the Carnegie Corporation bought from him, underwent a substantial transformation between the mid-1960s and the early 1980s. When it was donated to the New York Public Library, in 1926, the collection comprised five thousand books and a similar number of etchings and manuscripts, including letters by Toussaint L'Ouverture and poems by Phillis Wheatley. By the early 1970s, the collection was five times this size and was nationally recognized as "the biggest, most comprehensive collection" of its kind. Those who campaigned to improve the 135th Street branch, where it was stored during this period, understood the gravitas that this "very unique" collection conferred on Harlem, and they often mentioned the community's "fortunate position" of housing "the most prestigious collection of African and Afro-American art, artifacts, historical and literary documents in the world." This outlook was evident among those who ran similar institutions, such as the Studio Museum, whose director felt that being in Harlem meant the institution occupied two locations, one on Fifth Avenue and another that "invades history."[43] Working alongside the HUDC, the Harlem Cultural Council (HCC), and New York State's Urban Development Corporation (UDC), staff at the library established Harlem's credentials as a historic and therefore special site of black life. In time, their heritage-cum-development vision would, once more, extend Harlem's image as a forerunner or vanguard, this time for black urban regeneration groups.[44]

Efforts to preserve the library and collection were part of a much broader movement within Harlem that charged city officials with having allowed "a scandal of neglect and frustration" to fester. This movement began in the mid-1960s with the formation of the HCC, which led the way in lobbying the city for greater funding. When the HCC withdrew its support from the Metropolitan Museum of Art's exhibition *Harlem on My Mind*, after Harlem residents and artists were excluded from the event's planning, it helped turn the "shape of [Harlem's] cultural future . . . [into] a major question."[45] Under the leadership of Edward K. Taylor Jr., a producer with the Harlem Opera Society, the HCC led the way in responding to the neglect of the Schomburg collection, forming the Citizens Committee for the Schomburg in June 1968. Concern had been growing since at least February 1966, when the collection's long-serving curator, Jean Blackwell Hutson, confirmed what many had suspected: the library's physical structure and its small staff were inadequate for preserving the collection. Journalists who visited in subsequent months found a crumbling and cramped facility where "documents can't be found or fall apart in the user's hand" and witnessed "rotting newspapers" being retrieved for patrons from a dank basement and rare manuscripts perishing in the acid air of its storeroom.[46]

Responding to such accounts, campaigners, including the psychologists Kenneth and Mamie Clark, myriad groups of students, and ordinary patrons, set about raising funds and picketing the main branch of the New York Public Library. The Citizens Committee took out notices in the *Black Scholar* and the *Journal of Negro History*, and a special radio broadcast was organized to remind

New Yorkers this was "a heritage in peril of falling apart."[47] Amid these early campaigns, the association between the Schomburg collection and Harlem became ever more tightly drawn. The writer Albert Murray said the collection was "indigenous to Harlem." Julius Bloch, chair of the Queens College history department, equated the city's neglect with the community's wider deterioration, telling one journalist that "it is a collection of Negro material and is housed in Harlem. As such, it has not received the kind of professional services and financial support to which it is entitled." When *Ebony* described the unfolding crisis for a national audience, it explained that the collection's destruction would mean a "portion of the Negro's past may be gone forever."[48]

Such campaigns laid the foundations for a wider rhetoric of cultural loss, making Harlem's demise synonymous with the destruction of black heritage. In later years, organizers of Harlem Week, the cultural arts festival initiated in 1974, rallied supporters by pointing out that "it would be tragic to allow this, the community which was home to Ella Fitzgerald, Malcolm X, Sugar Ray Robinson, Adam Clayton Powell Jr., Duke Ellington ... to lose its glorious history," a claim echoed by later groups attempting to preserve Harlem's brownstones, with their efforts to "save history."[49] If the idea of Harlem as a historic place enjoyed some currency among ordinary residents, then these campaigns capture the strategic ways in which civic groups developed that image in these decades.[50]

While librarians and activists secured grants from the Ford Foundation, senior officials at the New York Public Library elevated the 135th Street Library from a branch to a research division and, in October 1971, renamed it the Schomburg Center for Research in Black Culture, moves that emphasized the uniqueness of its holdings. Accepting that the institution would need to be expanded, if not rebuilt, probably on the same site, the city also purchased a plot of land next to the existing building, paying $1.6 million for the block of Lenox Avenue between 135th and 136th Streets. Despite these developments, the following year, members of the HUDC approached the library's senior administrators with a proposal to construct the new facility on 125th Street, to the east of the recently opened State Office Building. Basing their plan for the "revitalization of Harlem" around 125th Street, "the focus of Black existence," the HUDC hoped to construct a hotel, convention center, and cultural center on the site and to persuade the Schomburg Center to relocate there. Library officials rejected the offer, deeming it inappropriate to place the new facility in a "commercial area," and insisting that "for historical reasons" the institution should remain on 135th Street. The institution's original site had a "history as a cultural and literary area," they explained, adding that "it was the scene of the Harlem Renaissance."[51]

This way of valuing space within Harlem, by emphasizing a block's historical significance, hardened in later years. In 1981, the National Register of

Historic Places awarded landmark status to the 1905 McKim, Mead and White building that was the site of the original library, describing it as "historically significant as a national center of black culture." One city official felt that the designation would help "to keep Harlem the Black capital of the world," underscoring the extent to which Harlem's "capital" status was now entrenched in institutions that exemplified and promoted knowledge of Harlem's past. Such designations expanded the neighborhood's stock of protected areas and began to fashion a corridor of historical landmarks through Central Harlem, granting the Schomburg Center status equivalent to the historic districts of St. Nicholas Avenue and Mount Morris Park.[52]

Such recognition imposed an imagined historic order on Harlem's built landscape, and, as in the rest of Manhattan, led to "developed pockets ... divided by swaths of neglect." J. Max Bond Jr., the architect eventually commissioned by the New York Public Library to design the new facility, was alert to this trend in urban planning and was opposed to such attempts to turn cities into "a series of distinct zones, each separate, each pure, each Puritanical."[53] Hailing from a family of prominent black educators and civil rights leaders, Bond understood architecture as a social and political activity, and he worried that urban design was increasingly "pitched to bourgeois sensibilities." Still, his firm's design for the new institution was attuned to the burgeoning economies of heritage tourism, something his later involvement in the Martin Luther King Jr. Center in Atlanta, Georgia, and the Civil Rights Institute in Birmingham, Alabama, confirmed. It was a stance that the historian Brian Goldstein has characterized as a combination of radical aspirations and moderate spatial vision. The final plans Bond's practice submitted to the New York Public Library, in April 1975, indicated both of these dynamics. The proposed new structure included two octagonal-shaped buildings, representing "the first churches (public buildings) built by Afro-Americans," both of which were to be constructed from brick "to reflect the materials of most of the nearby buildings" and to ensure the involvement of minority construction workers, many of whom were masons.[54]

Bond's plans hardly matched the dominant architectural style emerging across Harlem. Instead, like many New York restoration projects, they recycled varied historical features to "conjure up emotionally satisfying images of bygone times."[55] Architects commissioned to restore Harlem's other most iconic buildings, including the Apollo Theater and the Renaissance Complex, attempted, for example, to create "a modern environment with the ambience of the 1930s and '40s." By repairing original tile and brick, and using "restored existing signage of a historical significance," their designs tried to create a building that would "attain the spirit and excitement that once radiated throughout its Heyday." Such historicized pattern language had been made popular by other projects around Manhattan, particularly the South Street Seaport, which, as

M. Christine Boyer has shown, meshed several historical styles together, all with the aim to "repossess and return to New York's heyday." As Boyer argues, during these years, visual design codes became vital in shaping the "imageability" of urban environments, and renovations in Harlem likewise tended toward simplified simulations of its past. By the 1990s, some architects even presented "historically rich Harlem" as a sort of gritty Colonial Williamsburg.[56]

Construction at the 135th Street site began in June 1977, and in September 1980, after much delay, the new five-story Schomburg Center opened, at a cost of $3.7 million. The center's opening, alongside the relocation and expansion of The Studio Museum in Harlem, marked a moment when such institutions came to be regarded as highly valuable assets, with "places of historical significance" well suited to a burgeoning heritage tourism.[57] A Madison Avenue marketing company told HUDC officials, in the mid-1980s, that the Schomburg Center, along with the Harlem Performance Center and the historic brownstones of Strivers' Row, was one of Harlem's "most marketable amenities," of particular interest to European tourists drawn by "curiosity and a sense of history," their knowledge formed by the literary and filmic works about Harlem, which, as Paula J. Massood shows in the present volume, had long since entered their cultures.[58]

Such buoyant forecasts were widespread in the closing decades of the twentieth century, propelled by a belief that improvements to the neighborhood's historic cultural institutions would "re-establish Harlem as the attraction that it was in the 1920s and 1930s." Harlem and New York City power brokers usually proved eager supporters of heritage tourism, reasoning that such projects would benefit the neighborhood's economic future while also buttressing its symbolic capital. One senior official within Harlem's Uptown Chamber of Commerce thought Harlem's status as "the best known black community in the world" in fact depended on it receiving "its share of that [heritage] industry."[59]

While the Schomburg collection had long been regarded as one of Harlem's best-known attractions—featured on a 1950s tourist map and as the last stop on the Penny Sightseeing Company tours of the mid-1960s—the center's reopening in 1980 aligned with more concerted efforts to present the institution as "a main attraction for thousands of people who visit Harlem each year." Tourist brochures now reminded visitors that it was the events and institutions of a previous era that ensured Harlem's "unique spot in American history," while newly renovated apartments enticed middle-class African American buyers through allusions to Harlem's historic character, a claim sometimes illustrated with photographs of the new Schomburg Center.[60]

By the twenty-first century, as historian Robin D. G. Kelley has noted, the neighborhood's appeal was "tied to Harlem's black history."[61] Harlem's present was only ever elliptically mentioned, in upbeat accounts of the community. A 1989 article in *Time* magazine, for example, obliquely discussed the contemporary moment by telling "intrepid tourists" that "the place is *not what it was* during Harlem's toniest decades," and that it was not *"what it may become* in a looming decade of gentrification and white encroachment."[62] Harlem's discourses of futurity and wasness have not only limited consideration of the neighborhood's present-day setting; they often have also served as the main tributaries through which attempts to think about the present have been routed.

TEMPORAL CAPITAL

Time, then, has been foundational in each of the successive frameworks used to advance claims about Harlem's exceptionalism. It was time that structured the relationship between setting and symbol, reconciling narratives of Harlem's future promise with its present-day realities during the early twentieth century and asserting the exceptionalism of its decay in the late twentieth century by evoking the descent from its glorious past. In these ways, Harlem has been a powerful and persistent emblem of black life not only because the neighborhood was envisioned as a special place but also because it has provided a means of contemplating the condition and trajectory of the people of the African diaspora. In 1981, when the historian David Levering Lewis reflected on "urban America's future," it was to Harlem that he turned, "once the world's largest, most alive urban community of black people." Yet, while this neighborhood remained a crucial vector for plotting the temporal course of black life in the United States, the readings it gave were now uncertain. "What if the ravaged community [of present-day Harlem] represents, archetypally, not the past but the future of much of Afro-America?" Lewis pondered. As to Harlem's own future, he wrote, "Where did Harlem go? . . . Hope urges that the correct answer is not: to Gary, Newark, and East St. Louis."[63]

The commanding mythologies of futurity and wasness traced in this chapter rendered Harlem as an exceptional site of black life by placing it in time, making it a point at which people of African descent entered the historical imagination. In contrast to the temporal simplicity of these dominant Harlem mythologies, pushed by New Negro strategists and, later, Harlem's leading cultural institutions, which tended to represent the neighborhood straightforwardly as the past or future of black life, artistic treatments of the black past have often refused such neat teleologies. Aaron Douglas's mural *Aspects of Negro Life* (1934), Duke Ellington's extended composition *Black, Brown and Beige* (1943), and Bob Kaufman's poem "Walking Parker Home" (1965) all figured the neighborhood as one of several major epochs of black life. Like many artistic works that took Harlem as their subject, they depicted the neighborhood, and the broader sweep of black history, as a disjunctive temporality, deliberately placing their audiences in what literary scholar Lloyd Pratt, writing about mid-nineteenth-century black authors, has called a "conflict of time." Ellington refused a "continuous plot" to narrate the "symphonic saga of the African race . . . from the time of his life in the African jungle to present-day Harlem," while Douglas depicted Harlem's residents as simultaneously industrial workers and subjects haunted by "the clutching hand of serfdom." Placing their audiences "in time in more ways than one," these artists, and others, deployed the idea of Harlem to convey the dissonant sense of time that arose at the fraught intersection of racial particularity and universalism.[64]

In the U.S. context, W. E. B. Du Bois famously described this intersection as the challenge of being a "Negro and . . . an American," adding, in a less remarked-on passage, that this position was equivalent to being "swept on by the current of the nineteenth [century] while yet struggling in the eddies of the fifteenth century."[65] Richard Wright sharpened the contradiction, decades later, when he discussed the "Jim Crow lives that Negroes live in our crowded cities," lives propelled "toward the vortex of modern urban life" by industrial labor yet, as in Douglas's mural, anchored by cultural traditions that left many with a "consciousness . . . beyond the boundaries of the modern world."[66] Among a later generation of writers, it was the idea of Harlem that often signified the incongruity that people of African descent experienced in the modern world. Ellison wrote that living there provoked the realization, for many African Americans, that one was "full of the tensions of modern man but regarded as primitive," while Harlem's impoverishment amid Manhattan's wealth and power led Ann Petry to characterize it as an "anachronism" in 1949, an example of how racial inequalities arose from spatial *and* temporal constrictions.[67] As much as Harlem was a territorial symbol, then, it also summoned a temporal political community, locating people of African descent historically, while conveying their displacement and alterity and furnishing a framework within which the ambivalences of race and modernity collided and new forms of black subjectivity could be imagined.

NOTES

1. James Craig Gordon, "Key to the Enigma of Race's Future Hidden in Harlem, Race's Paris," *Pittsburgh Courier*, December 25, 1926. More generally, see James de Jongh, *Vicious Modernism: Black Harlem and the Literary Imagination* (Cambridge: Cambridge University Press, 1990), 214.
2. Alain Locke, "Harlem," *Survey Graphic* 6 (March 1925): 629 (emphasis added); James Weldon Johnson, "The Making of Harlem," *Survey Graphic* 6 (March 1925): 639 (emphasis added). For an explanation of this distinction, see Daniel T. Rodgers, "American Exceptionalism Revisited," *Raritan* 24 (Fall 2004): 21–47.
3. Paul Gilroy, *Darker than Blue: On the Moral Economies of Black Atlantic Culture* (Cambridge, MA: Harvard University Press, 2011), 131. The few studies that have examined temporality around Harlem's symbolism include Shane Vogel, *The Scene of*

Harlem Cabaret: Race, Sexuality, Performance (Chicago: University of Chicago Press, 2009); John L. Jackson Jr., *Harlemworld: Doing Race and Class in Contemporary Black America* (Chicago: University of Chicago Press, 2001). Sharifa Rhodes-Pitts similarly mentions the long tradition in which Harlem was "in the eternal process of becoming." Rhodes-Pitts, *Harlem Is Nowhere: A Journey to the Mecca of Black America* (New York: Back Bay, 2011), 37.

4. Ralph Ellison, blurb for Jervis Anderson, *This Was Harlem: A Cultural Portrait, 1900–1950* (New York: Farrar, Straus and Giroux, 1982).
5. Houston A. Baker Jr., "Modernism and the Harlem Renaissance," *American Quarterly* 39 (Spring 1987): 91; Mike Davis, *City of Quartz: Excavating the Future in Los Angeles* (New York: Vintage, 1992). More broadly, see Robert Beauregard, *Voices of Decline: The Postwar Fate of U.S. Cities* (Oxford: Blackwell, 1993).
6. Harold Cruse, "The Special Significance of Harlem—Its Place in the 'Theory of Black Cities,'" *Black World* 20 (May 1971): 21 (emphasis added); Amiri Baraka, *The Autobiography of LeRoi Jones* (New York: Freundlich, 1984), 297 (emphasis added).
7. Tracy Early, "Library Branch in Harlem Is Chief Repository of Black History," *Baltimore Sun*, December 28, 1980.
8. Henry Louis Gates Jr., memorandum, December 8, 1981, box 543, folder 7, Farrar, Straus and Giroux records, Manuscripts and Archives Division, New York Public Library.
9. Walter Johnson, "Time and Revolution in African America: Temporality and the History of Atlantic Slavery," in *Rethinking American History in a Global Age*, ed. Thomas Bender (Berkeley: University of California Press, 2002), 149.
10. Alain Locke, foreword to *The New Negro: An Interpretation* (1925; New York: Touchstone, 1992), xxvi; Alain Locke, "A Note on African Art," *Opportunity* (May 1924), reprinted in Charles Molesworth, ed., *The Works of Alain Locke* (New York: Oxford University Press, 2012), 101.
11. Daylanne K. English, *Each Hour Redeem: Time and Justice in African American Literature* (Minneapolis: University of Minnesota Press, 2013), 11.
12. Alain Locke, "Youth Speaks," *Survey Graphic* 6 (March 1925): 660; Locke, foreword to *The New Negro*, xxvi; Alain Locke, "Enter the New Negro," *Survey Graphic* 6 (March 1925): 631; DuBose Heyward, "An Epoch-Making Volume," *The Forum* (July 1926): 156–57; V. F. Calverton, "The Latest Negro," *The Nation* (December 30, 1925): 762.
13. Frederick Douglass, "The Future of the Negro," *North American Review* 139 (July 1884): 86; Nathaniel S. Shaler, "The Future of the Negro in the Southern States," *Popular Science Monthly* 57 (June 1900): 148.
14. Henry Louis Gates Jr., "The Trope of a New Negro and the Reconstruction of the Image of the Black," *Representations* 24 (Autumn 1988): 136. For an instance of how African Americans reworked this trope, see H. F. Kletzing and W. H. Crogman, *The Progress of a Race: or the Remarkable Advancement of the American Negro* (1897; Atlanta, GA: J. L. Nichols, 1920).
15. Alain Locke, quoted in "Dr. Locke Tells of the New Negro," n.d., box 164-146, folder 36, Alain Locke Papers, Moorland-Spingarn Research Center, Howard University, Washington, DC.
16. Alain Locke, "The New Negro," in Locke, *New Negro*, 4, 7; Locke, "Harlem," 630; Locke, "New Negro," 6; Paul Gilroy, *Against Race: Imagining Political Culture Beyond the Color Line* (Cambridge, MA: Harvard University Press, 2000), 95. See, for example, Ralph Ellison, "Harlem Is Nowhere," in *The Collected Essays of Ralph Ellison*, ed. John F. Callahan (New York: Modern Library, 2003), 321.
17. Alain Locke, "Race Contacts and Inter-Racial Relations: A Study in the Theory and Practice of Race" (1915–1916), reprinted in Molesworth, ed., *Works of Alain Locke*, 258; Michael

Hanchard, "Afro-Modernity: Temporality, Politics, and the African Diaspora," *Public Culture* 11 (Winter 1999): 265.

18. Alain Locke, "The Great Disillusionment" (September 1914), in *Race Contacts and Interracial Relations: Lectures on the Theory and Practice of Race*, ed. Jeffrey C. Stewart (Washington, DC: Howard University Press, 1992), 105.
19. Wilson Jeremiah Moses, *Afrotopia: The Roots of African American Popular History* (Cambridge: Cambridge University Press, 1998). See also Lloyd Pratt, *Archives of American Time: Literature and Modernity in the Nineteenth Century* (Philadelphia: University of Pennsylvania Press, 2010).
20. Alain Locke, "The Contribution of Race to Culture," *The Student World* (October 1930), reprinted in Molesworth, *Works of Alain Locke*, 294–95.
21. Locke, "New Negro," 7 (emphasis added).
22. Leonard Harris and Charles Molesworth, *Alain L. Locke: The Biography of a Philosopher* (Chicago: University of Chicago Press, 2008), 38; Alain Locke, "Our Little Renaissance," in *Ebony and Topaz*, ed. Charles S. Johnson (1927), reprinted in Molesworth, *Works of Alain Locke*, 212; "Irish Anticipations," *Survey Graphic* 17 (November 1921); "Mexico—A Promise," *Survey Graphic* 5 (November 1924). Emphases added. See also Bob Johnson, "Globalizing the Harlem Renaissance: Irish, Mexican, and 'Negro' Renaissances in *The Survey*, 1919–1929," *Journal of Global History* 1 (July 2006): 155–75.
23. Locke, "Harlem," 630; Locke, "New Negro," 6–7, 15; Davarian L. Baldwin, "Introduction: New Negroes Forging a New World," in *Escape from New York: The New Negro Renaissance Beyond Harlem*, ed. Davarian L. Baldwin and Minkah Makalani (Minneapolis: University of Minnesota Press, 2013), 13.
24. Locke, "Enter the New Negro," 633.
25. Locke, "Harlem," 630 (emphasis added); Locke, "New Negro," 10.
26. James Weldon Johnson, *Black Manhattan* (New York: Alfred A. Knopf, 1930), 281; James Weldon Johnson, "The Larger Success," *Southern Workman* (June 1923), reprinted in Sondra K. Wilson, ed., *The Selected Writings of James Weldon Johnson* (New York: Oxford University Press, 1995), 2:53.
27. James Weldon Johnson, "The Future Harlem," *New York Age*, January 10, 1920, reprinted in Wilson, *Selected Writings of James Weldon Johnson*, 100; Charles T. Magill, "Hidden Secrets in History of Harlem," *Chicago Defender*, July 29, 1922.
28. Johnson, "Larger Success," 53.
29. Johnson, *Black Manhattan*, xvii, 4, 260, 283.
30. Johnson, "Larger Success," 55; Johnson, *Black Manhattan*, 4, 283. It was instructive that a review of Johnson's book, by missionary Robert Speer, was entitled "The Negro and His Future," *Saturday Review of Literature* (October 18, 1930): 248.
31. Arturo Schomburg, "The Negro Digs Up His Past," *Survey Graphic* 6 (March 1925), 670. Locke played a crucial role in composing Schomburg's essay. See Jeffrey C. Stewart, *The New Negro: The Life of Alain Locke* (New York: Oxford University Press, 2018), 462–63. See also Thomas Allen, *A Republic in Time: Temporality and Social Imagination in Nineteenth-Century America* (Chapel Hill: University of North Carolina Press, 2008), chap. 5.
32. Mark Naison, *Communists in Harlem During the Depression* (Urbana: University of Illinois Press, 1983), 31; Cheryl Lynn Greenberg, *"Or Does It Explode?": Black Harlem in the Great Depression* (New York: Oxford University Press, 1991), 47, 66, 186.
33. St. Clair Bourne, "Harlem's 'Renaissance' Produced 'New Negro,'" *New York Amsterdam News*, January 24, 1942; Beauregard, *Voices of Decline*, 5.
34. Arna Bontemps, "The Two Harlems," *American Scholar* 14 (Spring 1945): 167–73; Robert C. Weaver, *The Negro Ghetto* (1948; New York: Russell and Russell, 1967), 3, 6.

44   Part I: Mythologies

35. "Lentement, Harlem prend son caractere. Il devient une capital—et la capitale d'un Etat dans L'Etat" (Slowly, Harlem is forming its character. It is in the process of becoming a capital—the capital of a state within a state). See Raymond Cartier, *Les Quarante-Huit Amériques* (Paris: Plon, 1953), 412.
36. Melvin Tolson, quoted in James Smethurst, *The New Red Negro: The Literary Left and African American Poetry, 1930–1946* (New York: Oxford University Press, 1999), 240, note 12. More generally, see Andrew M. Fearnley, "When the Harlem Renaissance Became Vogue: Periodization and the Organization of Postwar American Historiography," *Modern Intellectual History* 11 (April 2014), esp. 68–69.
37. Harlem Urban Development Corporation et al., "The Renaissance Complex" (November 20, 1991), box 4, folder 104, Harlem Development Archive, 1971–2009, City College of City University of New York; New York City Planning Commission, *Plan for New York City, 1969: A Proposal*, 6 vols. (Cambridge, MA: MIT Press, 1969); LeRoi Jones (Amiri Baraka), "Cold, Hurt, and Sorrow (Streets of Despair)" (1962), in *Home: Social Essays* (New York: William Morrow, 1966), 95 (emphasis in original); "New-Look Harlem Putting Out Tourist Maps, Folders," *Baltimore Sun*, November 13, 1978.
38. Larry Neal, "Cultural Conference Notes: Guidelines," 1968, typescript, box 6, folder 25, Larry Neal Papers, Schomburg Center for Research in Black Culture, New York Public Library (emphasis added).
39. Karen Odom, "A Special Time, A Special Place," *Ebony Jr.* (February 1979), 19.
40. Lewis, Turner, Partnership Architects and Planners, *125th Street Study Economic Revitalization Projects for Implementation*, February–November 1978, box 1, folder 22, Harlem Development Archive; Harlem Urban Development Corporation, *Harlem: The Next 10 Years—A Proposal for Discussion* (New York: Harlem Urban Development Corporation, 1974), 25.
41. *Time* magazine, quoted in Daniel Matlin, *On the Corner: African American Intellectuals and the Urban Crisis* (Cambridge, MA: Harvard University Press, 2013), 22; Michael Harrington, "Harlem Today," *Dissent* 8 (Summer 1961): 371–77.
42. Ruth Stewart to Museums Collaborative, July 14, 1975, box 20, folder 33, James W. Henderson Records, New York Public Library Archives, Astor, Lenox and Tilden Foundations; Carl Roberts, "Quiet Heroes Dedicated to Preserving Black Culture," *Sepia* (September 1973): 62.
43. Ad Hoc Committee for the Schomburg Collection, December 8, 1970, box 47, folder 12, Schomburg Center for Research in Black Culture Records, New York Public Library; Mary Holford, "Reappraisal of the Status of the Schomburg Collection and Preliminary Proposal for a Cultural Center in Harlem," January 17, 1968, typescript, box 19, folder 5, Schomburg Records; Randy Williams, "The Studio Museum in Harlem," *Black Creation* 4 (Winter 1973): 50.
44. Renewal efforts in black Chicago around heritage did not begin in earnest until the late 1980s. See Michelle Boyd, *Jim Crow Nostalgia: Reconstructing Race in Bronzeville* (Minneapolis: University of Minnesota Press, 2008).
45. Roberts, "Quiet Heroes," 62; McCandlish Phillips, "Future of Arts in Harlem Near Crossroads," *New York Times*, July 26, 1968. See also Bridget R. Cooks, "Black Artists and Activism: Harlem on My Mind (1969)," *American Studies* 48 (Spring 2007): 5–39.
46. "Visitors Crowd Repository of Negro Culture," *New York Times*, August 8, 1968.
47. See, for example, "Save the Schomburg Collection," *Black Scholar* 2, no. 5 (1971): 1; "The Schomburg Collection: A Heritage in Peril," WMCA broadcast, n.d., c. May 1968, box 21, folder 22, Henderson Records.

48. Albert Murray, quoted in C. Gerald Fraser, "Schomburg Collection Attracts Students of Negro Literature," *New York Times*, March 12, 1972; Julius Bloch, quoted in Ponchita Pierce, "Schomburg's Ailing Collection," *Ebony* (October 1967): 56.
49. "Harlem Week '85: Report," reel 4, Ademola Olugebefola Papers, 1967–1990, Schomburg Center for Research in Black Culture Records, New York Public Library; Josephine Jones, quoted in Nina Siegal, "Can Harlem's Heritage Be Saved?" *New York Times*, February 7, 1999.
50. For the uses to which Harlem's past has recently been put, see John L. Jackson Jr., "When Harlem Was in *Vogue* Magazine," present volume.
51. James Henderson to Frederick O'Neil, October 5, 1972, box 20, folder 29, Henderson Records; John Darnton, "Schomburg Files Get Harlem Site," *New York Times*, February 4, 1973; Lewis, Turner, Partnership Architects and Planners, *125th Street Study*; library memorandum, May 10, 1974, box 20, folder 9, Henderson Records; James Henderson, "The Schomburg Center for Research in Black Culture: Its Condition, Operation, and Needs" (1974), box 47, folder 9, Schomburg Records. On the institution's connection with this earlier movement, see Sarah A. Anderson, " 'The Place to Go': The 135th Street Branch Library and the Harlem Renaissance," *Library Quarterly* 73 (October 2003): 383–421.
52. Landmarks Preservation Commission, Designation List 139, LP-1133, February 3, 1981, http://s-media.nyc.gov/agencies/lpc/lp/1133.pdf; Ann Kheel, quoted in Charlayne Hunter, "Hopes and Fears on Rise with New Harlem Skyline," *New York Times*, November 20, 1973.
53. M. Christine Boyer, "Cities for Sale: Merchandising History at South Street Seaport," in *Variations on a Theme Park: The New American City and the End of Public Space*, ed. Michael Sorkin (New York: Hill and Wang, 1992), 184; J. Max Bond Jr., quoted in Priscilla Tucker, "Poor People's Plan," *Metropolitan Museum of Art Bulletin* 27 (January 1969): 268.
54. J. Max Bond Jr., "Working Cities: Density, Risk, Spontaneity" (2001), in *Writing Urbanism: A Design Reader*, ed. Douglas Kelbaugh and Kit Krankel McCullough (New York: Routledge, 2008), 12; J. Max Bond Jr., "Schomburg's New Home," *Schomburg Center Journal* 2 (Winter, 1983): 6; Brian D. Goldstein, *The Roots of Urban Renaissance: Gentrification and the Struggle over Harlem* (Cambridge, MA: Harvard University Press, 2017). See also Glenn Eskew, "The Birmingham Civil Rights Institute and the New Ideology of Tolerance," in *The Civil Rights Movement in American Memory*, ed. Renee Romano and Leigh Raiford (Athens: University of Georgia Press, 2006), esp. 42–43.
55. Boyer, "Cities for Sale," 184.
56. Harlem Urban Development Corporation et al., "The Renaissance Complex"; Boyer, "Cities for Sale," 200; Richard K. Dozier, "Riffin' on Urban Spaces," *Review of African American Art* 13 (January 1, 1997): 41–45.
57. Bert P. Highet and Walter H. Johnson, "Harlem—Tourism Market Assessment and Potential," *Tourism Management* 5 (June 1984): 147.
58. Quadrant Marketing, "A Marketing Plan for Harlem Tourism," April 1985, reel 4, Olugebefola Papers.
59. Sheila Rule, "Harlem, Tourist Center in 20s and 30s, Seeks Rebirth," *New York Times*, August 9, 1979; Lloyd Williams, quoted in Peter Bailey, "Harlem on My Mind," *Black Enterprise* (November 1979), 21.
60. Peter Bailey, *Harlem Today: A Cultural and Visitors Guide* (New York: Gumbs and Thomas, 1986), 3; Goldstein, *Roots of Urban Renaissance*, 219.
61. Robin D. G. Kelley, "Disappearing Acts: Capturing Harlem in Transition," in Alice Attie, *Harlem on the Verge* (New York: Quantuck Lane, 2003), 13.
62. Richard Corliss, "Welcome to Harlem!," *Time* (April 1989): 46 (emphasis added).

63. David Levering Lewis, "Harlem Today Resembles Nothing so Much as France After the Great War," *New York Times*, May 10, 1981.
64. Pratt, *Archives of American Time*, 167, 185; Duke Ellington, quoted in Mark Tucker, "The Genesis of 'Black, Brown and Beige,'" *Black Music Research Journal* 13 (Autumn 1993): 75; Ellington, quoted in Harvey Cohen, *Duke Ellington's America* (Chicago: University of Chicago Press, 2010), 204; Aaron Douglas, quoted in James Leggio, *Music and Modern Art* (London: Routledge, 2001), 210.
65. W. E. B. Du Bois, *The Souls of Black Folk* (1903; New Haven, CT: Yale University Press, 2015), 152.
66. Richard Wright, introduction to *Black Metropolis: A Study of Negro Life in a Northern City*, by St. Clair Drake and Horace Cayton (New York: Harcourt, Brace, 1945), xx; Richard Wright, *Twelve Million Black Voices* (1941; New York: Basic Books, 2008), 117, 135.
67. Ellison, "Harlem Is Nowhere," 322; Ann Petry, "Harlem," *Holiday* (April 1949): 168. See also Seymour Krim, "Harlem ist ein Anachronismus," *Merian: Städte und Landschaften* 23 (September 9, 1970): 52–57; Marc Singer, "'A Slightly Different Sense of Time': Palimpsestic Time in *Invisible Man*," *Twentieth Century Literature* 49 (Autumn 2003): 388–419.

2.

CLASS, GENDER, AND COMMUNITY IN *HARLEM SKETCHES*

Representing Black Urban Modernity in Interwar African American Newspapers

CLARE CORBOULD

In 1935, after two years of phenomenal success in the men's magazine *Esquire*, African American cartoonist E. Simms Campbell began publishing his work in the *New York Amsterdam News*, one of Harlem's weekly newspapers. Two weeks in advance, the newspaper advertised that it had secured the services of the rising star and promised "Harlem will laugh at itself through the clever contributions of Campbell."[1] Two years later, the *Pittsburgh Courier*, another black publication, poached Campbell and altered the title of the single-panel cartoon from *Harlem Sketches* to, simply, *Life*. The following week, however, the newspaper restored the original series title. Thus, a cartoon titled *Harlem Sketches* appeared in the weekly *Pittsburgh Courier* between October 1937 and late 1938, before returning to the *New York Amsterdam News* for a short stint in 1940. Its final run was again in the *Courier*, from September 1942 to late 1943, under the modified title *Sketches*.

What are we to make of a newspaper outside New York publishing cartoons titled *Harlem Sketches*? What, also, are we to make of the modification of that title after 1942? These questions are particularly intriguing, given that the content of Campbell's sketches only rarely described Harlem explicitly. Campbell depicted, rather, themes related to black urban life as a whole. The targets of his jokes ranged from gambling preachers to songsters who made ends meet by reprising southern work songs for white audiences; from the fraternal lodges and mutual aid societies that were legion in any town or city where African Americans congregated to black politicians; and from loafers and con men to the marks they duped. Campbell poked fun especially at a black elite, portraying them as lacking in taste and sense. Most frequently of all, he sketched misunderstandings between heterosexual men and women. Campbell also took aim, in wry images and captions, at white racism. None of these topics was peculiar to Harlem. Instead, the "Harlem" of the series title was an index or symbol of modern black life and of the distance African Americans had traveled from slavery.[2] *Harlem Sketches* implied that there was now a black community—however diverse—that was large, bold, cosmopolitan, and secure enough to, as the editors promised, "laugh at itself."[3]

Harlem was the modern black urban community par excellence, the one that best enabled Campbell to celebrate and critique, through humor, black life. Harlem was the most visually arresting of northern black enclaves, known for its gorgeous brownstones and wide boulevards. Proximity to Wall Street, Broadway, Tin Pan Alley, and the nation's most important book publishers, magazines, and newspapers distinguished Harlem further from other northern, black, urban sites. Having been occupied by a substantial African American community only since the 1910s, the neighborhood was also free from some of the tensions between new and old migrants that characterized a place like Chicago's South Side. It was more diverse than other black communities in another way, too, with its migrants coming from outside the United States as well as from the South. By 1930, one-quarter of Harlem's population was of Caribbean origin.[4] The neighborhood had an unusually large and renowned black elite, including some of the nation's most famed black writers, musicians, and politicians; a dense associational network; and the headquarters of many national organizations, as described by several other contributors to the present volume.

Residents of Harlem knew, however—as did their relatives and friends nationwide and beyond—that this black "city within a city" did not live up to the hype.[5] For many migrants from the islands, Harlem was just the northernmost urban development in "a connected Caribbean," a place where they experienced xenophobia even from African Americans and longed for home.[6] For all of Harlem's residents, whether from Bridgetown, Barbados, Durham, North Carolina, or San Juan Hill, west of Central Park, rents were steep, landlords miserly, and work precarious. As more and more people crammed in, the segregated neighborhood became ever more crowded. As poverty deepened during the Depression, and as drugs began to take their hostages, the delicate balance tipped more on the side of misery than pleasure.[7] Nevertheless, Campbell and his editors selected Harlem and not, say, Chicago's Bronzeville, Pittsburgh's Hill District, Philadelphia's Seventh Ward, Washington, DC's U Street, or Memphis's Beale Street to serve as shorthand for black urban modernity.

Although major black newspapers came out of cities such as Chicago, Pittsburgh, Baltimore, Philadelphia, Atlanta, Los Angeles, and Norfolk, it was Harlem that was considered important enough to feature in most, if not all, of them. When it came to gossip and social news, for example, every black newspaper printed local reports—who was visiting from out of town, who was hosting afternoon teas, where social groups were to meet, and what the book clubs were reading—but readers of the *Pittsburgh Courier*, *Atlanta Daily World*, *Chicago Defender*, and *Baltimore Afro-American* also had the opportunity, throughout the 1930s and as late as 1942, to enjoy tidbits of gossip in columns such as "Harlem Flashes," "Hi Hattin' in Harlem," "Harlem Shadows," "New York Page," "New York Society," "Ted Yates Covers New York Town," and "Billy Rowe's Harlem Notebook." While these newspapers featured society news and gossip from other locations, it was only Harlem that appeared in all of them.

Print culture, as scholars have long observed, played an essential role in forging links between people who did not know one another.[8] The black press did so by broadcasting achievements of African Americans—and of black people worldwide—but also simply by carrying news (including politics, sports, the arts, even gossip) among cities, towns, and regions, both within the United States and around the Atlantic.[9] By midcentury, there were 155 black newspapers nationwide.[10] Exact figures are hard to come by, but circulation of the major newspapers, including the *Pittsburgh Courier*, peaked at several hundred thousand each, some in the 1930s and others in the 1940s.[11] Distribution often went far beyond the primary city of publication. As scholars of African Americans' northward migration have noted, northern newspapers, helped along by train porters, reached ready audiences throughout the South.[12] Historian Kim Gallon reports that the *Pittsburgh Courier* sold only twenty thousand copies in the city during the 1920s and 1930s, with five to ten times that number reaching buyers elsewhere.[13] The *Negro World*, published in Harlem by Marcus Garvey's Universal Negro Improvement Association (UNIA), had pages in Spanish and French and was read all over the Atlantic; so, too, were West Indian and southern African papers. Circulation does not tell the whole story of readership, either, as newspapers were shared around and read aloud in groups, ensuring that "Harlem" became a subject familiar to black audiences across a wide geographic space.[14] It is not hard to imagine that Campbell's cartoons reached audiences around the Caribbean as well as all over the United States.

Comics and cartoon series played an important role in black print culture by ensuring that the black press was part of changing fashions in newspaper content, including the shared experience of humor among newspaper readers. *Harlem Sketches* appeared alongside single-panel and multipanel strips, and serial cartoons that went over weeks or even many months. At least a dozen male African American cartoonists, and one female, were featured often enough that their style and characters became well known to readers not just of the *Amsterdam News* or the *Pittsburgh Courier* but of all the black weeklies, even the relatively staid *New York Age*.[15] Although these illustrators, including Campbell, occasionally reprised unsavory stereotypes, together they refuted long traditions of black caricature in American visual and mass culture.[16] They did so by claiming, without apology, a space for black laughter, just as Langston Hughes and others were doing in literature.[17]

This chapter uses a selection of Campbell's 105 single-panel *Harlem Sketches* and *Sketches* cartoons to explore how the series used "Harlem" to form, as well as represent, a black community. That community was constituted in part by debate, which Campbell captured by sketching divisions of class, color, ethnicity, age, sexuality, geography, and, especially, gender. In the first section, I explore the cartoons in which Campbell deployed events and characters unique to Harlem, as opposed to the more usual cartoons in the series, in which "Harlem" was an index for urban black modernity more broadly. In the essay's second section, I consider Campbell's parodies of political activists and organizations to show how he suggested that, in the face of mercurial racism, laughter was a necessary remedy, perhaps better than many of the solutions put forward by activists, especially black nationalists and communists. The third section concentrates on those cartoons in which Campbell celebrated the ways black workers undermined racism, especially the unequal conditions in which they worked, whether as domestics or as boxers. In the fourth section, I examine Campbell's depiction of schisms within urban black communities, whether of gender, age, class, color, or a combination of these factors. The cartoonist used such tensions and conflicts to bring to life the kind of cosmopolitan community that was produced in urban settings, despite the forces of racial segregation.

As Campbell's series showed, the "Harlem" of the black press signified something far larger than the neighborhood itself in the 1930s and early 1940s: a mode of black life that was as far from plantation slavery as one could imagine. But the selection of Harlem to perform this work—to be the idealized home of the "New Negro" who had thrown off slavery's yoke and legacies—was not incidental. Much as Alain Locke, James Weldon Johnson, and others had heralded Harlem as the "race capital" and "great Mecca" of the black world during the 1920s, Campbell and the black newspapers that printed his work felt the need to locate the image of the "New Negro" geographically and, above all, in the place that signified, for them, urban black modernity at its most concentrated, diverse, and intense.[18]

Yet Campbell's Harlem was not the boosterish image furnished by the likes of Locke and Johnson. For all his pride in and affection for the neighborhood, he was intent on probing the frustrations and tensions that marked black urban life as well as celebrating its joys and achievements. In doing so, his cartoons relied on the realism and pathos characteristic of black humor.[19] Campbell skewered the pretentious and pressed hard on the fault lines of a community, including Harlem, that was beset by violent policing, corrupt politicians, and inequality at all levels. In poking fun, Campbell's cartoons, like those of his fellow illustrators Ollie Harrington and Jackie Ormes, reflected to black newspaper readers their own sense of the significance of Harlem as a symbol of black modernity and self-determination. At the same time, the images acknowledged those readers' equal awareness of Harlem's divisions and its failure to provide a life free from racism and inequality.

E. SIMMS CAMPBELL'S HARLEM

Campbell was born into a middle-class St. Louis family in 1906 and formed an early ambition to work as a visual artist. After the death of his father, he lived in Chicago with an aunt and completed high school, taking a particular interest in art classes. He briefly attended the Lewis Institute, spent a year at the University of Chicago, and studied longer at the School of the Art Institute of Chicago. During and after his studies, Campbell worked on short-lived magazines, including *The Phoenix* and *College Comics*.[20] He also served as art editor for a commercial publication, *Reflexus* magazine, which folded after a single 1925 issue, when *Chicago Defender* publisher Robert S. Abbott discovered that its founders had embezzled $100,000 from his company.[21]

Following that debacle, Campbell made his way back to St. Louis, where he worked as a railroad porter, until the owner of Triad Studios, J. P. Sauerwein, broke the conventions of the segregated commercial art world and hired him. In 1928, Campbell won first prize and $250 in the *St. Louis Post-Dispatch* cartoon competition. Late the following year, he hightailed it for New York, and within two years he was contributing a full page of cartoons to the *New York Sunday Mirror*. Soon after, he became a celebrated artist for the newly established men's magazine *Esquire*, where he would publish at least one illustration, if not a dozen, in nearly every edition until his death in 1971.[22] At the end of the 1930s, Campbell became the first syndicated African American artist when his series *Cuties*, about the travails of young white women as they sought husbands, appeared in 145 newspapers nationwide.[23]

By 1935, when Campbell began working at the *Amsterdam News*, his work had already demonstrated an insider's knowledge of Harlem, including an awareness of an impulse among the black elite and both black and white philanthropists and sociologists to uplift the neighborhood and its people. The first issue of a short-lived magazine, *Manhattan: A Weekly for Wakeful New Yorkers*, contained his foldout illustration *A Night-Club Map of Harlem* (figure 2.1). Its fanciful rendering of space rebuked the many maps of sociologists and urban reformers, who regarded Harlem as a problem to be solved.[24] Campbell included on his map hot spots such as Connie's Inn and the Lafayette Theatre, which were well known to white tourists to nighttime Harlem, but he also featured lesser-known clubs such as the Yeah, Man.

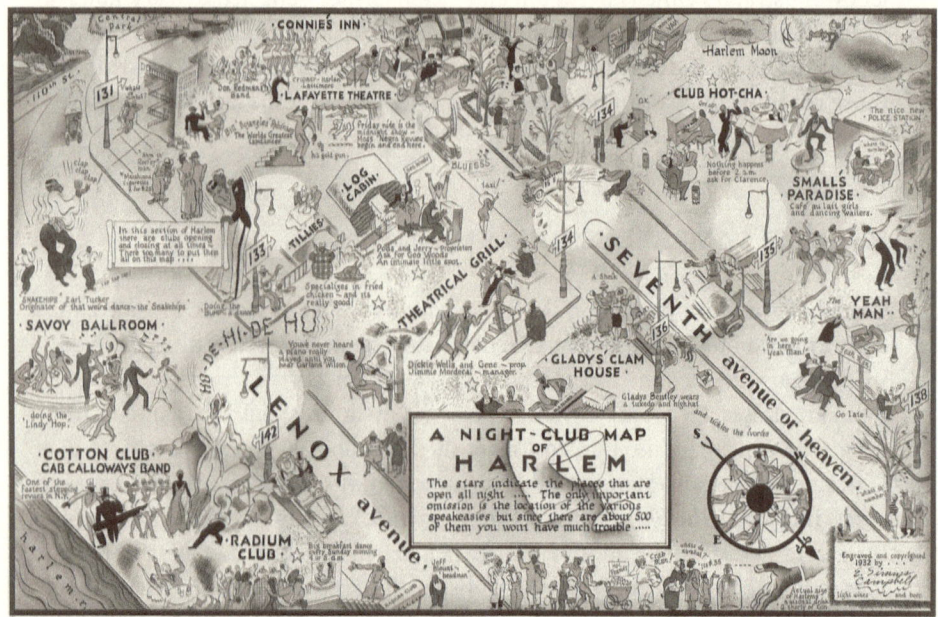

2.1 By the time E. Simms Campbell began publishing *Harlem Sketches*, he had an intimate knowledge of black New York, as well as having lived earlier in St. Louis and Chicago.

E. Simms Campbell, *A Night-Club Map of Harlem*, 1932. Reprinted with permission of the copyright holder.

According to Campbell's friend Cab Calloway, the Harlem bandleader, who would go on to use the map as endpapers in his 1976 memoir, the map rested on experience: Campbell was a hard-drinking connoisseur of all that Harlem had to offer.[25] Those who examined the image closely would also have noticed cross-street sites such as Tillie's Chicken Shack, where Harlem locals ate. The title box invited readers to contemplate the five hundred speakeasies whose whereabouts Campbell did not disclose. He also tempted readers of the downtown *Manhattan* magazine to make sense of the uniformed maid and white-collared priest discussing the day's "number"—a reference to the gambling game popular in Harlem.[26] The same topic preoccupied the pair near the pot dealer, in the top left-hand corner, and another two people on the image's bottom right, as well as the white and black policemen in "the nice new police station."[27] In short, the map denoted Campbell's ability to communicate with a white audience, but also his familiarity with the intricacies of the neighborhood that its black residents kept hidden from whites.

Regardless of Campbell's detailed knowledge of Harlem life and of the title of the comic series, only a few of his cartoons in these series, which appeared in the *Amsterdam News* and *Pittsburgh Courier*, were categorically about events that took place in New York. A 1938 panel showed the backs of two darkly colored figures on the banks of a waterway across from Manhattan's skyline. The two men ignore their fishing rods, instead tilting their heads to the sky as they trace the trajectory of a black kite nose-diving into the water. One remarks to the other, "There goes the Black Eagle again."[28] Here, they used the nickname of Hubert Julian, a black aviator whose exploits in Harlem and later Abyssinia brought him first fame and then notoriety among African Americans.[29] Campbell depicted a kind of laconic resignation on the part of the fishermen, as though by 1938 they knew well that Harlem's promise during the glitzy years of Julian's adventures had not panned out for most of the district's residents.

Some of Campbell's *Harlem Sketches* foregrounded phenomena that, while not exclusive to Harlem, were recognized as being especially pronounced there or as having originated in the neighborhood. In this way, a particular notion of Harlem as capital of black America—not as fundamentally different from, but as combining, concentrating, and sometimes elevating or elaborating the characteristics of black urban life more generally—was manifested in his work. Parades, for one, took on a special cast in Harlem because of their size, frequency, and the sheer breadth, grandness, and beauty of the avenues—from downtown all the way to Harlem—on which they occurred. Such events began in New York in 1917, with the Silent Protest Parade against lynching, organized by the National Association for the Advancement of Colored People; continued with the return of the "Harlem Hellfighters" (the 369th Infantry Regiment) two years later; and went on into the 1920s and 1930s, when organizations such as the UNIA and the Black Elks annually took to the streets. From downtown to uptown, marchers wore handsome uniforms and stepped to the accompaniment of bands.

While mutual aid societies certainly held parades in other cities, Harlem was distinctive because of the extensive network of political and social organizations headquartered in New York. The accounts and images that circulated after such parades further bolstered the unique prominence of Harlem in hosting the formal public life of African Americans.[30] Campbell even mocked the regularity of such events by sketching two tall African American men lounging on a park bench, taking a break from their work hauling a wagon and selling ice (figure 2.2). One remarks wearily to one another, "Boy—Ah'd give anything if that parade was only passin'."[31] The background implies the distinctive streetscape of Harlem, with the middle section taken up by uniformed marchers standing in a park and following the conducting of a drum major. Throngs of onlookers presumably add to the noise that so disturbs the workingmen's short break. The features that Campbell sketched were by this time widely known to black newspaper readers, from scores of photographs that had, since the 1910s, made New York synonymous with such occasions and thereby established Harlem as a black political hub.

"Boy—Ah'd give anything if that parade was only passin'?"

2.2 E. Simms Campbell occasionally depicted Harlem directly, but more often the title *Harlem Sketches* referred to modern, urban black life generally.

New York Amsterdam News, June 8, 1935. Reprinted with permission.

Likewise, numbers gambling took place in other cities, particularly Chicago, but it began in and was largely synonymous with black Manhattan. Because of the ingenuity of the numbers game and the use of daily figures published by Wall Street's financial institutions, it remained associated with black New York. In Campbell's take on the game, a sharply dressed numbers boss and his associate huddle around the telephone receiver in an office strewn with travel brochures. "Oh, so the bank was hit for $10,000?," says the boss, clutching his suitcase so that he can flee town without paying out on wagers placed at 1,000 to 1. "Thank you, thank you very much!"[32] Here was a theme Campbell expounded upon often: that regular African Americans were being taken for fools by those with the resources to do so, including other black Americans. The "Harlem" of his sketches was no utopia; it was a real place of conflicts, tensions, and rivalries, rather than an idyllic space free from oppression.

LAUGHTER IS SOME MEDICINE, AT LEAST

Campbell used his cartoon series to comment on the merits and pitfalls of various political movements established to improve the lot of African Americans, and for this he did not need to depict Harlem specifically. Rather, in training his satirical focus on what he regarded as overly extreme political groups, the "Harlem" of his sketches stood in for all urban (and even regional) areas in which modern black political life took place.

His illustrations make clear that although Campbell had reservations about particular political strategies and groups, he was nonetheless sympathetic to their basic cause, which was to right the inequalities that so disadvantaged African Americans. In one of the most touching *Harlem Sketches*, three children stand in the dark outside the window of a large, freestanding house. Their small frames cast shadows into the picture's foreground, toward the reader, thanks to the bright illumination inside. Lit up in silhouette inside is a grand Christmas tree. One child says to the others, "Ain't it bee-yootiful! The lady promised it to us when she throws it away!"[33] While the race of the tree's owner is not clear in the image, the lesser material circumstances of the children is a point Campbell makes amply. Another cartoon refers to the kinds of casual racism that could so dog black Americans looking to succeed in their chosen fields. Campbell sketched a dark-skinned football player, hand on hip, being talked down to by a coach, surrounded by four white players. "Why get sore?" asks the coach. "I simply said: 'Think how great you'd be if we played NIGHT football.'"[34]

Campbell was scathing about black nationalists who sought not to reform the United States but instead to leave it. Typically, he depicted them as unusually tall or shrunken men and corpulent women, an iconography out of sync with the modern city in the era of svelte flappers and dapper Lindy Hoppers. A 1935 cartoon features a photographic shop with a banner announcing, "We specialize in Lodges[,] Fraternal Groups & Clubs." The customer, whose portrait has just been taken, is a tall, thick-waisted man in full military regalia, including tasseled epaulets, embroidered wrist cuffs, a plumed helmet, medals, and a sword—a clear parody of Marcus Garvey, the self-appointed provisional president of Africa and head of the black nationalist UNIA. In the cartoon, the figure looks over a series of photographic negatives, bewildered. The sales assistant, a young man seeing an opportunity to save himself some time and money in developing the negatives into photographs, says in a wily way, "Negatives?

Why those are the POSITIVES, Man!"[35] Here, Campbell took aim at the inclination of black nationalists and Pan-Africanists to insist on the superiority of all things black.

Harlem, for Campbell, was the capital of black America but not necessarily of the black world. Garvey had been deported years before Campbell began working for black newspapers, but his influence lingered in urban areas, and it spiked after Italy's invasion of Abyssinia, in 1935.[36] In a complex cartoon, a man in a sharp suit, two-toned leather shoes, and a Panama hat is shown, reading a newspaper with the front-page headline "War in Ethiopia Inevitable." Alongside him stands a much taller man, in workers' clothes, head bandaged, and nursing a bruised fist. In the background, horses, police officers, and union organizers are shown in melees with African American men. In the foreground of this depiction of Harlem's 1935 riot, the injured man exclaims to the other, "You wants to go to ABYSSINIA to fight?"[37] Campbell suggested that it required a degree of material comfort and security at home, denoted by the newspaper reader's clothing, to be able to worry about circumstances abroad.

Campbell's rejection of the idea of a cohesive, global black community centered on Harlem continued from 1935 until the end of the cartoon series. By 1943, long after black troops had served in several theaters of war alongside people of color from around the world, Campbell pushed this theme even further.[38] Two African American GIs in the foreground of a cartoon from that year relax with their hands in their pockets, smoking. They gaze at the receding backs of three women, all very short and squat and with spiky black hairstyles that invert the shape of their grass skirts. The women seem to be melting into the foliage that drapes the borders of the image, invoking a long-held trope of racism that some people were closer to nature than others. One soldier says to the other, "By the way . . . who are you taking to the party tonight?"[39] Their slouching indicates a real weariness about the choice.

Pan-Africanists, black nationalists, and lodge members were not terribly bright, in Campbell's estimation, displaying a kind of backwardness that had come to be associated with the rural South rather than the fast-moving urban North. They were certainly nothing like, for example, the gangsters who populated black films, all now set in Harlem.[40] In a cartoon depicting a committee discussion at a black church, a congregant rises from the audience and, unaware of the etiquette of a formal general meeting, declares, "Ah THIRDS the motion!"[41] In another, a tuxedoed man stands up from behind a table draped in cloth, in front of the lodge's insignia hanging on the wall, to announce, "The president, governor, mayor, postmaster general and the board of aldermen are sorry they can't be here—but the meeting will go on irregardless!"[42] Even members of the lodges themselves might have laughed at the cartoon in which Campbell juxtaposed world affairs and the kind of internecine politics that could destroy organizations from within. In that image, the secretary, kitted out in a uniform similar to the man in the photographic shop, announces to the meeting room, "Most High And Worshipful Officiah Moses will now discuss Italy and Ethiopia, China and the Red Menace, and 'Who Took the Lodge's Punch Bowl From the Party last night!' "[43]

Campbell conveyed the deficiency of certain men's politics by representing them as unable to maintain appropriate relations with women and children. Their masculinity was inadequate, in other words. In a cartoon that again depicted members of an organization akin to the UNIA, Campbell sketched the office of the "Grand Exalted Ruler." A uniformed man finds himself beaten senseless and pinned under an overturned piece of furniture, after a robust woman in a uniform like that of the UNIA's Black Cross Nurses has flung open the door and wrenched the medals from his chest, only to hold them as though brandishing nunchakus (figure 2.3). He concedes, "Of course, if you feels that

2.3 E. Simms Campbell was pitiless in his mockery of black nationalists, communists, and other political groups he identified as extreme.

Pittsburgh Courier, January 29, 1938. Reprinted with permission.

way about it, why natchally the women's auxiliary can have medals, too!"[44] Two associates peek around the door in a cowardly fashion, relieved to have their headdresses still in place.

Other political groups, as Campbell portrayed them, also lacked the suppleness to answer the "race question," and once again they appeared in the newspapers as men incapable of fulfilling expected gender roles. Campbell parodied the soapbox speakers who dotted Harlem's street corners throughout the interwar years and who were often either black nationalists or communists. In an early cartoon for the *Amsterdam News*, yet another very overweight man stands atop a stepladder and holds court in front of a crowd of passers-by on foot and on bicycles. Two small children deflate his patriarchal pretensions by coming right up beside him, gazing up, and saying, "Mama says, 'You bring that ladder right home!' "[45] In a short story published five years later, Campbell used the same punch line, but this time the soapboxer was explicitly a communist. The story ends with Barbadian immigrant Montgomery Gaylord coming to the realization that "his wife was right. Perhaps if he had spent half as much time in trying to get a better job and being a better provider as he had in attending meetings, he'd amount to something. A dishwasher with his head in the clouds. That was it. His trouble was that his feet were up there, too."[46]

Campbell's inclination to disparage just about anyone who took themselves seriously may well have reflected a skepticism among many of his readers about the chances that politics of any stripe could improve life for African Americans, as well as a sense that anyone leading such an organization must be on the take. Thus, it was not just black nationalists, Pan-Africanists, and communists whom Campbell parodied. In a late cartoon in the series, one child says to another, about a pompous-looking man strolling past, "He takes both sides in everything. Mamma says he's a race leader."[47]

Campbell's cartoons drew on a long tradition in African American culture of building strength through shared jokes. With the United States deep in economic depression and African Americans suffering the worst of it, especially in the South, what else was there to do but laugh? This was not the laughter of comical stereotypes, which was designed to reassure uneasy white people of their superiority. It was, instead, a laughter that used Harlem to denote the existence of a large and politically diverse black community.

WEAPONS OF THE WEAK

Campbell may have poked fun at the loafers, drinkers, and numbers-playing clergymen of black urban spaces, or "Harlem," but he was nevertheless aware of the straitening circumstances that determined much of life for African Americans, including in the urban North. He well understood that not everyone could make a career drawing cartoons, even if he was content to permit the newspapers to suggest that his own success was solely the result of hard work.[48]

When Campbell noted and celebrated black workers' responses to their overbearing and often racist employers, the "Harlem" of the sketches' title became more symbolic than real. In a series of images, Campbell mocked the credulity of white employers, who seem shocked to find their underpaid and overworked black employees taking advantage of them whenever possible. The themes here would have been familiar to laborers in the rural South, right through to Harlem's "chorus girls."[49] In one, a maid in a smart dress, jacket, and hat, carrying two suitcases, is leaving behind a kitchen stacked high with unwashed dishes. She offers as a parting shot this remark to her stout employer: "Since Ah'm leaving, Ma'm—ah might as well tell you that the kitchen door key fits your liquor cabinet."[50] Along similar lines, a white man eyes his valet suspiciously as the man stammers, "Y-y-y-you knows how likker is w-w-w-when you leaves it open—it evaporates!"[51]

Many of Campbell's images provided a retort to white racism outside the workplace by alluding to assertions of black superiority that could not have been made in the South, and here, again, "Harlem" was an index rather than a real place. In one such image, a black basketball player toys with his white opponent: "I'm goin' 'roun' th' floor again, that's a pretty chick back there!"[52] If that cartoon did not specify the race of the attractive woman, in others Campbell did not hesitate. "Sorry, girls," says a heavyweight boxer to three young women hanging around after the bout, "mah manager says Ah gotta live like a monk!"[53] Two of the women have the line-shading on the face that Campbell favored when depicting light-skinned African Americans, but one appears to be white. In other cartoons published after the United States entered the war, Campbell was even more explicit in his use of the stereotype that black men made superior lovers. For example, an African American man in uniform, standing just inside a doorway with a bag at his feet reading "U.S. Army," and with his hat in his hand, admonishes the woman draped around his neck, "This is the very last kiss, babe. I've got to catch that train back to camp in two hours."[54] These urbane, sophisticated male figures were light years away from the buffoons or *Amos 'n' Andy* types that still peppered popular culture.

At times, Campbell's cartoons drew on Harlem as a place of unparalleled potential to reverse the usual course of racism and to display, if not great wealth, then at least immense style. The neighborhood was home, after all, to Strivers' Row and Sugar Hill, whose inhabitants were, by the late 1930s, if not earlier, associated with a style of photography quite distinct from the iconography of the Depression-era cotton South. In an early panel in the series, Campbell had a tall, well-dressed man in a white suit roll into Harlem in an impressive open-top car, puffing a cigar. As children and men pile around the car to admire it, the driver splays out his hand, saying laconically, "Yeah, It's Kinda' Nice—th' King of England Has One, Too."[55] That cartoon may well have called to readers' minds the kinds of sights that photographer James VanDerZee snapped in 1932 in his now iconic image *Couple in Raccoon Coats*, which depicted an impeccably dressed couple alongside a sleek car.

In an article for *Esquire* from 1936, Campbell wrote reverently of the ingenuity on display in the clubs and dance halls of Harlem, the "Homeland of Happy Feet." Offering up images that captured the new swing dance craze, Campbell closed his text with a description of the role such leisure played in the lives of black New Yorkers:

> Outside, on street corners, awaiting the dance hall's opening, the boy who runs the elevator in your building, the boot-black, the errand-boy, all of them in ankle-length overcoats and sporting pearl-gray, almost brimless hats, are as actors awaiting their cue. Throughout the long, weary day they have been menials and domestics in downtown white New York, but at night, in Harlem, they throw off the garb of servility and don royal raiment. Harlem is in the ascendancy at night.[56]

The *Harlem Sketches* series reflected Campbell's sense that, while it was possible everywhere to find ways to ameliorate racism, Harlem offered opportunities beyond those available in other cities, and especially in nonurban areas.

CAN YOU BE A BLACK WOMAN AND LAUGH AT THIS?

Opportunities for African American women in the Big Apple in the 1930s and 1940s, as everywhere, were constrained by forces that intersected where sex, race, and class met.[57] In cities, African American women tended to find work more easily than men, most often as domestics. While this provided a small measure of economic independence, the work was dull, sometimes grueling, or unsafe.[58] Campbell portrayed all of those complications in his images of black female domestics toiling unrewarded in the houses of white men and women. Urban black spaces did offer other work openings for African American women, including the cultural marketplace of bars and performance venues. These, too, were the target of Campbell's jokes. Many black women also participated in the illegal economy of numbers gambling and prostitution—a topic Campbell touched upon lightly.[59] When he sketched young women on the make, looking for husbands or generous lovers, or women too old to be successful in that arena, he addressed indirectly the limits of the choices available to African American women.

As Campbell depicted things, African American women who wished to marry well were required to maintain a degree of respectability while being courted by men who wanted more from them than they were willing—or able, given social conventions—to give. In these instances, the "Harlem" of the sketches' title was entirely symbolic; these images reflected the experience of African American women in all urban environments. In one of the *Sketches* cartoons, which very often featured servicemen, two young women are pictured indoors, preparing to go out. One sits at a dresser, arranging her hair, while the other rests atop a made bed, reading a book titled *Rough and Tumble Fighting*. The latter remarks, "I've been reading up on Commando tactics. I'm going out with a new fellow tonight."[60] Campbell used humor to draw attention to the particular challenges African American women faced in ever more populous cities.

Once they secured a domestic partner, women in Campbell's cartoons bore the brunt of those men's bad behavior. A 1942 sketch depicts a disheveled man in an armchair, and two children, beautifully dressed and with their arms tucked neatly behind them as they address their similarly well-turned-out mother, whose neat clothes are covered with an apron and who also carries a cleaning cloth. The children ask, "Guess what we gave Daddy for Christmas?" The gift is implied: an empty booze bottle sits on its side on the floor beside his chair.[61]

A similar domestic setting provides the scene for a classic New Year's Day illustration. This time the woman wears a handkerchief on her head while she sweeps up a broken bottle and party debris, pausing long enough to say to her husband's boss on the telephone, "No, mam, Henry won't be able to work for you today. Yes'm, it's his feet again!"[62] This theme continued right through the cartoon series, so that even Campbell's latest sketches, featuring a young, pretty girl and a GI, turned on the same joke. "There's no point in calling up your doctor," says the young lady to the serviceman on leave. "That's who you were out with last night!"[63]

In many cartoons, Campbell portrayed the undertone of violence and coercion that accompanied African American women in the workplace and in public life in general. In one of the *Harlem Sketches*, a young male patient grabs a nurse around the waist and pulls her onto the bed with him. She says in some alarm, "Of course this is the charity ward, Mr. Johnson, but you've got the wrong idea!"[64] Campbell depicted scenarios in which young women were sexually exploited by male employers. He drew a maid who is obviously fed up with having to avoid the predatory approaches of her boss's husband while simultaneously preventing her boss from finding out about them, which would entail the risk of losing her job. When her exasperated employer asks, "That's the seventh mop I've bought this week. What ever happens to them?," she replies, "I use them on your husband when he gets fresh, mam!"[65] In the most explicit of these images, one of three young dancers sobs in the dressing room, "Boo

SKETCHES — — By E. Simms Campbell

"You'll excuse me, won't you dear? I'm due back at camp in half an hour."

2.4 E. Simms Campbell portrayed the specific experiences of African American women.
Pittsburgh Courier, September 26, 1942. Reprinted with permission.

hoo—he fired me 'cause he didn't like my routine." An older woman chides her: "I done tole you 'bout concentratin' on your work so much."[66] The implication, especially given the state of undress of the two dancers who have kept their jobs, is abundantly clear.

Campbell occasionally found ways to portray women's sexuality, and he showed that racism, sexism, and ageism could combine to place a limit on the length of time women had to parlay their attractiveness into a mate or into partners who could satisfy their desires, even in cities, where women's choices multiplied. In one cartoon (figure 2.4), he sketched a young, light-skinned

African American woman, just married, beginning to take off her veil, when her uniformed husband says, "You'll excuse me, won't you dear? I'm due back at camp in half an hour." The look on her face suggests she is very taken aback at being denied the opportunity to consummate the marriage.[67]

Women might stray from husbands, too, such as the young wife who sits on the sofa in a pretty dress, with a gentleman's arm around her. They are listening to the radio together as he exclaims, "D——! Your husband sho has got some band!"[68] But when Campbell turned to picturing older African American women, their own sexual desire became the butt of the joke. In one cartoon, an expensively dressed, carefully coiffed, rotund woman reaches into her purse at the Christmas market and calls out, "Fo' dollahs wuth of mistletoe!," as though her only chance of being kissed would come from catching men underneath the doorway adorned with the foliage.[69]

Again, this was a theme that transcended the shift from *Harlem Sketches* to the *Sketches* series, a fact that conveys both the utility of "Harlem" as a signifier for this series and Campbell's attempt to use his drawings to address black urban life in toto. In a 1943 panel, Campbell showed yet another large woman, weeping on a sofa, with advice books, a bag of "love stones," and a bottle of "love potion" at her feet. The caption has her exclaiming, "Lawd, but Ah'm lonesome! Ah'd even like one that Uncle Sam rejected."[70] Campbell portrayed the ways that age, as well as gender, could shape experience for African Americans, even in places of supposed liberation such as Harlem.

Class, too, shaped the boundaries of the community that Campbell portrayed, and he paid particular attention to how denizens of an idealized urban space—the "Harlem" of the sketches' title—policed who belonged. According to myth, plucky black migrants to New York could get rich quickly. James Weldon Johnson, the educator, writer, lyricist, and diplomat turned political activist and Harlem booster, claimed in 1925 that the poor acclimatized rapidly and could almost as quickly become property owners.[71] Campbell used New York's reputation as the fashion capital of the United States to portray a potential pitfall of a swift rise into wealth.[72] In one cartoon, he sketched a well-dressed African American matron sitting in a milliner's oversize dressing room and examining her reflection in two mirrors. The sales assistant, carrying four hatboxes, says gently, "I'm sorry, Madam, but that isn't a hat, that's one of our wastebaskets."[73] In several images, Campbell suggested that inexperience at determining who was truly upper class meant there were plenty of pretenders, whose beautiful clothing and well-appointed residences were obtained only by a long line of credit. "Sorry Ah've only gin—Mah Relief Check didn't come today!" says one besuited man to a second, puffing a fat cigar, as they stand at the liquor cabinet in a well-decorated apartment.[74]

Alongside money—and often in the absence of deep wealth—one needed taste to belong to the newly emerged high society of places such as Harlem, and

2.5 E. Simms Campbell mocked the tendency of a new elite among urban black Americans to police the class boundaries of their newly stratified communities.

Pittsburgh Courier, July 9, 1938. Reprinted with permission.

Campbell pilloried as snobbery the policing of such boundaries. In one acutely observed cartoon, an attendant firmly leads away a man who has stripped down to skimpy leopard-print swimming jocks, while modestly dressed African Americans look on from the edges of the pool of an exclusive club (figure 2.5). The attendant, also black, exclaims, "I don't care what 'Esquire' says, Tarzan. You're going to put on a bathing suit."[75] By calling the man Tarzan and depicting him in a leopard print, overweight and barefooted, while the slimmer patrons wore high heels or flip-flops, Campbell suggested that some black Americans regarded others as primitive. These offenders, it seemed, might never adapt to Harlem society. It is difficult to tell in a black-and-white newspaper print, but "Tarzan" is darker skinned than the other pool users, with a hue similar to that of the guard leading him away. According to this cartoon, one needed taste and respectability—rather than, say, an ability to follow the latest fashion trends promoted in magazines such as *Esquire*—to enter the black elite. These attributes were necessary but not sufficient, and Campbell suggested, moreover, that lighter skin was a desirable quality, too.

HARLEM NO MORE?

When Campbell's series had its final run, in the *Pittsburgh Courier*, from September 1942 to October 1943, the title changed from *Harlem Sketches* to the more generic *Sketches*. It was not the only section of the newspaper that abandoned Harlem as the ultimate or exemplary manifestation of urban black life. Gossip columns changed their titles, too. "Billy Rowe's Harlem Notebook" became, in 1941, "Rowe's Notebook." The many tattle columns listed in this chapter's introduction all ceased publication by 1942.

Harlem did not, however, disappear as a symbol of black modernity. From 1943, Langston Hughes began publishing his "Simple" stories in the weekly *Chicago Defender*. This long-running series featured a loveable Harlem "everyman" whom Hughes used as a vehicle to discuss the events of the day. Other media also picked up the black city-within-a-city motif, such as New York radio station WMCA's program *Harlem USA*, which launched in 1948. Pictorial magazines such as *Life* began to include Harlem in multipage, glossy features that ranged from stories by Ann Petry to Gordon Parks's photo essays, as Paula J. Massood's chapter in the present volume shows. In that powerful visual genre, however, Harlem came to represent the apotheosis of urban decay. As in the newspapers, Harlem's centripetal force as a symbol of a diverse and hopeful black modernity was gone.

By the time Campbell moved his column for the final time, to the *Pittsburgh Courier*, the United States had joined the war and black soldiers were now a major feature of urban landscapes. The black serviceman quickly became the figure on which the black press hung the claims it made of the state.[76] If black men (and women) were to serve, once again, for the nation and for the principles of freedom and democracy, then was it not about time for nonblack Americans to recognize the equal claims to citizenship of their fellow citizens? In his treatment of modern black life, Campbell was quick to include soldiers, even when the cartoons' jokes remained the same. Campbell's transition from *Harlem Sketches* to *Sketches* indicated the fading away in the black press of Harlem as the hopeful, flourishing symbol of a modernity that was as far from slavery as one could imagine. That role, in black newspapers at least, was now taken up by the idealized figure of a uniformed African American GI. Where the promise of the cultural "renaissance" of black urban life had failed to convert the life chances of most African Americans, it was hoped that, this time around, military service might work, instead. The promise of Harlem was, for now, over.

NOTES

1. "E. Simms Campbell, Others Join Staff for New Paper," *New York Amsterdam News*, May 18, 1935.
2. Henry Louis Gates Jr., "Harlem on Our Minds," *Critical Inquiry* 24 (Autumn 1997): 1–12.
3. As Davarian L. Baldwin and Minkah Makalani's important anthology shows, the politics and aesthetics of the era's "New Negro" exceeded New York City. And yet, as so many of their own examples indicate, both politics and aesthetics found their loudest voice and/or coherence via the institutions that were situated in Harlem or elsewhere in New York. Davarian L. Baldwin, "Introduction: New Negroes Forging a New World," in *Escape from New York: The New Negro Renaissance Beyond Harlem*, ed. Davarian L. Baldwin and Minkah Makalani (Minneapolis: University of Minnesota Press, 2013), 1–27.
4. Winston James, "The History of Afro-Caribbean Migration to the United States," *In Motion: The African-American Migration Experience*, Schomburg Center for Research in Black Culture, http://www.inmotionaame.org/texts/viewer.cfm?id=10_000T&page=1. Accounts of the genesis and nature of Harlem's black community are legion. Key examples include Winston James, "Harlem's Difference," present volume; Shannon King, *Whose Harlem Is This, Anyway?: Community Politics and Grassroots Activism During the New Negro Era* (New York: New York University Press, 2015); David Levering Lewis, *When Harlem Was in Vogue* (New York: Oxford University Press, 1981); Kevin McGruder, *Race and Real Estate: Conflict and Cooperation in Harlem, 1890–1920* (New York: Columbia University Press, 2015); Gilbert Osofsky, *Harlem: The Making of a Ghetto—Negro New York, 1890–1930*, 2nd ed. (New York: Harper and Row, 1971); Irma Watkins-Owens, *Blood Relations: Caribbean Immigrants and the Harlem Community, 1900–1930* (Bloomington: Indiana University Press, 1996).
5. James Weldon Johnson, "The Making of Harlem," *Survey Graphic* 6 (March 1925): 635–39; Walter F. White, "Color Lines," *Survey Graphic* 6 (March 1925): 680–82.
6. Lara Putnam, "Provincializing Harlem: The 'Negro Metropolis' as Northern Frontier of a Connected Caribbean," *Modernism/Modernity* 20 (September 2013): 469–84. See also Watkins-Owens, *Blood Relations*.
7. Cheryl Lynn Greenberg, *"Or Does It Explode?": Black Harlem in the Great Depression* (New York: Oxford University Press, 1991).
8. Benedict Anderson, *Imagined Communities: Reflections on the Origin and Spread of Nationalism*, rev. ed. (London: Verso, 2006).
9. Lara Putnam, "Circum-Atlantic Print Circuits and Internationalism from the Peripheries in the Interwar Era," in *Print Culture Histories Beyond the Metropolis*, ed. James J. Connolly et al. (Toronto: University of Toronto Press, 2016), 215–39.
10. Thomas Sugrue, "Hillburn, Hattiesburg, and Hitler: Wartime Activists Think Globally and Act Locally," in *Fog of War: The Second World War and the Civil Rights Movement*, ed. Kevin M. Kruse and Stephen Tuck (New York: Oxford University Press, 2012), 90.

11. According to Patrick S. Washburn, after a peak circulation of 250,000 in four editions in 1937, and distribution in every state and abroad, the *Pittsburgh Courier* dropped to about 149,000 for the rest of the 1930s, with local city circulation at 20,000. Washburn, *The African American Newspaper: Voice of Freedom* (Evanston, IL: Northwestern University Press, 2006), 133–35. Andrew Buni writes that the *Pittsburgh Courier* outsold other black newspapers from 1937 to 1945, reaching a high point of 357,212 in 1947, which decreased to 280,000 by 1950. Buni, *Robert L. Vann of the* Pittsburgh Courier: *Politics and Black Journalism* (Pittsburgh, PA: University of Pittsburgh Press, 1974), 325. On the *Chicago Defender*'s circulation, see James R. Grossman, *Land of Hope: Chicago, Black Southerners and the Great Migration* (Chicago: University of Chicago Press, 1989), 74; 76–80; 302, note 32; 344, note 68; Ethan Michaeli, *The* Defender: *How the Legendary Black Newspaper Changed America* (New York: Houghton Mifflin, 2016), 256. For more general figures, see Roland E. Wolseley, *The Black Press, USA*, 2nd ed. (Ames: Iowa State University Press, 1972), 10.
12. Grossman, *Land of Hope*, 78; Mary G. Rolinson, *Grassroots Garveyism: The Universal Negro Improvement Association in the Rural South, 1920–1927* (Chapel Hill: University of North Carolina Press, 2007), 72–102, 119–20.
13. Kim T. Gallon, "Between Respectability and Modernity: Black Newspapers and Sexuality, 1925–1940" (PhD dissertation, University of Pennsylvania, 2009), 32.
14. "Put a wrapper on it and mail it" to others, advised Amy Jacques Garvey in the *Negro World*. See Ula Yvette Taylor, *The Veiled Garvey: The Life and Times of Amy Jacques Garvey* (Chapel Hill: University of North Carolina Press, 2002), 77.
15. Tim Jackson, *Pioneering Cartoonists of Color* (Jackson: University Press of Mississippi, 2016); Sheena C. Howard and Ronald L. Jackson II, eds., *Black Comics: Politics of Race and Representation* (London: Bloomsbury Academic, 2013). On particular artists, see M. Thomas Inge, ed., *Dark Laughter: The Satiric Art of Oliver W. Harrington* (Jackson: University Press of Mississippi, 1993); Brian Dolinar, *The Black Cultural Front: Writers and Artists of the Depression Generation* (Jackson: University Press of Mississippi, 2012), 171–224; Nancy Goldstein, *Jackie Ormes: The First African American Woman Cartoonist* (Ann Arbor: University of Michigan Press, 2008).
16. Henry Louis Gates Jr., "The Trope of a New Negro and the Reconstruction of the Image of the Black," *Representations* 24 (Autumn 1988): 129–55; Frances Gateward and John Jennings, "Introduction: The Sweeter the Christmas," in *Blacker the Ink: Constructions of Black Identity in Comics and Sequential Art*, ed. Frances Gateward and John Jennings (New Brunswick, NJ: Rutgers University Press, 2015), 5–6; Ian Gordon, *Comic Strips and Consumer Culture, 1890–1945* (Washington, DC: Smithsonian Institution Press, 1998), 59–79; Steven Loring Jones, "From 'Under Cork' to Overcoming Black Images in the Comics," in *Ethnic Images in the Comics*, ed. Charles Hardy and Gail F. Stern (Philadelphia, PA: Balch Institute for Ethnic Studies, 1986), 21–30; William H. Wiggins Jr., "Boxing's Sambo Twins: Racial Stereotypes in Jack Johnson and Joe Louis Newspaper Cartoons, 1908 to 1938," *Journal of Sport History* 15 (Winter 1988): 242–54.
17. Mike Chasar, "The Sounds of Black Laughter and the Harlem Renaissance: Claude McKay, Sterling Brown, and Langston Hughes," *American Literature* 80 (March 2008): 57–81.
18. On Locke and Johnson's characterizations of Harlem, see chapters by Andrew M. Fearnley and Daniel Matlin, present volume.
19. Lawrence W. Levine, *Black Culture and Black Consciousness: Afro-American Folk Thought from Slavery to Freedom*, rev. ed. (New York: Oxford University Press, 2007), 298–366; Glenda R. Carpio, *Laughing Fit to Kill: Black Humor in the Fictions of Slavery* (New York: Oxford University Press, 2008).

20. These biographical details come from Arna Bontemps, *We Have Tomorrow* (Boston: Houghton Mifflin, 1945), 1–14; and Elmer A. Carter, "Drawing Covers [rest of title illegible]," *Baltimore Afro-American*, April 16, 1932. The School of the Art Institute of Chicago has records showing that E. Simms Campbell attended during summer 1924, spring 1925, fall 1925, and fall 1926, though it holds no record of his graduation. Adam M. Torres, assistant director, Registration and Records, School of the Art Institute of Chicago, e-mail to author, July 21, 2015.
21. "Defender's Shake-Up Reveals 'Graft Ring,' " *Pittsburgh Courier*, May 2, 1925.
22. Arnold Gingrich, *Nothing but People: The Early Days at* Esquire: *A Personal History 1928–1958* (New York: Crown, 1971), 2, 94–100.
23. Reprints appeared in *Cuties in Arms* (1942) and *More Cuties in Arms* (1943), both republished in E. Simms Campbell, *The WWII Era Comic Art of E. Simms Campbell* (Landisville, PA: Coachwhip, 2012).
24. Shane Vogel, *The Scene of Harlem Cabaret: Race, Sexuality, Performance* (Chicago: University of Chicago Press, 2009), 147–49. Campbell completed *A Nightclub Map of Harlem* in 1932, and it was printed in *Manhattan: A Weekly for Wakeful New Yorkers* (January 18, 1933), 8–9.
25. Cab Calloway, *Of Minnie the Moocher and Me* (New York: Crowell, 1976), 117–20.
26. On numbers, see the chapter by Shane White, present volume.
27. Stephen Robertson, "Numbers on Harlem's Streets," Digital Harlem Blog, December 1, 2011, https://digitalharlemblog.wordpress.com/2011/12.
28. "Harlem Sketches," *Pittsburgh Courier*, September 24, 1938.
29. Shane White, Stephen Garton, Stephen Robertson, and Graham White, "The Black Eagle of Harlem," in *Beyond Blackface: African Americans and the Creation of American Popular Culture*, ed. W. Fitzhugh Brundage (Chapel Hill: University of North Carolina Press, 2011), 291–314.
30. Clare Corbould, "Streets, Sounds and Identity in Interwar Harlem," *Journal of Social History* 40 (Summer 2007): 859–94; Paula J. Massood, *Making a Promised Land: Harlem in Twentieth-Century Photography and Film* (New Brunswick, NJ: Rutgers University Press, 2013), 51–54.
31. "Harlem Sketches," *New York Amsterdam News*, June 8, 1935.
32. "Harlem Sketches," *Pittsburgh Courier*, October 1, 1938.
33. "Harlem Sketches," *Pittsburgh Courier*, December 25, 1937.
34. "Harlem Sketches," *Pittsburgh Courier*, November 13, 1937.
35. "Harlem Sketches," *New York Amsterdam News*, June 22, 1935.
36. Clare Corbould, *Becoming African Americans: Black Public Life in Harlem, 1919–1939* (Cambridge, MA: Harvard University Press, 2009).
37. "Harlem Sketches," *New York Amsterdam News*, August 24, 1935.
38. On black newspapers during World War II, see David J. Longley, "Vincent Tubbs and the *Baltimore Afro-American*: The Black American Press, Race, and Culture in the World War II Pacific Theatre," *Australasian Journal of American Studies* 35 (December 2016): 61–80.
39. "Sketches," *Pittsburgh Courier*, February 20, 1943.
40. Massood, *Making a Promised Land*, 75–83.
41. "Harlem Sketches," *New York Amsterdam News*, September 28, 1935.
42. "Harlem Sketches," *Pittsburgh Courier*, January 22, 1938.
43. "Harlem Sketches," *Pittsburgh Courier*, November 6, 1937.
44. "Harlem Sketches," *Pittsburgh Courier*, January 29, 1938.
45. "Harlem Sketches," *New York Amsterdam News*, October 26, 1935.

46. E. Simms Campbell, "A Communist Passes," *New York Amsterdam News*, April 20, 1940.
47. "Sketches," *Pittsburgh Courier*, February 27, 1943.
48. "Exclusive: The First Authentic Life Story of E. Simms Campbell, the Artist Who Painted Out the Color Line," *Baltimore Afro-American*, May 9, 1936; "Famed Cartoonist Campbell Tells Some of His Secrets," *New Journal and Guide*, April 5, 1941.
49. Robin D. G. Kelley, *Race Rebels: Culture, Politics, and the Black Working Class* (New York: Free Press, 1994).
50. "Harlem Sketches," *New York Amsterdam News*, May 11, 1940.
51. "Harlem Sketches," *Pittsburgh Courier*, February 12, 1938.
52. "Harlem Sketches," *Pittsburgh Courier*, February 26, 1938.
53. "Harlem Sketches," *Pittsburgh Courier*, October 23, 1937.
54. "Sketches," *Pittsburgh Courier*, February 13, 1943.
55. "Harlem Sketches," *New York Amsterdam News*, July 13, 1935.
56. E. Simms Campbell, "Swing, Mr. Charlie!," *Esquire* (February 1936), 100, 183; E. Simms Campbell, "Homeland of Happy Feet," *Esquire* (February 1936), 101–3.
57. Erin D. Chapman, *Prove It On Me: New Negroes, Sex, and Popular Culture in the 1920s* (New York: Oxford University Press, 2012); Farah Jasmine Griffin, *Harlem Nocturne: Women Artists and Progressive Politics During World War II* (New York: Basic Civitas, 2013), 79–131.
58. Jacob S. Dorman, "Back to Harlem: Abstract and Everyday Labor During the Harlem Renaissance," in *The Harlem Renaissance Revisited: Politics, Arts, and Letters*, ed. Jeffrey O. G. Ogbar (Baltimore, MD: Johns Hopkins University Press, 2010), 74–90; Greenberg, *"Or Does It Explode?,"* 22–26, 76–80; Cheryl D. Hicks, *Talk With You Like a Woman: African American Women, Justice, and Reform in New York, 1890–1935* (Chapel Hill: University of North Carolina Press, 2010); Watkins-Owens, *Blood Relations*, 24–25, 45–46.
59. LaShawn Harris, *Sex Workers, Psychics, and Numbers Runners: Black Women in New York City's Underground Economy* (Urbana: University of Illinois Press, 2016).
60. "Sketches," *Pittsburgh Courier*, March 13, 1943.
61. "Sketches," *Pittsburgh Courier*, December 26, 1942.
62. "Harlem Sketches," *Pittsburgh Courier*, January 1, 1938.
63. "Sketches," *Pittsburgh Courier*, February 6, 1943.
64. "Harlem Sketches," *Pittsburgh Courier*, June 11, 1938.
65. "Harlem Sketches," *Pittsburgh Courier*, April 9, 1938.
66. "Harlem Sketches," *Pittsburgh Courier*, April 2, 1938.
67. "Sketches," *Pittsburgh Courier*, September 26, 1942.
68. "Harlem Sketches," *New York Amsterdam News*, May 4, 1940.
69. "Harlem Sketches," *Pittsburgh Courier*, December 18, 1937.
70. "Sketches," *Pittsburgh Courier*, January 23, 1943.
71. Johnson, "Making of Harlem," 635–39.
72. Kathy Peiss has noted, for example, that zoot suits were originally called "Harlem Drape," being "identified with the capital of American fashion and hub of black life." Peiss, *Zoot Suit: The Enigmatic Career of an Extreme Style* (Philadelphia: University of Pennsylvania Press, 2011), 25.
73. "Harlem Sketches," *Pittsburgh Courier*, May 28, 1938.
74. "Harlem Sketches," *Pittsburgh Courier*, November 20, 1937.
75. "Harlem Sketches," *Pittsburgh Courier*, July 9, 1938. Campbell contributed a column about men's fashion to the *New York Amsterdam News* between April 6 and May 25, 1940.
76. For histories of activists' efforts to make use of the imagery of World War II–era black soldiers, see Stephen Tuck, " 'You Can Sing and Punch . . . But You Can't Be a Soldier or

a Man': African American Struggles for a New Place in Popular Culture," in Kruse and Tuck, *Fog of War*, 103–25. For a more general account of the symbolism of black military service in civil rights activism, see Steve Estes, *I Am a Man! Race, Manhood, and the Civil Rights Movement* (Chapel Hill: University of North Carolina Press, 2005). For an assessment of the efficacy of these campaigns, see Christopher Parker, "War and African American Citizenship, 1865–1965: The Role of Military Service," in *Oxford Handbook of African American Citizenship, 1865–Present*, ed. Henry Louis Gates Jr. et al. (New York: Oxford University Press, 2012), 425–63.

3.

HARLEM

The Making of a Ghetto Discourse

DANIEL MATLIN

Eunice Roberta Hunton is not among the canonical names of the Harlem Renaissance. What renown Hunton has centers on her work during the late 1930s as the first black female prosecutor in the New York district attorney's office, where she assisted in Thomas E. Dewey's prosecution of the mobster Charles "Lucky" Luciano. In 1925, four years out of Smith College and employed as a social worker, Hunton's single-page essay "Breaking Through" appeared toward the end of the *Survey Graphic*'s special Harlem number, guest-edited by Alain Locke. Yet when Locke revised the magazine issue that same year to produce his famous Harlem Renaissance anthology *The New Negro*, Hunton was one of four contributions he left out. The reasons for this omission are not difficult to discern. From its taut opening sentence—"Harlem is a modern ghetto"—her piece sat in uneasy relation to Locke's own, far more optimistic contention that Harlem "is—or promises at least to be—a race capital." Dropped from the team, Hunton has been no more than a footnote to Harlem Renaissance scholarship.[1]

And yet the inclusion of Hunton's essay in the *Survey Graphic* issue, the cover of which boldly labels Harlem the "Mecca of the New Negro," is not insignificant. Both veterans of the Harlem (or New Negro) Renaissance and scholars have described a linear shift in Harlem's iconography, whereby the neighborhood was revered, at the height of the renaissance, as an exceptional locus of black cultural production and empowerment, before the Depression and the 1935 Harlem riot recast the district as a symbol of tarnished hope and urban decay. "Nobody referred to Harlem as a ghetto then," remarked the columnist and satirist George Schuyler in an interview on the renaissance years, in 1974.[2] Writing in 1945, Arna Bontemps claimed that he and other young black artists and intellectuals had experienced the neighborhood during the renaissance period as a "foretaste of paradise," and that "none went so far as to suggest that there might be something wrong with Harlem." Only during World War II, Bontemps confessed, did he recognize what Harlem had "always been in essence: a black ghetto and a slum, a clot in the American bloodstream."[3]

Gilbert Osofsky, the historian who, in 1966, dated the "making of a ghetto" in Harlem to the 1910s and 1920s, nevertheless traced the making of a Harlem ghetto discourse to the Depression years, when a "new image of Harlem emerged" that had previously been known only to "stolid census-takers, city health officers and social workers" (and, presumably, to Harlemites themselves).[4] More recently, literary historians have plotted the trajectory of Harlem's symbolic meanings as a shift from, for example, "The Legendary Capital: The 1920s and 1930s" to "The Emerging Ghetto: The 1940s and 1950s," or from 1920s "city of refuge" to 1930s "everyghetto."[5] The more critical treatments of the Harlem Renaissance have long charged its representatives with the same "placid silence and Pollyanna complacency" about social and economic conditions in Harlem for which Locke himself issued a collective mea culpa in 1936.[6]

As a number of scholars have noted, only in the post–World War II era did reference to African American urban areas as "ghettos" become widespread. Authors such as James Baldwin and social scientists including St. Clair Drake and Horace Cayton increasingly employed "ghetto" during the 1940s, but it was amid the black uprisings engulfing hundreds of U.S. cities in the 1960s that the term became ubiquitously (indeed, almost exclusively, in reference to contemporary urban space) associated with black enclaves.[7] Hunton's insistent use of the phrase "modern ghetto" in 1925, however, provides not only an antecedent of these uses of "ghetto" but also a starting point for an alternative representational history of Harlem. Contrary to Schuyler's and Bontemps's recollections, the notion of Harlem as a "ghetto" was already in existence at the very moment when the neighborhood was first hailed as a "race capital"—not least, in the same issue of the *Survey Graphic*.

"Capital" and "ghetto" were the two master tropes of twentieth-century Harlem. Comprehending the relationship between them, and recognizing the synchronic as well as diachronic patterns of their use, is a necessary step toward understanding the meanings that have been invested in "Harlem" over time and the varied functions the neighborhood's symbolism has performed. The historian Nathan Irvin Huggins claimed, in 1971, that "the concept of Harlem becoming a ghetto would have seemed absurd" to Harlemites of the "renaissance generation," whereas in his own time, " 'ghetto' and 'Harlem' have become, to many, interchangeable words."[8] Yet linear narratives of a descent from 1920s "race capital" optimism to subsequent sober characterizations of Harlem as a "ghetto" obscure a significant and more complex history. That Hunton's bleak portrayal of Harlem was included in the *Survey Graphic* at all, against the grain of Locke's and most other contributors' buoyant depictions of the neighborhood, signals how, from the very outset, the notion of Harlem as a "race capital" was shadowed by the sharply contrasting notion of Harlem as a "ghetto."

Locke worked hard to suppress this ghetto imagery, which threatened his representational strategy of rendering the New Negro in a new, idealized black urban space. Yet the word "ghetto," and a broader ghetto discourse replete with images of social circumscription and physical enclosure, recurred and dogged the carefully constructed edifice of Harlem as a capital exempt from the prevailing black urban conditions of exclusion, disempowerment, and deprivation. "Race capital" and "ghetto" carried starkly divergent associations at this time, implying, respectively, the concentration of power and its absence; volition and compulsion; centrality and marginality.

In this chapter, I argue that the synchronicity of, and tension between, these two Harlem master tropes stems from the dynamics of a particular modality of African American life and politics that Earl Lewis has termed "congregation." As Lewis explains, in his history of black life in Norfolk, Virginia, congregation denotes a long-standing tradition whereby African Americans have sought to make a virtue of their enforced spatial concentration. Through civic and political associations, religious institutions, and cultural practices, African Americans have worked to make their communities and neighborhoods places of togetherness, empowerment, and psychological respite from domination; places that both enable and signify communal progress. They have struggled for ways to "frame their own reality" under circumstances where segregation has proposed to frame it comprehensively for them. "In the southern context," Lewis writes, "congregation was important because it symbolized an act of free will, whereas segregation represented the imposition of another's will."[9]

Black Harlem in the 1920s—both in actuality and in its depiction by Locke, James Weldon Johnson, and other renaissance publicists—was an enactment of congregation par excellence. What could speak more eloquently of African Americans' determination to frame their own reality than the rapid creation of this black "Mecca," "the greatest Negro community the world has known," where black women and men had congregated from the four corners of the country and the earth; where they established political clubs and fraternal orders, theaters and dance halls, street corner convocations and newspapers; and where the world's largest mass black political movement, Marcus Garvey's Universal Negro Improvement Association, was headquartered?[10]

Yet, as Lewis remarks of the South, "congregation in a Jim Crow environment produced more space than power."[11] In the North, the same equation obtained. As much as congregation was a creative response to segregation and not its automatic effect, segregation was still, incontrovertibly, the foundation on which congregation stood, and its basic structuring condition. As "Harlem" became, in the 1920s, a powerful, globally circulating symbol of African American life, it was enlisted simultaneously into two quite distinct, often directly opposed strategies of racial advancement. One, spearheaded by Locke, made Harlem Exhibit A in a bid for recognition of black worthiness for equal citizenship, through the publicizing of black accomplishment and self-reliance. The other, exemplified by Hunton, sought to expose the intolerable injustice of segregation. If "race capital" celebrated the energy and initiative that had given Harlem its vibrancy, the simultaneous and persistent "ghetto" undertone was a discordant note during the 1920s, interposed as a reminder of the coercive, restrictive, external forces that had also given black Harlem its being and its character. Harlem, Hunton could allow, was "a small city, self-sufficient, complete in itself—a riot of color and personality, a medley of song and tears, a canvas of browns and golds and flaming reds. And yet bound."[12]

SETTING AND SYMBOL

The appearance of Hunton's brief essay in the *Survey Graphic* may well have been contrary to Locke's wishes. Along with two other authors whose contributions he would excise in the revisions that produced *The New Negro*—the white journalists Konrad Bercovici and Winthrop D. Lane—Hunton's inclusion had likely been suggested by the magazine's editor, Paul Kellogg, who had commissioned Locke to compile an issue on black America. The monthly *Survey Graphic* was an offshoot of Kellogg's *Survey*, a publication aimed primarily at social work professionals, and while the illustrated *Graphic* reached out to a broader audience, it retained a strong emphasis on documenting social and labor conditions. As Locke's biographers remark, these dropped contributions were all "detailed sociological studies" that "probably originated from Kellogg's contacts."[13]

Moreover, these pieces all dwelled on segregation as a structuring condition of Harlem life and utilized images of enclosure that would become staples of the ghetto discourse. Bercovici, writing of his visits to Harlem, reported a pervasive "suspicion" of the outside world that constituted "a second wall to surmount; thicker even than the wall the white man has raised between himself and the colored population."[14] Lane, a contributing editor to the *Survey*, wrote of "the grim side of Harlem," describing systematic spatial confinement and consequent overcrowding and rent gouging. Unpersuaded by the Harlem exceptionalism dispensed elsewhere in the issue by Locke and Johnson, Lane folded Harlem into a generalized picture of racial segregation and exploitation endured by the "Negro in the northern city," who fell victim to "great congestion," "bad housing," and the false remedies of "quacks" and "fake druggists."[15]

Locke had hoped Hunton's piece would strike an affirmative tone. His April 1924 "syllabus" for the issue envisaged a three-page essay concerning "The Path-Breakers in the professions, sciences and in the new fields of social and race work and civic cooperation."[16] No draft of Hunton's essay has been located, but the published version was decidedly less effusive about Harlem than Locke had foreseen. Hunton did praise the achievements of those who broke the color bar in various professions. But she also employed the word "ghetto" no fewer than thirteen times, and she dwelled on the "race-bound" lives of those who "never leave the narrow confines of Harlem." Originally slated for the issue's second section, "The Negro Expresses Himself," the piece instead appeared with Bercovici's and Lane's in the less uplifting third section, "Black and White: Studies in Race Contacts." Locke did, at least, have the satisfaction of keeping the word "ghetto" off the contents page: Hunton's contribution, originally titled "Breaking the Ghetto Bonds," instead appeared as the sunnier "Breaking Through."[17]

Locke's aversion to this incipient ghetto discourse emanated from the core of his representational strategy and his conception of the New Negro Renaissance. Harlem, he wrote to prospective contributors, was to be both "setting and symbol" in the discussion of "our contemporary race development."[18] As is widely acknowledged, Locke believed the arts and letters of the renaissance would promote recognition of African Americans' capacity for "full initiation into American democracy." But no less important to him was Harlem itself, as a text (albeit one mediated by carefully curated writings) from which Americans could discern the race's progress and capabilities. At this nadir of American race relations, with the deadly outrages of the summer of 1919 fresh in the memory, with the Klan resurgent across the country and hopes of reward for black service in World War I extinguished, Locke pursued what has been termed a "culturalist" strategy. So entrenched and pervasive was Negrophobia that a radical transformation of black people's image was needed if there was to be any chance of persuading white Americans to accept equal citizenship. "Enter the New Negro," as Locke titled his own *Survey Graphic* essay.[19]

The term "New Negro" had emerged fitfully since the tail end of the nineteenth century, employed by a diverse cast ranging from Booker T. Washington to the socialists of the *Messenger*.[20] It appealed to Locke, specifically, as an apt tool with which to go about transforming the public image of black character, consciousness, and lifestyle. Heralding the arrival of the New Negro—a "type" encompassing both the "enlightened minority" of intellectuals and professionals and the metamorphosing "Negro peasant" who was suddenly transported to "the heart of the most complex urban civilization"—Locke seized what seemed like an opportunity to wipe the representational slate clean.[21] Years later, Langston Hughes's summation of the culturalists' approach was no less accurate for its sarcasm: "They were sure the New Negro would lead a new life from then on in green pastures of tolerance created by Countee Cullen, Ethel Waters, Claude McKay, Duke Ellington, Bojangles, and Alain Locke."[22]

The New Negro was to be seen as a figure already modern, already American, already sharing in the newest thoughts, processes, and feelings of the times and thus poised for full inclusion in national life. Introducing the literary works in the *Survey Graphic* issue, including poems by Cullen, Angelina Grimké, McKay, and Hughes, Locke saluted this generation of black writers who were "thoroughly modern, some of them ultra-modern," and remarked with satisfaction that "Negro thoughts now wear the uniform of the age."[23] Not only artists, but all New Negroes were in tune with contemporary American life and ideals. As befitted Locke's cultural pluralism, their "inner life" bore a distinctive race consciousness, while the objectives of their "outer life" were "none other than the ideals of American institutions and democracy."[24]

That the terrain of the New Negro must be a race capital, and by no means a ghetto, was clear to Locke for several reasons. First, he read the present mood of white America as beyond patience with, or interest in, the "Negro problem." Hence, if black America were to be accepted as part of the nation, it could only be on the basis of black self-reliance. As Kellogg wrote to Locke shortly before publication, the "purpose of the number" was to produce "something affirmative, and nascent, differing from the old protest psychology" that had yielded the "political approach of Negro rights, lynching, discrimination, and so forth."[25] The New Negro, Locke stressed, "lays aside the status of a beneficiary and ward for that of a collaborator and participant in American civilization."[26]

The forging of a race capital by African Americans signified, he believed, precisely this resourcefulness and initiative, in place of grievance and pleading. Black Harlem had "come into being and grasped its destiny with little heed from New York" in an achievement of the will comparable to that cherished American accomplishment, "the pushing back of the western frontier." The concentration of more than 100,000 black people in Harlem was not, Locke insisted, primarily a reaction to labor demand, the boll weevil, or the Klan. Rather, the "human tide" of northward migration of which Harlem's burgeoning was the greatest expression "is to be explained primarily in terms of a new vision of opportunity, of social and economic freedom," an intentional transition "from mediaeval America to modern."[27] Black Harlem's existence thus signified a self-willed and self-enacted congregation. It fell to Hunton to interject the contrary view, that Harlem was the product of externally imposed conditions of segregation: "prejudice has ringed this group around with invisible lines and bars."[28] It was a formulation that prefigured by forty years Kenneth B. Clark's renowned characterization of Harlem's "invisible walls" in *Dark Ghetto* (1965).[29] There was, meanwhile, an almost (Booker) Washingtonian aspect to Locke's willingness to downplay the force of segregation that had produced Harlem's hyperconcentration of black residents and to reassure white America that the New Negro was a willing "contributor," not an aggrieved "ward."

Second, to pronounce Harlem a "ghetto" not only rendered it a creation and symbol of white oppression rather than of New Negro initiative but also invoked a host of contemporary associations Locke was at pains to avoid. By the early decades of the twentieth century, "ghetto" had begun to displace "slum" as a signifier of the most problematic, feared spaces within America's industrial cities. Where "slum" continued to denote poverty, squalor, and moral hazard, "ghetto" imparted the additional meaning of an unassimilated presence, culturally and linguistically alien and maintaining parallel institutions seemingly impervious to Americanization. A letter of 1907 in which Locke refers to his friend Horace Kallen as a "Ghetto Jew I met at Harvard" indicates that Locke had himself employed the term in this way. Moreover, the *Survey Graphic* issue appeared less than a year after President Calvin Coolidge signed the Johnson–Reed Act, a sweeping measure of immigration restriction that was provoked by escalating public outcry over the surge of arrivals from Southern and Eastern Europe and Asia, which had transformed many U.S. cities over preceding decades. "Ghetto," which in its initial American usage had designated the urban settlements of Eastern European Jewish migrants, had, by the 1920s, gained wider application to the urban neighborhoods of other immigrant groups whose social, cultural, and religious practices were widely considered incompatible with an Americanism understood to be derived from Protestant Northern Europe.[30]

In their *Survey Graphic* contributions, both Locke and James Weldon Johnson were intent on insulating Harlem from such associations. With the New Negro's Americanism and modern orientation critical to their culturalist strategy, any comparison between the model black urban community and the putatively inward, tradition-bound, alien life of America's Jewish, Italian, Greek, or Chinese enclaves was to be resisted. Indeed, it was to be refuted, for beyond Hunton's essay, the *Survey Graphic* issue contained two further instances of Harlem's incipient ghetto discourse—in negation. Both Locke and Johnson voiced the notion of Harlem as a "ghetto" in the course of disavowing it, and they made clear, in the process, that the word's most damaging connotations were of a foreign, stagnant presence riddling U.S. cities. What "distinguishes Harlem from the ghettos with which it is sometimes compared," Locke wrote, conceivably prompted by Hunton's use of the term, was Harlem's "progressive," cosmopolitan character:

> The ghetto picture is that of a slowly dissolving mass, bound by ties of custom and culture and association, in the midst of a freer and more varied society. From the racial standpoint, our Harlems are themselves crucibles. Here in

Manhattan is not merely the largest Negro community in the world, but the first concentration in history of so many diverse elements of Negro life. It has attracted the African, the West Indian, the Negro American; has brought together the Negro of the North and the Negro of the South; the man from the city and the man from the town and village.[31]

Yet, even in Locke's account, the notion of Harlem as a ghetto could not be entirely submerged beneath the gleaming imagery of the race capital where "Negro life is seizing upon its first chances for group expression and self-determination." That the ghetto discourse shadowed and preyed on this sublime Harlem was evident even in the sentences in which Locke enshrined Harlem's preeminence: "In the final analysis, Harlem is neither slum, ghetto, resort or colony, *though it is in part all of them*. It is—or promises at least to be—a race capital." As briefly and superficially as he did so, Locke could not completely avoid acknowledging that Harlem's self-willed congregation was founded on the hard rock of externally imposed segregation. "Proscription and prejudice have thrown these dissimilar elements into a common area of contact," he wrote, before moving swiftly to a more sanguine register: "Within this area, race sympathy and unity have determined a further fusing of sentiment and experience. So what began in terms of segregation becomes more and more, as its elements mix and react, the laboratory of a great race-welding." Harlem, the emerging capital, was of a kind with those other crucibles of "emergent nationalities" now in the vanguard of a changing world. Though devoid of their "political significance," according to Locke, Harlem "has the same role to play for the New Negro as Dublin has had for the New Ireland or Prague for the New Czechoslovakia." Harlem, then, becomes the scene not of confinement, but of liberation.[32]

Following Locke's introduction and "Enter the New Negro" was James Weldon Johnson's contribution, "The Making of Harlem."[33] Johnson, then executive secretary of the National Association for the Advancement of Colored People and a prolific author, was even more fulsome than Locke in his panegyric to Harlem. That Johnson was married to the sister of John E. Nail—one of the property magnates who had profited handsomely from black Harlem's formation and whose firm, Nail and Parker, advertised its services in the *Survey Graphic* issue as "specialists in Harlem and colored tenement properties"—may have been one factor encouraging his unqualified praise of Harlem's living conditions.[34] But as George Hutchinson has discerned, Johnson was also anxious (with some foresight) that apologists for the white South would seize on Lane's depiction of "the grim side of Harlem" as confirmation that African Americans fared worse in the urban North than in Dixie.[35]

Johnson echoed Locke's portrayal of Harlem's magnetic pull by pronouncing Harlem "the great Mecca for the sight-seer, the pleasure-seeker, the curious, the adventurous, the enterprising, the ambitious and the talented of the whole Negro world." He also offered a vivid encomium to the elegance of Harlem's streetscape. In an article interspersed with photographs of benign Harlem scenes, including one showing a stretch of town houses designed by Stanford White—"a block which has few rivals in the city for distinction of line and mass and its air of quiet dignity"—Johnson painted a distinctly selective picture:

> Harlem is not merely a Negro colony or community, it is a city within a city, the greatest Negro city in the world. It is not a slum, or a fringe, it is located in the heart of Manhattan and occupies one of the most beautiful and healthful sections of the city. It is not a "quarter" of dilapidated tenements, but is made up of new-law apartments and handsome dwellings, with well-paved and well-lighted streets.

With its unqualified disavowal of "slum," Johnson's portrayal was even more blinkered than Locke's in its neglect of segregation and the latter's adverse impact on most Harlemites' daily lives. Johnson's Harlem was a site of dizzying black wealth accumulation, where even "Pig Foot Mary," a street vendor, had purchased a "five-story apartment house" for $42,000, and where, only a few years earlier, "it was not an uncommon thing for a colored washerwoman or cook to go into a real estate office and lay down from one thousand to five thousand dollars on a house."[36]

Lingering on this minority of property owners (and throwing in the wildly exaggerated claim that "Negro Harlem is practically owned by Negroes"), Johnson was silent about the grossly inflated rents endured by most Harlemites as a result of segregation—a word that appears nowhere in his article—and the overcrowding that made for less than "healthful" living. Instead, he offered Harlem as a beacon of good relations between the races, evidence that the "race problem" need not be "transferred" northward with the thousands of southern migrants. Far from protesting the northern variants of segregation and economic exclusion, Johnson warmly intoned that "New York guarantees its Negro citizens the fundamental rights of American citizenship" and that "in return the Negro loves New York. . . . He still meets with discriminations, but possessing the basic rights, he knows that these discriminations will be abolished."[37]

Much like Locke, Johnson sought to differentiate Harlem from immigrant neighborhoods and to emphasize its intrinsic Americanism. In its busy street life of colorful processions and brass band parades, Harlem bore similarities to New York's "Italian colony," he noted. Yet Johnson was more concerned with the dissimilarities. Harlem's "tendency is not to become a mere 'quarter,'" he continued. "Colony" and "quarter," like "ghetto," were words then routinely applied to immigrant urban settlements, and Johnson enumerated "three reasons" why these words did not fit Harlem. First, "the language of Harlem is not alien," for "Harlem talks American, reads American, thinks American." Second, Harlem was "not physically a 'quarter.' It is not a section cut off. It is merely a zone through which four main arteries of the city run." Here, Johnson implicitly contested Hunton's characterization of Harlem as "bound," "ringed around," and isolated from the surrounding city—imagery that evoked the original ghettos: the walled-in Jewish enclaves of early modern Europe. And third, the relative absence of black "gang labor" in New York's industries brought Harlem's workers into "the life and spirit of New York" as part of a larger, polyglot workforce.[38]

In these passages, Johnson challenged ghetto imagery obliquely, without direct reference to the term. But in one instance, the antithesis of Johnson's hopeful image of Harlem was made explicit. "Is there a danger," he asked, "that the Negro may lose his economic status in New York and be unable to hold his property? Will Harlem become merely a famous ghetto, or will it be a center of intellectual, cultural and economic forces exerting an influence throughout the world, especially upon Negro peoples?" Johnson answered, unsurprisingly, that "the Negro's advantages and opportunities are greater in Harlem than in any other place in the country" and that Harlem "will become the intellectual, the cultural and the financial center for Negroes in the United States," with "a vital influence upon all Negro peoples."[39] Though the phrase "race capital" does not appear in his essay, the identical version published in *The New Negro* carries the fitting title, "Harlem: The Culture Capital."[40] For Harlem to "become merely a famous ghetto" evidently meant just the opposite of what Johnson claimed Harlem was in fact becoming: a "center" of black cultural and economic empowerment, intermeshed with the surrounding city and the U.S. nation, and thus thoroughly distinct from the urban "colonies" of "alien" groups.

WESE TOO THICK TOGETHER IN HARLEM

The *Survey Graphic*'s Harlem number should be understood, then, as simultaneously inscribing and subtly effacing the image of sublime Harlem. It was not unique in this regard. Other renaissance-era texts that celebrated Harlem as a hopeful site of congregation and a race capital also carried an undertone of concern, varying in volume, about the bedrock of segregation on which this "greatest Negro city" was built.

When the publisher Albert Boni offered, even before the *Survey Graphic* issue had appeared in print, to bring out a revised version in book form, Locke saw an opportunity not only to disseminate the culturalist message more widely but also to refine the message by dispensing with those contributions that had deviated markedly from his own representational strategy. Free, now, of

Kellogg's editorial oversight and the need to accommodate the *Survey*'s sociological orientation, Locke was no longer bound to address what the magazine's editors, in their prefatory remarks to the Harlem issue, had called "the grim facts of exploitation which must be reckoned with in Harlem." Boni had a different requirement of Locke: that he tone down the emphasis on Harlem so that the book might offer a more comprehensive picture of African American life and thus, Boni believed, maximize its appeal to book buyers across the United States.[41]

Locke's solution, it seems, was to do what he no doubt wished to do anyway, namely, to drop the pieces by Hunton, Lane, and Bercovici that had accentuated Harlem's "grim" aspects. As a further measure, he commissioned new essays by Kelly Miller ("Howard: The National Negro University"), Robert Moton ("Hampton-Tuskegee: Missioners of the Masses"), and E. Franklin Frazier ("Durham: Capital of the Black Middle Class"), which celebrated three other exemplary sites of New Negrodom.[42] Yet if the resulting anthology, *The New Negro*, spanned a wider terrain of black America, the refrain of Harlem exceptionalism was scarcely diminished. Locke's foreword to the book no longer carried the title "Harlem," but it did carry the statement that "there are few [black] centers that can be pointed out approximating Harlem's significance."[43] Locke's homage to Harlem as an emerging "race capital" on a par with Dublin and Prague was imported, together with most of the material from "Enter the New Negro," into the book's opening essay, titled "The New Negro."[44] The renaming of Johnson's essay as "Harlem: The Culture Capital" amplified the effect further. With the "grim" accounts omitted and the strain of exceptionalism largely retained, the imagery of Harlem as sublime "race capital" was, if anything, even more pronounced than in the *Survey Graphic*.

Yet even these editorial modifications did not suppress all traces of the emerging Harlem ghetto discourse. The only unqualified application of the word "ghetto" in the magazine issue—Hunton's—had been excised, but two explicit disavowals remained. Johnson's expression of faith that Harlem would avoid becoming "merely a famous ghetto" survived intact.[45] And while Locke's proclamation of the "race capital" was no longer prefaced with an admission that it was "in part" also a "ghetto," he did invoke the ghetto discourse in a new passage in his foreword. Here, he once again presented the culturalist strategy as a direct alternative to remonstrating over segregation. "Liberal minds to-day cannot be asked to peer with sympathetic curiosity into the Ghetto of a segregated race life," he wrote. "That was yesterday," he continued, and with the onset of "cultural adolescence and the approach to maturity" had come "a development that makes these phases of Negro life only an interesting and significant segment of the general American scene."[46] Segregation and the ghetto were banished to the past; what now differentiated "Negro life" was only its "interesting" variation on American culture. In his eagerness to convey the extent of the New

Negro's cultural integration, Locke was prepared to mask the realities of a "segregated race life." "Liberal minds" were not to be troubled with such matters.

It was not only in negation that elements of the emerging ghetto discourse surfaced within *The New Negro*, however. While the book's two direct uses of the word "ghetto" were unequivocal disavowals, the burdens and injustices of "a segregated race life" nonetheless left their mark on its pages. It would not have been in Locke's power to insist on a purely celebratory account of Harlem from every contributor; nor, one assumes, would his willingness to deflect unsavory realities have extended quite that far. Even among the new batch of contributions were some that offered, at best, mixed messages about Harlem. Rudolph Fisher's short story "The City of Refuge" subtly reintroduced the harder appraisal that the exclusion of Hunton's, Lane's, and Bercovici's pieces had threatened to subdue.

The emergence of Fisher's protagonist, King Solomon Gillis, from the subway at Lenox Avenue and 135th Street at the story's opening is relayed with a sense of rapture to rival anything in the literary annals of the Harlem sublime. Less Mecca than Zion, Harlem appears to Gillis—a fugitive from Jim Crow injustice in North Carolina—as a miracle of deliverance, first rumored to him by a "traveling preacher" and now set before him in dazzling sunlight. Stunned by the sight of "Negroes . . . overwhelmingly everywhere," Gillis becomes transfixed by the figure of a white-gloved, black-skinned policeman confidently directing traffic: "Cullud policemans!" In Harlem, it seemed, "black was white. You had rights that could not be denied you; you had privileges, protected by law."[47]

The story's eighteen pages unfold a demolition of Harlem-as-Zion. Gillis reaches the cataclysmic realization that black is still black, that the miracle of congregation conceals an all-too-familiar matrix of white supremacy translated to new environs and confined spaces. His room in a boardinghouse is "half the size of his hencoop back home." The promise of empowerment, personified by the black policeman, is revealed to exist only within Harlem's apparatus of internalized exploitation. To secure a job at Tony's grocery store, Gillis must overcome his qualms and "steal" the position from a West Indian, whom he learns to call a "monkey-chaser." Unwittingly sucked into a drug-selling operation, Gillis himself falls prey to the machinations of fellow Harlemites who frame him as the culprit of their criminal acts and deliver him into the hands of three policemen—two white and one "cullud." As Gillis submits to arrest in a basement cabaret, he sees the black female dancer whom he has been admiring now being forced into an unwanted kiss by a white male patron, just as Harlem languishes in the clutch of ill-intentioned white power.[48]

The literary scholar Daylanne K. English noted, some years ago, that many Harlem Renaissance novels do not bear out the familiar criticism that their authors were "overly optimistic" and "socially blinkered." She points to Claude McKay's *Home to Harlem* and Nella Larsen's *Quicksand* and *Passing*, all published in 1928, as being far from straightforwardly optimistic in their evocation of Harlem. As English notes, the passage in McKay's 1937 memoir that relates his reasons for leaving Harlem—his need to escape "from the hot syncopated fascination of Harlem, from the suffocating ghetto of color consciousness"—echoes the character Billy Biasse's contention, in McKay's novel of nine years earlier, that "Wese too thick together in Harlem. Wese all just lumped together without a chanst to choose." Indeed, though the word "ghetto" does not appear in *Home to Harlem*, the emerging imagery of black ghettoization—of involuntary spatial confinement—does. For all its sensory pleasures, McKay's novel asserts, Harlem is a "pigpen," its residents hemmed in there "without a chanst to choose."[49]

Like the *Survey Graphic* issue and, indeed, *The New Negro*, McKay's and Larsen's novels were key texts in furnishing the imagery of sublime Harlem. "Oh, to be in Harlem again after two years away," muses McKay's Jake on his return from Europe, as he embraces the "noises of Harlem. The sugared laughter. The honey-talk on its streets. And all night long, ragtime and 'blues' playing somewhere.... Oh, the contagious fever of Harlem."[50] Helga Crane, in Larsen's *Quicksand*, is "fascinated" by Harlem's "continuously gorgeous panorama."[51]

And yet, even more than Locke's texts—and more deliberately—*Home to Harlem* and *Quicksand* also scrape away at the sublime Harlem they help to conjure. Complementing English's insights, Catherine Rottenberg has argued that many Harlem novels of the 1920s are in fact "shot through with ambivalence" about the neighborhood. For Rottenberg, this ambivalence is primarily a dynamic of "attraction and repulsion" toward the racialized condition of blackness, of which Harlem is symbolic. But she observes that what sometimes induces this repulsion in characters such as Helga is the "separation and racialization of space," as when, in Larsen's words, Helga's life becomes—like Harlem—"*bounded* by Central Park, Fifth Avenue, St. Nicholas Park, and One Hundred and Forty-fifth Street."[52]

"Ambivalence" might be said, then, to name something intrinsic to congregation itself, and to the particular spatial form it assumed in Harlem. That the *Survey Graphic* issue, despite Locke's best efforts to enshrine Harlem as a "race capital," had simultaneously conveyed the notion of Harlem as a "ghetto"—indeed, that Locke himself had allowed that his race capital was also "in part" a ghetto—is powerfully revealing of congregation's internal tensions. To idealize Harlem as a shining model of black autonomy and self-reliance was to invite the immediate rejoinder that congregation was conditioned by segregation. Thus, the discourses of Harlem as race capital and Harlem as ghetto became quickly entangled in the fractious call-and-response of congregation's possibilities and limitations.

THE CAPITAL OF EVERY GHETTO TOWN

Perhaps the most direct expression of this ambivalence toward Harlem during the 1920s belongs to Wallace Thurman. After arriving in Harlem from Los Angeles in 1925, Thurman eked out a living in part by penning newspaper and magazine articles in which he acted as tour guide and interpreter of this "popular and interesting section." What is striking is how these pieces lurch between the intensely laudatory and the bleakly sober, the imagery of the race capital and that of the ghetto. A lengthy article in the *Haldeman-Julius Quarterly* in 1927 begins with strong echoes of Johnson's "The Making of Harlem." This "great black city" is "located on one of the choice sites of Manhattan Island," Thurman relates. Relatively free of the "grime, smoke and oceanic dampness" that plague the Lower East Side, "where most of the hyphenated American groups live," in Harlem, "Little Africa has fortressed itself behind brick and stone on wide important streets where the air is plentiful and sunshine can be appreciated." The very next paragraph, however, seems to bridge the widest conceivable representational divide by anticipating James Baldwin's plaintive essay of 1960, "Fifth Avenue, Uptown." Thurman writes, "The tenement houses in this vicinity are darkened dungheaps, festering with poverty-stricken and crime-ridden step-children of nature. This is the edge of Harlem's slum district; Fifth Avenue is its board-walk. Push carts line the curbstone, dirty pushcarts manned by dirtier hucksters, selling fly-specked vegetables and other cheap commodities.... This is Harlem's Fifth Avenue."[53]

The juxtaposition is no less stark in an *American Monthly* essay, also from 1927: "Harlem is a ghetto struggling for more room and for more air. Harlem is a ghetto possible only in New York. Harlem is the capital of black America, the greatest Negro center in the world."[54] Indeed, Thurman's Harlem essays of the late 1920s are littered with references to the neighborhood both as capital and ghetto, often in close proximity, as though it were this duality that made Harlem "the city of constant surprises," a "multifaceted ensemble."[55]

As Avigail Oren's recent analysis of the black press has shown, the characterization of black urban areas as "ghettos," while not widespread, was slowly increasing during the 1920s in response to the northward spread of segregation. The *Pittsburgh Courier*, for example, employed "ghetto" some thirty-six times over the course of the decade.[56] That Harlem's ghetto discourse emerged concurrently with this in the writings of Hunton, Thurman, and others is of particular significance, given the loud celebrations of Harlem's exceptionalism and "capital" status that resounded across the United States and much of the world at this time. Still, this discourse remained fitful and incipient. Only in the 1940s did the *New York Times* begin to carry references to Harlem as a "ghetto" with any regularity, as events in Europe imbued the word with even more ominous connotations and as liberal groups such as the interracial City-Wide Citizens' Committee on Harlem gained attention with their assertion that Harlem was "a Black ghetto" whose residents were segregated, overcrowded, and subjected to exorbitant food prices and rents.[57]

Yet even in the mid-1930s Locke had abandoned his efforts to suppress the Harlem ghetto discourse. In the midst of the Depression and in the wake of the neighborhood's riot of 1935, Locke revisited Harlem in the pages of the *Survey Graphic*. It must have pained him, now, to write of "the Ghetto chain which fetters Harlem life," and to reflect, eleven years on from the Harlem issue, that "no emerging élite—artistic, professional or mercantile—can suspend itself in thin air over the abyss of a mass of unemployed stranded in an over-expensive, disease- and crime-ridden slum." There was, he conceded, "no cure or saving magic in poetry and art, an emerging generation of talent, or in international prestige and interracial recognition."[58]

In the years after World War II, the notion of Harlem as a ghetto proliferated and hardened in writings by the likes of James Baldwin and Ralph Ellison—though Ellison would later become the foremost opponent of ghetto discourse.[59] Meanwhile, the rapid suburbanization of America's white ethnics, coupled with the second, much bigger phase of the Great Migration, sealed what Eric Sundquist has called the "transference of the concept of the *ghetto* from Jews to African Americans."[60] By the time of the urban riots of the mid- and late 1960s, it was no longer necessary to preface "ghetto" with the adjectives "Negro" or "black."

The idea of Harlem as a "race capital" had lost much of its prophetic and exuberant force, but it did not disappear. For some, there remained hope that, as Langston Hughes imagined, the "dream" of Harlem had only been "deferred."[61] In black arts movement poetry of the 1960s, Harlem sometimes figures as a site of "phoenix-like rebirth."[62] Yet, in another development that crystalized during the 1960s, the imagery of the "race capital" and that of the "ghetto" became increasingly conflated, no longer expressing contradictory ideas or even, as in Thurman's writings, contrasting aspects of a "multifaceted" Harlem. The riots of that decade fundamentally remade the image of black America, exposing the magnitude of black migration and urbanization and making "urban crisis" a key signifier of America's racial strife and "ghetto" the archetypal domain of black life in literary, political, and popular discourse.

Under these circumstances, the meaning of "capital" in relation to black America often appeared to lose all signification of empowerment and to denote, instead, Harlem as simply the most famous or most damning example of black America's generally debased and ghettoized condition. For the authors of *Plan for New York City, 1969*, there seemed to be little tension, if any, between "the human disgrace of the Harlem slum ghetto" and the neighborhood's capital status. These two ideas could be run together in a single sentence, with no "but" to separate them, simply an "and," as if to signal that some elaboration was to follow: "Central Harlem is the capital of black America and a community chronically afflicted with physical and social problems that cry out for public attention."[63]

By the time Bobby Womack wrote and performed the title song of the blaxploitation film *Across 110th Street* (1972), Harlem's status as race capital no longer implied any qualitative exceptionalism, least of all any denial that Harlem was a "ghetto." The Harlem of which Womack sang was a landscape of exploitation and dejection, peopled by "pushers" and "junkies," "pimps" and "tricks." What now made Harlem black America's capital was, indeed, precisely that it embodied what had once seemed to threaten that claim: "In every city you find the same thing going down / Harlem is the capital of every ghetto town."[64]

NOTES

1. Eunice Roberta Hunton, "Breaking Through," *Survey Graphic* 6 (March 1925): 684; Alain Locke, "Harlem," *Survey Graphic* 6 (March 1925): 629; Alain Locke, ed., *The New Negro: Voices of the Harlem Renaissance* (1925; New York: Touchstone, 1997), originally published as *The New Negro: An Interpretation* (New York: Albert and Charles Boni). Eunice Roberta Hunton (1899–1970), later known as Eunice Hunton Carter, was born in Atlanta, moved to Harlem after graduating from Smith College, and earned a law degree from Fordham University School of Law in 1932. She was appointed by Fiorello La Guardia to serve as secretary to the Mayor's Commission on Conditions in Harlem, following the 1935 rioting, and became Dewey's deputy assistant that same year. After 1945, she worked in private practice and was active in the National Council of Negro Women, the National Association for the Advancement of Colored People, and other organizations. See Susan C. Puryear, "Eunice Roberta Hunton Carter, 1899–1970" (unpublished JD paper, Stanford University, 2001); Madison Gray, "Unsung Heroes: Eunice Hunton Carter, Mob Buster," *Time* (January 12, 2007), http://content.time.com/time/specials/packages/article/0,28804,1963424_1963480_1963450,00.html. For mentions of Hunton in Harlem Renaissance scholarship, see Barbara Foley, *Spectres of 1919: Class and Nation in the Making of the New Negro* (Urbana: University of Illinois Press, 2003), 226–27; Leonard Harris and Charles Molesworth, *Alain L. Locke: Biography of a Philosopher* (Chicago: University of Chicago Press, 2008), 195; George Hutchinson, *The Harlem Renaissance in Black and White* (Cambridge, MA: Belknap Press of Harvard University Press, 1995), 396.
2. Quoted in Andrew M. Fearnley, "When the Harlem Renaissance Became Vogue: Periodization and the Organization of Postwar American Historiography," *Modern Intellectual History* 11 (April 2014): 76–77.
3. Arna Bontemps, "The Two Harlems," *American Scholar* 14 (Spring 1945): 167, 170–71.
4. Gilbert Osofsky, *Harlem: The Making of a Ghetto—Negro New York, 1890–1930* (New York: Harper and Row, 1966), 187.
5. James de Jongh, *Vicious Modernism: Black Harlem and the Literary Imagination* (Cambridge: Cambridge University Press, 1990); James Edward Smethurst, *The Black Arts Movement: Literary Nationalism in the 1960s and 1970s* (Chapel Hill: University of North Carolina Press, 2005), 110.

6. Alain Locke, "Harlem: Dark Weather-Vane," *Survey Graphic* 25 (August 1936): 457. See, for example, Nathan Irvin Huggins, *Harlem Renaissance* (New York: Oxford University Press, 1971); David Levering Lewis, *When Harlem Was in Vogue* (New York: Alfred A. Knopf, 1981); Henry Louis Gates Jr., "Harlem on Our Minds," *Critical Inquiry* 24 (Autumn 1997): 1–12.
7. James Baldwin, "The Harlem Ghetto" (1948), in James Baldwin, *Collected Essays*, ed. Toni Morrison (New York: Library of America, 1998), 42–53; Horace R. Cayton and St. Clair Drake, *Black Metropolis* (1945; London: Jonathan Cape, 1946), 174–213; Mitchell Duneier, *Ghetto: The Invention of a Place, the History of an Idea* (New York: Farrar, Straus and Giroux, 2016), 24; Eric J. Sundquist, *Strangers in the Land: Blacks, Jews, Post-Holocaust America* (Cambridge, MA: Belknap Press of Harvard University Press, 2005), 391; Daniel Matlin, "Who Speaks for Harlem?: Kenneth B. Clark, Albert Murray and the Controversies of Black Urban Life," *Journal of American Studies* 46 (November 2012): 884; Fearnley, "When the Harlem Renaissance Became Vogue," 75–77; David Ward, *Poverty, Ethnicity, and the American City, 1840–1925: Changing Conceptions of the Slum and the Ghetto* (Cambridge: Cambridge University Press, 1989), 178.
8. Huggins, *Harlem Renaissance*, 4.
9. Earl Lewis, *In Their Own Interests: Race, Class, and Power in Twentieth-Century Norfolk, Virginia* (Berkeley: University of California Press, 1991), 90–91. Lewis's concept of "congregation" is also employed in Robin D. G. Kelley, " 'We Are Not What We Seem': Rethinking Black Working-Class Opposition in the Jim Crow South," *Journal of American History* 80 (June 1993): 75–112, esp. 79.
10. Locke, "Harlem," 629. On the dense tapestry of 1920s Harlem's associational and cultural life, see Clare Corbould, *Becoming African Americans: Black Public Life in Harlem, 1919–1939* (Cambridge, MA: Harvard University Press, 2009); Jervis Anderson, *This Was Harlem: A Cultural Portrait, 1900–1950* (New York: Farrar, Straus and Giroux, 1982); Winston James, *Holding Aloft the Banner of Ethiopia: Caribbean Radicalism in Early Twentieth-Century America* (London: Verso, 1998); Minkah Makalani, *In the Cause of Freedom: Radical Black Internationalism from Harlem to London, 1917–1939* (Chapel Hill: University of North Carolina Press, 2011); Jacob S. Dorman, *Chosen People: The Rise of American Black Israelite Religions* (New York: Oxford University Press, 2013).
11. Lewis, *In Their Own Interests*, 92.
12. Hunton, "Breaking Through," 684.
13. Harris and Molesworth, *Alain L. Locke*, 195. On the *Survey Graphic* and Paul Kellogg's editorial control over the Harlem issue, see Harris and Molesworth, *Alain L. Locke*, 188–90; Foley, *Spectres of 1919*, 224–25.
14. Konrad Bercovici, "The Rhythm of Harlem," *Survey Graphic* 6 (March 1925): 629.
15. Winthrop D. Lane, "Ambushed in the City: The Grim Side of Harlem," *Survey Graphic* 6 (March 1925): 692–94, 713–15.
16. Alain Locke, memorandum, n.d. [April 1924], in *The Survey Associates Records*, part 1, *The "Forget-Me-Not" Files* (microfilm, 57 reels) (Frederick, MD: University Publications of America, 1985), reel 39, frames 14, 16.
17. Hunton, "Breaking Through," 684; Kellogg to Locke, May 10, 1924.
18. Alain Locke, draft letter, October 25, 1924, box 164-88, folder 5, Alain Locke Papers, Moorland-Spingarn Research Center, Howard University, Washington, DC.
19. Alain Locke, "Enter the New Negro," *Survey Graphic* 6 (March 1925): 631–34. For a trenchant critique of Locke's "culturalism," see Foley, *Spectres of 1919*.
20. Henry Louis Gates Jr., "The Trope of a New Negro and the Reconstruction of the Image of the Black," *Representations* 24 (Autumn 1988): 129–55.

21. Locke, "Enter the New Negro," 630, 634.
22. Langston Hughes, *The Big Sea: An Autobiography* (1940; New York: Hill and Wang, 1993), 228.
23. Alain Locke, "Youth Speaks," *Survey Graphic* 6 (March 1925): 660.
24. Locke, "Enter the New Negro," 632. See also Ann Elizabeth Carroll, *Word, Image, and the New Negro: Representation and Identity in the Harlem Renaissance* (Bloomington: Indiana University Press, 2005), 122–55. The phrase "cultural pluralism," usually attributed to Horace Kallen, was in fact coined by Locke. See Foley, *Spectres of 1919*, 285.
25. Paul Kellogg to Alain Locke, February 5, 1925, box 164–88, folder 6, Locke Papers.
26. Locke, "Enter the New Negro," 634.
27. Locke, "Harlem," 629–30. Harlem's black population grew from 50,000 in 1914 to almost 165,000 in 1930. See Osofsky, *Harlem*, 105, 130.
28. Hunton, "Breaking Through," 684.
29. Kenneth B. Clark, *Dark Ghetto: Dilemmas of Social Power* (New York: Harper and Row, 1965), 11.
30. Locke, quoted in Jeffrey C. Stewart, *The New Negro: The Life of Alain Locke* (New York: Oxford University Press, 2018), 127. In 1903, the *New York Times* described as "appalling" the conditions in Brooklyn's Jewish "ghettos" of Williamsburg and Brownsville, "foreign cities within our city," where "American customs are unknown." "Immigration Problem Solved," *New York Times*, September 27, 1903. See also Ward, *Poverty*, esp. 2, 4, 7.
31. Locke, "Harlem," 630.
32. Locke, "Harlem," 629–30 (emphasis added). My references to the Harlem "sublime" borrow from Henry Louis Gates Jr.'s formulation: "Harlem as a site of the black cultural sublime was invented by those writers and artists at the turn of the century determined to transform the stereotypical image of Negro Americans as ex-slaves, members of an inherently inferior race—biologically and environmentally unfit for mechanized modernity and its cosmopolitan forms of fluid identity—into an image of a race of culture-bearers. To effect this transformation, the New Negro would need a nation over which to preside. And that nation's capital would be Harlem." Gates, "Harlem on Our Minds," 10.
33. James Weldon Johnson, "The Making of Harlem," *Survey Graphic* 6 (March 1925): 635–39.
34. Advertisements, *Survey Graphic* 6 (March 1925): 712; R. Jake Suddreth, "Nail, John E.," in *Encyclopedia of the Harlem Renaissance*, ed. Cary D. Wintz and Paul Finkelman (New York: Routledge, 2004), 2:855–56.
35. Hutchinson, *Harlem Renaissance*, 394.
36. Johnson, "Making of Harlem," 632, 635, 637–38.
37. Johnson, "Making of Harlem," 638–39. On living and working conditions in 1920s Harlem, see Jacob S. Dorman, "Back to Harlem: Abstract and Everyday Labor During the Harlem Renaissance," in *The Harlem Renaissance Revisited: Politics, Arts, and Letters*, ed. Jeffrey O. G. Ogbar (Baltimore, MD: Johns Hopkins University Press, 2010), 74–90.
38. Johnson, "Making of Harlem," 639. On "colony" and "quarter," see Ward, *Poverty*, 95, 186.
39. Johnson, "Making of Harlem," 639–40.
40. James Weldon Johnson, "Harlem: The Culture Capital," in Locke, *New Negro*, 301–11. For a defense of Johnson's notion of a "culture capital" that distinguishes it from Locke's "hierarchical" "race capital," see Cheryl A. Wall, "Harlem as Culture Capital in 1920s African American Fiction," present volume.
41. "The Gist of It," *Survey Graphic* 6 (March 1925): 627. For Boni's offer and conditions, see Paul Kellogg to Alain Locke, March 20, 1925, box 164–88, folder 6, Locke Papers. See also Martha Jane Nadell, *Enter the New Negroes: Images of Race in American Culture* (Cambridge, MA: Harvard University Press, 2004), 53–54. Other contributions written by the

magazine's staff—such as a description of Harlem as a community "hammered together by segregation"—also suggest that they were more comfortable than Locke with the imagery of the emerging ghetto discourse. See editorial, *Survey Graphic* 6 (March 1925): 698.
42. Kelly Miller, "Howard: The National Negro University," in Locke, *New Negro*, 312–22; Robert R. Moton, "Hampton-Tuskegee: Missioners of the Masses," in Locke, *New Negro*, 323–32; E. Franklin Frazier, "Durham: Capital of the Black Middle Class," in Locke, *New Negro*, 333–40. Also discarded by Locke was George E. Haynes, "The Church and the Negro Spirit," *Survey Graphic* 6 (March 1925): 695–97, 708–9.
43. Alain Locke, foreword to *New Negro*, xxvi–xxvii.
44. Alain Locke, "The New Negro," in Locke, *New Negro*, 3–16 at 7.
45. Johnson, "Harlem: The Culture Capital," 308.
46. Locke, foreword to *New Negro*, xxvi.
47. Rudolph Fisher, "The City of Refuge," in Locke, *New Negro*, 58–59. The story had originally been published in the *Atlantic Monthly* in February 1925.
48. Fisher, "City of Refuge," 61, 64.
49. Daylanne K. English, "Selecting the Harlem Renaissance," *Critical Inquiry* 25 (Summer 1999): 810, 814–15; Claude McKay, *Home to Harlem* (1928; New York: Pocket, 1965); Nella Larsen, *Quicksand* (1928; New York: Anchor, 2001); Nella Larsen, *Passing* (1928; New York: Modern Library, 2002). Among the critiques of Harlem Renaissance writers' "optimism" cited by English is Henry Louis Gates Jr.'s charge that "The 'Harlem' of literature and the Harlem of socio-economic reality were as far apart as Bessie Smith was from Paul Whiteman." Gates, "Harlem on Our Minds," 11.
50. McKay, *Home to Harlem*, 8.
51. Larsen, *Quicksand*, 77.
52. Larsen, *Quicksand*, quoted in Catherine Rottenberg, "Affective Narratives: Harlem and the Lower East Side," *Journal of American Studies* 44 (November 2010): 777, 785 (emphasis in original).
53. Wallace Thurman, "Negro Life in New York's Harlem: A Lively Picture of a Popular and Interesting Section," *Haldeman-Julius Quarterly* (Fall 1927), reprinted in Amritjit Singh and Daniel M. Scott III, eds., *The Collected Writings of Wallace Thurman: A Harlem Renaissance Reader* (New Brunswick, NJ: Rutgers University Press, 2003), 39–40; James Baldwin, "Fifth Avenue, Uptown: A Letter from Harlem," *Esquire* (July 1960), reprinted in Baldwin, *Collected Essays*, 170–79.
54. Wallace Thurman, "Harlem: A Vivid Word Picture of the World's Greatest Negro City," *American Monthly* (May 1927), reprinted in Singh and Scott, *Collected Writings*, 33.
55. Wallace Thurman, "Harlem Facets," *World Tomorrow* (November 1927), reprinted in Singh and Scott, *Collected Writings*, 35. See, more generally, Singh and Scott, *Collected Writings*, 32–78.
56. Avigail S. Oren, " 'Is a Negro District, in the Midst of Our Fairest Cities, to Become Connotative of the Ghetto . . . ?': Using Corpus Analysis to Trace the 'Ghetto' in the Black Press, 1900–1930," in *The Ghetto in Global History: 1500 to the Present*, ed. Wendy Z. Goldman and Joe William Trotter Jr. (Abingdon: Routledge, 2018), 206–22, esp. 214. Oren's essay is a useful counterpart to Mitchell Duneier's *Ghetto*, which impressively analyzes black social scientists' handling of the ghetto concept from the 1940s onward but gives little attention to earlier notions of the black ghetto.
57. "Drive Opens Today to Better Harlem," *New York Times*, May 24, 1942.
58. Locke, "Harlem: Dark Weather-Vane," 457–58, 462. In an earlier draft, Locke had used the wording "disease- and crime-ridden Ghetto." See Alain Locke, "Harlem: Dark Weather-Vane," typescript, n.d. [June 1936?], in *Survey Associates Records*, part 1, reel 39, frame 374.

59. Baldwin, "Harlem Ghetto"; Ralph Ellison, "Harlem Is Nowhere" (1948), in *The Collected Essays of Ralph Ellison*, ed. John F. Callahan (New York: Modern Library, 2003), 320–27, esp. 325; Daniel Matlin, *On the Corner: African American Intellectuals and the Urban Crisis* (Cambridge, MA: Harvard University Press, 2013), 23–24, 58. For a defense of "ghetto" as a characterization of the spatial forms created by U.S. urban segregation, see Loïc Wacquant, " 'A Black City Within the White': Revisiting America's Dark Ghetto," *Black Renaissance/Renaissance Noire* 2 (Fall/Winter 1998): 141–51.
60. Sundquist, *Strangers in the Land*, 391 (italics in original).
61. Langston Hughes, *Montage of a Dream Deferred* (1951), reprinted in Arnold Rampersad and David Roessel, eds., *The Collected Poems of Langston Hughes* (New York: Vintage Classics, 1995), 387–429, esp. 426.
62. De Jongh, *Vicious Modernism*, 178.
63. New York City Planning Commission, *Plan for New York City, 1969: A Proposal* (Cambridge, MA: MIT Press, 1969), 4:114, 134. On the imagery of the "urban crisis," see Matlin, *On the Corner*; Carlo Rotella, *October Cities: The Redevelopment of Urban Literature* (Berkeley: University of California Press, 1998). Smethurst has described a "symbolic merging of the earlier 'Negro capital of the world' of the Harlem Renaissance with the prototypical everyghetto 'home' of the 1930s and 1940s" in the postwar writings of Hughes, Baldwin, Ellison, and Chester Himes. Smethurst, *Black Arts Movement*, 111.
64. *Across 110th Street*, directed by Barry Shear (United Artists, 1972). The title song was cowritten by Bobby Womack and the jazz trombonist J. J. Johnson. For an appreciation of the film and its music, see Greil Marcus, *Mystery Train: Images of America in Rock 'n' Roll Music* (New York: Plume, 1997), 84–86.

4.

WHAT'S THE MATTER WITH *BABY SISTER*?

Chester Himes's Struggles to Film Harlem

PAULA J. MASSOOD

In a 1963 letter to filmmaker Shirley Clarke, Chester Himes observed, "U.S. distributors won't touch anything, at the moment it seems, that has anything to do with what is quaintly called 'The Negro Problem.' "[1] Though Himes was referring to Clarke's difficulties in distributing her film *The Cool World* (1963), he could just as easily have been referencing his own struggles to publish his novels and short stories and to bring his written works to the screen. From his failed attempts to adapt his first detective novel, *For Love of Imabelle* (1957), to his inability to successfully turn his screenplays into films—one an adaptation of his protest novel *If He Hollers Let Him Go* (1945), and the other, *Baby Sister*, an original script about Harlem, written in 1961—Himes faced insurmountable challenges in moving his unconventional renderings of Harlem from page to screen.[2]

In this chapter, I will explore the interconnected factors that contributed to Himes's inability to transfer his written works to the screen, from the aforementioned reluctance of film studios and distributors to deal with the "Negro problem" to the unwillingness of the National Association for the Advancement of Colored People (NAACP) to allow *Baby Sister* to be shot in Harlem. How did film, as a key and fraught medium of urban aesthetics, factor into the competing definitions of African American life at this time? And what was it about *Baby Sister*, the story—or Himes, the person—that ensured that the NAACP was unable to support the project during the early 1960s?

Since the Great Depression, the hopeful image of Harlem as a "race capital" characterized by black opportunity and achievement had been questioned, with film and photography often depicting the neighborhood as a problematic site of poverty, social fragmentation, criminality, and festering unrest.[3] Yet the reaction of the NAACP's leadership to Himes's script indicates just how invested some sections of the civil rights establishment and broader African American opinion continued to be in notions of Harlem as an exceptional locus of black achievement, respectability, and racial uplift. The conflict between Himes and the NAACP thus underscores the neighborhood's endurance as a crucial—and fiercely contested—spatial and visual metaphor for African American life well into the postwar period.

The origins and time line of the *Baby Sister* project are murky, though a number of facts are relatively clear. Like several notable African American artists at this time, including James Baldwin and Richard Wright, Himes migrated to Paris in 1954 and then led a peripatetic life over the next decade or so, spending time in France, Spain, Germany, Italy, and the United States. While in France, Himes was approached by filmmaker Pierre-Dominique Gaisseau and producer Arthur Cohn, who wished to make a film about Harlem. According to Himes, both Gaisseau and Cohn had recently seen the film adaptation of Lorraine Hansberry's *A Raisin in the Sun* (directed by Daniel Petrie, 1961), and the pair felt that the author could write a "better film about Harlem" (despite the fact that Hansberry's play and the adaptation were set in Chicago).[4]

By this point, Himes had already gained a following in France, based on his well-received series of detective novels published by Éditions Gallimard. Those stories, set in Harlem and focusing on the neighborhood's criminal elements, illustrated that he was unafraid to present contemporary Harlem, warts and all. This was a change from the neighborhood's more celebratory images, an enduring remnant of the music, art, and literature produced during the Harlem Renaissance years, which still existed in projects such as Langston Hughes and Roy DeCarava's photo-text collection *The Sweet Flypaper of Life* (1955), in which "Harlem returns to its roots as a promised land."[5] Himes began writing the screenplay for *Baby Sister* in 1961, while in a hospital in France recovering from injuries sustained in a car accident.

Before moving on to a consideration of *Baby Sister*, it is important to spend a moment discussing Gaisseau and Cohn, the pair who proposed the Harlem film project to Himes. Gaisseau was a French explorer and documentarian who had made a number of films about his various expeditions in South America, Papua New Guinea, and the African nations of Guinea and Mali. Cohn, a film producer based in Switzerland, was the younger brother of Harry Cohn, then president of Columbia Pictures. At the time that the pair contacted Himes, they were enjoying the success (Gaisseau as director, Cohn as producer) of *Le Ciel et la Boue* (The Sky Above—The Mud Below) (1961), a documentary detailing the seven-month journey of a French-Dutch expedition, which had included Gaisseau, through Dutch New Guinea (West Papua). The film, which won the Academy Award for Best Documentary in 1962, was notorious for the conditions endured by those involved in the production, resulting, for example, in the deaths of three porters and countless injuries and illnesses.[6]

Le Ciel et la Boue's sensational production details, however, belie a strictly conventional ethnographic film featuring a voice-over describing a land where "men still live in the Stone Age" and "nothing has changed since Captain Cook's day," and which refers to the island's inhabitants as headhunters, cannibals, and "real savages."[7] In its approach to its subject, which highlighted the disparity between the "rugged white men" and "naked black natives," the film was an example of traditional ethnographic filmmaking of the type that "reveals an obsession with race and racial categorization in the construction of peoples always already Primitive."[8] These were the forms of representations that the NAACP and other civil rights groups were fighting against.[9] While it is unclear what Himes meant when describing the pair's desire to make a "better film" than *A Raisin in the Sun*, we can surmise that Gaisseau and Cohn were influenced partially by an enduring European fascination with Harlem, and partially by an ethnographic primitivism toward nonwhite, non-European others.[10]

Himes later described *Baby Sister*, somewhat cryptically, as influenced by "memories of Faulkner, the writings of slaves, the novel of a[n unnamed] black woman writer,... Tennessee Williams's *Baby Doll* [at least the title], and the way I looked at Harlem."[11] The work's narrative is quite simple. It spans three days in the life of a seventeen-year-old Harlemite named "Baby Sister" Louis and her assorted friends and family members. Baby Sister and her family (three brothers and her mother) live in a cramped apartment in "the Valley," a neighborhood located around 116th Street and described as "shabbier than... 125th Street, louder, rougher; the automobiles parked along the curb are older, the goods for sale are inferior." Young and voluptuous, Baby Sister is "a juicy, tasty lamb in a jungle of hungry wolves."[12] The "wolves" include one of her brothers (Susie), who attempts to sell her to a local pimp (Slick Collins); her white cop boyfriend (Lieutenant Fischer), who impregnates her; and the local preacher (the Reverend Converted Sinner), who attempts to rape her. Baby Sister manages to survive what Himes described as a "Greek tragedy in blackface," but not before she inadvertently causes the deaths of her father, two of her brothers, and her police officer boyfriend.[13]

Himes's screenplay extends many of the themes found in his series of Harlem detective novels, which began with Gallimard's publication of *For Love of Imabelle* (*A Rage in Harlem*), in 1957, and continued through the next twelve years. In many ways, *Baby Sister* picks up from *Imabelle*, particularly in its depictions of Harlem. Indeed, Himes's descriptions of the area are almost identical across the two texts. For example, *Baby Sister* introduces the neighborhood in the following way:

This is Harlem, USA, a city of contradictions. A city of Negroes isolated in the center of New York City. A city of incredible poverty and huge sums of cash. A city of the meek and the violent.... Here is the part called the Valley, where the hungry eke out an existence and prey upon one another. The Valley is like a sea filled with cannibal fish. Put in your hand, draw out a stub.[14]

Just four years earlier, *Imabelle*'s Harlem setting was described as follows:

Looking eastward from the towers of Riverside Church, perched among the university buildings on the high banks of the Hudson River, in a valley far below, waves of gray rooftops distort the perspective like the surface of a sea. Below the surface, in the murky waters of fetid tenements, a city of black people who are convulsed in desperate living, like the voracious churning of millions of hungry cannibal fish. Blind mouths eating their own guts. Stick in a hand and draw back a nub. That is Harlem.[15]

Both passages present the neighborhood as a dangerous place that exists apart from the rest of the city. Harlem is New York's vicious underbelly, an area so stricken by poverty and neglect that it dehumanizes its inhabitants and forces them into lives of crime and venality. In this element of his work, Himes not only was echoing the arguments of urban sociologists of the time but also was stating a theme that would engage him for years to come. In his essay "Harlem: An American Cancer" (1963), for example, Himes extended the metaphor by arguing that the neighborhood exists "like a cancer on the body of a nation," where "discouraged, disillusioned, and defenseless people [live] Jim Crow."[16] And yet such imagery points to the ways in which the author was also interested in presenting a highly detailed and heterogeneous community, one in which saints reside next to sinners, the rich next to the poor, and strivers next to nihilists. With the backing of an Academy Award–winning director (albeit a French documentarian) and a producer with industry connections, it seemed as though *Baby Sister* would have a relatively easy path to production. This was not the case, however.

Once Himes completed *Baby Sister*, Cohn began the work of securing financial backing for the film. Despite the fact that the majority of the individuals attached to the project were based in Europe, Cohn, perhaps because of his Hollywood connections, sought funding from a number of major American studios.[17] According to Himes's account of the project in *My Life of Absurdity*, Cohn failed to find an investor because the Americans deemed the project "too much risk for its potential."[18] They were interested in films with more respectable projections of black life, such as those presented in *A Raisin in the Sun*, which details the story of an African American family determined to improve their lives by moving into an all-white Chicago suburb.

In order to parse what Himes meant by "too much risk for its potential," we first have to place the project in the context of Hollywood film at this time. Until World War II, African American characters were rarely seen in American film, except as uncredited extras or in minor roles that reinforced existing stereotypes (appearing as domestic help, for example).[19] Following the war, and after pressure from the Hollywood branch of the NAACP for more and improved African American representation, the industry began producing a series of low-budget films focusing on a variety of social ills, including racism, anti-Semitism, alcoholism, and drug abuse. As a result, the 1950s and 1960s saw a selection of "message movies," such as *No Way Out* (1950), *The World, the Flesh, and the Devil* (1958), *Odds Against Tomorrow* (1959), and *Guess Who's Coming to Dinner* (1967), which presented noble African American characters (often played by Sidney Poitier or Harry Belafonte) overcoming prejudice in all-white settings.[20]

Many of these films, including *A Raisin in the Sun*, stressed black achievement and integration, political tropes that had been central to the NAACP since its establishment in 1909. Unlike such examples, but in keeping with his popular fiction, Himes's *Baby Sister* presented a world peopled by many of the character types—criminal men, loose women, dysfunctional families—that the NAACP had been attempting to eliminate from American film since D. W. Griffith's infamous *The Birth of a Nation* (1915). Indeed, Cohn was referring to more than financial matters when discussing the screenplay's riskiness in Hollywood. He was alluding to what film scholar Michael Gillespie has described, in another context, as the "irreconcilable force of Himes's transgressiveness."[21]

In addition to Cohn's inability to secure financing for *Baby Sister*, the project also faced political opposition, particularly from the NAACP. After receiving a copy of the screenplay, the organization sent Cohn a letter, objecting to Himes's story. That the NAACP had issues with *Baby Sister* is hardly surprising. The screenplay's eponymous lead is presented as half victim of circumstance (living in a place with "no good shepherd") and half willing participant. For example, Baby Sister is described as a "hot-bodied, curly-haired, high-breasted brown-skin [sic] girl exuding an effluvium of sex urgency, with hips [that] are doing a hard slow suggestive shake in her skintight skirt. Her bedroom eyes are taunting and her big hard breasts molded in a tight sweater are haunting." Himes continues, "This is Baby Sister, Sing Sing quail, a lecher's dream, enough to make a preacher lay his Bible down." Her appearance and behavior result in stares and unwanted advances. In a later scene, Baby Sister climbs the stairs to her family's apartment and "every man she passes accosts her, tries to proposition her or rub against her.... The women avoid contact with her as though she is contaminated."[22] So, at seventeen, Baby Sister has firsthand experience of the benefits and curses of being an attractive young woman in Harlem.

Why would the NAACP object to Himes's characterization of Baby Sister and her family? In *Uplifting the Race*, historian Kevin K. Gaines argues that the core components of uplift ideology for many black elites included "an emphasis on self-help, racial solidarity, temperance, thrift, chastity, social purity, patriarchal authority, and the accumulation of wealth." In order to counter the degradations of slavery, along with the more egregious "minstrel-based constructions of blackness," black elites based their "status on . . . racialized conceptions of bourgeois morality," which privileged the male-headed household and marriage "as a sign of monogamous sexual purity."[23] Himes's rendering of Baby Sister's family situation in general, and Baby Sister in particular, would have challenged the ideological foundations of an elite organization like the NAACP, which was intent on countering the pervasive narratives around the dysfunctional black family.

Regardless of this, and despite the times when Baby Sister uses her sex appeal to her benefit (acquiring clothes, meals, drinks, and other gifts from her many admirers), she is presented sympathetically—or as sympathetically as any of Himes's characters can be. In the scene just described, for example, her response is to "fend off [her male neighbors], some angrily, some laughingly, some flirtingly."[24] This is also the case in her affair with a local police officer, which is depicted with more sensitivity than one would expect, given the subject matter and the time period. Lieutenant Fischer, a white man "handsome enough to be a movie actor," is in love with Baby Sister but is neither brave enough to be seen in public with her nor chivalrous enough to stand by her once he learns she is pregnant with his child. Instead, he pays for an abortion, telling her that "it's the wrong world" for their love and a biracial offspring.[25] The narrative is curious here because it not only indicates Baby Sister's genuine (if perhaps immature) feelings for Fischer but also suggests that his attraction to her extends beyond sex. In fact, Fischer is a far more sympathetic white character—or police officer—than Himes usually wrote (and his detective novels stand in contrast here).

As this suggests, the screenplay presented complex characters along with its more one-dimensional treatments of Harlemites. Despite this, there remains an element of the narrative that focuses on—and celebrates—Harlem's more degraded aspects. Indeed, *Baby Sister* resonates with sexual innuendo, drinking, drugs, violence, and death, much of which is relayed in Himes's characteristic lampooning style. Again, such components link the screenplay to Himes's novels, which, argues Christopher Breu, are "designed to shock or disturb, producing narratives that not only resist categorization but also flaunt conventional morality and eschew easy recuperation by any single ethical or political position."[26] This is on full display, for example, in Baby Sister's aforementioned introduction. But this technique, complete with its aspects of parody (for instance, in the scenes of amateur night at the Apollo Theater), satire (especially around the hypocrisy of the black church), and humor, could have tipped the scales against the project for investors who may have worried about the screenplay's more minstrel-like moments at a time when the film industry was making cautious (though glacial) attempts to change racial representation on the screen. Even more important for this discussion is *Baby Sister*'s tone, which likely alienated members of the NAACP who were given to conventional uplift melodramas and thus opposed to Himes's strategic use of the absurd to combat racism. As Gaines suggests, for black elites, "claiming respectability often meant denouncing nonconformity to patriarchal gender conventions and bourgeois morality."[27]

Himes was no stranger to the NAACP, particularly members of its New York branch, and some of the organization's opposition may also have been personally directed at him.[28] Even though he wrote about Harlem, Himes was not from Harlem, although he had briefly lived there at different times, "storing up," as he put it, "all the imagination and observations and absurdities which were destined to make my Harlem novels a success."[29] He spent time in the neighborhood in the early 1940s, for example, visiting his cousin Henry Lee Moon and his cousin's wife, socialite Mollie Lewis.[30] The Moons were influential members of New York's black community, with Henry serving as the NAACP's national publicity director and Mollie as the director of the New York chapter of the Urban League. Both were also active in national politics and worked as advisors to President Roosevelt as part of what was informally known as his "Black Cabinet."[31] During the summer of 1944, Himes stayed in the Moon household, where he became acquainted with members of Harlem's political and cultural elite, including NAACP Executive Secretary Walter White, political scientist Ralph Bunche, and author Ralph Ellison.[32]

Later, after a falling out with the Moons over his sexual indiscretions (Himes was married but had numerous affairs), Himes drew upon his experiences there as the basis for his French-language novel *Mamie Mason* (1962). The novel was a sexually explicit burlesque of Harlem's black bourgeoisie that included scenes of debauched parties and interracial sex, all of which Himes described as a "Rabelaisian treatment of the sex motivation of New York's inter-racial set."[33] Himes admitted that the main character, socialite Mamie Mason, was based on Mollie Lewis, and a number of the characters in the novel were loosely veiled references to Harlemites he had met while staying with the Moons. As Gaines argues, "Black elites defended elite black women against scholarly and journalistic accusations of unchastity," with concerns over miscegenation "plac[ing] a judgmental scrutiny on the conduct of black women."[34] In short, *Mamie Mason* may have cut too close to the bone for Harlem's respectable set, many of whom were well connected to the NAACP and were invested in a strictly heteronormative definition of black sexuality.

If Himes's bawdy subject matter and tendency to show the underbelly of African American life were not enough to turn the NAACP against *Baby Sister*, the U.S. publication of *Pinktoes* (1961), the English-language version of

Mamie Mason, certainly was. As the author wrote in a 1962 letter to writer and journalist John A. Williams, Cohn showed a copy of the screenplay to Herbert Hill, labor secretary of the NAACP, in the hope of gaining the association's support for the project and winning industry funding and technical support.[35] Himes claimed that Hill, aware of the controversy surrounding *Pinktoes*, then "wrote to Cohn . . . that he and his colleagues in the association objected to [*Baby Sister*'s] story and [promised that] they would do everything in their power to keep it from being produced."[36] Indeed, Hill described the screenplay as "nothing more than a travesty on Negro life in Harlem . . . hav[ing] no relationship to reality and . . . not redeemed by any literary values."[37] Cohn dropped the project not long afterwards, and the screenplay then ended up in the hands of Joseph E. Levine of Embassy Pictures, a distributor of foreign films, who had moved into film production. Again, according to Himes, Hill intervened in the name of the NAACP and the project died.[38]

In his letters, and then again in his autobiography, Himes clearly laid the blame for *Baby Sister*'s failure on the NAACP. The organization either was unhappy with the author's "debased" representation of middle-class Harlemites in *Pinktoes* or was more generally distressed at Himes's depiction of the underbelly of Harlem life in his detective novels and in *Baby Sister*. Their intervention undoubtedly contributed to the project's failure. But the issue is more complicated than a case of informal blacklisting or respectability politics, and it can be connected back to Himes's letter to Shirley Clarke from 1963—written not long after the *Baby Sister* project had died, in which he cites the reluctance of U.S. distributors to touch anything that might explore the "Negro problem."

In his letter to Clarke, Himes was addressing the director's recent troubles finding distributors for her new feature film (cowritten with Carl Lee) *The Cool World*, an adaptation of Warren Miller's 1959 novel.[39] The narrative of both the novel and the film focuses on a young gang member in Harlem named Duke Custis, and it tracks his attempts to buy a pistol as a means of wresting the leadership of the gang from its drug-addled president. For Duke, the gun is a ticket to his version of the American Dream, where the interconnected elements of masculinity and success are defined by the weapon one carries. The film was shot on location in Harlem and featured the neighborhood's streets, residents, and buildings (it was set in one of the New York Housing Authority's abandoned tenement buildings). Such settings contributed to the film's sense of despair, its decaying interiors and rubble-strewn exteriors suggestive of the economic destitution of Duke's surroundings. This is supplemented by an overwhelming emotional poverty, exemplified in the teen's home life, which is defined by an overworked and distracted mother, an absent father, and a Bible-thumping grandmother. *The Cool World* thus presents a grim and hopeless existence in which young black men and women drift into lives of crime and prostitution for lack of better options or role models. Like *Baby Sister*, it is also a film about the "Negro problem," and it utilizes Harlem as a metaphor for larger forces of urban exclusion and disorder weighing down on American political and social discourses during the early 1960s.

With its focus on black urban criminality and a realist style consisting of location shooting, direct sound, and use of nonprofessional actors, Clarke's film continued an already familiar trope in visual culture, one that had been evident in photojournalism, which from the 1930s on had described America's "ghettos" with almost sociological detail. Clarke's film sets a serious tone, utilizing elements of environmental determinism and discourses of black pathology already familiar to the American public from photo magazines such as *Life*, *Fortune*, and *Look*. Gordon Parks's "Harlem Gang Leader," published in 1948, serves as a good example of the way Harlem was treated as a visual ghetto, even before films such as *The Cool World* or *Baby Sister* put (or attempted to put) these images on screen.

"Harlem Gang Leader" was Parks's first photo feature for *Life* magazine. While Parks's images focus on Red Jackson (and Parks spent weeks with the young man), the gang leader of the title, the accompanying text introduces its human subject through a description of his urban surroundings. One side of the article's two-page title spread features Red in profile, while the other side includes a long-shot photo of Harlem's cityscape, overlaid with text that reads:

> The tower in the upper right-hand corner of this page belongs to New York City's famous Riverside Church. Stretching off to the left of it are the classic buildings of Columbia University and the elegant apartments of some of the city's leading citizens. Nestled just below these, under the smoke and haze, are the crowded tenements and the cluttered, dreary streets of Harlem, the U.S.'s biggest Negro community. Here 500,000 people live, crammed into a ghettolike section built originally to hold less than half that number. Schools, like housing, are crowded and run-down, and at the close of each day overworked teachers are glad to turn their restless pupils back into the streets. With little to do but roam around, the children often band together into street gangs—at their best, organized athletic teams, at their worst, roving bands of hoodlums held together by a common spirit of rebellion and a need for security. Leonard ("Red") Jackson, 17, is the tough and successful leader of such a gang.[40]

The text describes Harlem as a cramped ghetto and Red as the inevitable product of the "Negro problem." Miller's *The Cool World* echoed this language, as did Clarke's later film. As the quoted passages from *For Love of Imabelle* and *Baby Sister*, discussed earlier, indicate, Himes employed similar imagery in his own Harlem fiction a decade later. Unlike what appears in "Harlem Gang Leader," however, Himes rejected earnest representations based on realist aesthetics in favor of a stylistic manifestation of his view that "not only does racism express the absurdity of the racists, but it generates absurdity in the victims."[41] Only absurd narratives could capture an absurd situation in which "poverty and ghettoization [are seen] as pathologies of family disorganization rather than as the result of systematic factors such as exclusion from the labor market and housing discrimination."[42]

Focusing on a simplified interpretation of Clarke's film as presenting black pathology obscures the complex factors behind both *The Cool World*'s production and its failure to find an audience, reasons that may also provide insight into Himes's own experiences with *Baby Sister*. *The Cool World* is a seemingly straightforward cautionary tale about a young man's criminal turn—in this way it conformed to the social science–inflected discourses of urbanists and politicians—and this may be one of the main reasons that the project was made in the first place (and why producer Frederick Wiseman was interested in adapting the novel to film). Yet the film's avant-garde aesthetics were far less conventional, and in the end these aesthetics, rather than the story, may have contributed to its difficulty in securing wide distribution in the United States.

In creating what has been described as a "tone poem of the slums," Clarke drew from her background in documentary film and experimental narrative to create a layered and complex set of aesthetics.[43] *The Cool World* combines stylistic elements from a number of cinematic modes, including voice-over narration and the mobile camera and location shooting of contemporary documentary practices, nonnarrative visual and aural montage sequences from avant-garde cinema, and more conventional dramatic scenes that propel the story forward by providing motive and conflict. Despite these latter, more classical narrative elements, the film often looks and sounds like an experimental documentary.

Because of its unconventional approach to its subject, *The Cool World* proved to be a hard sell to both general and "targeted" (i.e., theaters in black neighborhoods) audiences. Clarke and Wiseman's decision to take the film through the festival circuit may also have affected its chances for a wider release because it situated the film as art cinema. Moreover, Wiseman's promotion of Clarke as the film's director and his effective neglect of her collaborator, Carl Lee, may have unduly affected the film's appeal among African American audiences. In the end, *The Cool World* was seen and sold as an art film, and this, along with its style, may have worked against Clarke's desire for a wider audience that could have included African American patrons.

How do Shirley Clarke's difficulties with *The Cool World* relate to Chester Himes's experiences with *Baby Sister*? Although it may be difficult to draw a direct line between the two projects, beyond their creators' correspondence, one can make plausible connections relating to subject matter and aesthetics, especially since both projects were in the works at the same time. It is undeniable that *The Cool World*—the novel and the film—draws on the tradition of social problem literature, especially that which focuses on the perils of urban living. This was acceptable subject matter for organizations like the Urban League and the Congress of Racial Equality, both of which supported the film.[44] Duke's problems stem from impoverished surroundings and an American economic and political system that has failed him and other Harlemites like him, and in this way the film tells a familiar story without providing extended analysis or solutions. The main problem lay with the film's unconventional style and structure, which made it difficult to find a suitable market. In short, the film's aesthetic style meant that it did not *look* like a problem picture or a documentary, and this worked against it. Even so, it was eventually made (on a very small budget, financed by Wiseman), and the problems it encountered occurred after its release.

Baby Sister, on the other hand, never succeeded in being produced, a fate that was due to a combination of its subject matter and its style. When Himes wrote *Baby Sister*, he had already shifted away from his more overtly political subject matter, like that in *If He Hollers Let Him Go*, and toward genre fiction, such as the detective novel and the sexual farce (exemplified by *Pinktoes*), with the detective genre allowing him to, as Gillespie suggests, present "a sense of the absurd as a black existential trope and as a narrative device."[45] Though *Baby Sister* is not a detective film, it contains many of the elements of Himes's genre work, including a focus on Harlem's criminal milieu and an explicit interest in sex—so much so, in fact, that it is hard to take it seriously at times. And yet the screenplay also contains moments when Himes attempts to place Baby Sister's story within a larger political and cultural context. For example, *Baby Sister*'s Harlem is described again, later in the screenplay, in the following way:

> The inhabitants of this community, restricted, exploited, prostituted, violated and violent, timid and vicious, living in their rat-ridden, hotbox, stinking flats, are either the hungry wolves themselves, or are struggling to save themselves from hungry wolves. And it is perfectly reasonable and natural these people should be hungry ... If your own food—food for the soul and food for the spirit as well as food for the stomach—had been held just out of reach for three hundred years, or longer, you would be hungry too.[46]

Such political consciousness runs throughout the story (as it does through most of Himes's detective fiction), but it is often overshadowed by the more salacious elements of the narrative. Thus, while Baby Sister's story is ultimately tragic—indeed, a "Greek tragedy in blackface"—her overdetermined appearance and behavior, along with the story's violence and sexual context, are some of the most memorable elements of the screenplay.

As Himes suggests in his autobiography, his move to France coincided with his shift away from protest fiction. When approached by Marcel Duhamel at

Gallimard, the author—initially reluctant to write detective novels—soon began regularly contributing to the editor's *Série noire* imprint. In a European context influenced by the traces of surrealism and existentialism, Himes began honing a different style, one that "embrac[ed] absurdity as both a social condition and as a narrative apparatus." For Himes, absurdity was more than a style or a plot device; it pertained, argues Jonathan P. Eburne, "specifically to the conditions of black life in America, through which African Americans are interpolated into racist relations independently of their will, even in spite of their recognition of its effects."[47] As Himes wrote, in the early 1970s, "racism generating from whites is first of all absurd. Racism creates absurdity among blacks as a defense mechanism. Absurdity to combat absurdity. . . . So it was with me."[48] In other words, the parody and satire, the violence and crime, and the language found in *Baby Sister* are employed to describe living conditions that would otherwise be overwhelmingly stifling.

Himes's shift from social realism to a more caustic form of social satire was also a move away from the moralistic posturing and earnestness often associated with uplift literature. In the process, such a move upended deep-seated cultural and political questions over the symbolic importance of Harlem in black life. In "Who Speaks for Harlem?," historian Daniel Matlin identifies a split in the early 1960s between social scientists like Kenneth B. Clark, who saw black cityspaces like Harlem as socially dysfunctional ghettos, and cultural critics like Albert Murray, who argued against such discourses of pathology. Murray also dismissed the idea that films like *The Cool World* were examples of "realistic documentation," arguing that it was "no more realistic than the book itself, which was more concerned about being cute about everything than about being accurate about anything."[49]

Although Himes was not actively involved in Murray and Clark's dispute, his descriptions of the cityspace as a "sea filled with cannibal fish" suggest that he saw the city, like Clark, as a place that bred sickness in its inhabitants.[50] But Himes transforms the pathological into the absurd by injecting humor into moments of violence, rage, and moral turpitude. Moreover, he never intended his rendering of the city to be taken as anything other than fiction. As he states, "The Harlem of my books was never meant to be real; I never called it real," thus providing a counterpoint to Herbert Hill's earlier equation of "literary values" with "a relationship to reality."[51] In effect, Himes "question[ed] writing's ability to either channel or represent the 'deadly venom' of racism and rage alike."[52] Yet, despite his descriptions of Harlem, he never directly ascribes the behavior of characters to the place. Rather, he attributes it to larger systemic effects of antiblack racism, segregation, and discrimination. In short, Himes's Harlem stories were neither celebrations nor critiques of black life. This tonal, generic, and political "unplaceability" may have been the stories' undoing, particularly where cinematic adaptation—often reliant on the "real"—was concerned.

Less than a decade later, and in a different industrial and political context, Himes's transgressive style and subject matter were finally translated to the screen in Ossie Davis's 1970 adaptation of Himes's *Cotton Comes to Harlem* (1964). Davis's version of the novel remains fairly faithful to the original story, which involves the theft of $87,000 from a fraudulent "Back-to-Africa" movement and the mysterious appearance of a bale of cotton on the streets of Harlem. The filmic version differs, however, in its overall tone and in the ways in which Harlem is portrayed on the screen. Unlike Himes's use of noir tropes to provide a sense of the black absurd (what Gillespie has described as a "historically and culturally precise sense of angst [via] irrationality [and] disorienting skepticism"),[53] Davis's *Cotton Comes to Harlem* removes many of the narrative's noir elements and replaces them with a carnivalesque rendering of a detective story, communicated in bright colors, Afrocentric clothing, and contemporary music and idioms. Likewise, Himes's Harlem is largely stripped of its more visceral aspects. Instead, Davis's Harlem was intended, according to the director, to show the neighborhood as a "complete world, one which includes moments of joy and laughter as well as misery and discontent."[54]

One of the major factors in the successful adaptation of *Cotton* was the industry's increased interest in African American subject matter in the late 1960s and early 1970s.[55] But an even more forceful influence on the film may have been Ossie Davis's involvement. *Cotton* was Davis's directorial debut, but his acting career (on stage and screen) stretched back two decades and included theatrical writing and directing credits. Moreover, his decades-long civil rights activities, including his involvement in the 1963 March on Washington, provided him with political and artistic gravitas within the African American and white communities. While Himes may have been a pariah among the NAACP leadership and black bourgeoisie, Davis was a well-respected and admired race man. At this time, there may have been no safer bet for ushering Himes's Harlem stories onto the screen.

But Davis was not without his own controversies, especially related to the fraught nature and history of what Gillespie calls "film blackness," or the attempt to reframe black film away from the "presumption that the fundamental value of a black film is exclusively measured by a consensual truth of film's capacity to wholly account for the lived social experience or social life of a race."[56] In short, Davis's films also tended to strain what Hill called the "relationship to reality." Davis's play *Purlie Victorius* (1961) and its subsequent screen adaptation serves as an example of the continuing concern over appropriate aesthetics for African American narratives. It tells the story of a traveling con man/preacher who returns home to Georgia to claim an inheritance, with the intention of saving the community's church and becoming its spiritual leader. The play is broadly farcical, and it self-consciously appropriates stereotypes such as the Uncle Tom and racist southern whites to "comment meaningfully on them."[57] Davis, with partner Philip Rose and producers Milton and Thomas Hammer, adapted the play for the screen, selecting Nicholas Webster as the director.

The film version, titled *Gone Are the Days*, opened in 1963 to a lackluster response. In *Soul Searching*, Christopher Sieving examines the reasons behind the film's box office troubles, from its producers' inability to draw African American audiences to the film's use of stereotypes that, while being self-consciously deployed, were seen as "too controversial" by some distributors. Sieving also suggests that the film's failure was partially due to the fact that it "in no way satisfied the criterion of 'accuracy' or 'authenticity' established by the NAACP as the prime objective for African American–themed filmmaking." In other words, rather than draw upon the preferred aesthetics of realism or uplift, the film's self-conscious style and performance modes (direct address, use of sets rather than locations) worked against it, much as aesthetics had worked against *Baby Sister*.[58]

Davis did not direct a film until 1970, when he and Arnold Perl adapted *Cotton Comes to Harlem* for the screen, from a preexisting screenplay. As I have suggested, Davis's version of the work reduces many of the novel's more transgressive elements and replaces them with a farcical tone that celebrates Harlem and its residents while occasionally also pointing to the neighborhood's shortcomings. Davis's reasoning behind these changes wavered. On the one hand, they were in keeping with his own style, which often used farce and comedy as a means of examining race relations through a "pro-nationalist or anti-assimilationist" lens. On the other hand, Davis's experiences with *Gone Are the Days* made him aware of the limitations of stylistic experimentation.[59] For Davis (and *Cotton*'s backers), therefore, Himes's particular use of the absurd to examine black life in America may have been too much in its original form. The result of Davis's changes, argues Gillespie, is a "lack of a substantial sense of the black absurd, resulting in carnivalesque slapstick [rather] than a brutal allegory of vicious irrationality."[60]

This final point takes us back to Himes's observations about the "Negro problem." It could be that there was no market for Clarke's *The Cool World*, based on its subject matter alone, but it would seem that the film's style ultimately had just as much to do with its inability to find its place among viewers. Likewise, *Baby Sister*'s subject matter no doubt contributed to its difficulties, particularly with the American investors Arthur Cohn targeted for financing. Its story of a sexy, young, and tragic heroine was too much of a risk for such investors, who were looking for politically safer (and therefore more profitable) projects about Harlem.

But *Baby Sister*'s aesthetics undoubtedly played a role in its failure as well. Not only could its absurd elements be read as lacking the seriousness needed for African American subject matter at the time, but also its stylistic resemblance to Himes's other works offended influential elements in the NAACP, a group that, from its beginnings, had been involved in determining the boundaries of African American visual aesthetics, particularly as they related to Harlem. The representational stakes were high, and Himes's attempt to navigate a path between urban dysfunction and earnest realism may have been too complex or overdetermined for black elites, even in the 1960s. Perhaps, in the end, the "Negro problem" Himes faced was not so much the stories he told as the complex and unconventional forms he used to tell them, forms which projected a surreal Harlem, deformed by the absurdities of antiblack racism, rather than one that had "no relationship to reality."

NOTES

1. Chester Himes to Shirley Clarke, December 1963, quoted in Christopher Sieving, *Soul Searching: Black-Themed Cinema from the March on Washington to the Rise of Blaxploitation* (Middleton, CT: Wesleyan University Press, 2011), 44.
2. *Baby Sister* was not Himes's first interaction with the film industry. In the early 1940s, and prior to the publication of his first novel, Himes traveled to Los Angeles and tried to find work in the studios, first as a publicity writer for *Cabin in the Sky* (directed by Vincente Minnelli, 1943), and then as a script reader at Warner Bros. Although he was initially offered the script reader position, the offer was rescinded after Jack Warner learned that Himes was black. For more on this, see James Sallis, *Chester Himes: A Life* (New York: Walker Books, 2000), 75–76. Moreover, as Edward Margolis and Michel Fabre suggest, Himes's Hollywood experiences "reinforced [his] convictions about American race relations." Margolis and Fabre, *The Several Lives of Chester Himes* (Jackson: University Press of Mississippi, 1997), 47.
3. As Daniel Matlin argues in the present volume, the area's negative aspects were recognized in the 1920s but were not widely acknowledged until the 1940s. In Paula J. Massood, *Making a Promised Land: Harlem in Twentieth-Century Photography and Film* (New Brunswick, NJ: Rutgers University Press, 2013), I trace this visual discourse of black urban pathology back to the 1930s, when photojournalism visually cast Harlem as a problem.
4. Chester Himes, *My Life of Absurdity: The Autobiography of Chester Himes* (1976; New York: Thunder's Mouth, 1995), 2:237.
5. Massood, *Making a Promised Land*, 102.
6. According to Himes, Pierre-Dominique Gaisseau's film "earned him [Gaisseau] the name of murderer by the French crew" because he refused to abandon the project, despite the dangerous conditions they faced. See Himes, *My Life*, 237.
7. The film's conventional approach is surprising, considering that ethnographic film as a whole had begun to shift to a more self-conscious style. For example, the same year that *Le Ciel et la Boue* (The Sky Above—The Mud Below) was released, Jean Rouch and Edgar Morin directed *Chronique d'un été* (Chronicle of a Summer). The film focused on a heterogeneous group of people living in Paris over the course of one summer. It was notable for including the presence of the filmmakers in scenes and for asking its subjects to

    participate in the filming. It is credited with sparking a new movement in documentary film, *cinéma vérité*.
8. Bosley Crowther, "The Sky Above Documentary on a New Guinea Trip Opens," *New York Times*, June 20, 1962.
9. Fatimah Tobing Rony, *The Third Eye: Race, Cinema, and the Ethnographic Spectacle* (Durham, NC: Duke University Press, 1996), 12.
10. Gaisseau traveled to New York sometime in 1962 or 1963 to shoot another documentary, *Only One New York* (1964), a film that examines the multiple ethnic and racial enclaves located in the city and includes two sections on Harlem—one on "El Barrio" in East Harlem and another on the area's African American neighborhoods. The latter section, which is roughly five minutes long, focuses on what it identifies as "Harlem style," particularly as it related to music, dance, and gospel culture. Himes traveled to New York to serve as a "contact man" for the Harlem filming, but his involvement in the final work remains unclear. See Margolis and Fabre, *Several Lives*, 125–26.
11. Himes, *My Life*, 238.
12. Chester Himes, *Black on Black: Baby Sister and Selected Writings* (New York: Doubleday, 1973), 10, 26.
13. Himes, *My Life*, 238. The screenplay opens on the funeral services for Baby Sister's father, who was killed by street thugs while trying to defend his daughter's honor. Baby Sister also has an older sister, Lil, and another brother, both of whom escape the story unscathed.
14. Himes, *Black on Black*, 11.
15. Chester Himes, *A Rage in Harlem* (New York: Vintage Crime, 1991), 93. Originally published as *For Love of Imabelle* (1957).
16. Chester Himes, "Harlem: An American Cancer," *Presence Africaine* 17 (First Quarter 1963): 46.
17. Himes and Gaisseau could have sought funding from the French government, which had supported their small film projects.
18. Himes, *My Life*, 243.
19. From the 1910s to the 1940s, a separate "race" film industry existed, making films for African American audiences, who often viewed these in segregated screenings or theaters. Companies such as the Lincoln Motion Picture Company and the Micheaux Film and Book Company produced a wide variety of films, including melodramas, comedies, gangster films, and Westerns, featuring African American performers. For more on the race film industry, see Pearl Bowser and Louise Spence, *Writing Himself into History: Oscar Micheaux, His Silent Films, and His Audience* (New Brunswick, NJ: Rutgers University Press, 2000); Jacqueline Najuma Stewart, *Migrating to the Movies: Cinema and Black Urban Modernity* (Berkeley: University of California Press, 2005); Paula J. Massood, *Black City Cinema: African American Urban Experiences in Film* (Philadelphia, PA: Temple University Press, 2003).
20. For more on message movies, see Thomas Cripps, *Making Movies Black: The Hollywood Message Movie from World War II to the Civil Rights Era* (New York: Oxford University Press, 1993).
21. Michael Boyce Gillespie, *Film Blackness: American Cinema and the Idea of Black Film* (Durham, NC: Duke University Press, 2016), 88.
22. Himes, *Black on Black*, 10, 12, 38. In *Imabelle*, the eponymous character is described similarly: "She was a cushion-lipped, hot-bodied, banana-skin chick with the speckled-brown eyes of a teaser and the high-arched, ball-bearing hips of a natural born *amante*." See Himes, *Rage*, 6.

23. Kevin K. Gaines, *Uplifting the Race: Black Leadership, Politics, and Culture in the Twentieth Century* (Chapel Hill, NC: University of North Carolina Press, 1996), 2, 76–78. See also Massood, *Making a Promised Land*, chap. 2.
24. Himes, *Black on Black*, 38.
25. Himes, *Black on Black*, 20, 93.
26. Christopher Breu, *Hard-Boiled Masculinities* (Minneapolis: University of Minnesota Press, 2005), 143–44.
27. Gaines, *Uplifting the Race*, 5.
28. Himes had a solid middle-class background, although he was conflicted throughout his lifetime about what he saw as the hypocrisies of the black bourgeoisie. See Sallis, *Chester Himes*, 95.
29. Himes, *My Life*, 29.
30. Henry Lee Moon was an early supporter of Himes and helped his cousin gain employment with the Works Progress Administration. The Moons also helped Himes secure a Rosenwald Fellowship, allowing him to complete his first novel, *If He Hollers Let Him Go*. See Sallis, *Chester Himes*, 255.
31. Jodi Melamed, *Represent and Destroy: Rationalizing Violence in the New Racial Capitalism* (Minneapolis: University of Minnesota Press, 2011), 76.
32. Himes's friendship with Ellison lasted for decades and endured both writers' moves from the United States to France.
33. Quoted in Margolis and Fabre, *Several Lives*, 94. *Mamie Mason* was written in 1956 but was shopped around until 1958, when it received a contract with the French publisher Plon. Himes also sold the rights to Olympia Press, which released an English-language version, entitled *Pinktoes*, in 1961. Plon did not publish the French language version until 1962, doing so under the title *Mamie Mason ou Un exercice de la bonne volonté*.
34. Gaines, *Uplifting the Race*, 122.
35. Herbert Hill was labor secretary from 1951 to 1977, where he worked to put pressure on unions, like the International Ladies' Garment Workers' Union and others in the film industry, to diversify. Additionally, the Hollywood branch of the National Association for the Advancement of Colored People exerted some influence over the industry, particularly in the postwar years.
36. Himes, quoted in John A. Williams and Lori Williams, eds., *Dear Chester, Dear John: Letters Between Chester Himes and John A. Williams* (Detroit, MI: Wayne State University Press, 2008), 3.
37. Hill, quoted in John A. Williams, "Chester Himes Is Getting On," *New York Herald Tribune Book Review* (October 11, 1964), 21.
38. Himes, quoted in Williams and Williams, *Dear Chester*, 3. Levine was the North American distributor for Gaisseau's *Le Ciel et la Boue*. He was relatively new to producing, having founded Embassy in 1956, and was primarily known at this time for distributing low-budget films such as *Godzilla* (1956) and for introducing Sophia Loren to an American audience through his promotion of Vittorio De Sica's *Two Women* (1961).
39. Most of the personnel for *The Cool World* project, including Warren Miller, Clarke, and producer Frederick Wiseman, were white. Carl Lee, who played a significant role in the production, was effectively sidelined in the film's publicity. This may have been due to Wiseman's desire to market the film as an art project by stressing Clarke's directorial links to the documentary and experimental film worlds. For more on this, see Sieving, *Soul Searching*; and Lauren Rabinovitz, *Points of Resistance: Women, Power, and Politics in the New York Avant-Garde Cinema, 1943–71* (Urbana: University of Illinois Press, 2003).

40. Gordon Parks, "Harlem Gang Leader," *Life* (November 1, 1948), 96–97.
41. Himes, *My Life*, 1.
42. Gaines, *Uplifting the Race*, 11.
43. Albert Johnson, "The Negro in American Films: Some Recent Works," *Film Quarterly* 18 (Summer 1965): 26.
44. The responses of various political groups to *The Cool World* can be found in Sieving, *Soul Searching*, 69.
45. Gillespie, *Film Blackness*, 89.
46. Himes, *Black on Black*, 11–12.
47. Jonathan P. Eburne, "The Transatlantic Mysteries of Paris: Chester Himes, Surrealism, and the *Série noire*," *PMLA* 120 (May 2005): 807, 814.
48. Himes, *My Life*, 1.
49. Albert Murray, "White Man's Harlem," *New Leader* (December 7, 1964): 28.
50. Himes, *Black on Black*, 11.
51. Margolis and Fabre, *Several Lives*, 103.
52. Eburne, "Transatlantic Mysteries," 815.
53. Gillespie, *Film Blackness*, 149.
54. Ossie Davis, quoted in Massood, *Black City Cinema*, 87.
55. Hollywood's interest in African American subject matter during the late 1960s and early 1970s was partially fueled by an industry-wide financial crisis that led studios to invest in smaller-budget films made by recent film school graduates. This crisis also led to an interest in previously overlooked market sectors, including youth and African American audiences. Before the industry turned its attention to blaxploitation production, it produced a selection of comedies, such as *Putney Swope* (Robert Downey Sr., 1969) and *Watermelon Man* (Melvin van Peebles, 1970), which took a satirical approach to American race relations. *Cotton Comes to Harlem* belongs to this moment, but it also contains characteristics of what would become blaxploitation following the release of van Peebles's *Sweet Sweetback's Baadasssss Song*, in 1971. See Massood, *Black City Cinema*, chap. 3.
56. Gillespie, *Film Blackness*, 4.
57. Sieving, *Soul Searching*, 20–21.
58. Sieving, *Soul Searching*, 23, 27. Sieving argues that the box office failure of *Gone Are the Days* affected the nascent emergence of black-themed film productions. He also argues that the producer of *The Cool World*, Frederick Wiseman, "reported diminished interest by distributors in his film following the media reports on *Gone Are the Days*." See Sieving, *Soul Searching*, 24.
59. Sieving, *Soul Searching*, 38.
60. Gillespie, *Film Blackness*, 184, note 25.

PART II
MODELS

5.

HARLEM'S DIFFERENCE

Winston James

Harlem is not to be seen. Or heard. It must be felt.
WALLACE THURMAN, 1927

Dankey seh worl' no level.
AFRICAN-JAMAICAN PROVERB[1]

You have pure-blooded Africans, British Negroes, Spanish Negroes, Portuguese Negroes, Dutch Negroes, Danish Negroes, Cubans, Porto Ricans, Arabians, East Indians and black Abyssinian Jews in addition to the racially well-mixed American Negro. You have persons of every conceivable shade of color. Persons speaking all languages, persons representative of many cultures and civilizations. Harlem is a magic melting pot, a modern Babel mocking the gods with its cosmopolitan uniqueness.
WALLACE THURMAN, 1927

"Negro Mecca," "Negro Metropolis," "Black Capital of the World," "City of Refuge," "Queen of the Black Belts," even "Nigger Heaven" and "Pickaninny Paradise," represent merely a small sample of the more popular sobriquets that were attached to Harlem in its heyday. Each suggests that this "city within a city" was something out of the ordinary, not only remarkable but unique, and positively so. For Harlem's significance transcended its limited geographic and population base in northern Manhattan as it became the center of African American political movements and black artistic expression for much of the twentieth century. For black people elsewhere in the African diaspora—in the Caribbean, Central and South America, Britain, and France—as well as on the African continent itself, Harlem acquired the legendary status of a modern Timbuktu.

No other black community on the planet has so captured the imagination of poets, novelists, playwrights, filmmakers, musicians, artists, and photographers as has Harlem.² Home to Marcus Garvey, W. E. B. Du Bois, Grace Campbell, Cyril Briggs, Amy Jacques Garvey, Richard B. Moore, Langston Hughes, Zora Neale Hurston, Hubert Harrison, A. Philip Randolph, Claude McKay, Duke Ellington, Billie Holiday, Adam Clayton Powell Jr., Benjamin Davis, and Malcolm X—to name only a few—Harlem provided the space for a bewildering variety of innovative artistic expressions—notably in dance, music, poetry, and prose—and accommodated and cultivated dissident political ideologies and practices, from the more mainstream "integrationist" to revolutionary socialist, communist, Pan-Africanist, and black nationalist. Harlem not only drew artists and political activists to its bosom but also captured and stirred their imaginations. Additionally, it was the site of the most expansive black proletarian dreaming and yearning, as captured so well in the fiction of Rudolph Fisher, the poetry and prose of Hughes and McKay, and the neighborhood's exuberant music and dance.

But despite the celebration of Harlem and its extraordinary global profile and reputation, no one has adequately explained how and why the black community in this relatively small section of northern Manhattan stands so distinctively apart from all others. The doings and achievements of the community have been amply recorded, but there is little by way of explanation as to why they happened in Harlem's black community as opposed to, say, those of Chicago, Boston, Philadelphia or, for that matter, London or Paris.

In this chapter, I shall attempt to explain how and why Harlem became so different from all other black communities within and outside the United States, and why its formation and trajectory were more conducive to the realization of its astonishing achievements—political, intellectual, and artistic. This undertaking is more complex than it perhaps at first appears. Among other things, it entails the recognition of New York City as a pioneer and symbol of modernity and how such a status affected its black denizens and would-be denizens; the physical and human geography of black Harlem; the provenance and characteristics of its population; the exceptional density of Harlem's population and therefore its propinquity—living cheek by jowl, to the extent that young lovers often resorted to St. Nicholas and Riverside parks to have sex; the rich black public sphere that emerged—newspapers, magazines, debating societies, public forums, churches, clubs, theaters, bars, cabarets, dance halls, and so forth; and the rich and often overlapping networks of friendships and associations.

Harlem was one of those sites I have elsewhere called "black contact zones," where, in this case, black America not only learned about itself—indeed got to *know* itself for the first time—but was also afforded a unique opportunity to learn about the wider African diaspora and world. By black contact zones, I mean sites where peoples of African descent from different geographic spaces meet, interact, and commingle with one another, often for the first time.³ They are generally sites of work and/or residence. Sugar and banana plantation complexes, seaports, and spaces of major construction projects, such as the Panama Canal Zone, are key examples of black contact zones during the early twentieth century. But metropolitan cities and their discrete black quarters, such as in London, Paris, and especially New York, also operated as black contact zones.[4] Within these zones one may also identify smaller and more intimate units, such as barracks, hostels, tenements, apartment buildings, workingmen's halls, clubs, lodges, mutual aid societies, and churches. They facilitate and constitute denser networks of intraracial and transnational interactions among their members. Because these institutions constitute units within the larger zone, we may call them "inner black contact zones," the inner rings, as it were, of a series of concentric circles denoting graduating levels of sociability and intimacy.

Black contact zones are often sites of shared suffering, of sorrow as well as joy, and generally are sites of black solidarity. While they are not without their tensions and even open conflicts, inherent within them are structural conditions conducive to collaboration, mutuality, and community—a "balm in Gilead," as the spiritual expresses it, where tears are wiped away. Thus constituted, they are congenial spaces for the development of black internationalism and Pan-Africanism. It is therefore not surprising that organizations such as the Universal Negro Improvement Association (UNIA) found ready adherents and fervent recruits in such environments—on the Panama Canal, on the large sugar plantations of eastern Cuba and the Dominican Republic, on the massive banana plantations of Costa Rica, and in the port cities of Lagos, Nigeria, and Cape Town, South Africa, with their black workforces from different regions and nations.[5]

An important dimension of life in black contact zones is the mixing or exchange of cultures, which results in the transmutation of the cultures of all members over time, to a greater or lesser extent, leaving no group culturally unchanged in the process. Culture—conceived broadly as a way of life—is inherently dynamic, always in the process of becoming, never static. Following Fernando Ortiz, we may call this process "transculturation," which was, as we shall see, very evident in places such as Harlem during the 1920s. Ortiz mobilized the concept to more accurately capture the observable cultural dynamics in Cuban history—the melding of indigenous native Caribbean (in particular Taino), Iberian, African, and Asian cultural forms, from the sixteenth to the twentieth centuries—contrasting the term to the more conventional anthropological concepts of acculturation and assimilation, which suggest unidirectional cultural change involving one or more ethnic groups adopting the culture of another or others (generally the dominant group) without reciprocation.[6] But the tempo of cultural change tends to increase in black contact zones. Cuisine, sartorial practices, music, dance, ideologies, and language are often observed to undergo discernible and relatively rapid transformations.

Given the necessarily limited length of this chapter, I would like to focus on a particularly neglected dimension of the Harlem experience, namely the status of Harlem as one of these black contact zones with distinct characteristics that help to explain its extraordinary political and cultural dynamism, especially during the 1920s. In so doing, and in order to bring into sharper relief Harlem's peculiarities, I shall contrast this community with the second-largest urban black settlement in the United States at the time, black Chicago. In some influential recent scholarship, Harlem is depicted as merely one point in the circuit of black internationalism. Paris and, if to a lesser extent, London are conceptualized as essentially equivalent sites to Harlem in the circuit. I argue that such a conceptualization is flawed and grossly misleading.

BLACKENING HARLEM AND MAKING CONTACT

At the turn of the twentieth century, no one could have foreseen or even imagined the astonishing transformation that would overtake Harlem—a white, genteel, bourgeois community in upper Manhattan—within the space of less than a generation.[7] As Claude McKay observed, "This patchwork of humanity was planned by no expert mind. It did not evolve from any blue print of interracial and international adjustment. It is the crude, bold offspring of necessity."[8] Manhattan's black population, which rapidly concentrated in Harlem in the early decades of the twentieth century, underwent an explosive increase. From just over 36,000 people in 1900, it grew to more than 60,000 in a decade and to 109,000 by 1920, which by 1930 was more than doubled to 225,000. (Another 100,000 lived elsewhere in New York City, with Brooklyn accounting for more than two-thirds of them.) In fact, during those years, spanning a mere generation, the black population in Manhattan increased by a staggering 520 percent.

As is well documented, this demographic growth was propelled by extraordinarily large waves of migration, mainly from the South and the Caribbean. By 1930, New York City had a black population of almost 328,000—almost ten times that of 1900.[9] When one bears in mind the pervasive and draconian restrictions that were placed upon African American movement prior to the Great Migration, and the relatively recent escape from such confinements, during World War I, one gains an appreciation of the dramatic break with the past that the formation of black Harlem signaled and portended.[10] Similarly dramatic changes simultaneously took place in Chicago. Numbering just over 30,000 in 1900, Chicago's black population reached 44,000 in 1910, climbed to more than 109,000 by the census of 1920, and soared to 234,000 by 1930. Chicago's black population had increased, over those thirty years, by 676 percent.[11]

The reasons for the exodus from the South are well documented. The Great War generated new employment opportunities in the North that attracted black southerners; the economic hardship and political terror in the South pushed enterprising black people to the North; the opportunity for their children to gain an education was a major incentive for them to leave; the desire for freedom and the ability to vote all played their part, to varying degrees, in providing energy to the black stampede northward. As Richard Wright, who as a young man left Mississippi for Chicago (by way of Tennessee), put it, black migrants sought the invigorating "warmth of other suns."[12]

But despite the extraordinarily rich literature on the Great Migration, there has been virtually nothing by way of comparative analysis of migrants' northern destinations. There are, for instance, exceptional analyses of the migration to Chicago and, to a lesser extent, to New York, but there is little or nothing analyzing the similarities and differences between the movements to these chief destinations. When one looks at the movements in a comparative frame, one quickly discovers that the patterns of these migrations had important differences. Significantly, the provenance of those who went to Harlem was very different from that of those who went to Chicago. And this difference is of major importance in understanding the cultural and political forms that developed in these new black cities-within-cities.[13]

Whereas almost a quarter of New York City's black population in 1930 was born in the state of New York, less than a fifth (18 percent) of Chicago's black population was born in Illinois. New York City's African American migrants came overwhelmingly from the southern Atlantic seaboard states (Virginia being the single largest source), whereas Chicago's came largely from the south central states (Mississippi being the single largest source), with a significant portion coming from the Mississippi Delta region. But above all, and remarkably, while New York City's foreign-born black population stood at 54,754 in 1930 (16.7 percent of the city's black residents), that of Chicago was only 1,338 (or 0.6 percent of black residents). Furthermore, while New York State had 15,305 black residents who were born in "Outlying Possessions" such as Puerto Rico, the U.S. Virgin Islands, and the Panama Canal Zone (more than 13,000 of whom lived in Manhattan), Illinois had a mere 97 residents from these areas.[14]

As I have documented elsewhere, this foreign-born black population in New York City, and in Harlem in particular, though overwhelmingly Caribbean in origin, was not exclusively so. There were hundreds, if not thousands, of West Africans, mainly from British colonies. There were also black Cape Verdeans, though the majority of these immigrants to the United States settled in New England. Black people also came from South America, in addition to those, largely of Caribbean ancestry, who came from Central America. And the Caribbean migrants were by no means a homogenous group; they emanated from different islands (with Jamaicans and Barbadians making up the largest island groupings) and also from the Caribbean continental enclaves of British Honduras (now Belize), Dutch Guiana (now Suriname), and British Guiana (now

Guyana). They spoke different languages, in accord with colonial heritage—English, French, Spanish, Dutch, and Danish—in addition to the local creoles and variants of the colonizers' languages. Alongside French (and Creole) speakers from Martinique and Guadeloupe were citizens from the Republic of Haiti. Spanish-speaking Afro-Cubans and Afro-Puerto Ricans were also members of the Harlem community, though most of the latter were concentrated in East (or "Spanish") Harlem, a contiguous and somewhat distinct community.[15]

As early as 1915, 28 percent of residents of one key block of Harlem apartments were foreign born, including people from the British Caribbean as well as from "Cuba, Panama, Martinique, West Africa, France, England, Canada, Portugal [probably Cape Verdeans], and even China."[16] A. Philip Randolph (who soon became one of the community's leading black radicals) and his wife Lucille had a lodger who was an Afro-Cuban cigar maker. Caribbean lodgers on the block generally rented from someone from their homeland. Nevertheless, as Irma Watkins-Owens has found, "there are enough census examples of immigrants lodging with natives to show the proximity with which diverse ethnic groups shared the limited space in Harlem." Jamaican Claude McKay, for one, preferred to lodge with African Americans rather than with his fellow Caribbeans. Writing to Nancy Cunard in 1932 from his Moroccan exile, he disclosed that when he lived in the United States he had "always preferred the American Negroes to the West Indians who on all occasions display too much 'class' spirit for my liking."[17]

Although Virginians and South Carolinians were the largest groupings of African American migrants born outside of the state of New York, every single state within the union provided members to the emergent black Manhattan. Indeed, alongside the 30,490 black Virginians living in Manhattan also lived, among others, 166 black Californians, thirty-nine from Washington State, eleven from Utah (including the distinguished writer Wallace Thurman), and three from Nevada, the lowest representation registered.[18] These migrants not only lived and worked together but also bonded as friends and neighbors, married one another, and had children together.

That African Americans met and established romantic and marital partnerships with others from a different state was not, of course, unique to Harlem. What set Harlem apart was the sheer variety of states from which the migrants came and the large number of cross-state unions that developed. Harlem was the U.S. community most likely to witness a marriage between a black man from Boston and a black woman from Charleston, largely because this was the place where they were most likely to meet. This dynamic, generally overlooked by scholars, was also a feature of Harlem that set it apart and contributed to Harlem's unique role as the site of what Alain Locke, in another context, would call "a great race-welding," and that Roi Ottley wrote of as Harlem's "distinct worldliness."[19]

Despite the still-enduring stereotype of West Indian "clannishness," a substantial number of "intermarriages," not to mention romantic relationships, also took place between African Americans and Afro-Caribbeans. Afro-Puerto Rican Arturo Schomburg, the great Pan-Africanist and bibliophile, was married three times, each time to an African American woman. Although they never married, for almost a decade Zora Neale Hurston had a torrid relationship—"the real love affair of my life"—with a brilliant and handsome young Antiguan, Percival Punter.[20] Jacob Lawrence, a child of the Great Migration he would so tenderly portray, married fellow artist Gwendolyn Knight, a child of the Barbadian migration to New York. Romare Bearden, another gifted, artistic child of the Great Migration, married Nanette Rohan, who hailed from French Saint Martin. Tellingly, they first met at an event expressing Pan-African solidarity, a benefit for victims of a Caribbean hurricane.[21]

Such unions ought not to surprise. As McKay noted, writing of the relationship between African Americans and Afro-Caribbeans in Harlem, "They work together, play together, marry one another and share equally the joys and sorrows of the group."[22] What is remarkable is the frequency with which these partnerships occurred. A foreign-born black population of 98,620 lived in the United States in 1930, the majority in New York City. But, significantly, another 39,909 black people were born in the United States to one foreign-born black parent and one native-born black parent. This was almost the same as the 43,452 who were born to two foreign-born parents. That is to say, roughly half of the black children born to foreign parents also had an African American parent. Almost twice as many children were born to African American women with foreign-born male partners (26,310) as were born to foreign-born black women married to African American men (13,599).[23] These figures cannot tell us of partnerships without children, such as that of the childless Hurston and her Antiguan lover.

Two important social phenomena facilitated these cross-cultural relationships. First, the female African American population consistently outnumbered that of African American males in New York City. In 1910, there were eighty-six black men for every one hundred black women in Manhattan, a number which rose only to ninety-one in 1920 and to ninety-three in 1930.[24] Second, black men generally outnumbered black women entering the United States, especially in the early years of black immigration.[25] With the "surplus" of African American women, on the one hand, and a "surplus" of foreign-born black men, on the other, this pattern in partnerships is easy to understand. But the differences in demographic characteristics only helped to facilitate this pattern; they did not *cause* it.

These partnerships were clearly the fruits of romantic connections that developed between African American men and women, on the one hand, and foreign-born black men and women (mainly from the Caribbean), on the other.

Though unremarked, such relationships have always been part of the history of the African diaspora in the United States. Among others, W. E. B. Du Bois was the child of such a union (mother from Massachusetts, father from Haiti, with Bahamian roots), as was James Weldon Johnson, whose parents met in New York City (mother from the Bahamas, father from Virginia). Grace Campbell, a mainstay of the African Blood Brotherhood (ABB), was born in Georgia (mother from Washington, DC, father from Jamaica), and the great actor and political activist Leonard Lionel Cornelius Canegata, better known as Canada Lee, was born in New York City to a South Carolinian mother and a father from Saint Croix. Malcolm X, a later example, had a Grenadian mother and a father from Georgia. There is also the very unusual case of Andy Razaf (born Andreamenentania Paul Razafinkeriefo, in Washington, DC), poet, pioneering jazz lyricist, and political activist, whose mother was from Kansas (with Missourian roots) and whose father was from the Madagascar royal family.[26] The scale of the black migration in the twentieth century made such partnerships more likely and frequent. "Like New York City Harlem is a cosmopolitan city," Wallace Thurman observed, in 1927. The "American Negro"—already, Thurman noted, an "ethnic amalgam"—was, in Harlem, "intermixing with Negroes from the Caribbean, from Africa, Asia, South America, and any other place dark-skinned people hail from."[27]

Of course, there were also cases of people from different parts of the Caribbean and the wider African diaspora—the "Ishmaelite remnants," McKay called them—meeting in Harlem and striking up romantic relations.[28] Harry Belafonte is only one of many offspring of such unions. His mother was from Jamaica and his father from Martinique. Barbadian Richard B. Moore married Jamaican Kathleen James. His close friend and comrade Surinamese Otto Huiswoud married Guyanese Hermina Dumont. Eric Walrond (Guianese-born of Barbadian parents and brought up in Panama) married Jamaican Edith Cadogan.

In short, interwar Harlem was the site of an extraordinary and unique mixture of people of African descent—a black ethnic mixture far more heterogeneous than that which obtained in Chicago, its closest counterpart—and not only from across the United States itself but also from around the globe. Additionally, there were Chinese, Japanese, Indian (both Hindu and Muslim), Filipino, and Mexican residents in Harlem conspicuous enough to be registered by contemporaries. According to McKay, there was even a "miniature Chinatown at the bottom of Lenox Avenue," with Thurman providing a vivid portrait of the Bamboo Inn, "a Chinese-American restaurant that features Oriental cuisine, a jazz band and dancing," while Roi Ottley writes of the colorful religious festival (Eid al-Adha) put on annually by Harlem's Indian Muslims. Harlem was the "melting pot of the darker races," observed Eric Walrond.[29]

Crucially, Harlem's black population was also notoriously densely packed—"a boundary bursting coop," Thurman called it. "Y'all live like bees in a hive, don't y'?" noticed the visiting Miss Cynthie, one of Rudolph Fisher's fictional characters. Harlem's population density of 336 people per acre was five times that of black Chicago.[30] The differential is due in part to the fact that Harlem was a vertical city (like much of Manhattan), with people living literally on top of one another in multistory or tenement apartment buildings, whereas black Chicago, including the densely populated South Side, was more horizontally laid out, with relatively low-rise residential buildings. But Harlem's scandalously high rents (significantly higher than those in Chicago) also meant families often had to take in lodgers, and take them in greater numbers and proportion than in Chicago, to stay in their homes. Even the vaunted "romping ground of the fashionable set," Sugar Hill in West Harlem, was, as McKay noted, "vinegar sour to many of its residents pinching themselves to meet the rent." Charged as much as "four times" the amount paid by the area's previous white tenants, "the majority of the families up there in sweet Sugar Hill are packed together like sardines," he wrote, with "the unit of private family life the rarest thing. Almost all families take in lodgers. All available space must be occupied." And this applied even to the most "dicty" block in Harlem, Strivers' Row (139th Street, between Seventh and Eighth Avenues), where, according to McKay writing in 1940, rooms were rented, as they were on every other block in Harlem.[31]

TRANSCULTURATION

These characteristics of Harlem created an environment that enabled the most remarkable level of transculturation anywhere within the African diaspora. Writing in 1925, W. A. Domingo, one of the distinguished Caribbean radicals of interwar Harlem, remarked, "Ten years ago it was possible to distinguish the West Indian in Harlem, especially during the summer months. Accustomed to wearing cool, light-colored garments in the tropics, he would stroll along Lenox Avenue on a hot day resplendent in white shoes and flannel pants, the butt of many a jest from his American brothers who, to-day, have adopted the styles that they formerly derided."[32] No longer the signifier of a "monkey-chaser," this tropical attire had been so widely adopted by others that "visibility of dress no longer makes the Negro immigrant conspicuous."[33]

Conversely, black immigrants adopted the cuisine of African Americans. The foods that delighted McKay on his return from London to Harlem in 1921 were an amalgam of Caribbean and African American dishes, though mostly the latter: "Spareribs and corn pone, fried chicken and corn fritters and sweet potatoes were like honey to my palate."[34] Certainly, this reflected the difficulty and expense of acquiring foodstuffs from the Caribbean.[35] But Caribbean migrants' new culinary habits also came from their discovery of new and delicious African American dishes in the bosom of Harlem. The influence went both ways. Domingo had a thriving Harlem business—aptly named the West Indies Produce Corporation—that imported Caribbean produce, and his customers went well beyond his Caribbean compatriots. From various ingredients, he also prepared and bottled chutneys and sauces—from his "own little factory" in Harlem—that were even carried by Woolworths.[36]

Ira Reid's pioneering study attributes Harlemites' greater use of condiments—chives, garlic, curry, peppers, and lime juice—to the influence of black immigrants, along with "yams, West Indian pumpkins, Guatemalean [sic] black beans, pigeon peas, mangos, pawpaws, ginger root ... choyos ... green peppers, plantains, papaya, guava, eddo, alligator pears, breadfruit, cassava, black pudding, red fish and tannias." As a knowledgeable observer remarked at the time, "Negroes are becoming more cosmopolitan in eating. They are branching out and trying all sorts of new foods and ways of preparing the old standbys."[37]

Alongside the conjugal links and culinary encounters between the different segments of Harlem's African diaspora should be placed the professional and workplace relations that developed among them. They worked together in the garment factories downtown, in the post office, and on the railways as Pullman porters and waiters. Together, African Americans and Afro-Caribbeans formed the Brotherhood of Sleeping Car Porters, in 1925. African American and Caribbean lawyers formed partnerships, as did doctors opening clinics and hospitals together. Black nurses and social workers rallied together without regard to ethnic origin, and they fought together to allow the integration of the profession, especially in Harlem Hospital, where black doctors were barred until the mid-1920s.[38] Out of all these experiences emerged not only a tradition of solidarity but also one of genuine friendship and a strong sense of common purpose, with many emerging as Pan-Africanists and socialists.

I have elsewhere documented the enormous contribution made by black immigrants to Harlem's radical political culture, which, furthermore, contributed to its growth not only elsewhere in the United States but also globally. This was particularly true of the Garvey movement, which spread nationally, especially in the South, and also internationally.[39] Part of the attractiveness and success of this black internationalism emanated from the wide international experience and networks of black immigrants to the United States, especially British Caribbeans, who had previously experienced the brutal racism in Central America, Cuba, and the Dominican Republic.[40] On the other side, black immigrants (especially Caribbeans) learned from African Americans—particularly working-class African Americans, who had centuries of inherited practice—how to endure what we might call the peculiar travails of racial adversity in the United States, with wisdom, dignity, and poise and with the capacity to partake in the pleasures of living, without cynicism, paralyzing incapacity, or resignation. McKay captured this in a number of his writings, but most profoundly in his novel *Banjo*, where he admired his black proletarian characters' capacity to cope with and survive the "long life-breaking tragedy of Africa."[41]

In entertainment and amusement, a similar dynamic of transculturation took place. Caribbean immigrants were as enamored with the blues and jazz as their African American counterparts. And they introduced calypso to Harlem, which became a popular form within the community in the 1920s. They all went to the cabarets; they all went to the speakeasies; they all danced at the Savoy and did the Lindy Hop and the Charleston; they all went to see the Harlem-born Fats Waller, one of their own, do his mischievous magic on the piano; they all went to see the drag duo Gladys Bentley (a Trinidad-born singer dressed as a man) and "Gloria Swanson" (a "Mr. Winston," an African American man from Chicago, dressed as a woman) and laughed at their bawdy jokes.[42] The immigrants introduced "numbers," a form of gambling within the community, but it quickly spread beyond its Caribbean enclave to the community as a whole. And they all dabbled in the occult, though occultist practitioners were disproportionately Caribbean.[43] They all strolled in their finery along Seventh Avenue, especially on Sunday afternoons and summer evenings. McKay believed that this promenading was probably introduced by the "Spanish" Negroes, by which he means black Puerto Ricans, with their Iberian tradition of the *paseo*.[44] Regardless of its source, everybody partook in the ritual. As James Weldon Johnson wrote, in a powerful evocation of the Harlem stroll:

> Strolling in Harlem does not mean merely walking along Lenox or upper Seventh Avenue or One Hundred and Thirty-fifth Street; it means that those streets are places for socializing. One puts on one's best clothes and fares forth to pass the time pleasantly with the friends and acquaintances and, most important of all, the strangers he is sure of meeting. One saunters along, he hails this one, exchanges a word or two with that one, stops for a short chat with the other one.... The hours of a summer evening run by rapidly. This is not simply going out for a walk; it is more like going out for adventure.[45]

All of this contributed to Harlem's rich sociability and public sphere, reinforcing the communion of its heterogeneous peoples; the observation of styles and fashions and their imitation, adoption, and adaptation; its race-welding.

Perhaps more than anything else, residents all swam in the sea of Harlem's effervescent political culture—they heard street corner orators such as Hubert Harrison, saw and often partook in Garvey's political parades, and read Harlem's radical newspapers and magazines. The extensive travel and experience of many of the black migrants (especially those from the British and French Caribbean who had worked and lived in Central America) made Harlem fertile ground for the cultivation of black internationalism.[46] Moreover, their children grew up together, went to school together, played on the streets together, suffered together, and became not only New Yorkers but also Harlemites together, shaped by the community's unique heritage and cultural amalgamation.[47]

And, like any people placed in such confined spaces, they also had their fights. The "Garvey Must Go" campaign that peaked in 1922 to 1923 was an especially public flare-up, but it proved to be transient and of limited social reach. McKay, a reliable witness on such matters, noted that the disagreements, where they existed, were sharpest between the African American and Afro-Caribbean petty bourgeoisie, who were struggling for "place and elbow room."[48] This was intraclass tension—especially among the politicians—and the use of ethnicity as a weapon, rather than genuinely interethnic rivalry, a key point missed by scholars who have addressed the subject.[49] There was less tension among the "ordinary types of both groups," observed McKay. "The natives call the West Indians 'monkey-chasers' and the West Indians call them 'coons' and they fight or laugh over it. But they work together, play together, marry one another and share equally the joys and sorrows of the group." Thus the rivalry between them, though "stupid," was "more comic than tragic."[50] In 1924, due to racist immigration laws, the black flow into the United States had virtually come to a standstill. By the early 1930s, more black immigrants were leaving than were entering the country.[51] Along with the shared calamity of the Great Depression, all these developments eased Harlem's ethnic tensions.

There were, moreover, plenty of moments that focused African American and Caribbean minds alike on their common black predicament. There is no better example of the shared sorrow and joy of which McKay spoke than the responses to the defeats and triumphs of the African American boxer and Harlem resident Joe Louis. Both African Americans and Afro-Caribbeans in Harlem fell into a trough of inconsolable despondency when Louis lost, in 1936, to the German Max Schmeling—no Nazi, but a man loved and hailed by Hitler *and* by American white supremacists. Both groups in Harlem rose in ecstatic joy when Louis slaughtered Schmeling in the rematch, two years later.[52]

NEW NEGROES

This unparalleled degree of black cosmopolitan interaction and transculturation was central to Harlem's emergence as the preeminent site of "New Negro" consciousness, organizing, and activism during the interwar period. Far from being solely (or even principally) a cultural movement, the New Negro refrain sounded throughout all spheres of black life, from poetry to nightlife and from organized politics to the informal politics of everyday encounters. Along with (and in relation to) its cosmopolitanism, two further factors help explain Harlem's status as the center of New Negrodom: its youthfulness and its literacy.

We are apt to forget that the New Negro movement was quintessentially a youth and young adults' movement—a generational revolt. It was led by men and women in their twenties and early thirties. Marcus Garvey was just twenty-six when he founded the UNIA, in 1914, and he celebrated his thirty-third birthday during the historic Negro Peoples of the World convention, in August 1920, when his movement was at its height. His partner, "cofounder," and later wife, Amy Ashwood, was only seventeen when they launched the organization.[53] Langston Hughes captured the bravado and optimism of his peers in his poem "Youth" when he was twenty-two years old. His friend Wallace Thurman was only twenty-four when he edited the audacious magazine *Fire!!* and twenty-six when his first novel *The Blacker the Berry* appeared, and he had written a trove of other works in multiple genres when he died at just thirty-two. And McKay penned his sonnet "If We Must Die," the "anthem of the New Negro movement," when he was twenty-nine.

Not coincidentally, the Harlem community itself stood out for the youthfulness of its population, and especially for its large cohort of young and single adults. According to sociologists, young adults, especially unmarried men, are the most inclined to engage in dissenting political and cultural activities.[54] The United States census for 1930 reports that 37 percent of America's 12 million black people were between the ages of fifteen and thirty-four. In Chicago the figure was 43 percent, whereas Manhattan's (effectively Harlem's) was 45.5 percent. Nationally, 52 percent of this population of fifteen to thirty-four years old was in its twenties. Chicago had 57 percent of this group in its twenties, but Harlem exceeded that, with 59 percent. Similarly, for the nation as a whole, 32.2 percent of African American men fifteen years and older were single, whereas the figure for Manhattan was 37 percent, and 30.2 percent for Chicago. Among black women nationally, the figure was 23.3 percent. But Chicago, at 16.8 percent, had a lower proportion of single black women than the nation as a whole, whereas Manhattan exceeded the national average, with 27 percent. The contrast continues when we look at single young adults. In 1930, 66.4 percent of young black men between the ages of fifteen and thirty-four in Manhattan were single. For Chicago, the figure was 61.4 percent. Among young black women (fifteen to thirty-four), the gap was even greater, with 49.1 percent of this cohort of black female Manhattanites being single, compared to 37.8 percent of their Chicagoan sisters.[55]

These demographic differences are striking, and their cultural and political impact, which cannot be fully engaged here, cries out for deeper exploration. One thing is clear, however: these young men and women in Harlem and elsewhere appreciated the power of their generation, which expressed itself both politically and culturally in the New Negro movement. This movement articulated its demand for new leadership largely in generational terms and had its seat in Harlem. It was there that the most radical black organizations and publications were based: the Liberty League, founded and led by Hubert Harrison, and its organ, the *Voice*; the UNIA and its paper, the *Negro World*; the ABB and the *Crusader*; the black socialists around A. Philip Randolph and Chandler Owen, who edited the *Messenger* magazine; the *Emancipator*, edited by W. A. Domingo and Richard B. Moore; plus somewhat more ephemeral publications such as the *Challenge* and the *Promoter*.

The New Negroes were emphatically against the Old Negroes, or the Old Crowd, as the *Messenger* referred to them. It was a bitter ideological struggle waged by the young against their disparaged elders for the reins of political leadership. In the crosshairs were the old Booker T. Washington establishment, the "Tuskegee machine," led by Robert Russa Moton after Washington's death in 1915; and also the National Association for the Advancement of Colored People (NAACP), represented by Du Bois, along with a host of others. The New Negroes did not mince their words. The thirty-year-old Randolph, in 1919, spoke of the need to "scrap the Old Crowd. For not only is the Old Crowd useless, but like the vermiform appendix, it is decidedly injurious, it prevents all real progress."[56] At age thirty-one, Cyril Briggs, one of the most eloquent voices of the era, elaborated upon the generalized discontent of the New Negro with the Old Negro. In an editorial in the *Crusader*, he wrote:

> The Old Negro and his futile methods must go. After fifty years of him and his methods the Race still suffers from lynching, disfranchisement, jim-crowism, segregation and a hundred other ills. His abject crawling and pleading have availed the Cause nothing. He has sold his life and his people for vapid promises tinged with traitor gold. His race is done. Let him go.... For us the future and all the great tasks that lie ahead. For the Old Leader *Requiescat [i]n pace!*[57]

How typical were these sentiments, and how widely was such literature disseminated? Precise answers to such questions are, of course, impossible. But there is compelling evidence to suggest that these ideas were by and large shared by a majority of black people, especially northern youth. While some of the more expansive claims about the circulation of interwar black periodicals should be treated with caution, the popularity and rapid increase in the number and circulation of black publications by the start of the 1920s is not in doubt. In 1900, there were two hundred black newspapers and magazines nationally; by 1921, there were nearly five hundred. In Chicago alone, the number increased from four black newspapers in 1912 to fifteen (including five weeklies) by 1921. New York City—where the nation's first black newspaper, *Freedom's Journal*, had been founded, in 1827—had seventeen black newspapers and magazines in 1921, including the weekly *New York Age, Amsterdam News, New York News*, and *Negro World*. In addition, there were the important monthlies, the *Crisis, Messenger*, and *Crusader*. There was an estimated combined circulation of

1.6 million for the black press nationwide in the 1920s, compared to 300,000 to 500,000 in 1910. One informed contemporary reported that "these papers are read, and passed from hand to hand, and re-read until they are worn out." Given that each issue of these black newspapers and magazines had, on average, no fewer than five readers, one gets a sense of the remarkable influence and accommodation of such ideas among black people at the time.[58]

A significant decline in illiteracy facilitated the growth of these new organs. Between 1910 and 1930, the rate of illiteracy among black people age ten and older halved, falling to 16.3 percent. The corresponding drop among those age twenty-one and older was almost as dramatic—from 35.7 to 20 percent.[59] And Harlem had the highest rate of black literacy in the nation, with practically zero illiteracy by 1930.[60] The concentration of black people in northern urban centers facilitated the more rapid and effective circulation of these newspapers by reducing the distance between the publishers and their market. This did not mean, of course, that there was not a wide circulation of newspapers such as the *Negro World* and the *Chicago Defender* far from their northern bases, especially in the South.[61]

But beyond the number and size of these publications, they distinguish themselves *qualitatively* from their prewar predecessors as being, in the words of the Indianapolis *Freeman* in 1919, "more militant" and "more wide awake for race progress" than ever before.[62] And Harlem was the home of the most radical organs in the nation, beginning with Harrison's short-lived but pioneering and influential *Voice* and *New Negro*; the *Messenger*, edited by Randolph and Owen, which Attorney General A. Mitchell Palmer called "by long odds the most able and the most dangerous of all the Negro publications;"[63] the *Crusader*, the organ of the ABB, edited by Briggs; the *Emancipator*, edited by Richard B. Moore and W. A. Domingo; the *Challenge*, edited by William Bridges; and the *Promoter*, edited by Hodge Kirnon. In addition, there was Garvey's *Negro World*, which by the mid-1920s was published in English, French, and Spanish, a testament to its international and Pan-Africanist reach and ambition.

These publications not only came out of New York; they came straight out of Harlem. It is therefore not surprising that Harlem publications (especially the *Messenger*, *Negro World*, *Crusader*, and *Challenge*) took up virtually all of the attorney general's report "Radicalism and Sedition Among the Negroes as Reflected in Their Publications," submitted to the United States Senate in 1919. Harlem had developed a rich and radical print culture as one facet of a "black public sphere" of unrivaled scale and intricacy.[64]

Indeed, like its tightly packed residents, Harlem had an exceptionally dense network of social institutions, churches (of all denominations), and mutual aid societies—associations based on state or island origins as well as more inclusive ones such as the UNIA.[65] The community was also famous, even during the 1920s, for its street corner forums, where the likes of Garvey, Harrison,

Randolph, and (later) Audley "Queen Mother" Moore, to name a few, would speak on a wide range of topics but focused on attacking white supremacy from socialist or black nationalist vantage points.[66] Professor Kelly Miller of Howard University, a Booker T. Washington disciple, complained that, during this period, "Harlem was filled with street preachers and flamboyant orators haranguing the people from morning till night upon Negro rights and wrongs." The Justice Department intelligence reports bear eloquent testimony to this fact and to the large crowds that gathered to listen.[67]

The radical forums also operated inside, at Garvey's Liberty Hall, at Ethelred Brown's Unitarian church, at the Lafayette Theatre, where the People's Educational Forum, founded in 1920, met every Sunday afternoon. Under the leadership of Arturo Schomburg, the 135th Street Library became not only an exceptional repository of knowledge about the global black experience but also a forum for meetings, poetry readings, and art exhibitions. Tenants' associations were established early in the community's history, to combat poor housing conditions and high rents.[68] Harlem was never short of rallies and demonstrations. The UNIA always put on a good show, especially at its annual international conventions, which boasted the bringing together of the "Negroes of the world" through their delegates from the four corners of the earth.

In short, Harlem developed a remarkable number of public institutions, religious and secular, that supported and bound its people together. Given such a thick network of social interactions, Harlem afforded an opportunity for the development of group consciousness not previously encountered by any community of black people; it was a unique rendezvous for peoples of African descent. Outside Harlem, how often would an African American from South Carolina get the chance to meet another from Oregon, or black people from Aruba, Carriacou (from where Audre Lorde's parents left for Harlem), or Lagos? Prior to the Harlem encounter, how many African Americans and Trinidadians had the chance to meet a black Brazilian or a black sailor from the port city of Liverpool, England, or Freetown, Sierra Leone? Because of the unique and varied composition of its black population, Harlem, more than any other place in the world, provided an opportunity not only for African Americans to know themselves as a group, and the wider black world, but also for members of the general African diaspora to get to know one another and continental Africans, and for continental Africans to get to know their sisters and brothers of the diaspora.

AMONG THE BLACK CONTACT ZONES

Harlem's preeminence among the world's black contact zones emerges starkly when the neighborhood is viewed alongside its nearest international analogues, the black communities of London and Paris. Both of these cities had relatively tiny black populations. The precise sizes of Britain's and France's black populations in the early twentieth century are difficult to determine because of their patterns and protocols of enumeration.[69] However, it is fair to assume that from 1911 to 1931 Britain's black population hovered around 14,000 (roughly 9,000 from the Caribbean and 5,000 from Africa). Even in 1951, there were only around 15,000 to 17,000 Caribbean immigrants in all of Britain.[70] In France, the pattern was rather similar. In 1924, the colonial migrant population of every origin was estimated at less than 10,000, excluding French citizens from the Caribbean. Paris had a black population of between 10,000 and 15,000 in 1926. This included only twenty-five African students, which fell to twenty-one students in 1932.[71] Until the 1950s, both capitals were more crossroads than sites of black settlement.[72] Neither Paris nor London enjoyed the same rich mixture of black humanity that Harlem accommodated.

Moreover, the black populations of both London and Paris, even more than the population of Chicago, were far more geographically dispersed than their concentrated, segregated, and densely packed counterparts in Harlem. Paris, in addition, was riven by intra-ethnic and class division and conflict (especially between West Africans and Afro-Caribbeans) to an extent foreign to black Harlem, even during the divisive days of "Garvey Must Go."[73] Furthermore, Harlem's rhythm of development differed markedly from those of Paris and London. Harlem was at its height, politically and culturally, during the 1920s, whereas black Paris gave birth to the *négritude* movement in the 1930s (the term itself was not coined until 1939), heavily influenced by the Harlem Renaissance writers, especially McKay, just when Harlem and the movement it hosted were being decimated by the Great Depression.[74]

Similarly, the height of the anticolonial movement in London was reached in the 1930s and the postwar years. Thus, the maturation of the black movements in London and Paris occurred *after*, and was substantially inspired by, Harlem's awakening. This is not to deny linkages and even cross-fertilization between Harlem and Paris or London, which have long been established and have recently been reemphasized.[75] But it is noteworthy that the chief protagonists in the *négritude* movement, Aimé Césaire and Léopold Senghor, were always explicit in their acknowledgement of Harlem's pioneering role. When Senghor declared, in a 1950 essay, "Claude McKay can be considered rightfully as the true inventor of *négritude* . . . not of the word . . . but of the values of *négritude*," he expressed the shared view of the group.[76] Similarly, it was in the 1930s (following George Padmore's arrival in 1935) that black London started to flex its political muscles, ramping up its antiracist and anticolonial struggles during the Ethiopian crisis and the labor revolts in the Caribbean and sub-Saharan Africa.[77]

It is, therefore, strange, misleading, and disappointing to read, in a book published as recently as 2013, that "the New Negro experience in the United States [was] *just one nodal point* within a dynamic and uneven circuit of black internationalism."[78] As the author of these remarks acknowledges, this depiction of

Harlem and the New Negro movement is not new. As early as 1955, the proud Washingtonian Sterling Brown described Harlem as only the "show-window, the cashier's till" of a wider movement, and more recently his disciple Robert Stepto described the Harlem Renaissance as "*merely* the North American component of something larger and grander."[79] After quoting and endorsing Stepto's remarks, another writer, having registered the estimates of the black population in Paris, admits, "Still, these numbers are nowhere near the concentration of peoples of African descent in Harlem"—without telling his readers that Harlem's population was around *one hundred times* that of black Paris and far more densely packed. Do not differentials of such magnitude deserve disclosure and command greater attention and analysis? The same author then tries to undermine Harlem's demographic weight by stating that Paris's significance in this period "is not a question of sheer population size." He suggests that Paris is "crucial because it allowed boundary crossing, conversations, and collaborations that were available nowhere else to the same degree."[80]

But what is meant by "boundary crossing, conversations, and collaborations?" Whatever they were, did these activities not also happen in New York City? Was Paris so self-evidently superior to Manhattan in such matters? And were such supposed boundary crossings, conversations, and collaborations sufficiently important to elevate the status of black Paris relative to black Harlem? Although the author's book otherwise resists the tendency, such assertions bring to mind the archetypical African American caricatures of a nonracist France and a paradisiac Paris—"the myth of French culture and hospitality," as Michel Fabre once put it.[81]

What assertions such as "*just* one nodal point" and "*merely* the North American component" do is to elide the uneven, if combined, development of black internationalism itself, to flatten spatial differences, differences across international boundaries, in the name of "transnational studies," as well as to ignore divergent temporalities. Whether through historical ignorance or conceptual failure, such arguments, at best, proffer false equivalences; at worst, they are clumsy sleights of hand. Transnational approaches hold unquestionable value—especially in combatting Euro- and U.S.-centrism—but must always maintain an eye toward differences as well as similarities across space and time. Each social formation possesses its own history and peculiarities, and these must always be acknowledged if our scholarship is not to do violence to the lived historical experiences of individuals and groups.

Thus, to suggest that Harlem was "just one nodal point" is akin to saying that Jupiter is merely a planet in our solar system. Because of its magnitude, its peculiar composition, and the conjuncture of its formation, black Harlem occupied a distinct position within black internationalism. We may dare say that Harlem was *exceptional*—not superior, but divergent—in the sense that its process and rhythm of development and its distinct constitution departed radically from all other black urban formations in the United States and elsewhere in the 1920s.[82] Yes, it was only *a* nodal point in the network of black internationalism, but it was a crucially important, arguably even a pivotal one; some nodal points are more important than others.

The most traveled (and arguably the most curious and observant) black intellectual of his generation was Claude McKay, who not only visited but also *lived and worked* in all three places—Harlem, London, and Paris—among others, for considerable periods. After returning to Harlem, and after an absence abroad of more than twelve years (1922–1934), in addition to a previous sojourn of more than a year in London (1919–1921), McKay concluded, in his most sober and unsentimental book (written during the dark days of the Great Depression), that not only was Harlem a black community with "no counterpart in any other of America's black belts" but also it was "the queen of the black belts" and remained a "magnet," despite the Depression. He went further: "Harlem is more than the Negro capital of the nation. *It is the Negro capital of the world*. And as New York is the most glorious experiment on earth of different races and divers groups of humanity struggling and scrambling to live together, so Harlem is the most interesting sample of black humanity marching along with white humanity."[83]

It was these peculiar qualities, and the special gift Harlem afforded, that had led Alain Locke, in 1925, to rejoice. That Locke was a man who knew both Paris and London intimately again lends his words a special authority. He is worth quoting at length:

> Here in Manhattan is not merely the largest Negro community in the world, but the first concentration in history of so many diverse elements of Negro life.... Within this area, race sympathy and unity have determined a further fusing of sentiment and experience.... [W]hat began in terms of segregation becomes more and more, as its elements mix and react, the laboratory of a great race-welding. Hitherto, it must be admitted that American Negroes have been a race more in name than in fact, or to be exact, more in sentiment than in experience. The chief bond between them has been that of a common condition rather than a common consciousness; a problem in common rather than a life in common. In Harlem, Negro life is seizing upon its first chances for group expression and self-determination.[84]

If anything, Locke *understated* the matter. For what took place in Harlem was more than a "fusing of sentiment and experience." It was also, in important ways, the development of *new* sentiments and *new* experiences generated by the new, intimate, and dense social interactions among a large group of black people of culturally and geographically diverse backgrounds.

A great deal remains to be said about how such new sentiment and experience emerged from the seedbed of Harlem's unique social and spatial character, and I will elaborate on much of this elsewhere. For the purposes of this chapter, a few points warrant attention, albeit by way of previewing the more sustained analysis to come.

First, Harlem attracted a remarkable number of artists and intellectuals from around the country and abroad, who contributed profoundly to its cultural life. With a few notable exceptions, all of the artists and intellectuals connected to the so-called Harlem Renaissance were born outside of New York State, much less Harlem. "Harlem is a piece of New York," McKay noted. "And exactly as New York is not the typical American city ... so Harlem is no black Chicago or Durham, N.C."[85] These artists, intellectuals, and political activists were attracted by the excitement, freedom, adventure, and opportunity that New York City and Harlem provided—the best theaters in the country as well as the leading publishing houses, magazines, and journals were all based in Manhattan.

Almost from the start, New York City, a dynamic, cosmopolitan port city, was, if not in name, the de facto capital of the colony and later of the United States. It was the capital of capital and the purveyor of high modernism in all its forms. It was America's primate city, rising above all others by almost every measure, "the Macedonia of the USA."[86] A rich and exciting immigrant city that constantly replenished itself, it also was the site of the new, especially culturally and politically.[87] These qualities made New York City, more than Chicago or any other city, a major attraction, especially to black artists and intellectuals. "Harlem was like a great magnet for the Negro intellectual," said Langston Hughes. He conceded that the real magnet might well have been Gotham itself, but because of residential racism, once the black intellectual arrived in the city, he or she had to live in Harlem anyway.[88]

On top of this, there was the conscious effort to recruit black "talent" to New York on the part of leading figures of the NAACP and the New York Urban League. The brilliant artist Aaron Douglas, for instance, moved to Harlem from Kansas as a result of such inducement.[89] Harlem provided the political and intellectual freedom that was absent elsewhere—in the South, in the colonial Caribbean, and in Africa. This feature of Harlem was crucial to the success of Garvey and the UNIA. And Harlem's reputation and success only enhanced its reputation and success further by attracting more and more ambitious and frustrated artists, intellectuals, and activists. Many of the politically discontented and radicalized (particularly black veterans of the Great War) went to Harlem, some explicitly to join the UNIA and other radical groups, such as the ABB and the black socialists around the *Messenger*.[90] No other place enjoyed Harlem's magnetic pull of this category of migrants.

The second point is that black Harlem's abrupt newness—the stunning rapidity with which this site of black urban life established itself in northern

Manhattan—is crucial to understanding the distinctive sociopolitical formations the neighborhood engendered. Without a long-established black elite of the kind that existed in Washington, DC, Philadelphia, Boston, and indeed Brooklyn, black life in 1920s Harlem was far less constrained by the snobbishness and censorious moralizing of the black bourgeoisie. Certainly, Harlem had its "aristocrats of color," but they, too, were newcomers, and they struggled to establish institutional and cultural hegemony over a rapidly swelling, overwhelmingly proletarian and rambunctious black community jealously guarding its newfound freedom. Hughes, who devoted an entire essay to skewering the haughtiness of Washington's black upper crust, was relieved to return to Harlem, "where people are not so ostentatiously proud of themselves, and where one's family background is not of such great concern."[91]

Third, the unusual rapidity and density of black Harlem's formation ensured that its intellectuals, no less than its social elite, were thrust together—banged up, as it were—with greater physical propinquity to the working class and poor. Such propinquity has always been a catalyst for the radicalization of intellectuals, providing a depth of knowledge of working-class experience that often elicits a sense of moral outrage. As I have written previously, a conjuncture of occurrences within and outside the United States—from the scourge of southern lynching and the return of disillusioned African American servicemen, to the Russian Revolution and uprisings in India and Ireland—fueled Harlem's radical ambience in powerful ways.[92]

The more immediate environment of Harlem itself contributed to the process of radicalization in ways that have yet to be fully captured. Harlem, unlike black Washington, was effectively a black frontier society, with all the social fluidity that comes with such formations, heightened further by its rapid population growth, ethnic heterogeneity, and endless churning. All of this, and the relative weakness of elite social policing, afforded its residents a greater sense of freedom, exploration, and experimenting. The rise of the dark-skinned, proletarian protagonist (the laborer, the prostitute, the porter, the maid, the jazz musician) in the writings of McKay, Hughes, Rudolph Fisher, and others was a strikingly new phenomenon of the 1920s, and one with substantial roots in these authors' experiences of Harlem. Moreover, black intellectuals had, by and large, been forced to experience *directly* the working life of the masses of black people, precisely because of the exclusionary practices of racism. This led to what one might call their "forced proletarianization." McKay, for instance, despite his formal education and gifts, worked as a "porter, houseman, janitor, butler, waiter—anything that came handy."[93] Such experiences lay at the heart of these residents' artistic production and depiction of black working-class life. They were worker-intellectuals. To the "nice Negroes" who criticized his proletarian realism, McKay responded:

132   Part II: Models

I did not come to knowing Negro workers in an academic way.... I knew the unskilled Negro worker of the city by working with him as a porter and longshoreman and as a waiter on the railroad. I lived in the same quarters and we drank and caroused together in bars and at rent parties. So when I came to write about the low-down Negro, I did not have to compose him from an outside view.[94]

Finally, black Harlem's incipience and fluidity in the 1920s made for an extraordinarily prolific and varied queer culture. Just as lines of ethnicity and class were troubled and tested in Harlem's crucible of encounters, so too did gay and bisexual men and women enjoy a level of freedom and tolerance unheard of elsewhere—even among their white counterparts in Greenwich Village.[95] Black Harlemites were, to a remarkable extent, a culturally masterless people. As the Hamilton Lodge Balls demonstrated, with their massed, resplendent drag queens, Harlemites did as they pleased, within the bounds of the law—and sometimes outside it. Harlem was, arguably, the closest that black people, especially the working class, came to having a liberated space within the United States.[96] Where structures of authority are inchoate or embryonic, pleadings for respectability are ineffectual. Even Harlem's most "influential" pastor, Adam Clayton Powell Sr., to his great disappointment and consternation, was largely ignored on matters of morality.[97] Bruce Nugent would recall of 1920s Harlem, "People did what they wanted to with whom they wanted to do it.... Nobody was in the closet. There wasn't any closet."[98]

In such ways, for many of the writers who would make the name of Harlem ring out across and beyond the black world, it was the very forms of connections within this black contact zone that had inspired new sentiments, new visions of black actualities, new possibilities. "Strange," Langston Hughes pondered in "Aesthete in Harlem,"

> That in this nigger place,
> I should meet Life face to face
> When for years, I had been seeking
> Life in places gentler speaking
> Until I came to this near street
> And found Life—stepping on my feet![99]

CONCLUSION

Harlem, through its fortuitous and small beginnings, exercised extraordinary and unique power in attracting African Americans from all over the United States. It also welcomed the children of Africa from elsewhere in the Americas and from the continent itself. Harlem afforded, like nowhere else on earth, the opportunity for people of African descent to know themselves beyond the narrow bounds of village, town, county, region, and nation. It enhanced and facilitated a more global understanding of the black experience and offered chances to participate in it and shape its future. Harlem provided the space for the development of what might be called a new "Afropolitanism," a condition of belonging and sharing among peoples of African descent—"race-welding," to use Locke's term.[100] It is hardly surprising, then, that Harlem would become the home of the most transnational black organization the world has ever known, the Universal Negro Improvement Association.

The first adjective in this name warrants pause. Though it was founded by a Jamaican, the organization was not named the "Jamaican," or "West Indian," or "Caribbean," or, for that matter, "American" or "African" Negro Improvement Association but the *Universal* Negro Improvement Association, thus (quite deliberately) announcing the inclusive, aggregating ambition and centripetal promise that allowed it to attract black people from all over the world, and in the millions. Already fired up by racist proscriptions and oppression from his time in the Caribbean, Central America, and Europe, it was while journeying back to Jamaica from England in the summer of 1914 that Garvey had an epiphany that led to the name:

> It was while speaking to a West Indian negro who was a passenger with me from Southampton, who was returning home to the West Indies from Basutoland with his Basuto wife, that I further learned of the horrors of native life in Africa. He related to me in conversation such horrible and pitiable tales that my heart bled within me. Retiring from the conversation to my cabin, all day and the following night I pondered over the subject matter of that conversation, and at midnight, lying flat on my back, the vision and thought came to me that I should name the organization the Universal Negro Improvement Association and African Communities (Imperial) League. Such a name I thought would embrace the purpose of all black humanity. Thus to the world a name was born, a movement created, and a man became known.[101]

This message resonated with Harlem's multinational, transnational, heterogeneous, and oppressed members of black humanity. There was not a more congenial home for the UNIA than Harlem. The shrewd Garvey quickly realized this, decided to stay in the United States instead of returning to Jamaica after his 1916 speaking and fund-raising tour, and moved its headquarters to Harlem, formalizing the arrangement two years later. Harlem became the UNIA's beachhead, enabling multiple conquests with a rapidity and élan that astonished—and to a great extent overwhelmed—even its ever-confident general.

The Afropolitan character of Harlem contributed profoundly to its dissenting political culture and vibrant social life, enhanced by the density of its population and the cooperation, sociality, and forced proletarianization of its members. Not only its Pan-Africanism and black bolshevism but also its music, dance, cuisine, sartorial tastes, and religious life were all shaped by this distinction. Harlem might not have been Locke's hyperbolic "race capital" or McKay's "Negro capital." After all, a "capital" implies the prior existence of a nation-state. We may have nations without states, but can there be a capital without a clearly delineated geographic and sovereign space? I do not think so, if the concept is not to be divested of meaning. Harlem, however, was the closest thing to a "black capital." Through its enormous black population, its intrablack ethnic variety, amalgamation, vitality, and dynamism ("melting pot Harlem—Harlem of honey and chocolate and caramel and rum and vinegar and lemon and lime and gall"), it has shaped not only the United States but also the wider world in a multitude of ways, including politically as well as culturally.[102]

NOTES

1. "Dankey seh worl' no level" (The donkey says the world is not level). The world is not flat; it has hills and valleys, peaks and troughs, and things are not equal.
2. For a brilliant survey and analysis of Harlem's hold on the literary imagination, see James de Jongh, *Vicious Modernism: Black Harlem and the Literary Imagination* (Cambridge: Cambridge University Press, 1990).
3. Winston James, "Culture, Labor, and Race in the Shadow of U.S. Capital," in *The Caribbean: A History of the Region and Its People*, ed. Stephan Palmié and Francisco Scarano (Chicago: University of Chicago Press, 2011), 445–58. The concept of "contact zone" was adapted from the field of linguistics by Mary Louise Pratt to refer to "spaces of colonial encounters" between colonizers and colonized or travelers and "travelees," characterized by "radically asymmetrical relations of power." Pratt, *Imperial Eyes: Travel Writing and Transculturation* (London: Routledge, 1992), esp. 6–7. My conceptualization is rather different. The term "black contact zone" is focused on *horizontal* relations and networks (as opposed to the hierarchical ones between black subordinates and superordinate whites) that developed among peoples of African descent from different backgrounds—geographic, linguistic, cultural, national, colonial—within a specified space.
4. I have undertaken preliminary explorations of London, the Panama Canal Zone, and Costa Rica as black contact zones. Winston James, "Black Contact Zones: Their Role in the Development of Pan-Africanism, Transnationalism, and Internationalism—The Case of London, 1897–1939," paper presented at the conference Writing Post-National Narratives: Other Geographies, Other Times, University of Witwatersrand, Johannesburg, November 1–3, 2010; Winston James, "Black Contact Zones: Their Role in the Development of Pan-Africanism, Transnationalism, and Internationalism—The Cases of Panama and Costa Rica, 1880–1939," paper presented at the conference Reimagining the Hemispheric South, University of California, Santa Barbara, January 20–21, 2011.
5. The literature on the subject is substantial and growing, but see, in particular, Robert Hill, ed., *The Marcus Garvey and Universal Negro Improvement Association Papers*, esp. vols. 9–13 (Berkeley: University of California Press; and Chapel Hill: University of

North Carolina Press, 1995-2016); Tony Martin, *Race First: The Ideological and Organizational Struggles of Marcus Garvey and the Universal Negro Improvement Association* (Dover, MA: Majority, 1986), chap. 7. For a good overview of the movement in the Spanish-speaking Caribbean and Central America, see Jorge L. Giovannetti and Reinaldo L. Román, eds., "Garveyism and the Universal Negro [Improvement] Association in the Hispanic Caribbean," *Caribbean Studies* 31 (special issue, January–June 2003).

6. Fernando Ortiz, *Cuban Counterpoint: Tobacco and Sugar* (New York: Alfred A. Knopf, 1947), 97–103.
7. For good overviews of the prehistory of black Harlem and its transformation into a black community, see James Weldon Johnson, *Black Manhattan* (1930; New York: Da Capo, 1991); Gilbert Osofsky, *Harlem: The Making of a Ghetto—Negro New York, 1890–1930*, 2nd ed. (New York: Harper and Row, 1971); Jeffrey Gurock, *When Harlem Was Jewish, 1870–1930* (New York: Columbia University Press, 1979).
8. Claude McKay, *Harlem: Negro Metropolis* (New York: E. P. Dutton, 1940), 29.
9. See U.S. Department of Commerce, Bureau of the Census, *Negro Population, 1790–1915* (Washington, DC, 1918), 101; U.S. Department of Commerce, Bureau of the Census, *Negroes in the United States, 1920–1932* (Washington, DC, 1935), 62.
10. On these restrictions, see William Cohen, *At Freedom's Edge: Black Mobility and the Southern White Quest for Racial Control, 1861–1915* (Baton Rouge: Louisiana State University Press, 1991).
11. It should be noted that Chicago's black population slightly exceeded that of Manhattan in 1920 and 1930, with Chicago having a black population of 109,458 to Manhattan's 109,133, in 1920, and 233,903 to Manhattan's 224,670, in 1930. However, the black population in New York City as a whole (that is, including that of all five boroughs) exceeded that of Chicago by more than 40 percent—327,706 to Chicago's 233,903. See Bureau of the Census, *Negroes in the United States, 1920–1932*, 57, 62.
12. Richard Wright, *Later Works: Black Boy (American Hunger), The Outsider* (New York: Library of America, 1991), 880.
13. For good analyses of the migration to New York, see Johnson, *Black Manhattan*, and Osofsky, *Harlem*. The classic studies of the movement to Chicago are Allan H. Spear, *Black Chicago: The Making of a Negro Ghetto, 1890–1920* (Chicago: University of Chicago Press, 1967); James R. Grossman, *Land of Hope: Chicago, Black Southerners, and the Great Migration* (Chicago: University of Chicago Press, 1989). See also Chicago Commission on Race Relations, *The Negro in Chicago: A Study of Race Relations and a Race Riot* (Chicago: University of Chicago Press, 1922); Emmett J. Scott, *Negro Migration During the War* (1920; New York: Arno, 1969), esp. chap. 10.
14. See Bureau of the Census, *Negroes in the United States, 1920–1932*, 23, 31–32, 34–36.
15. See Winston James, *Holding Aloft the Banner of Ethiopia: Caribbean Radicalism in Early Twentieth-Century America* (New York: Verso, 1998). See also Irma Watkins-Owens, *Blood Relations: Caribbean Immigrants and the Harlem Community, 1900–1930* (Bloomington: Indiana University Press, 1996); Ira De A. Reid, *The Negro Immigrant: His Background, Characteristics and Social Adjustments, 1899–1937* (New York: Columbia University Press, 1939).
16. Watkins-Owens, *Blood Relations*, 45–48.
17. Claude McKay to Nancy Cunard, August 20, 1932, Nancy Cunard Collection, Harry Ransom Humanities Research Center, University of Texas at Austin.
18. Bureau of the Census, *Negroes in the United States, 1920–1932*, 34–36.
19. Alain Locke, ed., *The New Negro: An Interpretation* (New York: Albert and Charles Boni, 1925), 7; Roi Ottley, *New World A-Coming: Inside Black America* (Boston: Houghton Mifflin, 1943), 41.

20. Zora Neale Hurston, *Dust Tracks On a Road: An Autobiography* (1942; New York: Harper Collins, 1996), 205–11. See also Valerie Boyd, *Wrapped in Rainbows: The Life of Zora Neale Hurston* (New York: Scribner, 2003), where Punter's identity is first revealed. Hurston had referred to him simply by his initials, as "P. M. P.," in her autobiography.
21. Ellen Harkins Wheat, *Jacob Lawrence, American Painter* (Seattle: University of Washington Press, 1986), 63; Myron Schwartzman, *Romare Bearden: His Life and Art* (New York: Harry N. Abrams, 1990), 176.
22. McKay, *Harlem*, 132.
23. Bureau of the Census, *Negroes in the United States, 1920–1932*, 22.
24. Bureau of the Census, *Negroes in the United States, 1920–1932*, 85.
25. Sixty percent of black immigrants who entered the United States in 1900 or earlier were men. The proportion gradually fell over the years, to roughly half by 1926. See James, *Holding Aloft the Banner of Ethiopia*, 363.
26. W. E. B. Du Bois, *Darkwater* (New York: Harcourt, Brace, 1920); W. E. B. Du Bois, *Autobiography of W. E. B. Du Bois: A Soliloquy on Viewing My Life from the Last Decade of Its First Century* (New York: International, 1968); James Weldon Johnson, *Along This Way: The Autobiography of James Weldon Johnson* (1933; New York: Penguin, 1990); James, *Holding Aloft the Banner of Ethiopia*, 174–75; Mona Z. Smith, *Becoming Something: The Story of Canada Lee* (New York: Faber and Faber, 2004); Barry Singer, *Black and Blue: The Life and Lyrics of Andy Razaf* (New York: Schirmer, 1992).
27. Wallace Thurman, "Harlem Facets," *World Tomorrow* (November 1927), reprinted in Amrijit Singh and Daniel M. Scott III, eds., *The Collected Writings of Wallace Thurman: A Harlem Renaissance Reader* (New Brunswick, NJ: Rutgers University Press, 2003), 35; Edgar M. Grey, "Harlem—Negro Melting Pot," *New York Amsterdam News*, April 20, 1927.
28. McKay, *Harlem*, 30.
29. McKay, *Harlem*, 135; Thurman, "Negro Life in New York's Harlem: A Lively Picture of a Popular and Interesting Section," *Haldeman-Julius Quarterly* (Fall 1927), reprinted in Singh and Scott, *Collected Writings*, 49; Ottley, *New World A-Coming*, 52–58; Eric Walrond, "The Black City," *Messenger* (January 1924), 13. See also Vivek Bald, *Bengali Harlem and the Lost Histories of South Asian America* (Cambridge, MA: Harvard University Press, 2013), esp. chaps. 5 and 6.
30. Thurman, "Harlem Facets," 35; Rudolph Fisher, "Miss Cynthie," in *City of Refuge: The Collected Stories of Rudolph Fisher*, ed. John McCluskey Jr. (Columbia: University of Missouri Press, 1987), 73; T. J. Woofter, *Negro Problems in Cities* (1928; New York: J. & J. Harper, 1969), 79.
31. McKay, *Harlem*, 23, 26–28. In the early 1920s, black residents in Harlem paid almost a quarter of their income in rent. Black Manhattanites paid a median monthly rent of $46.91, compared to $38.72 for black Chicagoans, in 1930. In Manhattan, 64.3 percent of black family homeowners took in lodgers, whereas only 35.5 percent of their Chicagoan counterparts did so. Just under 40 percent of black tenants in Manhattan had lodgers, compared to 36.6 percent of black tenants in Chicago. Remarkably, less than 1 percent of black residents in Manhattan owned their own homes in 1920, compared to 27 percent of black Chicagoans. For data and a good comparative analysis, see Bureau of the Census, *Negroes in the United States, 1920–1932*, 281, 285; Woofter, *Negro Problems in Cities*, 121–35, 137–41.
32. W. A. Domingo, "Gift of the Black Tropics," in Locke, *New Negro*, 346.
33. Reid, *Negro Immigrant*, 113.
34. Claude McKay, *A Long Way From Home* (New York: Lee Furman, 1937), 96.
35. Viola Glenn, "The Eating Habits of Harlem," *Opportunity* 13 (March 1935): 82–85.

36. Ras Makonnen, *Pan-Africanism from Within* (New York: Oxford University Press 1973), 89. The name of Domingo's business and its address (1692 Park Avenue) are revealed in the letterhead of his correspondence. See Domingo to Richard Hart, May 27 and July 13, 1938, provided by Hart to the author and now contained in the Richard Hart Papers, Institute of Commonwealth Studies, University of London.
37. Reid, *Negro Immigrant*, 129; Glenn, "Eating Habits of Harlem," 84.
38. Watkins-Owens, *Blood Relations*, chaps. 4 and 5.
39. James, *Holding Aloft the Banner of Ethiopia*. See also Mary G. Rolinson, *Grassroots Garveyism: The Universal Negro Improvement Association in the Rural South, 1920–1927* (Chapel Hill: University of North Carolina Press, 2007); Adam Ewing, *The Age of Garvey: How a Jamaican Activist Created a Mass Movement and Changed Global Black Politics* (Princeton, NJ: Princeton University Press, 2014).
40. For a recent contribution to this scholarship, see Lara Putnam, "Provincializing Harlem: The 'Negro Metropolis' as Northern Frontier of a Connected Caribbean," *Modernism/Modernity* 20 (September 2013): 469–84.
41. Claude McKay, *Banjo: A Story Without a Plot* (New York: Harper and Brothers, 1929), esp. 321–22. On the differences in the articulation of race and racism in the Caribbean and the United States, see James, *Holding Aloft the Banner of Ethiopia*, chap. 4. See also Richard Wright's searing testimony of the socialization and everyday survival strategies of African Americans, especially in the South. Wright, "The Ethics of Living Jim Crow: An Autobiographical Sketch," in *Uncle Tom's Children* (New York: HarperCollins, 1993), 1–15.
42. Langston Hughes, *The Big Sea: An Autobiography* (New York: Alfred A. Knopf, 1940), 225–26; Jeff Kisseloff, *You Must Remember This: An Oral History of Manhattan from the 1890s to World War II* (New York: Schocken, 1989), 323; Richard Bruce Nugent, *Gay Rebel of the Harlem Renaissance*, ed. Thomas H. Wirth (Durham, NC: Duke University Press, 2002), 221–23.
43. McKay, *Harlem*, 73–81, 101–16; Shane White, Stephen Garton, Stephen Robertson, and Graham White, *Playing the Numbers: Gambling in Harlem Between the Wars* (Cambridge, MA: Harvard University Press, 2010); LaShawn Harris, *Sex Workers, Psychics, and Numbers Runners: Black Women in New York City's Underground Economy* (Urbana: University of Illinois Press, 2016), chaps. 2 and 3.
44. McKay, *Harlem*, 29. It is possible that the Italian tradition of the *passeggiata*, brought by Italian immigrants living in Italian Harlem (East Harlem), had an influence upon the practice. For a history of Italian Harlem, see Robert Anthony Orsi, *The Madonna of 115th Street: Faith and Community in Italian Harlem, 1880–1950* (New Haven, CT: Yale University Press, 1985). For an analysis of the history and meaning of the *passeggiata* in Italian life, see Giovanna P. Del Negro, *The Passeggiata and Popular Culture in an Italian Town: Folklore and the Performance of Modernity* (Montreal: McGill-Queen's University Press, 2004).
45. Johnson, *Black Manhattan*, 162–63.
46. See Richard B. Moore, "Africa Conscious Harlem," in *Harlem: A Community in Transition*, ed. John Henrik Clarke (New York: Citadel, 1970), 77–96.
47. Reid, *Negro Immigrant*, 144–45; McKay, *Harlem*, 31; Grey, "Harlem—Negro Melting Pot."
48. McKay, *Harlem*, 132.
49. See David J. Hellwig, "Black Meets Black: Afro-American Reactions to West Indian Immigrants in the 1920s," *South Atlantic Quarterly* 77 (Spring 1978): 206–24.
50. McKay, *Harlem*, 132–34. Privately, he called the rivalries and jealousies between the groups "so stupid and idiotic" (McKay to Cunard, August 20, 1932). In his novels, such tensions are resolved through humor and reconciliation. See, for instance, *Banjo*, 77–78.

51. James, *Holding Aloft the Banner of Ethiopia*, esp. 12, 355, 367.
52. Anderson, *This Was Harlem*, 285–89; Kisseloff, *You Must Remember This*, 332–33.
53. Tony Martin, *Amy Ashwood Garvey: Pan-Africanist, Feminist and Mrs. Marcus Garvey No. 1 (Or a Tale of Two Amies)* (Dover, MA: Majority, 2007).
54. See, for instance, Karl Mannheim, "The Problem of Generations," in *From Karl Mannheim*, ed. Kurt H. Wolff, 2nd ed. (New Brunswick, NJ: Transaction, 1993), 351–98; "Generations in Conflict," *Journal of Contemporary History* 5, no. 1 (special issue, 1970); and, especially, Philip Abrams, "Rites de Passage: The Conflict of Generations in Industrial Societies," *Journal of Contemporary History* 5, no. 1 (special issue, 1970), 175–90.
55. Calculated from Bureau of the Census, *Negroes in the United States, 1920–1932*, 90, 147, 174, 179.
56. A. Philip Randolph, "A New Crowd—A New Negro," *Messenger* (May–June 1919), 27. The *Messenger* carried a regular "Who's Who" column, under which this article appeared, and was forthright and merciless in its appraisal of both friend and foe.
57. *Crusader* (October 1919), 9–10.
58. Robert Kerlin, *The Voice of the Negro 1919* (New York: E. P. Dutton, 1920), ix; Frederick G. Detweiler, *Negro Press in the United States* (Chicago: University of Chicago Press, 1922), 1–13; Theodore Vincent, ed., *Voices of a Black Nation: Political Journalism in the Harlem Renaissance* (San Francisco: Ramparts, 1973), 23, 37.
59. U.S. Department of Commerce, *Fifteenth Census of the United States: 1930* (Washington, DC: Government Printing Office, 1932), 2:1219, 1224.
60. Bureau of the Census, *Negroes in the United States, 1920–1932*, 210, 252.
61. Detweiler, *Negro Press*, 15.
62. Cited in Vincent, *Voices of a Black Nation*, 24.
63. U.S. Senate, *Investigative Activities of the Department of Justice*, 66th Cong., 1st Sess., Sen. Doc. 12, no. 153 (Washington, DC: Government Printing Office, 1919), 172.
64. "Radicalism and Sedition Among the Negroes as Reflected in Their Publications," exhibit no. 10, in *Investigative Activities of the Department of Justice*, 161–87. See also Winston James, "Being Red and Black in Jim Crow America: On the Ideology and Travails of Afro-America's Socialist Pioneers, 1877–1930," in *Time Longer than Rope: A Century of African American Activism*, ed. Charles Payne and Adam Green (New York: New York University Press, 2003), 336–400, esp. 364–86. On Harlem's "black public sphere," see Clare Corbould, *Becoming African Americans: Black Public Life in Harlem, 1919–1939* (Cambridge, MA: Harvard University Press, 2009).
65. Watkins-Owens, *Blood Relations*, chap. 4; Roi Ottley and William J. Weatherby, eds., *The Negro in New York: An Informal History, 1626–1940* (New York: Praeger, 1969), 193–94; Osofsky, *Harlem*, 131–33.
66. See McKay, *Harlem*; James, *Holding Aloft the Banner of Ethiopia*, chap. 5; Watkins-Owens, *Blood Relations*, chap. 6; James, "Being Red and Black"; Ralph L. Crowder, "The Historical Context and Political Significance of Harlem's Street Scholar Community," *Afro-Americans in New York Life and History* 34 (January 2010): 34–71.
67. Kelly Miller, "After Marcus Garvey—What of the Negro?" *Contemporary Review* 131 (April 1927): 494; James, *Holding Aloft the Banner*.
68. Ronald Lawson, ed., *The Tenant Movement in New York City, 1904–1984* (New Brunswick, NJ: Rutgers University Press, 1986).
69. Michael Banton, *The Coloured Quarter: Negro Immigrants in an English City* (London: Jonathan Cape, 1955), 66–67; Winston James, "The Black Experience in Twentieth-Century Britain," in *Black Experience and the Empire*, ed. Philip D. Morgan and Sean

Hawkins (Oxford: Oxford University Press, 2004), 349–50; Philippe Dewitte, *Les mouvements nègres en France, 1919–1939* (Paris: L'Harmattan, 1985), 24–26.

70. Banton, *Coloured Quarter*, 66–67; E. J. B. Rose et al., eds., *Colour and Citizenship: A Report on British Race Relations* (London: Oxford University Press, 1969), 96–97; Ceri Peach et al., "Immigration and Ethnicity," in *British Social Trends Since 1900: A Guide to the Changing Social Structure of Britain*, ed. A. H. Halsey (Basingstoke: Macmillan, 1988), 578–79.

71. Dewitte, *Les mouvements nègres en France*, 24–26; Jennifer Anne Boittin, *Colonial Metropolis: The Urban Grounds of Anti-Imperialism and Feminism in Interwar Paris* (Lincoln: University of Nebraska Press, 2010), xviii; Gary Wilder, *The French Imperial Nation-State: Negritude and Colonial Humanism between the Two World Wars* (Chicago: University of Chicago Press, 2005), 341.

72. I developed this argument in the case of London, and Britain as a whole, in James, "Black Experience in Twentieth-Century Britain."

73. See Martin Steins, "Brown France vs. Black Africa: The Tide Turned in 1932," *Research in African Literatures* 14 (Winter 1983): 474–97; Martin Steins, "Black Migrants in Paris," in *European-Language Writing on Sub-Saharan Africa*, ed. Albert S. Gérard (Budapest: Akadémiai Kiadó, 1986), 1:354–78; J. Ayo Langley, "Pan-Africanism in Paris, 1924–36," *Journal of Modern African Studies* 7 (April 1969): 6–94. Frantz Fanon provides a fine analysis of the roots of the tension. Fanon, "West Indians and Africans," in *Toward the African Revolution* (Harmondsworth: Penguin, 1970), 27–37.

74. For a measure of the havoc wrought and suffering engendered, see Cheryl Lynn Greenberg, *"Or Does It Explode?": Black Harlem in the Great Depression* (New York: Oxford University Press, 1991).

75. The pioneering accounts are Lilyan Kesteloot, *Black Writers in French: A Literary History of Negritude*, trans. Ellen Kennedy (1963; Philadelphia, PA: Temple University Press, 1974); Imanuel Geiss, *The Pan-African Movement* (1968; London: Methuen, 1974), esp. part 2. Notable recent additions are Brent Hayes Edwards, *The Practice of Diaspora: Literature, Translation, and the Rise of Black Internationalism* (Cambridge, MA: Harvard University Press, 2003); Minkah Makalani, *In the Cause of Freedom: Radical Black Internationalism from Harlem to London, 1917–1939* (Chapel Hill: University of North Carolina Press, 2011); Marc Matera, *Black London: The Imperial Metropolis and Decolonization in the Twentieth Century* (Berkeley: University of California Press, 2015).

76. Léopold Sédar Senghor, *Liberté I: Négritude et Humanisme* (Paris: Seuil, 1964), 116. Senghor, Aimé Césaire, and Léon-Gontran Damas could recite McKay's poetry by heart, as well as passages from his novel *Banjo* (1929). See also, among other works, Kesteloot, *Black Writers in French*; Jacques Louis Hymans, *Léopold Sédar Senghor: An Intellectual Biography* (Edinburgh: Edinburgh University Press, 1971); Jacqueline Kaye, "Claude McKay's *Banjo*," *Présence Africaine* 73 (First Quarter 1970): 165–69; Bridget Jones, "With *Banjo* by My Bed: Black French Writers Reading Claude McKay," *Caribbean Quarterly* 38 (March 1992): 32–39.

77. Hakim Adi, *West Africans in Britain, 1900–1960: Nationalism, Pan-Africanism and Communism* (London: Lawrence and Wishart, 1998); Makalani, *In the Cause of Freedom*; Matera, *Black London*.

78. Davarian L. Baldwin, "Introduction: New Negroes Forging a New World," in *Escape from New York: The New Negro Renaissance Beyond Harlem*, ed. Davarian L. Baldwin and Minkah Makalani (Minneapolis: University of Minnesota Press, 2013), 3–4 (emphasis added). Putnam similarly uses the metaphor of "node" in reference to Harlem. But unlike

Baldwin, she describes Harlem as "certainly a key node" within what she calls the "interconnected circum-Caribbean." Unfortunately, Putnam does not elaborate upon the modifier "key." She writes that "we cannot assume that Harlem's 'jazzin-sheiks,' cosmopolitan crowds, street-corner oratory, and international vision were unique within its blocks. Wages were higher in New York, buildings taller, night classes more common. Yet jazz, anticolonial critique, radical black politics, class-laden languages, and a self-aware black press were under construction at multiple sites" (Putnam, "Provincializing Harlem," 481). This kind of argument does indeed amount to "provincializing" Harlem. Yet this is achieved by ignoring the unequal or asymmetrical exchange between Harlem and the Central American communities on which Putnam focuses. It elides the sheer scale and peculiar ethnic, regional, national, and linguistic makeup of black Harlem. Most importantly, it ignores the greater reach and influence of black Harlem in comparison to the sites she mentions. Limón was not Harlem and the *Panama Tribune* was not the *Negro World*. The Universal Negro Improvement Association, to this day the largest black organization the world has ever seen, was not headquartered in Panama City but in Harlem. Post Menelik, the seat of the African Blood Brotherhood, was not in Bocas del Toro; it was in Harlem. The *Messenger* and the *Crusader* were not published in Colón; they emanated from Harlem. Black South Africans did not run into the streets crying, "The Panamanians are coming!" They shouted, "The Americans are coming!"—referring to the Garveyites. See Robert Trent Vinson, *The Americans Are Coming! Dreams of African American Liberation in Segregationist South Africa* (Athens: Ohio University Press, 2012).

79. Sterling A. Brown, "The New Negro in Literature (1925–1955)," in *The New Negro Thirty Years Afterward*, ed. Rayford W. Logan, Eugene C. Holmes, and G. Franklin Edwards (Washington, DC: Howard University Press, 1955), 57; Robert B. Stepto, "Sterling A. Brown: Outside in the Harlem Renaissance," in *The Harlem Renaissance: Revaluations*, ed. Amritjit Singh, William S. Shriver, and Stanley Brodwin (New York: Garland Publishing, 1989), 73 (emphasis added).

80. Edwards, *Practice of Diaspora*, 2–4. Among others, George Hutchinson adduces evidence to strongly contest this argument. Hutchinson, *The Harlem Renaissance in Black and White* (Cambridge, MA: Belknap Press of Harvard University Press, 1995).

81. Michel Fabre, *From Harlem to Paris: Black American Writers in France, 1840–1980* (Urbana: University of Illinois Press, 1991), 2, and esp. 92–113.

82. I use the term "exceptionalism"—despite the dark freight connected to its use in the United States, as in the term "American exceptionalism"—simply to indicate a departure from the norm, not in the nationalistic and chauvinistic way in which it is often used in American political and historical discourse. See Daniel T. Rogers, "American Exceptionalism Revisited," *Raritan* 24 (Fall 2004): 21–47.

83. McKay, *Harlem*, 16 (emphasis added), 30.

84. Locke, *New Negro*, 6–7.

85. McKay, *Harlem*, 15. Harlem, declared black Washingtonian Sterling Brown, was "no more Negro America than New York is America" ("New Negro in Literature," 57). This was not meant as a compliment to Harlem.

86. These words are John Gunther's, quoted in John F. Davis, "The Changing Face and Role of America's Primate City," in *New York: City as Text*, ed. Christopher Mulvey and John Simons (Basingstoke: Macmillan, 1990), 177.

87. Within the vast literature on New York City, see, especially, Edwin G. Burrows and Mike Wallace, *Gotham: New York City to 1898* (New York: Oxford University Press, 1999); Francois Weil, *A History of New York* (New York: Columbia University Press, 2004); Ann

Douglas, *Terrible Honesty: Mongrel Manhattan in the 1920s* (New York: Farrar, Straus and Giroux, 1995).
88. Hughes, *Big Sea*, 240.
89. David Levering Lewis, *When Harlem Was in Vogue* (New York: Oxford University Press, 1981), 121–55; Hutchinson, *Harlem Renaissance*; Amy Helen Kirschke, *Aaron Douglas: Art, Race, and the Harlem Renaissance* (Jackson: University Press of Mississippi, 1995), 55–59.
90. James, *Holding Aloft the Banner of Ethiopia*, chap. 2; Chad Williams, *Torchbearers of Democracy: African American Soldiers in the World War I Era* (Chapel Hill: University of North Carolina Press, 2010), chaps. 5–7. Black veterans were conspicuous as editors and contributors of prose, poetry, and correspondence in the *Negro World*, *Messenger*, and *Crusader*. For a while, they even had their own militant mouthpiece, the *Veteran*. An engrossing firsthand account of one such veteran is Harry Haywood, *Black Bolshevik: Autobiography of an Afro-American Communist* (Chicago: Liberator, 1978).
91. Langston Hughes, "Our Wonderful Society: Washington," *Opportunity* 5 (August 1927): 226–27.
92. James, *Holding Aloft the Banner of Ethiopia*.
93. Claude McKay, "A Negro Poet Writes," *Pearson's Magazine* (September 1918): 276.
94. McKay, *Long Way From Home*, 228. For a similar retort, see Hughes, *Big Sea*, 267–68.
95. I build here on the invaluable study by George Chauncey, *Gay New York: Gender, Urban Culture, and the Making of the Gay Male World, 1890–1940* (New York: Basic Books, 1994).
96. It should be noted that black people *possessed* Harlem but never *owned* it. In 1920, less than 1 percent of black Manhattanites owned their homes and only 2 percent of Harlem's apartment units were black owned. See Woofter, *Negroes in Cities*, 141; Kevin McGruder, *Race and Real Estate: Conflict and Cooperation in Harlem, 1890–1920* (New York: Columbia University Press, 2015), 177.
97. Adam Clayton Powell Sr., *Against the Tide: An Autobiography* (New York: Richard R. Smith, 1938), 209–17.
98. Kisseloff, *You Must Remember This*, 288–89.
99. Langston Hughes, "Aesthete in Harlem," in *The Collected Poems of Langston Hughes*, ed. Arnold Rampersad and David Roessel (New York: A. A. Knopf, 1995), 128.
100. I conceived of the term "Afropolitanism" to name the condition being described—of belonging, intermingling, transculturation, and sharing among diverse peoples of African descent, particularly within a dense urban setting such as Harlem—only to discover that it has been used by others for rather different purposes. The term is most widely associated with the Nigerian-Ghanaian writer Taiye Selasi, who used the expression (but denies coining it) to denote the life-world of young, professional people with direct African lineage living in the diaspora. Selasi, "Bye-Bye Babar," *The LIP Magazine* (March 3, 2005). As she later explained, she did not use the term in connection with the "original" African diaspora, which came out of the slave trade, but with a new, late twentieth-century and early twenty-first-century movement. See Aaron Bady, "From That Stranded Place: A Conversation with Taiye Selasi," *Transition* 117 (2015): 157–60. Since then, the Afropolitan has come to be largely associated with the consumer and popular culture of young, transnational, professional African immigrants in the West. The term has had some more critical scrutiny of late. For a good sample of the range of discussion, see *Journal of African Cultural Studies* 28, no. 1 (special issue, 2016). In my own rendering, Afropolitanism is not incompatible with cosmopolitanism—one can simultaneously be of the African world as well as the wider world. What my use of "Afropolitanism" draws attention to, however, is a particular set of relationships among peoples of

African descent and the new structures of feeling that they generate. Black contact zones provide the most conducive conditions within which Afropolitanism, thus defined, develops and thrives.
101. Marcus Garvey, "The Negro's Greatest Enemy," *Current History* 18 (September 1923), reprinted in Hill, *Marcus Garvey and Universal Negro Improvement Association Papers*, 1:5–6.
102. Langston Hughes, "My Early Days in Harlem," in Clarke, *Harlem*, 64.

6.

BLACK WOMEN'S INTELLECTUAL LABOR AND THE SOCIAL SPACES OF BLACK RADICAL THOUGHT IN HARLEM

MINKAH MAKALANI

In *A Long Way from Home* (1937), Claude McKay recalls his return to Harlem, in 1921, after a brief sojourn in England. Strolling along uptown's wide avenues, he encountered once more the "familiar voices and the shapes of houses and saloons" that left him "inflated with confidence." There was, for McKay, a comfort that came with being "lost in the shadows of Harlem again." One particular shadow was a speakeasy on Seventh Avenue, run by a childhood friend, a woman named Sanina. Sanina's establishment "was always humming like a beehive with brown butterflies and flames of all ages from the West Indies and from the South." Having spent "ten days of purely voluptuous relaxation" at Sanina's, which left him penniless and depending on her for food, McKay admitted, "I was uncomfortable. I began feeling intellectual again."

His discomfort was not with his friend Sanina, whose speakeasy offered him a reprieve from Harlem's Talented Tenth. Nor was it with the revelry in this most familiar of shadows—at one point Sanina even agreed to entertain a group of white writers for McKay. Rather, McKay's discomfort seems to have issued from the realization that he *had* to throw himself back into his intellectual activism. There is a resonance here with Langston Hughes's famous call for black artists to "let the blare of Negro jazz bands and the bellowing voice of Bessie Smith singing the Blues penetrate the closed ears of the colored near intellectuals until they listen and perhaps understand." McKay's suggestion that his time at Sanina's spurred his "feeling intellectual again" invites us to contemplate the importance of this social world—and of the work black women performed to make that world possible—wherein he experienced the "rare sensation [of being] just one black among many," to the more radical strains of black thought then being elaborated in Harlem.[1]

One of Harlem's more alluring mythical figures is the male autodidact, an individual who, through self-guided study and keen intellect, appears uniquely positioned to assume a major role in black political life. If acceptance by and citizenship within a modern nation-state required demonstrating that black people were, in fact, modern people, it stands to reason that many early twentieth-century thinkers would have considered it essential that any display of the "New Negro" portray black men of letters. This certainly guided Alain Locke's approach to his *Survey Graphic* number, "Harlem: Mecca of the New Negro," and the collection that grew from it, *The New Negro: An Interpretation*. For sleeping car porters or union organizers who had never received a university education, the need to display erudition, self-taught or otherwise, was as paramount as it was for a high school teacher. Thus, the Fisk- and Harvard-educated W. E. B. Du Bois was compelled to spar with the self-taught Marcus Garvey for the hearts and minds of black America, and both men had to contend with detractors like Hubert H. Harrison, Richard B. Moore, and Cyril V. Briggs, none of whom ever attended university.

Yet, for this portrait to hold, one must accept as a mere accident of history that so many self-taught men happened to gather in Harlem. It would seem that the Negro Mecca, unlike so many other places, such as Washington, DC, or Chicago, either produced or drew to its environs male intellectuals who largely were from outside the academy. As enticing as such a tale might be, it loses sight of the intellectual societies, lyceums, debate forums, and black periodicals that functioned as an educational network facilitating the rise of New Negro radicalism. Also lost in this telling is any sense of the vital role that black women played in building and sustaining those institutions.

Black women thinkers remain among the score of casualties from the scholarly habit of limiting the realm of the intellectual to those who leave behind a corpus of easily accessible and archived writings. As the editors of the recent collection *Toward an Intellectual History of Black Women* have noted, "Black women have rarely worked out of the academy or research institutes," the gendered, racialized structures of academia confining "the scenes of their intellectual labor [to] the intimate spaces of parlors [and] to highly public podiums, where the oral expression of ideas often mixed with the material demands of communities."[2]

If black women's ideas "grew out of challenges to both the body and mind," grasping the complexity of their responses to those challenges requires that we adopt alternative methodological approaches. We might follow Davarian Baldwin's example in *Chicago's New Negroes*, where he finds that in the Windy City's "streets and in its cinemas, beauty salons, Sanctified churches, and sports stadiums," spaces not traditionally considered as generative of thought, people pursued a "marketplace intellectual life," where they debated and struggled over questions of class, race, gender, and nation and produced "theoretical insights" unto themselves.[3] Similarly, in her discussion of Amy Ashwood Garvey and Ella Baker in interwar Harlem, Ula Taylor reveals that the social practice of street strolling also involved entering a place where one could "mature intellectually," given Harlem's cultural "atmosphere that allowed stepladder speakers to occupy busy street corners," and that "political meetings and lectures took place in public parks all over town." Taylor widens our understanding of intellectual life by showing how, through walking Harlem's streets, black women not only learned of the contemporary issues that faced ordinary residents but also, through snatches of conversation and their later published responses, emerged as "organic intellectuals."[4]

The approaches pursued by these scholars help to guard against the tendency to see black women simply as behind-the-scenes organizers, a view that separates the creation and maintenance of social spaces—work that black women often undertook—from the intellectual debates that emerged within those arenas. This tendency, Dayo Gore warns, serves to render "invisible the national and international aspects of their activism and ... [their] intellectual and philosophical contributions to black radicalism." If we can view organizational work as a strain of intellectual labor, we might better appreciate black women as thinkers whose practices, as Joy James argues, "provided models and strategies for resistance" by improvising "integrative analyses of race, gender ... and class."[5]

In this chapter, I challenge the notion that Harlem possessed some mysterious quality that lured black male autodidacts, and instead I redirect attention toward those who organized meetings in the back rooms of local businesses, held socials in their homes, put on street corner debates, and built institutions that served various political, intellectual, and social needs. By recovering such activities, I hope to move us beyond the shallow pastiche of Harlem's social and intellectual life—its stepladder orators and ephemeral periodicals, modes of socializing and places of leisure—which is often glossed in accounts of this community, and instead try to model an approach to such history that brings into focus the institution building of black women as itself a form of intellectual work, the fashioning of spaces in which they, and others, could debate a variety of issues and modulate between the local and the global and that furnished them with a framework within which they could articulate a black radical feminist politics. It is an orientation that allows us, for example, to celebrate Arturo Schomburg's magnificent contribution as a collector of books and manuscripts, while recovering the work of the women librarians, such as Ernestine Rose and Jean Blackwell Hutson, who made the 135th Street Library "the place to go" for the neighborhood's thinkers, and that recovers the work Lodie Biggs performed at the Frederick Douglass Bookstore on 125th Street, which continues to be mentioned predominantly in accounts of her better-known husband, Richard B. Moore.[6]

Following Claudia Jones's observation, in 1949, that black women were "the real active forces—the organizers and workers—in all the institutions and organizations of the Negro people," I propose that the recovery of black women's intellectual work must attend to the social spaces women helped to create and maintain.[7] Doing so orients the analysis of black radical thought to the social terrain in which it emerged, which often took the social as a key theoretical frame in pursuit of African diasporic liberation. My emphasis on social space follows Anthony Bogues's observation that a key feature of black radical thought is its coupling of freedom with equality—broadening claims to citizenship and the right to participate in governance so that they encompass demands for the rights to life, including those of housing, education, and health care.[8]

The focus on black radical thought, rather than social movements or organizations, also allows for a genealogical approach that attends to the peculiarities of Harlem without necessarily reinforcing any sense of this place as exceptional or, indeed, locating it at the center of black radical thought. As I have argued elsewhere in regard to Amy Ashwood Garvey's Florence Mills Social Parlour and Afro-Restaurant in 1930s London, and as several scholars have shown with regard to the Martinican sisters Paulette and Jane Nardal in Paris around the same time, black women in many urban centers were crucial in creating and sustaining the institutions that shaped and advanced antiracist and anticolonial politics.[9] This was no less true of those in Harlem during the interwar years.

The genealogical approach, though, encourages us to contemplate the "conditions of possibility" for black radical thought and therefore prompts us to recognize that, although the direction of thought has no boundaries, it always emerges in *specific* locations, is provoked in part by local issues, is shaped by certain conditions, and is discussed by distinct audiences. This is a perspective that allows for an understanding of Harlem as a specific location in the circulation of ideas throughout the African diaspora—alongside other U.S. cities such as Chicago or Washington, DC, the cosmopolitan metropoles of Paris, London, and Hamburg, and locales like Port-au-Prince, Haiti, Fort-de-France, Martinique, or Havana. In this respect, what distinguished Harlem's social spaces from those of its contemporaries was its uniquely varied African diasporic population and the social density of its inhabitants that Winston James calls the neighborhood's "propinquity."[10] Together these ensured that even a leisurely stroll along one of Harlem's avenues would bring one into contact with a range of black people, a host of competing political ideals, and a constellation of overlapping, often competing social spaces.

Here, I focus on the work and thought of Grace Campbell, Elizabeth Hendrickson, and Williana Jones Burroughs, three women who stand out as community feminists whose politics reverberated in both national and diasporic arenas.[11] Grace Campbell, a black clubwoman and social worker, helped establish some of the more dynamic political and intellectual institutions in 1920s Harlem. She would work with Elizabeth Hendrickson, a Caribbean immigrant, seamstress, entrepreneur, and socialite, who focused on political issues in Harlem and the Caribbean. Campbell and Hendrickson both joined the Communist Party (CP), as did the schoolteacher and longtime radical activist Williana Jones Burroughs, whose turn toward the party was informed by her encounter with both Campbell and Hendrickson. Each of these women found her way to Harlem under radically distinct circumstances, and they worked to build institutions that allowed them to respond to their immediate contexts and to address larger political questions that spoke to the worlds they had left behind as well as to African diasporic life more broadly.

The institution building of Campbell, Hendrickson, and Burroughs was itself a mode of intellectual work that provided a space in which they, and others, discussed a variety of issues, both immediate and abstract, and that furnished them with a framework for pursuing a more critically developed activism. This intellectual labor allowed them to articulate a nascent black radical feminism that would shape, if only subtly, an explicitly global, diasporic orientation that we later find in the lives and thought of such black intellectuals as Louise Thompson Patterson and Claudia Jones.

What I propose is something other than a story that follows the archival grain and the corresponding methodological protocols of historical narration, whereby one can discern a clear line of contact and transmission of ideas from Campbell, Hendrickson, and Burroughs on through to a subsequent generation of black radical women like Patterson and Jones. That such lines of connection rarely leave more than a faint trace in the archives suggests that, rather than work through the epistemological violence of such silences, a genealogical approach—one concerned with identifying those practices, events, and even missed opportunities that establish not so much a link between one period (the beginning of a historical arc) and the next (its culmination), as the conditions of possibilities for myriad events—might prove more appropriate to telling any story of New Negro women's radical thought.

GRACE CAMPBELL AND THE SOCIAL SPACES OF BLACK RADICAL THOUGHT

For much of its organizational life, the Harlem-based African Blood Brotherhood (ABB) was a small group of activist intellectuals who maintained memberships alternatively in the Socialist and Communist Parties. Campbell, along with her numerous organizational memberships and her work as a parole officer, was the sole woman on the ABB's Supreme Council. Like many of its contemporaries, the ABB envisioned itself as engaged in a struggle for racial "manhood." When its founder, the Caribbean émigré radical Cyril Briggs, ran an advertisement in the *Crusader* magazine in 1919 announcing the group's formation, black men from Philadelphia to the Dominican Republic responded, pledging their commitment to fight for African redemption and the "rescue of our women and children." Yet, at its height in 1923, fully 2,000 of its 3,000 members were women.[12] In light of this, it may not be surprising that, if Briggs is most readily associated with the ABB, it was Grace Campbell who made its theoretical innovations and very survival possible.

Born in Georgia in 1882 to an African American mother, Emma Dyson Campbell, and a Jamaican-born father, William Campbell, Grace Campbell had instilled in her early on the values of womanly comportment and race work. The Campbells had moved to Texas and to Washington, DC, by the time Grace was in her midteens. It was in the nation's capital that she encountered a highly organized network of black clubwomen who emphasized uplift and the responsibilities incumbent upon the "better class" of the race. After graduating from Howard University, she started working as an elementary schoolteacher in Washington, before moving to Chicago, and by 1905 she had found her way to New York.[13]

Her career as a social reformer began in 1911, when she started working as a probation officer for the New York Court of General Sessions and took a position in the National League for the Protection of Colored Women. As Cheryl Hicks notes, Campbell soon turned her attention away from the criminal justice focus of her colleagues to address the discriminatory treatment of black women within the judicial system. Dismissed in 1913 for refusing to show deference to her white supervisors, Campbell went on to establish the Empire Friendly Shelter for delinquent women, in 1916, and a year later became an official parole officer for New York City. This is likely around the time Campbell moved to Harlem; she and her sister lived in the Empire Friendly Shelter until at least 1920, before she took up residence in her own home at 206 West 133rd Street. In Harlem, her concern with discriminatory policies toward black women in the criminal justice system signaled her burgeoning radicalism.[14]

Like many politically minded black people in Harlem, Campbell often found herself at the public lectures of Hubert Harrison, a Virgin Islander who, by 1910, had emerged as the most prominent black member of the Socialist Party of America. Popularly known as the "black Socrates" for his captivating public lectures that effortlessly linked local racial concerns to world events, and which James Weldon Johnson celebrated as "equivalent to a year of college, and of incalculable benefit to the community," Harrison's erudition appealed to

Campbell, who joined several other burgeoning Harlem radicals in becoming Socialists.[15]

One of the first black women Socialists, Campbell also experienced a political shift during this period; her concern with uplift and personal responsibility soon gave way to a gendered critique of a racialized criminal justice system. Early in her career, she had distinguished between respectable working-class black women and those in the criminal justice system. In a 1917 report, she described two black women in her charge as "in need of strong discipline," noting that they "used profane language, called people from the street . . . [and were] unpleasant with other inmates."[16] Her concern with self-discipline and comportment reflected a more general emphasis among black elites on chastity, social purity, and self-help in race advancement.[17]

By 1925, Campbell would stress economic rights, group struggle, discriminatory social structures, and, as Hicks observes, the gendered, racialized ways that class impacted black women's experiences in the criminal justice system. Writing in the *New York Age* in 1925, she explained that the high number of black women convicted in New York City courts was the result of low wages and poverty that drove many to crime and sex work. Of paramount importance, however, was how the courts treated black women. "In cases of prostitution" in particular, she explained in this rare editorial, "the offense against the law is made possible only through the participation of men." Yet, in the courts, the "woman alone is accountable, and she alone bears the humiliation and punishments." Such discriminatory judicial practices were compounded by reformatory institutions that refused to take in both white and black women, which left "unfortunate young colored women" to serve their sentences "in the workhouse with hardened offenders."[18] Campbell joined her concern for black women's limited economic opportunities with a keen insight into the gendered structures of the criminal justice system.

This shift in Campbell's thinking did not result simply from her membership in the Socialist Party, or from listening to Harrison's lectures. Rather, her political views grew out of her radical organizing activities and intense intellectual engagements with other New Negro radicals. A formidable public speaker herself, Campbell gave lectures around the city, sponsored lyceums, and even held a position on the New York City school board, which allowed her to sponsor lectures by various radicals throughout the city. She served as secretary for the Socialist Party's 21st Assembly District in Harlem and twice ran for the New York State Assembly on its electoral ticket. Drawing on these multiple networks, her national reputation, and her own oratorical skills, in 1920 Campbell recruited a number of black women into the Socialist Party, many of whom were likely among the black women making up the ABB's core membership.[19]

While the array of her professional obligations and multiple organizational commitments left Campbell little time to record her ideas in print, she brought her considerable administrative skills to organizing and maintaining key institutions that fostered New Negro radical thought. In the summer of 1917, working with Louise Jackson, another black woman in the Socialist Party, Campbell launched the People's Educational Forum (PEF), a Sunday afternoon lecture series that also sponsored debates at Harlem's Lafayette Hall on Seventh Avenue and 131st Street. Campbell may have taken the idea for the PEF from her own Empire Friendly Shelter, which had occasionally sponsored lyceums.[20] For the PEF, she scheduled speakers such as W. E. B. Du Bois, who lectured on "The War and the Darker World," and the Columbia University anthropologist Franz Boas, who discussed "Supposed Racial Inferiority." Other speakers included Egbert Ethelred Brown, the Unitarian minister of the Harlem Community Church, and William H. Ferris, the editor of *Negro World*, who discussed the "Four Phases of Negro Radicalism." Reflecting black radicals' concerns with race and class, the PEF also held a discussion on "The Relation of the Race Problem to the Proletarian Movement," where participants identified the ties between black liberation in the United States and anticolonial struggles in Africa and Asia.[21] Encouraging debate and the free exchange of ideas, the forum was known as an "intellectual battleground" that, as Richard B. Moore would recall, provided black radicals with a venue where they could approach "socialist theory as a method of social analysis of the Afro-American situation and [the] oppressed colonial peoples in Africa, the Caribbean, and elsewhere."[22]

What few accounts there are of the PEF provide no insight into which debates or discussions Campbell participated in, though she almost certainly would have found room there for thinking through her nascent radical analysis of black women in the criminal justice system. We may never know the extent to which Campbell urged ABB members to think about gender, though it is hardly a stretch to imagine her bringing the struggles of black working-class women into the ABB's meetings and the PEF's discussions. These were the institutional spaces she created that initiated a process whereby questions and concerns about race opened up onto issues related to black women and the home. The group of black women she recruited into the Socialist Party likely would have also joined her in addressing concerns about raising families, discriminatory wages, and unsanitary living conditions and expressed a sense of their own political importance to black struggle, as something other than wives. Indeed, it is against this backdrop that we can see Cyril Briggs's editorials on housing in the *Crusader* reflecting both his reading of Friedrich Engels's *The Housing Question* (1872) and, possibly more importantly, the influence of Campbell and other black women in the ABB.[23]

Campbell's keen intellect and impressive organizational skills are difficult to exaggerate, though there is the risk of falsely implying that her energies were inexhaustible. Among her numerous professional and organizational obligations, she was also the ABB's treasurer, making all of that group's logistical arrangements—scheduling meetings, securing lecture halls, collecting dues, paying bills—and overseeing its activities from her home, where fellow members occasionally roomed when between apartments. She was also involved in establishing the American West Indian Association, located at 149 West 139th Street, in 1921, which quickly became an important institution in Harlem's Caribbean community and served as a key venue for elaborating a black radical politics. When ABB members first began joining the Communist Party, this association doubled as the headquarters of the Party's Harlem branch, which Campbell helped to establish in 1922, along with Briggs, Moore, and McKay.

Still, resources were always scarce, and the ABB's male members gave only minimal support. By the end of 1920, Campbell stopped running the PEF, leaving it to Moore and W. A. Domingo to revive a year later, albeit only briefly. Among the many reasons why ABB members left the Socialist Party for the Communist Party, the most practical was the promise of greater resources for their work. Yet by 1925, when Briggs dissolved the ABB and urged its members to join the communist-controlled American Negro Labor Congress (ANLC), Campbell was still forced to convene meetings of the Party's Harlem branch at her home.[24]

When ABB radicals abandoned independent black political formations to work solely within the CP, few were surprised to find that the most progressive white-led political party, especially in terms of its policies on race, was led by radicals who were at times imperious and often condescending toward black Communists, if not outright dismissive of their contributions. An interaction between Campbell and Rose Pastor Stokes, a high-ranking, white CP official, is particularly telling. One evening, while walking to Campbell's home in Harlem (see figure 6.1), Stokes, who constantly feared that she was under surveillance, was convinced that a black man following her was a federal agent. Campbell tried to calm Stokes, suggesting to her, perhaps playfully, maybe facetiously, "That colored man, maybe he was attempting—kind of—to get friendly with you." Stokes took umbrage at Campbell's remark. As Claude McKay recalls, in Stokes's response, in "her voice, and her manner, was the most perfect bourgeois expression of the superior person." Campbell drew the point more finely: "I didn't mean to insinuate anything, but any person is likely to be mistaken for something else."[25]

Campbell may have taken a bit of guilty pleasure in suggesting that Stokes could be seen as loose or be mistaken for a prostitute. She well knew how black women, regardless of class or self-presentation, were seen as sexually available to white (and black) men, either by force or, in Harlem, for a price. Campbell may have seen in Stokes her former white supervisors from the National League for the Protection of Colored Women, or a municipal court judge who could

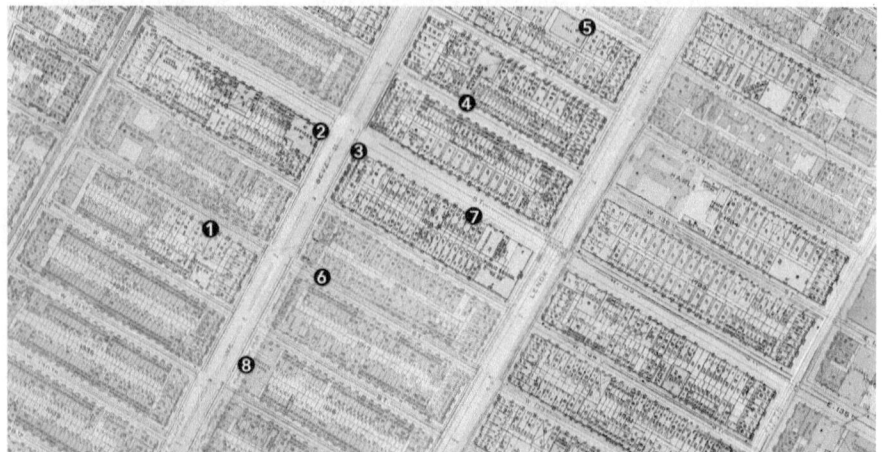

6.1 Map of selected social spaces of Harlem's interwar intellectual life: 1. Grace Campbell's home on West 133rd Street. 2. Harlem Educational Forum meeting at room 212 of the New York Public Library, 200 West 135th Street. 3. Offices of the African Blood Brotherhood, 2299 Seventh Avenue. 4. American West Indian Association Hall, 149 West 136th Street. 5. Universal Negro Improvement Association Liberty Hall, 112 West 138th Street. 6. Harlem Tenants League Office, 196 West 133rd Street. 7. Empire Friendly Shelter, 116 West 135th Street. 8. Lafayette Theatre, 2225 Seventh Avenue.

Background map from http://digitalharlem.org. Used by permission.

only conceive of black women as morally weak, promiscuous charges. Whatever Campbell's motivations, she had certainly grown tired of dealing with coworkers and comrades who viewed black women as subordinate, if not outright inferior.

It is not entirely surprising, given the frequency of such exchanges, that black radicals grew increasingly concerned about the party's work in black communities. They must have been troubled, too, by the continued atrophy of the radical intellectual culture that Campbell had helped to build in Harlem. Many black radicals, therefore, were likely enthused when, in April 1926, Campbell resurrected the People's Educational Forum, renaming it the Harlem Educational Forum (HEF). Tapping into her network of black clubwomen around the city, she ensured that the forum would again be seen as a major venue for black radical thought.

Like its earlier iteration, the HEF featured intense intellectual exchanges and debates, taking as its motto a line from Shakespeare's *Macbeth* (act 5, scene 8): "Lay on, Macduff, and damn'd be him that first cries, 'Hold, enough!' " Campbell again drew on her contacts within Harlem to hold the forum's meetings at the Utopia Neighborhood House at 170 West 130th Street. The HEF exhibited the same breadth as the earlier group, with topics ranging from civil liberties to the relationship between race and labor, the New Negro, the future of China and its impact on black people, and even a talk by the National Association for the Advancement of Colored People's William Pickens, entitled "What I Saw in Russia." Campbell also organized concerts and dances through the HEF, revealing a concern for the social life of the mind. Indeed, the relationships black radicals had formed over the years would prove fortuitous, for, by scheduling Harrison to give the inaugural lecture ("Is the White Race Doomed?"), Campbell inadvertently brought her contemporary, Williana Burroughs, a Queens schoolteacher and close friend of Harrison's, into a context where she began to contemplate joining the Communist Party.[26]

WILLIANA BURROUGHS AND NEW YORK'S INTERSECTING SOCIAL SPACES

Born Williana Jones in 1882, in Petersburg, Virginia, Burroughs's early life was marked by poverty and social upheaval. Williana's mother, who had been a slave, moved the family to Manhattan after the death of Williana's father. Williana was just four years old, and whatever grief she felt from losing her father was compounded by what came next. When her mother found it nearly impossible to support the family, the young Williana was forced to spend several years in Harlem's Colored Orphan Asylum.

Despite her circumstances, she excelled academically. In 1902, after graduating from Hunter College, she began a teaching career that granted her entrance into New York's black elite circles and, soon enough, brought her into contact with its more radical denizens. It was in this environment that she would meet Hubert Harrison and his close friend and coworker at the United States Post Office, the stage actor Charles Burroughs. When Jones and Burroughs wed in 1909, however, Williana Burroughs encountered yet more institutional discrimination, this time through a New York public school ban on married women in the classroom.[27] Following her dismissal from teaching, she began a brief career as a social worker, her early experiences likely fostering a concern with the plight of poor and working-class black women.

Still, it would be a mistake to consider her radicalism a mere function of biography. Rather, her politics were nurtured in the dynamic network of Harlem radicals gathered around Harrison. Even though she moved to Jamaica, Queens, following her marriage, her ties to Harrison kept her looped into Harlem's vibrant radical intellectual culture, while her career as a social worker almost certainly made her aware of Campbell well before either had joined any leftist organization.

Soon after Burroughs joined the Socialist Party, in 1920, she became secretary of the Institute for Social Study, a group led by Harrison and Moore, which counted Campbell as a member. If Burroughs had not come into contact with Campbell before, she now worked alongside possibly the most important black radical woman in New York. The institute's focus on the "lives and welfare of the great masses of the people" mirrored the discussions in many of Campbell's forums and provided a framework within which Burroughs could synthesize the array of black radical debates and the numerous New Negro formations that dotted Harlem's political cartography.[28] There is no way to know whether she ever attended one of Campbell's lyceums at the Empire Friendly Shelter or a PEF meeting, though it is hard to imagine otherwise, given how these various formations and their social space overlapped in the bustling Harlem community.[29]

As with several other Harlem radicals, Burroughs slowly gravitated to the growing U.S. communist movement. In 1925, after New York City repealed its ban on married women teaching in public schools, Burroughs returned to the classroom as an elementary teacher in Queens's PS 48 and promptly joined the New York City Teachers Union. That same year, she witnessed black Communists assume greater leadership roles in the newly formed ANLC. The organization convinced her that the Communists "were sincere in their interest towards the Negro people," and her work with black Communists at the Institute for Social Study offered her a unique perspective on the group.

It is not surprising, then, that she was in attendance for Harrison's inaugural lecture at the 1926 meeting of the revamped HEF. Within weeks of that lecture, HEF participants and members of the ANLC selected Harrison to draft a resolution demanding government protection for a group of black workers in New Jersey who had recently been attacked by white mobs. In addition to such organizational work, that summer Burroughs also helped to organize a series of lectures by Harrison on "The World Problems of Race," which covered the rise of modern racial ideology; European expansion and empire in Asia, Africa, and India; and the global dimension of black racial oppression and liberation.[30]

Burroughs benefited from Harlem's vibrant black radical milieu, its social and institutional spaces cultivating her radical politics. It was in this milieu that she arrived at her own sense of the diasporic scope of black liberation. And it was out of this context that she would find herself on the international stage. After joining the Communist Party, in 1926, Burroughs rose rapidly within its ranks, writing regularly for the *Daily Worker* and serving on several committees dedicated to Negro work. Under her party name, Mary Adams, she wrote articles on education, racial discrimination, and black workers in South Africa and Haiti, and even her occasional reports on labor organizing in the United States conveyed a diasporic orientation, framing the organization of foreign-born black workers in terms of the long international history of black workers' revolts.[31] Burroughs's rise within the CP would lead her to become the first black woman to address a congress of the Moscow-based Communist International, in 1928. But during the two years between joining the party and traveling to Moscow, she worked largely with black Communists and other community organizers in the Harlem Tenants League (HTL), which was formed on February 12, 1928, by longtime Harlem organizer and black clubwoman Elizabeth Hendrickson.[32]

ELIZABETH HENDRICKSON AND CEMENTING SISTERHOOD, FROM THE VIRGIN ISLANDS TO THE HARLEM TENANTS LEAGUE

Hendrickson was born in Saint Croix, Virgin Islands, and immigrated with her family to New York in 1899. In time, like Campbell and Burroughs, she gravitated to Harlem's radical circles and thrust herself into community organizing and uplift work, modeling what LaShawn Harris calls a practice of black radical women's politics "by combining leftist reform with the traditional organizing patterns among black women."[33] She cofounded the Virgin Islands Protective League and served as president of the American West Indian Ladies Aid Society (AWILAS), mutual aid societies that focused on social and political issues in Harlem and the Caribbean. These New York–based social spaces also grounded her in the debates that encircled Harlem's residents and informed her later work as vice president of the Harlem Tenants League.

Hendrickson's attention to Caribbean and other black folk in the United States suggests that she had a sense of the complexity of the country's racial and imperial power. Rather than viewing British Caribbean colonies as separate from the logics that guided racial oppression within the United States, she considered Caribbean immigrants and African Americans to be involved in a mutually constitutive political struggle against empire and racial capitalism. This budding radicalism was aided by her involvement in Caribbean political networks, which may have led her to take classes at the Socialist Party–controlled Rand School of Social Science, along with numerous other Caribbean radicals.[34] She worked with many black socialists, even helping Domingo and Moore publish their short-lived *Emancipator* newspaper. And later, along with Campbell and Howard University graduate Maude White, Hendrickson became one of the first black women to join the Communist Party.[35]

While her radical politics were clear, most in Harlem knew Hendrickson through her work in the American West Indian Ladies Aid Society, a mutual aid organization set up in 1917 that provided Harlem's Caribbean immigrant women with a vibrant social network and, in times of need, with moral and financial support. Organized by a group of women from the Virgin Islands with the intention of "cementing a spirit of Sisterhood . . . and for the purpose of assisting one another," AWILAS also gave considerable attention to political issues in the Caribbean, alongside those issues confronting black people in the United States. As the islands felt the impact of the Depression, AWILAS sponsored events to raise funds to send food and clothing to the Caribbean during the Christmas holidays.[36] Hendrickson, possibly reflecting her close ties to Campbell, also worked with several New York–area organizations to secure funds to establish a home for black women convicted of crimes, citing the lack of alternatives available for black women to avoid serving jail time at Rikers Island.[37]

Hendrickson was soon equally well known for her radical political orientation, fusing her work in mutual aid societies and social work with her more systemic perspective on poverty and black working-class struggles around New York City. Labor organizers, political activists, and community groups routinely approached her and AWILAS for support; as early as 1927, she led AWILAS in contributing funds to a unionizing effort by black painters, and provided assistance for the Brotherhood of Sleeping Car Porters to investigate the lynching of a Pullman porter in Locust Grove, Georgia.[38]

In early 1928, along with Campbell and Burroughs, Hendrickson helped to establish the Harlem Tenants League, which carried the work performed by black Communists beyond the organization of black industrial workers and began to articulate a vision of radical politics geared toward community and place. Hendrickson and those leading the HTL envisioned a formation that would address the daily needs of Harlem residents and mobilize as wide a swath of the black community as possible. One result was that, by focusing on poor housing conditions and high rents, and showing that such factors led to disproportionately higher mortality among black residents, the HTL drew black women into the group in far larger numbers than had been achieved by any previous group tied to the CP—approximately five hundred members at its height, the majority of whom never joined the party.[39] Although this community-level approach left untheorized the confluence of race and gender within capitalism or imperial domination, on a practical level it shifted the analytical frame toward what Van Gosse has called "an awareness of shifting gender constraints and possibilities" that, in turn, fostered a sense of black women being just as important as black men to working-class struggles.[40]

At its founding in early 1928, Richard B. Moore was elected as the HTL's president, while Campbell and several other black women Communists, including Hendrickson, took up leadership positions. Moore and Campbell were the driving force behind the HTL's earliest efforts, which included establishing tenants' committees throughout Harlem to pressure landlords to make basic repairs, lower rents, and address overcrowding. These committees functioned as "militant, fighting tenants leagues" capable of exerting pressure at both state and local levels "for the protection of the welfare and lives of the masses of the people." The HTL led rent strikes, boycotts, and protest marches, all of which were designed to galvanize Harlemites and, according to the historian Shannon King, "best exemplifies Harlemites' struggle for community rights" during these years.[41]

The league's mode of community organizing not only drew black women into the group but also offered an alternative for how black radicals might think about class consciousness. Organizationally, the HTL stood apart from other Communist-led formations. As Maude White put the problem years later, "few blacks held leading positions" within the party, and what leadership positions they did hold (largely in the ANLC) were closed to black women.[42] The HTL, despite electing Moore as its president, provided black women communists, and black women in Harlem more generally, with the opportunity to develop practical organizing skills and instilled a sense of their capacity to effect change. Hermina Dumont Huiswoud, a young British Guianan immigrant who had been active in the CP since 1925, recalled that "we had a big league and did a lot of good work," which included her taking the lead in organizing a May Day march by the HTL.[43]

The HTL blocked evictions, and when Harlem tenants returned home to find that a landlord had removed their possessions to the street, league members would move them back in. Even black male communists began to think about housing and health as working-class issues. Otto Hall attributed the growing class consciousness among Harlemites to "paying 50 percent more for rent for dirty, stuffy quarters than white residents" while "suffering a higher death rate and a tremendous rate of child mortality."[44] Cyril Briggs implored black men not to "sacrifice our babies and see our women starve and scrimp until their nipples run dry," imagery that continued to see black women as mothers in need of male protection, a view entirely at odds with the work black women were carrying out in Harlem.[45] The prevalence of black Communist men writing about these issues, while black Communist women carried out the daily work of the HTL, reflected the gendered structures of black radicalism and communist organizing and would soon take its toll.

By July 1929, the HTL had organized committees in several buildings across Harlem. In possibly its most dynamic action, as New York City's emergency rent laws were set to expire in 1929, the HTL led a march of more than two hundred local residents that ultimately forced some property owners to withdraw rent increases and compelled the city's board of aldermen to enact moderate relief measures. Yet, by this time, Hendrickson and others were growing tired of Moore's impractical organizing habits, his flooding of the league's leadership with communists, and his habit of carrying factional disputes from the CP into the HTL. In addition, Moore and Campbell were in opposing Communist Party factions that were vying for control of the party. When, in a blatantly sectarian move, Moore tried to remove Campbell from the HTL, league members instead removed him as president. In turn, Campbell, Hendrickson, and others left the party and led what became one of two groups known by the name of the Harlem Tenants League.[46]

One can only imagine what the HTL might have accomplished had it not fallen victim to the vagaries of left factionalism. It is nonetheless clear that the league provided a dynamic model for organizing working-class black communities and highlighted, at least for some, the value of black women in political movements. Even before its demise, the black Communist Otto Huiswoud would urge the Communist Party to "develop similar leagues in other large cities where Negroes are segregated and forced to pay exorbitant rents," while CP leader William Foster would hold up the HTL as a model for organizing black people. Ultimately, the Communist International's Trade Union Unity League would adopt the HTL model in organizing its Unemployed Councils in 1929, through which the party made its greatest strides in organizing in black communities.[47] As Robin D. G. Kelley explains, the Unemployed Councils' focus on relief, housing, and municipal power structures often provided black women with an opportunity to serve "as local leaders of ... neighborhood relief committees" and fostered a belief "in their collective ability to obtain basic necessities."[48]

We should not, however, take this to mean that Harlem provided a template that was straightforwardly imposed on places like Birmingham, Detroit, or Chicago. Harlem's population density, its proliferation of social and political organizations, its intellectual networks, and the vibrant black radical print culture headquartered there all came together to foster an organizational style that spoke to the immediate social needs of the neighborhood itself. This provided insights that could inform organizing efforts in other black communities whose equally vibrant black political cultures were rooted in, and responded to, the social spaces that grew up in those municipalities.

CODA: CLAUDIA JONES ON SUPEREXPLOITATION AND THE BLACK HUMAN

The genealogical approach pursued here, which views black women's institution building as intellectual labor, helps us to better understand diasporic liberation struggles that began with black women thinkers, organizers, and political activists. The concerns such women expressed about the social holds important lessons for thinking about any progressive political struggles.

The Unemployed Councils formed an important moment in the genealogy of these women's roles in developing the social spaces for black radical thought. In recounting her early experiences on the left, Louise Thompson Patterson, a writer and activist during the 1920s who later joined the CP, paints a compelling portrait of how black intellectuals in Harlem responded to black working-class struggles in the Unemployed Councils for "jobs and welfare, relief." Thompson recalls that the people she knew "began to establish discussion groups and that sort of thing," turning their attention to both local and international questions and establishing "a whole series of home study groups." As she put it, at that time in Harlem, "there was really a ferment of activity."[49] Her work in Harlem also involved drawing a link between black women's local struggles and African diasporic liberation movements. She would help to establish a branch of the Society of American–Soviet Friendship uptown, organize protests as part of the international Scottsboro defense campaign, work on the Council on African Affairs, and participate in the 1937 Congress Against Racism and Anti-Semitism in Spain.

Still, several years would pass before another black woman Communist, Claudia Jones, would elaborate a conceptual frame that could address the range of concerns raised by Campbell, Hendrickson, and Burroughs. Jones and her family emigrated from Trinidad to the United States when she was a young girl, and they settled in Harlem at the height of its intellectual and political vibrancy in the 1920s. Quite early in life, Jones became a political organizer, and she thrived in Harlem's rich intellectual and political culture, moving easily within its activist circles and working for radical publications before joining the CP in 1936—a membership that came in response to both the Scottsboro case and the Italian invasion of Abyssinia. By 1945, Jones had emerged as a major thinker within the party, and as the only black woman on its National Committee, she focused on the lives and labors of black women. It was in this position that she grappled with gender oppression, Marxism–Leninism and the woman question, and racial and gender hierarchies within the CP.[50]

Jones's most innovative theoretical work in this period was her essay "An End to the Neglect of the Problem of the Negro Woman!" (1949), which presented black women's labor exploitation in terms of their position "as workers, as Negroes, and as women." Jones explained that for an organization supporting "full economic, political and social equality of the Negro people and . . . equal rights for women," it only stood to reason, given their "triply-oppressed status," that "the Negro Woman, the most exploited and oppressed, belongs in our Party."[51]

Yet, by working through the triple-oppression framework, Jones located class alongside race and gender in an alternative understanding of exploitation and value. It was an approach that led Jones, as Carole Boyce Davies notes, to stress that black women were not "remunerated in any way equivalent to their labor power."[52] Jones argued that it was in the area of domestic labor that black women experienced the greatest degree of exploitation. But, as if recognizing the disjuncture between domestic labor and the kind of labor that Karl Marx argued produced surplus value, Jones introduced her corresponding concept of "super-exploitation."[53]

In Marx's labor theory of value, labor exploitation occurs when a worker imparts labor power to an exchangeable commodity, the difference between the wages paid to a worker and the price that a commodity brings on the market appearing as a surplus value, or capital.[54] Rather than attempt to explain black domestic labor in these terms, Jones focused on black women's social value. Of particular importance were the gendered forms of racial oppression that structured capitalism so as to render black women available as more than simply exploitable labor power. Beyond cleaning homes, black domestics performed the range of activities necessary for social reproduction, such as "washing windows, caring for the children, laundering, cooking, etc., and all at the lowest pay." Not only the elite white families who employed black women as domestics but also working-class (even Communist) white women, as well as black men, extracted social value from black women's domestic labor. On top of her exploitation in white homes, the black domestic often returned to her own home to "begin housework anew to keep her own family together."[55] Jones's framework of superexploitation thus indexed a measure of exploitation beyond unremunerated labor power.

In identifying black women's underpaid labor in white homes, and their unpaid labor in their own, as fundamental strictures on black life, Jones exceeded the conceptual limits of Marxism. Erik McDuffie rightly notes that, with superexploitation, Jones captured how black women were exploited "as mothers and as the breadwinners" in poor black communities.[56] In conjoining the increased rates of exploitation black women experience with "the conditions of ghetto-living—low salaries, high rents, high prices, etc.," which limit the life, health, and spiritual well-being of black people, Jones outlined how antiblack racial attitudes aided the exploitation of black women, leaving them socially ostracized and organizationally marginalized.

The array of social relationships and racialized, gendered practices that Jones gathered into a coherent frame with her twin concepts of triple oppression and superexploitation registers a "maternity death rate for Negro women ... triple that of white women" and the reality that "one out of every ten Negro children born in the United States does not grow to manhood or womanhood!" In responding to this reality, Jones argued, black women's organizations assumed their *"special character,"* where black women address "all questions pertaining to the economic, political, and social life of the Negro people, and particularly the Negro family," which included working "to provide social services denied to Negro youth as a result of the Jim-Crow lynch system in the U.S."[57] Insisting on other modes and regions of exploitation, Jones's attention to black people's full human potential focused on the structures forestalling any sense of black humanity.

What is crucial here is that Jones, in writing against the grain of Marxist orthodoxy, addressed the struggles of black women as oriented toward the potential for black humanity in its fullness. Thus, she realized in their breadth the insights that earlier had been suggested by the work of Campbell, Burroughs, and Hendrickson, who refused to limit their organizing around New York simply to black men or workers, and who made social issues like housing, sex work, legal discrimination, and organizing black women at the community level integral to such modes of thought. In taking the working class in its most capacious terms, Jones's theoretical insights brought into view the essential *social* class character of black political struggle. Through her insistence that party members "acquire political consciousness as regards [black women's] special oppressed status" and recognize that black women "in their churches, communities and fraternal groups are leaders of masses, with an invaluable mass experience to give to our party," she also indicated how the intellectual work of black women radicals shaped their social organizing.[58] In this sense, Jones's intersectional approach to race, class, and gender went even further than that label suggests. By attending to those questions that might seem outside the political, or separate from a normative conception of freedom, Jones fashioned a notion of equality that took the social being of black people, the ability to socially reproduce oneself, as constitutive of, rather than incidental to, a radical politics.

Following her arrest in 1948 under the Smith Act and her 1955 deportation to England, Jones would continue her political activism and maintain social institutions and spaces that she considered essential to black life. In her newspaper, the *West Indian Gazette*, and her founding of the Notting Hill Caribbean Carnival, Jones continued to organize and sustain the social and institutional spaces necessary for black radical thought.

NOTES

Sections of this essay were previously published in Minkah Makalani, "An Apparatus for Negro Women: Black Women's Organizing, Communism, and the Institutional Spaces of Radical Pan-African Thought," *Women, Gender, and Families of Color* 4 (Fall 2016): 250–73. Copyright 2016 by the Board of Trustees of the University of Illinois. Used with permission of the University of Illinois Press.

1. Claude McKay, *A Long Way from Home* (1937; New York: Harcourt Brace, 1970), 95–97, 130–31; Langston Hughes, "The Negro Artist and the Racial Mountain," *The Nation*, June 26, 1926, reprinted in Nathan Irvin Huggins, ed., *Voices From the Harlem Renaissance* (New York: Oxford University Press, 1976), 309.
2. Mia Bay et al., eds., *Toward an Intellectual History of Black Women* (Chapel Hill: University of North Carolina Press, 2015), 4–5.
3. Davarian L. Baldwin, *Chicago's New Negroes: Modernity, the Great Migration, and Black Urban Life* (Chapel Hill: University of North Carolina Press, 2007), 5, 19.
4. Ula Taylor, "Street Strollers: Grounding the Theory of Black Women Intellectuals," *Afro-Americans in New York Life and History* 30 (July 2006): 155.
5. Dayo Gore, *Radicalism at the Crossroads: African American Women Activists in the Cold War* (New York: New York University Press, 2011), 6; Joy James, *Shadowboxing: Representations of Black Feminist Politics* (New York: Palgrave Macmillan, 2002), 41, 43.

6. Sarah A. Anderson, " 'The Place to Go': The 135th Street Branch Library and the Harlem Renaissance," *Library Quarterly* 73 (October 2003): 383–421; Richard B. Moore, *Richard B. Moore, Caribbean Militant in Harlem: Collected Writings, 1920–1972*, ed. W. Burghardt Turner and Joyce Moore Turner (Bloomington: Indiana University Press, 1992), 69–70.
7. Claudia Jones, *An End to the Neglect of the Problems of the Negro Woman!* (New York: National Women's Commission, CPUSA, c. 1949), 9. This pamphlet originally appeared as an article under the same title in *Political Affairs* (1949). The passage cited here does not appear in the abridged version reproduced in *Claudia Jones: Beyond Containment*, ed. Carole Boyce Davies (Banbury: Ayebia Clarke, 2011), 74–86.
8. Anthony Bogues, "And What About the Human?: Freedom, Human Emancipation, and the Radical Imagination," *boundary 2* 39 (Fall 2012): 45.
9. Minkah Makalani, *In the Cause of Freedom: Radical Black Internationalism from Harlem to London, 1917–1939* (Chapel Hill: University of North Carolina Press, 2011), 202–3. On the Nardal sisters, see T. Denean Sharpley-Whiting, *Negritude Women* (Minneapolis: University of Minnesota Press, 2002); Brent Hayes Edwards, *The Practice of Diaspora: Literature, Translation, and the Rise of Black Internationalism* (Cambridge, MA: Harvard University Press, 2003), 119–86; Jennifer Wilks, "Black Modernist Women at the Parisian Crossroads," in *Escape from New York: The New Negro Renaissance Beyond Harlem*, ed. Davarian L. Baldwin and Minkah Makalani (Minneapolis: University of Minnesota Press, 2013), 227–45.
10. Winston James, "Harlem's Difference," present volume.
11. On community feminism, see Ula Taylor, *The Veiled Garvey: The Life and Times of Amy Jacques Garvey* (Chapel Hill: University of North Carolina Press, 2002), 2, 64.
12. Makalani, *In the Cause of Freedom*, 52–53.
13. Winston James, *Holding Aloft the Banner of Ethiopia: Caribbean Radicalism in Early Twentieth-Century America* (London: Verso, 1998), 174–75; Cheryl Hicks, *Talk with You Like a Woman: African American Women, Justice, and Reform in New York, 1890–1935* (Chapel Hill: University of North Carolina Press, 2010), 161–76.
14. *Chicago Defender*, April 19, 1919; Hicks, *Talk with You Like a Woman*, 16, 161–76. Winston James cites the 1920 census as listing Grace Campbell living at the Empire Friendly Shelter with her sister and twenty-six other people. James, *Holding Aloft the Banner of Ethiopia*, 326, note 152.
15. James Weldon Johnson, "An Open Air Lecture Course," *New York Age*, May 6, 1915, quoted in Jeffrey B. Perry, *Hubert Harrison: The Voice of Harlem Radicalism, 1883–1918* (New York: Columbia University Press, 2009), 245–46.
16. Campbell, quoted in Hicks, *Talk with You*, 171.
17. Kevin K. Gaines, *Uplifting the Race: Black Leadership, Politics, and Culture in the Twentieth Century* (Chapel Hill: University of North Carolina Press, 1996).
18. Campbell, quoted in Hicks, *Talk with You*, 173.
19. Makalani, *In the Cause of Freedom*, 54; Hicks, *Talk with You*, 172; James, *Holding Aloft the Banner of Ethiopia*, 175.
20. *Chicago Defender*, January 31, 1920.
21. Makalani, *In the Cause of Freedom*, 39–40.
22. Moore, *Richard B. Moore*, 217.
23. *Crusader*, May 1919, 4; November 1918, 7; December 1918, 6.
24. *Worker*, July 15, 1922; August 5, 1922. Department of Justice Files, National Archives, Washington, DC, report of March 4, 1921, RG 65, File BS 202600-677-30X; report of March 29, 1921, File BS 202600-677-32; report of June 25, 1921, File BS 202600-677-59; report of June 24, 1921, File BS 202600-677-60; report of July 2, 1921, File BS 202600-677-62. Earl

Titus to Justice Department, November 3, 1923, and November 19, 1923, File 61-50-477, in *Federal Surveillance of Afro-Americans, 1917–1925: The First World War, the Red Scare, and the Garvey Movement*, ed. Theodore Kornweibel (Frederick, MD: University Publications of America, 1985), microfilm reel 3.
25. McKay, *A Long Way from Home*, 161.
26. *New York Amsterdam News*, May 19, 1926; June 23, 1926; February 23, 1927; March 16, 1927. Makalani, *In the Cause of Freedom*, 147–48.
27. *Daily Worker*, September 27, 1933.
28. "The Institute for Social Study Special Seminar on World Problems of Race," brochure in box 16, folder 46, Hubert H. Harrison Papers, Rare Books and Manuscript Library, Columbia University, New York.
29. Perry, *Hubert Harrison*, 90–93; LaShawn Harris, "Running with the Reds: African American Women and the Communist Party During the Great Depression," *Journal of African American History* 94 (Winter 2009): 34–35; Erik McDuffie, *Sojourning for Freedom: Black Women, American Communism, and the Making of Black Left Feminism* (Durham, NC: Duke University Press, 2011), 35.
30. *Daily Worker*, September 27, 1933; *New York Times*, May 3, 1926; *Harlem Liberator*, November 18, 1933; Clarence Taylor, *Reds at the Blackboard: Communism, Civil Rights, and the New York City Teachers Union* (New York: Columbia University Press, 2011), 59; Joyce Moore Turner, *Caribbean Crusaders and the Harlem Renaissance* (Urbana: University of Illinois Press, 2005), 148–49; Harris, "Running with the Reds," 24.
31. *Daily Worker*, August 5, 1927; May 1, 1928.
32. *New York Amsterdam News*, January 8, 1930.
33. Harris, "Running with the Reds," 21.
34. Makalani, *In the Cause of Freedom*, 29–30; Joyce Moore Turner, *Caribbean Crusaders and the Harlem Renaissance* (Urbana: University of Illinois Press, 2005), 41–45.
35. Harris, "Running with the Reds," 33–34.
36. Margaret Samuel to American West Indian Ladies Aid Society (AWILAS), November 11, 1930, box 1, folder 3, American West Indian Ladies Aid Society Collection, Schomburg Center for Research in Black Culture, New York.
37. Minnie Wilkerson to AWILAS, May 7, 1928, box 1, folder 3, AWILAS Collection; "Program for Fourteenth Annual Sermon of the American West Indian Ladies Aid Society," November 17, 1929, box 2, folder 8, AWILAS Collection.
38. V. C. Gasper to Elizabeth Hendrickson, October 1, 1927, box 1, folder 3, AWILAS Collection; V. C. Gasper to Elizabeth Hendrickson, October 28, 1927, box 1, folder 8, AWILAS Collection.
39. Makalani, *In the Cause of Freedom*, 148.
40. Van Gosse, " 'To Organize in Every Neighborhood, in Every Home': The Gender Politics of American Communists between the Wars," *Radical History Review* 50 (Spring 1991): 113.
41. *Liberator*, December 7, 1929; *Negro Champion*, September 8, 1928; Mark Solomon, *The Cry Was Unity: Communists and African Americans, 1917–1936* (Jackson: University Press of Mississippi, 1998), 97, 99; Shannon King, *Whose Harlem Is This, Anyway?: Community Politics and Grassroots Activism During the New Negro Era* (New York: New York University Press, 2015), 93.
42. Harris, "Running with the Reds," 31.
43. Hermina Dumont Huiswoud, quoted in Turner, *Caribbean Crusaders*, 136.
44. Otto Hall, quoted in Mark Naison, *Communists in Harlem During the Depression* (New York: Grove, 1985), 23.

45. *Liberator*, December 7, 1929.
46. *New York Amsterdam News*, January 8, 1930; Makalani, *In the Cause of Freedom*, 148–49.
47. "Program of Action," n.d., Russian State Archive of Socio-Political History 515/1/3356; W. Foster, "Draft Report: The 4th Convention of the Trade Union Unity League," November 28, 1929, Russian State Archive of Socio-Political History 515/1/1565.
48. Robin D. G. Kelley, "A New War in Dixie: Communists and the Unemployed in Birmingham, Alabama, 1930–1933," *Labor History* 30 (Summer 1989): 376–78.
49. Louise Thompson Patterson, interview by Ruth Prago, November 16, 1981, series 1, box 2, 30, Oral History of the American Left, Tamiment Library and Robert F. Wagner Labor Archives, New York University.
50. Carole Boyce Davies, *Left of Karl Marx: The Political Life of Black Communist Claudia Jones* (Durham, NC: Duke University Press, 2007), 43; McDuffie, *Sojourning for Freedom*, 138, 167–69.
51. Jones, *An End to the Neglect*, 4, 18. For Jones's use of the term "triply oppressed," from which the term "triple oppression" is drawn, see Claudia Jones, "We Seek Full Equality for Women" (1949), reprinted in Davies, *Claudia Jones*, 87. For a fuller discussion of the triple-oppression frame within black left feminist thought, see McDuffie, *Sojourning for Freedom*.
52. Davies, *Left of Karl Marx*, 43; McDuffie, *Sojourning for Freedom*, 138, 167–69.
53. Jones, *An End to the Neglect*, 4.
54. Karl Marx, *Capital* (New York: International, 1987), 1:149–53, 173–92.
55. Jones, *An End to the Neglect*, 11.
56. McDuffie, *Sojourning for Freedom*, 167.
57. Jones, *An End to the Neglect*, 5, 9 (emphasis in original).
58. Jones, *An End to the Neglect*, 18–19.

7.

HARLEM AS CULTURE CAPITAL IN 1920S AFRICAN AMERICAN FICTION

CHERYL A. WALL

Zora Neale Hurston never lived in Harlem, and although Claude McKay wrote three books with Harlem in the title (*Harlem Shadows*, *Home to Harlem*, and *Harlem: Negro Metropolis*), he spent more time in Marseilles and Morocco than in uptown Manhattan during the 1920s. Wallace Thurman, who spent most of his too-short adult life in Harlem and cowrote a Broadway show and edited a magazine, both titled *Harlem*, sometimes found the place itself too hectic. In our historical moment, scholars are reassessing the importance of Harlem and are recasting it as just one among many loci of a movement that redefined people of African descent as modern subjects during the first decades of the twentieth century.[1] Yet I argue that for the writers who lived there, and even for those who did not, Harlem in the 1920s exerted an imaginative pull that no other single location did. One might refer to "Paris Noir" or "Colored Philadelphia" or the South Side of Chicago, but "Harlem" signified all by itself.

From its beginning as a black metropolis, the idea of Harlem exceeded its geographic boundaries. It was the "City of Refuge," the "Mecca of the New Negro," the "Negro metropolis," and the "promised land." These symbolic meanings resonated with writers and ordinary folk alike. Yet fiction writers and poets, who were moved as much by the power of their own invention as by everyday realities, understood that they were creating a literary landscape. They incorporated Harlem cultural practices—the numbers game, religious rituals, rent parties, and Sunday promenades—into plots that explored traditional themes of romance and coming-of-age. These practices were not unique to

Harlem; as one commentator notes, "the rent party tradition did not originate in Harlem, though rents were so high that Harlem would surely have had to invent the tradition if it had not already existed."[2]

The alienation produced by hard labor, low wages, and racism existed elsewhere as well, but the population density of Harlem heightened the psychological drama and gave many of these cultural practices a distinctive inflection. Writers tuned their ears to Harlem sounds: its music and its language, which some dubbed "Harlemese," a mix of southern idiom and urban slang, which, with varying degrees of success, writers transcribed and stylized. As a result, fiction writers, including Hurston, McKay, Rudolph Fisher, and Wallace Thurman, offer a more complex and candid portrait than did Alain Locke and James Weldon Johnson, Harlem's best-known promoters. Indeed, the elements of Harlem life that these promoters wished to suppress—its proletarian and queer aspects, for example—sparked writers' imaginations.

Although almost all who wrote about it considered Harlem to be both a symbol of black modernity and an incipiently diasporic space, the implications of its diasporic identity registered differently. For Alain Locke, Harlem had the potential of becoming a "race capital," where African Americans would represent the vanguard of African peoples. Sounding a note that James Weldon Johnson and Thurman would echo, Locke's essay "The New Negro" emphasizes the "many diverse" elements concentrated in Harlem: "It has attracted the African, the West Indian, the Negro American; has brought together the Negro of the North and the Negro of the South; the man from the city and the man from the town and village; the peasant, the student, the business man, the professional man, artist, poet, musician, adventurer and worker, preacher and criminal, exploiter and social outcast."[3]

As a consequence of these diverse people in a tight space—a consequence, as Locke acknowledges, of segregation—Harlem had become "the laboratory of a great race-welding" (*New Negro*, 7). The common condition that people of African descent shared would be complemented by a "common consciousness" that could overturn the condition of oppression and exploitation. By the time Locke homes in on this potential, however, he posits a disturbingly hierarchal relationship among people of African descent. Blacks in the United States become "the advance-guard of the African peoples in their contact with Twentieth Century civilization." As a consequence of their movement from medieval to modern within the United States, they are prepared to lead the mission of "rehabilitating the race in world esteem" (14). Locke's formulation is as vague as it is utopian, and his idea of Harlem as race capital exemplifies U.S. black exceptionalism at its worst.

By contrast, Johnson's conception of Harlem as a "culture capital" retains its utility and may deepen our understanding of the art and literature produced there. As he famously wrote, "Harlem is indeed the great Mecca for the sightseer, the pleasure-seeker, the curious, the adventurous, the enterprising, the ambitious and the talented of the whole Negro world; for the lure of it has reached down to every island of the Carib Sea and has penetrated even into Africa."[4] Johnson's Harlem was cosmopolitan. Most of its residents had migrated from the rural South and others were native New Yorkers. A significant number came from the Caribbean, and a small number from Africa. The demographic mix produced myriad opportunities for exchange as well as conflict, as people became aware of a black world much wider than they had imagined. Johnson, himself a cosmopolite who had achieved success in education, the law, the theater, and the diplomatic service, knew at first hand how broadly diverse black cultures were. As blacks from different backgrounds interacted in Harlem, they recognized the breadth of their collective experiences as well.

Unlike Locke's idea of a race capital, Johnson's idea of a culture capital is not hierarchal; it is vernacular and democratic. While most of his essay in *The New Negro* is devoted to a spurious argument that Harlem was approaching economic self-sufficiency, Johnson also recognizes "a growth of group consciousness and community feeling" in Harlem (*New Negro*, 309). While the essay is short on specifics in support of this assertion, two details stand out: the mention of the community's weekly brass band parades and a reference, earlier in the essay, to the Marshall Hotel, a gathering place for actors, athletes, and musicians, located on West 53rd Street, a center of black life in New York City in the first decades of the twentieth century.[5]

Considered in light of Johnson's other writings, these details suggest a conception quite distinct from Locke's race capital. Most important, they are cultural rather than political. In *Black Manhattan* (1930), Johnson recounted the career of James Reese Europe, whose Clef Club orchestra was an incubator for jazz. An officer in World War I, Lieutenant Europe led the band of the all-black 369th Infantry Regiment, the "Harlem Hellfighters," on their triumphal return to New York City. After marching up Fifth Avenue in strict formation, the band segued into a syncopated rhythm as it reached 130th Street and Lenox Avenue.[6] Earlier, Europe had been one of the musicians who gathered at the Marshall Hotel, a site that Johnson fictionalized in *The Autobiography of an Ex-Colored Man* (1912).[7] Long after Europe's death, in 1919, Harlemites continued to thrill to the sounds of a brass band. At the core of Johnson's culture capital, then, are vernacular expressions created by working-class people.

In *The Book of American Negro Poetry* (1922), Johnson had shown his capacious understanding of black poetry by including poems written in black vernacular idiom, such as Paul Laurence Dunbar's "When Malindy Sings," as well as poems that follow Anglo-American literary conventions, such as Phillis Wheatley's sonnets. For Johnson, poetry is democratic in its character; its forms are frequently derived from vernacular sources. His preface also cites important poets from Brazil, Cuba, and Haiti as well as France and Russia. What he deems black poetry is a multinational and multilingual project. Equally important, in identifying the contributions black Americans had made to U.S. national culture, he listed the Uncle Remus stories, the spirituals, ragtime, and the cakewalk, which he averred were "the only things artistic that have yet sprung from American soil."[8] These terms can be updated and more usefully understood as folklore, sacred music, jazz, and social dance. In various forms, these contributions defined much of the national culture throughout the twentieth century. Focusing on 1920s Harlem, Johnson defined a culture capital that could host a broader array of cultural expressions than those conventionally associated with U.S. blacks. The framework Johnson constructs provides a critical touchstone for analyzing the literature of Harlem.

In a series of essays, Thurman offered views of Harlem that sometimes reverberated with and sometimes diverged from Johnson's. For example, in the multipart article "Negro Life in New York's Harlem: A Lively Picture of a Popular and Interesting Section" (1927), Thurman mapped the neighborhood's commercial and residential streets, marking blocks with modern apartment buildings and those with overcrowded tenements. Similarly, he highlighted the positive and negative aspects of the community's social life. He titled a section "House Rent Parties, Numbers, and Hot Men," the last referring to purveyors of "hot," or stolen, merchandise. Highly visible on the streets of Harlem, such figures were invisible in the essays of Locke and Johnson. What stood out for Thurman as well as his peers was the community's heterogeneity: "You have pure-blooded Africans, British Negroes, Spanish Negroes, Portuguese Negroes, Dutch Negroes, Danish Negroes, Cubans, Porto Ricans, Arabians, East Indians and black Abyssinian Jews in addition to the racially well-mixed American Negro. You have persons of every conceivable shade and color. Persons speaking all languages, persons representative of many cultures and civilizations. Harlem is a magic melting pot, a modern Babel mocking the gods with its cosmopolitan uniqueness."[9]

For Thurman, this cosmopolitanism derived in part from Harlem's location in New York City, an opinion he shared with Johnson, whose essay "Harlem: The Culture Capital" he quotes freely. But Harlem's cosmopolitanism is unique because of its racial cast. It is the crossroads of the black world. What neither Johnson nor Thurman could have foreseen was the impact of the Johnson–Reed Act of 1924, which introduced quotas that dramatically curtailed immigration to the United States from the Caribbean and Africa. Harlem in the next generation would not strike observers as a melting pot, magical or otherwise.

Among poets and fiction writers, Harlem is also drawn as a diasporic space, but it is hardly utopian. The idea—or perhaps more aptly, the ideal—of a "Negro world," which was so alluring that Marcus Garvey used the phrase as the title of his internationally distributed newspaper, published in Harlem, proved daunting to achieve on a day-to-day basis. The Harlem that writers depict is the site of ethnic conflicts, which along with the class and gender tensions that urban life exacerbated, proved difficult, if not impossible, to resolve. Rejecting the Lockean view of the Great Migration as a victory march from the feudal to the modern, writers represented the psychological as well as physical dislocation that rural people from the U.S. South and the Caribbean experienced in Harlem: the anonymity, the shredding of old values, and the disintegration of families. They represented, in particular, the ways that new conceptions of gender roles proved at once liberating and divisive. Consequently, Harlem gained symbolic value through their works—not as a model community and political vanguard of the black world but as the most important and resonant site at which the tensions, conflicts, and constraints as well as the energies, opportunities, and dynamism of modern cosmopolitan black life and subjectivity could be explored.

The remainder of this chapter examines the ways in which specific writers used Harlem as "setting and symbol"; how they represented the ideal of "race-welding" as well as the conflicts that threatened its fulfillment. It starts with Rudolph Fisher's signature short story "The City of Refuge," first published in the *Atlantic Monthly* in 1925, then republished in *The New Negro* that same year. It should be noted that Locke, as editor, championed the work of the "younger generation of Negro writers," including Fisher and Hurston. But Hurston, along with McKay and Thurman, quickly rejected Locke's prescriptive attitude toward art. The chapter also considers a recently rediscovered Hurston story set in Harlem and first published in the black newspaper the *Pittsburgh Courier*, in 1927, and then briefly analyzes McKay's best-selling novel *Home to Harlem* (1928). It ends with a discussion of Thurman's play, cowritten with William Jourdan Rapp, *Harlem: A Melodrama of Negro Life in Harlem* (1928).

All of these texts highlight their authors' experiments with language; the latter two texts exemplify the generic innovations that Harlem life inspired. For example, although *Home to Harlem* may be considered a picaresque novel, several of its most memorable passages demonstrate McKay's attempts to render in prose the sounds of Harlem's jazz clubs or cabarets. Thurman and Rapp collaborated on a play that fused the conventions of melodrama with the rhythms and movement of jazz.

• • •

"The City of Refuge" is the ur-story of the Great Migration. A rural naïf, ironically named King Solomon Gillis, arrives in Harlem and is mesmerized by its sounds and sights: the subway, the buildings, the crowds, and, most of all, black policemen. Gillis, who has killed a white man in self-defense, is on the lam from North Carolina, where he knows he cannot expect justice from the all-white legal system. The black policemen are the metonym for the justice he associates with the North.[10]

The plot is unsurprising. A con man named Mouse, claiming to be from Gillis's hometown, sizes him up and soon has the unsuspecting Gillis peddling drugs. On one level, "City of Refuge" retells the familiar story of the young man from the provinces overwhelmed by life in the big city. But the discourse of the story reveals how appealing the idea of Harlem as a "laboratory of a great race-welding" was to ordinary blacks, as well as exposing how the plenitude of blackness in Harlem obscured the differences within.

The story makes clear that Gillis has heard about Harlem before he gets there, but the reality is more than he could imagine: "Negroes predominantly, overwhelming everywhere. There was assuredly no doubt of his whereabouts. This was Negro Harlem."[11] Some of the people on the street speak an urban vernacular that Gillis needs to decode: "shines" are working-class blacks and "jay birds" are new arrivals like himself (*New Negro*, 60). As the plot unfolds, Gillis discovers that his new world is not simply black and white. If blacks are not simply black, whites are not simply white, either. Mouse manipulates Gillis into a job with an Italian grocer, who speaks his own vernacular and proves as gullible about the underside of Harlem life as Gillis is. The strict binary between black and white that governed Gillis's life in the South is thus unsettled. Too late, Gillis realizes that, in the North, it is black people whom he cannot trust.

Even as Mouse begins to betray him, he introduces Gillis to the term "monkey-chaser" (64), a then-common epithet for blacks from the Caribbean. It associated West Indians with the jungle and primitivism—in other words, the same associations that white Americans used to denigrate U.S.-born black Americans. While Gillis does not analyze his reasons, he is initially put off by the intraracial prejudice the term expresses. Yet, as if to suggest the fragility of the race-welding Locke prophesied, by the end of the story the phrase rolls easily off Gillis's tongue.

Fisher continued to explore the psychology of southerners in the city that thwarted their expectations of community and morality. "Vestiges," four brief sketches also published in *The New Negro*, limn the conflict between the strict conservative values of the South and the more flexible mores of Harlem. To elders who view their children's beliefs and behavior with alarm, Harlem is a "city of Satan." Slick preachers prey on credulous believers. A granddaughter chooses the cabaret over the church. Parents take pride in their educated children but worry about their loss of faith. In the final sketch, the vestige of faith proves disorienting to a young man, who, out for a night on the town with a bootlegger friend, finds it impossible to mock the tent revival they visit on a lark. Difficult as it is to sustain the values of faith and community that characterized life in the South, it is not quite possible to leave them behind.[12]

■ ■ ■

Zora Neale Hurston understood this as well. While her best-known fiction is set in the all-black town of Eatonville, Florida, where she was raised, she published several short stories set in Harlem. "Muttsy" (1926), published in *Opportunity*, recounts the migration of an innocent young woman from Eatonville to Harlem. "Story in Harlem Slang" (1942), which appeared in *American Mercury*, is also a migration tale, but its laugh-out-loud humor derives more from its characters' verbal turns than from their circumstances. Several other Harlem stories by Hurston appeared in 1927 in the *Pittsburgh Courier*, a nationally circulated African American newspaper, which suggests that the Harlem setting appealed even to black readers who had never been there. "The Book of Harlem," "The Back Room," "Monkey Junk," and "The Country in the Woman" were originally published in 1927, at a time when Hurston, as a student at Barnard, lived on the West Side of Manhattan, before she began fieldwork in the South. "She Rock" appeared in 1933, after that fieldwork was completed.[13]

With the exception of "The Back Room," which features a worldly, upper-middle-class protagonist who at thirty-eight feels she has missed her chance at marriage, the stories represent migrants who try to negotiate the added pressure that urban life places on their domestic relationships. Even more than Fisher, Hurston plays up the humor in her stories, perhaps because she is writing for black readers who may have seen themselves and their neighbors mirrored in her tales. The humor is exaggerated in "Book of Harlem," "Monkey Junk," and "She Rock" by the use of biblical language and form (the paragraphs of the stories are numbered like verses in the Bible). But the humor does not mask the seriousness of the issues at stake.

The form of "The Country in the Woman" is more conventional, but the story is also an incisive exploration of gender relations in the context of urban migration. The title revises the adage that you can take the man out of the country but you cannot take the country out of the man. As the story opens, Caroline Potts stands unkempt but "arrogantly akimbo" on Seventh Avenue and 134th Street, between her husband and his other woman, who is "heavy built and stylish in a Lenox avenue [sic] way." Testifying to Harlem's wide renown as a center of black glamour, the writer assumes her readers can picture what is stylish on Lenox Avenue. They can certainly imagine Caroline standing with her hands on her hips, as well as the other woman's fear, which sends her "easing on down 134th Street."[14] In the backstory Hurston fills in, readers learn that Caroline and her husband, Mitchell, have emigrated from rural Florida to Harlem, where they rent an apartment in the "Car[ibb]ean Forties" (*Amerikastudien*, 587), a reference to the district's sizable West Indian population. Mitchell has long been a philanderer, and Caroline has always exacted revenge in cruel and original ways. Yet, in Harlem, she must fight against the city's different definitions of womanhood as well as her husband's infidelities.

Like female characters in Hurston's novels, Caroline can fight, verbally and physically. On Seventh Avenue, she lets loose a series of vernacular blasts at her rival, including "she might be a big cigar, but I sho kin smoke her" (587). Her verbal parries delight the crowd that gathers, as much as they embarrass her husband. For his part, Mitchell has counted on the anonymity of the city to protect him from Caroline's detection. When that fails, he lectures her on the protocols of urban life: "Folks up heah don't run after they husbands and carry on cause they sees him swappin' a few jokes wid another woman. You aint down in de basement no more—youse in New Yawk" (588). Although the motives behind Mitchell's words are selfish, the sentiment they express was widely held, that is, that New York in general, and Harlem specifically, represent the apex of progress. Caroline is not persuaded on either count.

In response to her husband's rejection, and in the manner of later Hurston protagonists, including Janie Crawford in *Their Eyes Were Watching God* (1937), Caroline withdraws into herself. Mitchell moves outward, adopting (as best he can) the air of a man-about-town. He hangs out on the corner, learns to speak Harlemese ("Well, so long Tweety, see you in the funny papers"), and continues his affairs (*Amerikastudien*, 590). When he buys a fur coat for his side-woman, though, he overplays his hand. Caroline reverts to her country ways. She strolls down Seventh Avenue with an axe over her shoulder. Mitchell's friends know he is in danger but are too afraid of Caroline to warn him, let alone to disarm her.

The story does not represent the encounter; instead, the narrator describes the crowd watching Caroline returning home just as leisurely as she set out, only this time she is wearing the fur coat and "over her shoulder, like a Roman lector, she bore the axe, and from the head of it hung the trousers of Mitchell's natty suit, the belt buckle clacking a little in the breeze" (590). The elements of her two lives—the rural and the urban—cannot be synchronized. If she carries herself like a Roman bodyguard, it is because Caroline has learned that she must be the source of her own protection.

Though unmanned and humiliated, Mitchell does not leave her. He accepts the fact that he "caint git de country out dat woman" (590). Hurston's story thus counters Locke's teleology of the movement from rural to urban and medieval to modern. It suggests, instead, that black southerners brought their cultural practices and identity to the North, where they became constitutive elements of Harlem life.

Hurston's stories in the *Pittsburgh Courier* reflect, in particular, her burgeoning interest in what she would later call "Negro idiom." What is striking about "The Country in the Woman" is its juxtaposition of rural southern black speech with its northern variant, Harlemese. The story uses these idioms to highlight the conflict between the characters: when he moves to New York, Mitchell Potts begins to speak a different language, one in which his spouse is not conversant. Hurston's exploration of this idiom later animated "Story in Harlem Slang." Both stories reflect her belief that vernacular expression was the wellspring of

African American art in general. They demonstrate, as well, the ways in which Harlem in particular could fire Hurston's imagination.

■ ■ ■

Claude McKay's *Home to Harlem* (1928) is an experimental novel that takes a conventional literary genre, the picaresque novel, and reanimates it by drawing on black vernacular expressive forms. It focuses on characters drawn from the black working class and demimonde. It represents almost continuous conflicts among characters across lines of difference drawn by class, ethnicity, gender, and sexuality. Yet it also features transcendent moments—some following literary convention, sparked by experiences with nature and romantic love, and others unconventionally, occurring on the jazz floor in Harlem cabarets. Not coincidentally, one project of the novel is to invent a literary equivalent for jazz.

Numerous scenes in *Home to Harlem* unfold in bars and cabarets. The text quotes blues extensively, making clear how central the blues is to the lives of its characters. In a gesture toward the diasporic cultures of Harlem, the novel also quotes "Ring the Bell Again," a song it identifies as being from Port of Spain. The narrator links the music of Trinidad with that of black America when he observes that, like so many songs of its kind, it was curious "for the strange strengthening of its wistful melody by a happy rhythm that was suitable for dancing."[15] At some moments in the text, the novel attempts to represent this combination of melody and rhythm. In these passages, it represents all of the elements of jazz performance.

One example comes early in the novel, as the protagonist, Jake, sits in a cabaret named the Baltimore and watches the singer leave the dance floor, "humming back to her seat." The band takes over: "The saxophone was moaning it. And feet and hands and mouths were acting it. Dancing. Some jigged, some shuffled, some walked, and some were glued together swaying on the dance floor" (*Home*, 32). The narrator attempts, here, to help readers hear the sound of the instrument and visualize the moves the dancers make. Simply to call the movements "dancing" is insufficient; readers need to see bodies in motion. To convey the effect of the performance, the novel's narrator describes the visceral impact it has on Jake: he feels as though he is burning up with fever. In other scenes, dancers achieve moments of ecstasy, and at these moments McKay shows himself to be as adept at writing jazz-inspired prose as Langston Hughes in *Not Without Laughter*.[16]

In a letter to James Weldon Johnson, McKay explained, "I consider *Home to Harlem* a real proletarian novel, but I don't expect the nice radicals to see that it is."[17] Neither McKay's colleagues at the *Liberator*, the downtown leftist magazine, nor the Harlem leftists A. Philip Randolph and Chandler Owen claimed the novel as such. In fairness, more of the novel's scenes are set in speakeasies and buffet flats (private apartments offering food, liquor, and sex) than in the workplace. But Jake, an ex-soldier who is returning to the United States after enlisting in World War I, is a worker and a sometime acute social observer. If the novel partakes of primitivist myths and depicts the black and brawny Jake as a "natural man," it also pauses to consider the conflicts that erupt because, as Jake acknowledges, "wese too close and thick in Harlem" (*Home*, 287).

Finding a place to live is a frequent challenge for the novel's characters. The places they find are overcrowded and substandard. Jake usually finds a room to rent, but another character has to sleep on a cot in a hallway when he loses his job. Most of the characters choose sexual partners based on whether they can offer them a place to live. Threats of being evicted either for nonpayment of rent or for alienation of affection loom large. Unlike the blacks in Johnson's essays, who catch the "fever" to buy property, McKay's characters scramble for a place to sleep. Strivers' Row might as well be on another planet.

The novel depicts Jake's ongoing struggles with employment. In one scene, he quits a job as a longshoreman when he realizes that he and his fellow blacks are being used as scabs, yet he refuses to join a union because it assigns black workers the worst piers. In the second section of the novel, Jake leaves Harlem and finds a job as a cook on the Pennsylvania Railroad, "just to break the hold that Harlem had upon him" (125). During a layover in Pittsburgh, he suffers the abhorrent conditions of the dormitory the company runs for its black employees. Rather than sleep with the bedbugs, Jake spends the night on the town. He reports to work the next day tired but with his pride intact.

The novel represents, as well, the tensions that simmer between working-class and middle-class blacks, tensions that are exacerbated by intraracial color prejudice. It shows how different cabarets appeal to different strata of the black population and satirizes the working-class characters who pretend to associate with the elites. Despite its jabs at the pretensions of the bourgeoisie, the novel takes pains to remark on the existence of a striving middle class. It is less forgiving in its treatment of intraracial prejudice. The novel mocks Susie, an older female character, for never getting over a light-skinned lover of her youth; she remains forever vulnerable to the blandishments of men who resemble him.

While this character is derided for color prejudice, the novel's treatment of her is part of a larger pattern of misogyny woven through the text. Women are frequently depicted as predators; they are as jealous as they are controlling. They fight one another in order to lay claim to the men they want, and male characters succeed when they escape the grasp of females. For his part, Jake avers that "a woman could always go further than a man in coarseness, depravity and sheer cupidity" (68). Such sentiments stud the text. The only positive female character, symbolically named Felice, is a prostitute with whom Jake hooks up on his first night in Harlem. She proves her value by returning the money he pays her for her services. Then she disappears. Jake spends the rest of the novel in pursuit of her. In a novel filled with ecstatic moments, none is more important or more romanticized than the initial coupling between Jake and Felice.

The novel's other key male character is Ray, a Haitian-born intellectual, working as a dining car waiter and living in Harlem. Ray opens Jake's mind to new historical and political vistas, a broader sense of a black world, and a Pan-African sensibility informed by the anticolonialist politics of the Caribbean. The U.S. intervention in Haiti has uprooted Ray's family and caused Ray to drop out of Howard University. Ray regales Jake with episodes from Haiti's heroic history. As he sits and eagerly drinks in tales of Toussaint L'Ouverture, Jake exclaims, "A black man! A black man! Oh, I wish I'd been a soldier under sich a man" (132). In their initial conversation, Ray talks about not only Toussaint but also Sappho, whose poetry is part of the literary history of homosexuality that he sketches. Ray's literature lesson helps to contextualize a blues lyric that floats through the novel: "And there is two things I don't understan' / It is a bulldyking woman and a faggoty man." While at face value the lines might suggest a negative attitude toward homosexuality, the novel's representation proves otherwise.[18]

For example, the novel depicts a scene in the Congo cabaret: "All round the den, luxuriating under the little colored lights, the dark dandies were loving up their pansies. Feet tickling feet under tables, tantalizing liquor-rich giggling, hands busy above." When the singer approaches the table where Jake is also sitting, the excitement intensifies: "She danced a jagging jig before him that made the giggles rise like a wave in the room. The pansies stared and tightened their grip on their dandies. . . . They looked the favored Jake up and down. All those perfection struts for him. Yet he didn't seem aroused at all" (*Home*, 31–32). The club's clientele is both gay and straight, and the atmosphere welcomes public gestures of affection from all. The Congo is a metaphorically free space where, fueled by liquor and jazz, patrons experience ecstatic moments. While scenes like this could have taken place in communities other than Harlem—the novel refers to a similar gathering in Philadelphia, though it does not depict it in detail—Harlem's gay nightlife was made central to its cosmopolitan uniqueness.[19]

Other than Pittsburgh, the novel depicts few of the stops Jake and Ray make as they travel on the railroad. The narrator compares the homosocial world of the railroad crew to a ship's crew, and most of the action occurs in the confined space in which the characters work. Indeed, the sketchiness with which other locations are described serves to foreground Harlem. For Jake, especially, Harlem stands apart. He is soon yearning to be back in the place that, though he was not born there, is his home.[20] He does not stay. Perhaps the same concentration and energy that make Harlem so attractive to Jake ultimately overwhelm him. Taken as a whole, the novel does not idealize Harlem; instead, it represents it as a place where the problems of black modernity are distilled.

■ ■ ■

Wallace Thurman and cowriter William Jourdan Rapp dramatized these problems in their play *Harlem: A Melodrama of Negro Life in Harlem* (1928). Although the play was once titled *City of Refuge*, its tone is closer to McKay's novel than to Rudolph Fisher's short story of that name. By any measure, the play was the greatest commercial success of the short career that preceded Thurman's death in 1934, at age thirty-two. He joined with Rapp, a white freelance journalist, playwright, screenwriter, and producer who had published an earlier drama titled *Osman Pasha*.[21] While the details of their collaboration cannot be documented, scholars presume that Thurman contributed most of the play's content while Rapp shaped its structure. Essayist, editor, and novelist Thurman, who had been part of the Harlem scene since his arrival in New York from Salt Lake City (via Los Angeles), in 1925, was almost certainly the source of the allusions to Fisher's work.

Featuring a large cast of twenty-six actors, *Harlem* was a three-act play that its subtitle aptly described. It was doubtless the music, dancing, and dialogue rich in the idiom of Harlemese (a term Thurman coined) that made the play the Broadway success it became when it started its run in 1929. The protagonist is drawn from the short story "Cordelia, the Crude" that Thurman had published in *Fire!!*, the legendary little magazine he edited in 1926. Written in the first person, the story bears the influence of Jean Toomer. Much like the sketches in the first section of Toomer's novel *Cane*, "Cordelia, the Crude" is told from the point of view of a male narrator observing the stunted life of a young woman.[22] Unlike the sketches, however, the play is stuffed with plot, and Cordelia's actions are the plot's catalyst rather than its main focus. *Harlem* overflows with conflicts between men and women, parents and children, the God-fearing and the godless, whites and blacks, and American and West Indian blacks. It exemplifies the reasons Harlem became such an important setting and symbol. The conflicts, contradictions, and frictions of black modernity were lived out in heightened form in the densely concentrated yet most diverse black community in the world.

The play's main characters have all arrived in Harlem from elsewhere. The Williams family has migrated from the U.S. South to a Harlem that falls far short of their dreamed-of promised land. Indeed, apart from an elder brother, no one in the family admits to wanting to come north at all. Not only are they materially no better off but also the move has disrupted the family dynamic. Unable to find a job, the father hosts rent parties to support the family. One such party provides the setting for the play's first and third acts. The stage directions describe the mother as the stronger parent, but the character's actions evince no strength: she mainly bemoans her situation and relies on a faith that brings no deliverance.

Both parents stand by helplessly as eighteen-year-old Cordelia flaunts her sexuality and boldly entertains a series of lovers in the family home. In part a fallen woman and in part a woman striving for sexual and personal autonomy, Cordelia, in her dress, behavior, and language, is less her parents' child than a daughter of Harlem. She refuses to settle for the menial jobs available to her. "I'm cut out for something big, something more excitin' and beautiful dan bein' a washwoman or a lady's maid," she proclaims.[23] Because productions of the play cast singers in the role, the character seems to harbor ambitions for a career in show business.[24] But by leaving her aspirations inchoate, the script underlines Cordelia's confusion. She is fatally attracted to Harlem's hustlers, and the play represents no future for her but prostitution. Tellingly, the parents hope to save Cordelia by marrying her to a West Indian suitor, Basil Venerable. Ambitious and hardworking, if dangerously naive, he represents the upward mobility the Williams family cannot attain by themselves. But Cordelia's recklessness dooms everyone's chances.

Apart from Cordelia's betrayal, Basil suffers from the prejudice directed toward him as a West Indian.[25] If the stage directions describe the character as being "extremely conscious" of his background, the dialogue shows how the U.S.-born blacks make it impossible for him to forget it. When he angrily objects to Cordelia's infidelity and threatens her physically, she answers in kind: "Don't you pull no rough stuff. Hurt me? Remember this! The day you hurts me is de day Marcus Garvey'll be minus a monkey hip eating countryman." Basil warns her against making "any more remarks about me or my countrymen." He does not finish his next thought: "Just because I'm not a bootlicking American nigger—"[26]

Like other moments in the play, this exchange depicts the stereotyped views blacks held of one another. For their part, the U.S.-born blacks professed a nativist superiority vis-à-vis blacks from the West Indies. At the same time, these black nativists perceived West Indians as more industrious and more likely to succeed than U.S.-born blacks were. Although the play never follows up on the reference to Garvey, its casualness serves to convey what a well-known figure he was to ordinary Harlemites.[27] Basil expresses his own sense of superiority, as one who has migrated from a place unlike the southern United States, where blacks outnumbered whites and the power relations were less visible. In Harlem, where southern-born blacks outnumber blacks from anywhere else, Basil shores up his identity by drawing on memories of home. Yet, despite the suspicions they hold about each other, blacks make common cause in Harlem, so much so that none of the characters finds the prospect of an interethnic marriage unusual.

In every other measure, the play's Harlem inverts the optimistic portraits drawn by Locke and Johnson. Apart from the gangsters, the play's characters live on the edge of poverty. Crime, a pervasive feature of everyday life that neither essayist acknowledged, bubbles always beneath the surface. The gun introduced in the first act belongs to the father, who fears violence might erupt during his party. It becomes the weapon that seals Basil's fate. The play treats the danger the streets pose to the moral lives of Harlem's children unsentimentally. Cordelia is hardly a victim; she chooses the "sweet men" who flirt with her and happily trades in one when a better one comes along. Her attention shifts from the rent party pianist to a petty gangster to the numbers boss, Kid Vamp. In a move unusual for the time, the play does not punish Cordelia. At its end, ignoring her parents' entreaties, she leaves home with Kid Vamp, who the audience knows has committed the murder of which Basil stands accused.

As the play makes clear, crime in Harlem thrives because of the relationship between the police and the criminals. The black gangsters and the white detective are well acquainted. Moreover, the white detective is cavalier in his treatment of the murder scene. The black patrolman is too distracted to concentrate on the facts of the case, because his main concern is to document his own actions lest he be accused of misconduct.

The play is equally unsentimental in its depiction of the relationships among the members of the Williams family. Unlike Rudolph Fisher, who took seriously the fear that parents and grandparents had for a younger generation seduced by the streets of Harlem, Thurman and Rapp depict parents who do not deserve the audience's sympathy. They are ineffectual and, in the father's case, insincere. The mother's religiosity would cause most teenagers to flee. The play depicts nothing about southern folkways that is worth preserving. Nevertheless, even if many of the play's characters regret the migration, the play endorses it. Harlem may be dangerous and amoral, but it is urgently alive.

Harlem did not succeed because of the serious topics it addresses. The play's producers pressured the authors to sensationalize the material, and they did. In advertisements and playbills, the production was touted with a flurry of exclamations: "Harlem! . . . The City that Never Sleeps! . . . A Strange, Exotic Island in the Heart of New York! . . . Rent parties! . . . Sweetbacks! . . . Primitive Passion! . . . Number Runners! . . . Chippies! . . . Jazz Love! . . . Primitive Passion! . . . Voodoo! . . . Hot-Stuff Men! . . . Uproarious Comedy! . . . Powerful Drama!"[28] By representing Harlem as a never-ending display of passion and exoticism in the heart of New York, the play encapsulated Harlem's lure, in two hours, from the vantage point of a safe seat in the theater, where playgoers could experience danger without risk. The marketing strategy was to mix the strange with the familiar in order to lure those who wanted a harmless thrill. The publicity's references to rent parties, sweetbacks, numbers runners, chippies, jazz, and voodoo were racially marked, while the "city that never sleeps" (now a staple of New York City public relations), as well as "uproarious comedy" and "powerful drama," made the strange familiar.

Critics responded with enthusiasm peppered with the racial stereotyping characteristic of the 1920s. "Downright entertainment," wrote one, who closed his review with the advisory, "If you like the quaint humor of the Negro, you'll find it doubly a treat." Another cited a publicity release from Rapp and Thurman that sallied, "If they offend any by the realism they have snitched from the negro [sic] community for use in their play . . . they could, had they wanted to, have done much worse." For his part, the reviewer described the play's rent party scene as a "dancing orgy." The *New York Times* headlined its review "A White Man's Holiday," which aligned the play with other productions, unnamed, but clearly Eugene O'Neill's *The Emperor Jones* and DuBose Heyward's *Porgy*, which allegedly presented "a civilization still happy in the joyous rhythms and rich colors and free forms that have been vanishing, alas, out of our less primitive white civilization."[29]

As a counter to these tropes—and perhaps even to their own publicity letter—Rapp and Thurman cowrote an article that promised to reveal the "real Harlem, the city of surprises." It provided demographic information, citing a population of 250,000 people who were "as varied and polyglot as could be found anywhere." Its estimate that 40 percent of Harlemites were "foreign-born" is unusually high but useful for the purposes of their play, and they offered a gloss for the ethnic conflict it dramatized. Identifying the nativist impulse on the part of U.S.-born blacks, it noted that West Indian immigrants, used to a lower standard of living, were often willing to work for lower wages; the latter, on the other hand, chided the native born for having been enslaved longer and for seeming to accept the realities of lynching and segregation. Here and elsewhere in the article, Thurman and Rapp dealt in perceptions rather than in fact—one wonders how much lower living conditions were in rural Jamaica than in rural Mississippi. More straightforwardly, they describe cultural practices from rent parties to the numbers—and shouting.[30]

The article takes a surprising turn when it spends five paragraphs lauding the "innumerable Harlem Negroes [who] live in expensively appointed homes and apartments, have maids and chauffeurs, entertain lavishly, and send their sons to Columbia, Harvard, and Yale, while their daughters go to Barnard, Vassar, and Wellesley."[31] The Harlemites who enjoyed this level of material success could in fact have been quickly counted, and the discussion serves mainly to remind readers today of the risks the playwrights had taken in staging the underside of Harlem life, the blowback they anticipated from black intellectuals and the black middle class, and their own compulsion to demonstrate to whites that what they were representing in their play was not all there was to black life.

Constrained though they were by commercial pressures, audience prejudices, and the ideology of uplift, Thurman and Rapp were among a handful of playwrights who sought to integrate African American music, dance, and drama. Their ambition was notably different from that of Eubie Blake and Noble Sissle, whose *Shuffle Along* (1921) and *Chocolate Dandies* (1924) were popular and innovative musicals. Instead, like Hughes and Hurston in the ill-fated *Mule Bone* (1930) and Hurston in the never-produced *Color Struck* (1926), Thurman and Rapp experimented with black vernacular forms to produce a new form of drama.[32] Unlike Hughes and Hurston, however, Thurman and Rapp chose an urban setting and, consequently, urban folkways that demonstrated what had been gained, lost, and revised in the transition of rural southerners to big city life in its most heightened, exaggerated form: that of Harlem.

■ ■ ■

Harlem never fulfilled the romanticized ideal of a "race capital," but fiction writers and playwrights as diverse as Thurman and Rapp, Fisher, Hurston, and McKay all recognized that the distinctive cultural mélange produced in Harlem was a result of the intense intermingling of black people from across the globe. They perceived the drama inherent in the miscommunications and conflicts that attended their daily interactions. They appreciated, as well, the sense of common purpose forged in response to the racism that all people of African descent faced in the nation's largest city. Moreover, they documented the ways in which urban life exacerbated tensions that exist in all communities, between young and old, rich and poor, male and female. More specifically, they heard in the speech of ordinary Harlemites a vernacular that combined southern black idiom, West Indian idiom, and urban slang and that could be put to literary use. They experimented with language to produce literary equivalents for that speech as well as for blues and jazz. Their work testifies to the centrality of representations of Harlem as "culture capital" in the black fiction of the 1920s.

NOTES

1. As its title announces, this is the project of Davarian L. Baldwin and Minkah Makalani, eds., *Escape from New York: The New Negro Renaissance Beyond Harlem* (Minneapolis: University of Minnesota Press, 2013). That reassessment continues in the present volume.
2. Jervis Anderson, *This Was Harlem: A Cultural Portrait, 1900–1950* (New York: Farrar, Straus and Giroux, 1982), 152. See also Shane White, "City of Numbers: Rethinking Harlem's Place in Black Business History," present volume.
3. Alain Locke, "The New Negro," in *The New Negro: An Interpretation*, ed. Alain Locke (1925; New York: Atheneum, 1992), 6. Subsequent parenthetical citations are to this edition.
4. James Weldon Johnson, "Harlem: The Culture Capital," in Locke, *New Negro*, 301.

5. For more on the Marshall Hotel as a cultural site, see Kevin McGruder, *Race and Real Estate: Conflict and Cooperation in Harlem, 1890-1920* (New York: Columbia University Press, 2015), 125.
6. James Weldon Johnson, *Black Manhattan* (1930; New York: Atheneum, 1969), 119-24, 235-36.
7. James Weldon Johnson, *The Autobiography of an Ex-Colored Man* (Boston: Sherman, French, 1912).
8. James Weldon Johnson, preface to *The Book of American Negro Poetry* (1922; New York: Harcourt Brace, 1931), 10. For a compelling analysis, see Brent Hayes Edwards, "The Seemingly Eclipsed Window of Form: James Weldon Johnson's Prefaces," in *The Jazz Cadence of American Culture*, ed. Robert G. O'Meally (New York: Columbia University Press, 1998), 580-601.
9. Wallace Thurman, "Negro Life in New York's Harlem: A Lively Picture of a Popular and Interesting Section," *Haldeman-Julius Quarterly* (Fall 1927), reprinted in Amritjit Singh and Daniel M. Scott III, eds., *The Collected Writings of Wallace Thurman: A Harlem Renaissance Reader* (New Brunswick, NJ: Rutgers University Press, 2003), 44. For a thorough analysis of the demography of Harlem in the 1920s, see Winston James, "Harlem's Difference," present volume.
10. The story seems to mock King Solomon Gillis's belief in the significance of black policemen. But Johnson attributes the absence of a violent outbreak in New York City during the Red Summer of 1919 to the "large proportion of Negro police on duty in Harlem" (Johnson, "Harlem," 310).
11. Rudolph Fisher, "The City of Refuge," in Locke, *New Negro*, 58. Subsequent parenthetical citations are to this edition.
12. Rudolph Fisher, "Vestiges: Harlem Sketches," in Locke, *New Negro*, 75-84.
13. Zora Neale Hurston, "The Book of Harlem," *Pittsburgh Courier*, February 12, 1927; "The Back Room," *Pittsburgh Courier*, February 19, 1927; "Monkey Junk," *Pittsburgh Courier*, March 5, 1927; "The Country in the Woman," *Pittsburgh Courier*, March 26, 1927; "She Rock," *Pittsburgh Courier*, August 5, 1933. These stories were reprinted in Glenda R. Carpio and Werner Sollors, eds., "African American Literary Studies: New Texts, New Approaches, New Challenges," *Amerikastudien/American Studies* 55, no. 4 (special issue, 2010): 566-81, 587-97. "Book of Harlem" was earlier reprinted in Cheryl A. Wall, ed., *Zora Neale Hurston: Novels and Stories* (New York: Library of America, 1995), 979-84. I mistakenly noted there that the story had not been previously published, an error for which I here apologize.
14. Zora Neale Hurston, "The Country in the Woman," reprinted in *Amerikastudien/American Studies* 55, no. 4 (special issue, 2010): 587. Subsequent parenthetical citations are to this edition.
15. Claude McKay, *Home to Harlem* (1928; Boston: Northeastern University Press, 1987), 292. Subsequent parenthetical citations are to this edition.
16. Langston Hughes, *Not Without Laughter* (1930; New York: Alfred A. Knopf, 1968).
17. McKay, quoted in Wayne F. Cooper, *Claude McKay: Rebel Sojourner in the Harlem Renaissance* (Baton Rouge: Louisiana State University Press, 1987), 247.
18. The lyric alludes to a stanza in Bessie Smith's "Foolish Man Blues" (1927): "There's two things got me puzzled, there's two things I can't understand . . . / That's a mannish-actin' woman an' a skippin', twistin', woman-actin' man." Two important studies that engage the subject of homosexuality in *Home to Harlem* are Gary Holcomb, *Claude McKay, Code Name Sasha: Queer Black Marxism and the Harlem Renaissance* (Gainesville: University Press of Florida, 2007); and Eric H. Newman, "Ephemeral Utopias: Queer Cruising,

Literary Form, and Diasporic Imagination in Claude McKay's *Home to Harlem* and *Banjo*," *Callaloo* 38 (Winter 2015): 167–85.

19. As Shane Vogel argues convincingly, McKay's novel exemplifies the "Cabaret School," an aspect of writing inspired by performance practices that countered the uplift ideology set forth by Johnson, Locke, and, perhaps preeminently, W. E. B. Du Bois. Instead, it proposed alternate models of identity by queering factors of race and sexuality. Vogel, *The Scene of Harlem Cabaret: Race, Sexuality, Performance* (Chicago: University of Chicago Press, 2009), esp. 132–66.

20. Thabiti Lewis has argued that McKay's novel does not represent Harlem as the sole site of black artistic and political energy; instead, Harlem "offered cramped quarters and limited opportunity." Lewis, " 'Home to Harlem' Again: Claude McKay and the Masculine Imaginary of Black Community," in Baldwin and Makalani, *Escape from New York*, 376. I agree, but neither Brooklyn nor Pittsburgh, two alternative locations the novel depicts, captures Jake's imagination the way that Harlem does. For McKay, Harlem is the place where black artistic and political energy *as well as* the problems of black modernity are at their height.

21. William Jourdan Rapp (1895–1942) was an established journalist, editor, and playwright when he began his collaborations with Thurman, which, in addition to *Harlem*, included the unproduced plays *Jeremiah, the Magnificent* and *Black Mecca*.

22. Wallace Thurman, "Cordelia, the Crude," *Fire!! A Quarterly Devoted to the Younger Negro Artists* 1 (November 1926): 5–6.

23. Wallace Thurman and William Jourdan Rapp, *Harlem: A Melodrama of Negro Life in Harlem*, reprinted in Singh and Scott, *Collected Writings*, 325.

24. In the original production of *Harlem*, Cordelia was played by Isabel Washington, a Cotton Club dancer, who performed the role of the "other woman" in the film *St. Louis Blues*, starring Bessie Smith, and later married the Reverend Adam Clayton Powell Jr.

25. The history of ethnic conflict and cooperation that the play dramatizes is documented in Irma Watkins-Owens, *Blood Relations: Caribbean Immigrants and the Harlem Community, 1900–1930* (Bloomington: Indiana University Press, 1996).

26. Thurman and Rapp, *Harlem*, 319.

27. *Harlem* was the first play of a projected trilogy. A fictionalized Marcus Garvey was the protagonist of the second play, *Jeremiah, the Magnificent*, also cowritten by Thurman and Rapp. Performed only once, in 1933, the play is published in Singh and Scott, *Collected Writings*, 378–439.

28. Singh and Scott, *Collected Writings*, 305–9.

29. The reviews cited are "Harlem," *American Recorder*, February 23, 1929; Burns Mantle, "Realism and the Negro Drama," *New York Daily News*, March 1, 1929; "A White Man's Holiday," *New York Times*, March 5, 1929.

30. William Jourdan Rapp and Wallace Thurman, "Few Know Real Harlem, the City of Surprises: Quarter Million Negroes Form a Moving, Colorful Pageant of Life," *New York World*, March 3, 1929, reprinted in Singh and Scott, *Collected Writings*, 66–67.

31. Rapp and Thurman, "Few Know Real Harlem," 68.

32. *Shuffle Along* was the most popular black show of the 1920s. As George Wolfe's production *Shuffle Along, or, the Making of the Musical Sensation of 1921 and All That Followed* (2016) underscores, Eubie Blake and Noble Sissle created a musical that, unlike the vaudeville entertainments that preceded it, had a book; it was not simply a series of unconnected acts. Still, its script, like its title and like the title *Chocolate Dandies*, reflected the lingering influence of minstrelsy. Despite Hurston's desire that she and Hughes create "real Negro theater," their collaboration resulted in a broken friendship but no show.

8.

CITY OF NUMBERS

Rethinking Harlem's Place in Black Business History

SHANE WHITE

On March 20, 1948, the film director Abraham Polonsky phoned the writer Ira Wolfert. Polonsky was filming *Force of Evil* (1948), a spirited attack on monopoly in American life, couched as a story of the numbers racket in New York, loosely based on a Wolfert novel, and Polonsky had a serious problem. We know this because a Federal Bureau of Investigation operative tapped and recorded the call. Polonsky explained to Wolfert that he could not get anyone to make sense of the details of numbers: "Nobody understands it, you see, except those people who lived in New York and played it. The other people just can't make head nor tail about it." What made matters worse was that, notwithstanding their ignorance, people "just have got some kind of feeling about it" and mistakenly thought they knew what was going on. This had been Polonsky's "constant beef" throughout the whole project.[1]

Seventy years on and the problem the radical (for Hollywood at least) director had to grapple with remains intractable. Although numbers is simple and elegant, blindingly obvious once you know how it works, the game remains opaque to almost everyone else. Not that this has inhibited commentators, many of whom apparently also harbor "some kind of feeling about it," from declaiming authoritatively about the mechanics of numbers while often dismissing what the game meant to Harlem, the place where it first emerged in 1920 or 1921.

Take, for example, Jonathan Gill's *Harlem: The Four Hundred Year History From Dutch Village to Capital of Black America* (2011). According to the author, the numbers "king" Casper Holstein made his money from "an informal West Indian gambling scam called *bolito*, which he expanded into numbers," a game in which Harlemites "would bet their hard-earned nickels and dimes on a lucky number and hope it matched the figure that represented the daily volume at the New York Stock Exchange." Gill then explained that the odds of winning were 900 to 1, but Holstein paid off at 600 to 1, and "the difference—up to $15,000 a day—paid the salaries of an army of employees who would take bets, transport cash, and count and launder money."[2]

It is difficult to know where to start in pointing out what is wrong with this brief account. But the number did not "represent" anything so simple as stock exchange turnover; it was a combination of digits drawn from different places. For almost all of the time that Holstein was involved in numbers, the source of the day's number was not the New York Stock Exchange but another financial institution, the New York Clearing House. Although Holstein and the other numbers kings and queens did pay off at 600 to 1, the odds of winning were one in a thousand, not one in nine hundred. The only way Gill's explanation of the daily profits from the game—as the "difference" between 600 to 1 and 900 to 1—makes any sense is if one thousand (or, as he has it, nine hundred) gamblers were each allocated a different number, meaning that the take would be $1,000 and the winner would walk away with $600, leaving a profit of $400. In fact, this was how *bolito*, a game associated mostly with Spanish speakers (often Cubans) was organized originally, in New York and elsewhere. Much of the attractiveness of numbers for ordinary African Americans, though, was that individual gamblers picked their own number.

Is it worth worrying about such details? Quite possibly not. It is a problem, though, when mistakes contribute to a slighting of the importance of numbers to Harlem, and a corresponding failure to recognize the importance of Harlem to African American business history. Gill's characterization of numbers as "an informal West Indian gambling scam" hardly augurs well for a careful assessment of the game's role, and the consequent allocation of a few lines to the subject, out of more than 450 pages on the history of Harlem, comes as no surprise. I dwell on Gill's book only because it is a popular account, a synthetic overview of Harlem's history that has been and will be read by many people. He drew on academic studies to write *Harlem* and, unsurprisingly, the authors of most of them have paid similarly scant attention to numbers.[3]

The neglect of this part of Harlem's history is not just a pity; it is a lost opportunity. To be sure, the recent turn against Harlem exceptionalism has been productive, opening up new terrain in African American studies, and rightly reminding us to resist all-too-easy assumptions of Harlem's preeminence, even uniqueness.[4] Yet, for all the scholarship devoted to Harlem, the case of numbers shows that there are still important absences in our understanding of what went on above 125th Street. Attending to numbers reinforces the importance of Harlem as a major site of African American innovation—if one wanted to be provocative, perhaps even the *leading* site. Not only did the numbers kings and queens blaze a trail followed by many other urban black communities but also they generated, literally, a good deal of black America's "race *capital*." Numbers both exemplified and—through its infusion of this capital to other spheres of activity—intensified the rich associational life that placed Harlem at the forefront of black advancement during the interwar years.

Outsiders have been misunderstanding and underestimating numbers for close to one hundred years. Back in the 1920s, as the craze for the game initially took off, policemen sent up to Harlem—unless instructed to the contrary, when some big push was on—often preferred to turn a blind eye to what looked to be very small beans. While colleagues were on the trail of murderers or bootleggers, they were seemingly stranded, filling out paperwork to prosecute a black housewife for betting a nickel on 444. It was hardly the way to promotion, let alone peer recognition. Many in the district attorney's office, similarly, were not enamored with the idea of prosecuting people involved in numbers. It all seemed a waste of effort.

In Harlem itself, there were some African Americans who frowned on what they viewed as an illegal and sordid game. Numbers played no part in the Harlem that Alain Locke chose to promote and celebrate. The only mention of it in the *Survey Graphic*'s special Harlem issue, published in March 1925 and guest-edited by Locke, was in Winthrop D. Lane's "Ambushed in the City: The Grim Side of Harlem." Lane opened his sharp sociological piece with a nearly thousand-word explanation of the game, reporting that Harlem was "ablaze" with numbers: "People play it everywhere, in tenements, on street corners, in the backs of shops." For Lane, this evidenced Harlem's grim side; indeed, "the whole game, as it is staged, smells of exploitation." Later in 1925, when Locke repurposed his *Survey Graphic* issue into the famous anthology *The New Negro: An Interpretation*, Lane's article was one of the four pieces he dropped quietly. Numbers did not fit in with the Harlem Renaissance grandee's idea of Harlem as a race capital.[5]

Similarly, for a black leader and spokesman such as W. E. B. Du Bois, the racket was a deplorable criminal infraction, part of the seamy side of Harlem life, something that impeded the more important project of Negro uplift. But anyone more sympathetic to the way life was lived in Harlem understood that all those pennies and nickels added up to a lot of money and that numbers was important to Harlem's residents. As Langston Hughes, not much interested in whether numbers was legal or not, or indeed what whites thought of the game, recognized with characteristic style, "The numbers is the salvation of Harlem, its Medicare, and its Black Draught, its 666, its little liver pills, its vitamins, its aspirins and its analgesic balm combined."[6] In addition—and here was a tragedy that would exact a heavy toll on Harlem over ensuing decades—Dutch

Schultz and other white gangsters given their start by the folly of Prohibition did not underestimate the importance of the game. They knew to a penny how lucrative was the business of numbers.

Misunderstandings about numbers, though, are but part of a larger problem, for, until very recently, scholars have paid little attention to the story of black business. Over the past four decades, historians have almost completely rewritten African American history. Yet few of the scads of published pages have touched on black business history. The action has been elsewhere, first in social history and more recently in cultural history. This seeming lack of interest in the details of black business life continues to perplex, for economic history opens up new ways of viewing the larger social and cultural structures of society.[7] That unrealized potential remains the signal attraction of investigating black economic life.

Part of the reason for the neglect of black business life in New York City's history is that, at least from the end of slavery there, in 1827, the story of free black impoverishment and decline at the hands of a modernizing economy was, to contemporaries, strikingly obvious and well known.[8] The early stirrings of the northern economy's transformation into an industrial powerhouse gave every sign of leaving blacks floundering off to one side, of reducing African Americans to a dwindling and beleaguered minority in dynamically expanding centers such as New York City.

Surveys of northern black business life from the antebellum period down to the recent, impressively encyclopedic work of Juliet E. K. Walker have told an essentially similar story, albeit with varying degrees of sophistication and elaboration.[9] Of course, there were a few African Americans who, against the odds, started businesses, made money, and got ahead. But, for the most part, such successful individuals were concentrated in service-sector niche markets, not in the engine room driving the American economy. Overall, scholars have emphasized discrimination, exclusion, and consequent black impoverishment, demonstrating that, having shucked off slavery, northern blacks, and more particularly New York blacks, were consigned to a slow death in a hard place. These accounts carry considerable explanatory power.

And yet there was more to black life, particularly black business life, than this. The recovery of pioneering black firms and individuals by the likes of Juliet Walker is anything but complete. There are still successful African Americans who were well known in their own time but who have since fallen between the cracks and are now completely forgotten.[10] Yet the problem is more than simply one of ignored or forgotten individuals. There needs to be rather more flexibility in the definition of economic achievement. Although most will readily admit that African Americans have faced enormous discrimination, much of it specifically designed to prevent blacks from getting ahead economically, there remains a reluctance to allow that such discrimination affected the contours of black economic development by directing efforts into other channels. African American entrepreneurs, be they the beauty product purveyor Madam Walker or Casper Holstein, moved into areas where they would not be in direct competition with white firms.[11] Sometimes white authorities deemed those areas to be illegal.

While it is true that American blacks founded neither a Ford Motor Company nor a Coca-Cola Company, a Harlemite did invent numbers. African Americans should be assessed not for their shortcomings, measured against some impossible white standard, but for what they achieved. And numbers was an achievement. A *New York Times* reporter labeled it, in the years before 1931, "a brilliant Harlem success story," and he was right.[12] Denied ready access to the financial institutions everyone else was able to use, African Americans created their own forms of financial organization. Although they were on the margins of—maybe even outside—the formal market, in the case of numbers between the wars, such activity was of a size and importance that requires it to be seen alongside the much more familiar work of another Harlem institution, Marcus Garvey's Universal Negro Improvement Association, in powerfully shaping everyday life.

■ ■ ■

It was clear enough to Polonsky and Wolfert what they had to do to make numbers less confusing in *Force of Evil*. The novelist had immediately pointed out, "You'll have to take a number up from the playing of it to the odds."

Polonsky agreed. "That's right. And we will also have to explain the distribution of the odds and that kind of stuff—without making an exposition." He then added that they had to show "just exactly how the whole racket plays out at every single point." It was as though you had "to explain it to someone in Azusa, California—taking nothing for granted."[13]

Let me follow their advice.

Numbers was a form of gambling in which individuals wagered on which numeral between **0** and **999** would turn up as the day's number. The standard transaction was to bet anything from one cent to a few dollars on a three-digit number. The chance of any number hitting was one in a thousand, but the wager was paid off at 600 to 1. Later on, in the 1930s, box plays (betting on all six possible combinations of a three-digit number) or single-digit plays (betting on just the first, middle or, most often, last digit) became more common. Numbers runners working for various "bankers" spread out all over Harlem and San Juan Hill, collecting bets from individual gamblers.

Casper Holstein's act of genius had been in working out a way to generate the number, randomly and in a fashion that was, as far as ordinary gamblers were concerned, impossible to rig or fix. Founded in 1853, the New York

Clearing House was a financial institution that facilitated the daily exchanges and settlements of money between the city's banks. In the years after World War I, at precisely 10:00 every workday morning, an employee descended to the lobby of the Clearing House building at 77 Cedar Street, in Lower Manhattan, and chalked up on a blackboard three freshly calculated figures, each of which acted as a basic economic indicator and two of which, to the embarrassment of this august financial institution, were used in the game of numbers. The daily number, avidly awaited by tens of thousands of Harlem residents, was worked out by combining the second and third digits from the bank clearings with the third digit from the Federal Reserve Bank balance. For example, on the last Monday before Christmas 1930, the clearings were $**589** million and the balance was $**116** million; hence, the winning number was **896**. Within seconds of 10:00 A.M., the daily Clearing House figures were telephoned through to Harlem numbers bankers and to the afternoon newspapers.

That ability to telephone the number through to the newspapers hints at some of the advantages of this new game. The one played in Chicago, called "policy," required physical apparatus, "wheels" as they were called, in the different territories of the city, from which usually twelve out of seventy-eight balls were drawn. This equipment had to be located in the city, requiring a physical presence and necessitating relationships with police and politicians. Then the results of the daily draws had to be publicized throughout a wheel's catchment area. Numbers was less cumbersome and, particularly early on in the 1920s, left a lighter footprint on the city. Organized and substantial police and political involvement was not obvious until the end of the 1920s.

For the newspapers, printing the results of illicit lottery draws in Chicago was obviously encouraging illegality, but the Clearing House numbers or, later, race results were news, not of themselves contrary to the law. In New York, major newspapers quickly became complicit in the numbers racket by printing the number in as timely a fashion as possible. On placards at Harlem newsstands, the *New York Sun* shamelessly boasted that it was "FIRST with the BANK Clearing NUMBER."[14]

Holstein, a migrant from the Virgin Islands, had invented numbers around 1920, and for the next decade everyone from newspaper reporters to blues singers referred to the game as the "Clearing House numbers." But as of January 1, 1931, the Clearing House, increasingly embarrassed by its links to numbers, ceased publication of the daily figures. Although some initially believed that the game would cease, this was wishful thinking. Bankers quickly came up with alternative ways of generating a daily number, and, over ensuing decades, figures taken from the New York Stock Exchange, from the pari-mutuel totals paid out on horse races at tracks throughout the country, and even from the Cincinnati Clearing House were all used to drive New York's gambling racket. But no source ever achieved the cachet of the New York Clearing House.

During the 1930s, Harlem was rife with rumors of rigged numbers, and what gave legs to the rumors was that, once white gangsters moved in and took over, the whispers of crooked goings on often had more than a modicum of truth to them—in fact, the fix was put in regularly. Most days of the year the people running numbers had a license to print money. In February 1925, a collector who had left a good job to get involved in the lucrative racket spoke to a *New York Age* reporter: "Last week I collected over $400 and paid out only $6—all the rest was velvet." In other words, this African American had accepted several thousand bets of a penny, nickel, dime, or more from his clients and only one wager of a penny had "hit," necessitating a payoff. A penny at 600 to 1 is $6. Although this was indeed rather more velvet than was usually the case, he added that he had still "cleared over a thousand dollars in the past four weeks," many times what he would have earned in his previous regular job.[15]

And yet, for all its lucrativeness, numbers was an inherently unstable scheme. People did not choose numbers at random to bet on. There were always concentrations on certain numbers thought to be "lucky," and when one of those hit, the extraordinarily high odds of 600 to 1 created a financial disaster for the banker. On March 3, 1928, the Clearing House number was 333. Many African Americans had "followed a popular hunch, based on Saturday being the third day of the third month and coming right after Friday" and bet on that number. Harlem bankers took heavy losses, one prominent figure losing about $11,000. Interestingly, the largest winning wager that he had on his books was a ten cent play, paying off $60. In other words, several hundred African Americans had bet a penny, nickel, or dime on 333. Much the same pattern had occurred in Atlantic City, Boston, and Philadelphia, cities in Gotham's orbit that also used the New York Clearing House numbers. In Atlantic City, when 333 hit, bankers had lost more than $100,000.

Further adding to numbers' instability, bankers did not always pay off their losses. In this case, when the *New York Age* reporter asked the banker who had lost $11,000 if he was going to give his customers "a square deal" and meet his obligations, the African American muttered something to the effect that "certain employees of the Clearing House were in cahoots with some of the policemen" and there had been a leak, resulting in "this heavy play." This was unlikely. By the banker's own admission, no one had bet more than ten cents on 333 with him, and similar plunges on the number had occurred in several other cities, making it improbable that there was anything untoward going on. After all, with inside knowledge of a certain return of 600 to 1, who bets only a dime? The banker was weighing up whether he could welch on his debts.[16]

Numbers, then, was a very large and highly remunerative, if volatile, business. The writer and essayist Wallace Thurman guessed, in the late 1920s, that "there must be in Harlem over a thousand numbers runners daily collecting slips from 100,000 clients." There was probably a score or more bankers, the most important of whom were known as the "black kings and queens." These black entrepreneurs grossed staggering sums of money. Estimates of the volume of an illegal activity are always problematic, but in 1926 the *New York Age* suggested that numbers in Harlem turned over about $75,000 a day, or roughly $20 million a year. Five years later, the figure was probably four times that. As early as 1924, the *Age* had noted that it was "freely reported" that some of Harlem's bankers "show a weekly profit of from $10,000 to $15,000, or even more."[17] But every now and then, almost the entire business would be flattened when a heavily backed number hit. Some bankers would remove themselves quietly from Harlem for a few months, while others brazenly refused to pay and challenged the aggrieved to do something about it. Numbers bankers did not have a good reputation for paying off large losses—occasionally violence ensued.

The most important feature of the business, and the one that contributed substantially to its popularity, was that an individual gambler chose the number she or he would back. It was different from a lottery, where tickets were allocated randomly. Outsiders dismissed "Nigger Pool," as it was often called, as a game of pennies, but the crucial point was that black men and women determined the details of how they "invested," to use the term Harlemites often used, their nickels and dimes. Although they had little chance of winning—well, one in a thousand—they still had control over picking their number, certainly more control than they had over most aspects of their lives. Scores of thousands of ordinary black New Yorkers made their decision about which number to back on the basis of an array of traditional beliefs that had been developed and refined over at least a century of African American involvement in what we might call games of chance.

It cannot be emphasized too strongly, though, that for perhaps a majority of black participants in the 1920s and 1930s, numbers was not a game, nor did it involve chance. For thousands of African Americans, the daily number was not random, and hitting it did not depend on luck. As early as June 1923, a writer in the *New York Age* noted that "by all imaginable methods these bettors pick the numbers they are to play the next day." He continued, "They are mostly superstitious and almost any odd incident may be interpreted as a tip by them." This was particularly the case with dreams. In fact, Harlem's best-sellers during its renaissance years were not novels but dream books, pamphlets that facilitated converting a dream into a three-digit figure. Numbers were everywhere. They were on buses, in addresses, on license plates, in baseball scores, in dates of birthdays, and even in hymn numbers in church. Harlem became the city of numbers and, north of Central Park, the game was simply embedded in the warp and woof of everyday life.[18]

Records such as the parole case files in the Municipal Archives of the City of New York allow access to the behavior of ordinary, if not quite random, African Americans. Take, for instance, the case of Edward Day.[19] Originally from

Tarboro, North Carolina, he had joined the Great Migration and moved to Harlem around the time of World War I. Day worked as an elevator operator in an apartment building on Fifth Avenue near 128th Street, for which he received a rent-free room in an apartment with other building employees and $8.75 a week. On his thirty-eighth birthday, on December 24, 1934, he had sexual intercourse with a fourteen-year-old African American girl. He claimed that he thought she was seventeen years old. The judge placed him on probation for two years.

On May 6, 1935, an apartment in the building was robbed and the police searched Day's room. Although they found no evidence at all of any link to the robbery, a policeman stumbled across six policy slips containing sixty-one numbers. Since possibly as many as one in three Harlemites gambled on numbers and probably had slips on their person or wherever they lived, the game's illegality rendered a very large proportion of the population vulnerable to police harassment. In this case, a Detective Tunney arrested Day. He thought that the black man was a runner who had held back a bet or two on his own account and, when the number had hit, was liable and had to pay the winnings himself. That day, Day had withdrawn $4 from his bank account and pawned a suit for $10.

Day admitted gambling on numbers and knowing runners, who allowed him to play numbers at a discount (he would pay twenty cents for a twenty-five-cent slip), but he denied being either a robber or a runner. Two days after his arrest, he received a suspended sentence for the numbers. However, his arrest for numbers meant that Day had violated probation, and he spent quite a few days in prison, waiting for his case to be heard, which threatened his job and, consequently, his lodging. The result of it all was that his probation period was extended.

Perhaps it all seems penny ante to us. But the parole records demonstrate conclusively how precarious life was in Harlem, especially in the 1930s. A dollar here or there was a matter of some moment. The records also show, time and time again, that the parole officer and the probationer inhabited different worlds. In Day's case, his officer kept hammering away about the importance of saving, more or less forcing Day to open a thrift account at the post office branch at Lenox Avenue and 126th Street. At least, on one occasion, his officer had the good grace to admit, "The question of thrift was also discussed with him but inasmuch as he only earns $8 per week, it is rather difficult to budget whereby savings could be incorporated." The officer, with what must have been a galling level of interference in his charge's life, also urged Day to join some organization "where he may have proper recreational outlets and be able to surround himself with good associates." He did not have numbers in mind. Indeed, the parole officer considered Day to be "a weak, acquiescent individual, [who] in his effort to accommodate lodgers and tenants in these premises, collects numbers from them which he in turn delivers to runners."

The parole officer completely failed to recognize the significance of the sociability of numbers, as gamblers passed their slips on to Day—gossip and chat about who had hit, what tomorrow's number might be, and the new suit that one of the numbers kings had worn strolling down Seventh Avenue last Sunday—and the importance an extra dollar or two from collecting numbers slips for the runner might make to the life of someone earning $8 a week. Whether the parole officer acknowledged it or not, knowing how to place a bet on numbers was pretty much part of the job of being an African American elevator operator—and not just in Harlem.

Throughout, I have used the word "business" advisedly. In fact, there was a strange disjuncture between the myriad individual decisions to back a number, influenced by a centuries-old African American culture, and the business of collecting and keeping track of all those nickels and dimes, which was as sophisticated and modern an enterprise as existed in Harlem and throughout black America at this time. This facet of numbers was revealed most clearly by police raids on numbers banks.

Take, for example, a police raid in 1935. At about 5:15 P.M. on August 23, Officer Sidney Cusberth knocked on the door of a first-floor apartment at 70 Lenox Avenue. After barging in, Cusberth found a hive of activity. At this time, the daily number was derived from the amount of money bet on nominated horse races, and 5:15 P.M. was at the beginning of rush hour for numbers banks. The apartment looked like a busy modern office. A thirty-three-year-old black man, the strikingly named Herman McTootle, ran the establishment. He and a Bessie Smith were operating adding machines, and four black women were sorting slips and calling off the numbers to the machine operators. On the table were 5,547 mutual horse race policy slips detailing 44,546 numbers. In addition, the officer found $12.62 in silver, dating stamps and pads, a punch, a ledger, and sixty-five pads of policy banking instructions.

McTootle employed five black women to keep track of his bank's transactions, all American-born and each described as a "housewife." After a check of their fingerprints, the district attorney's office determined that not one of them had a criminal record. On being asked, each of these women informed the arresting officer that she was paid $25 per week for working "from 5:00 P.M. till 7:30 P.M. when the last number was out."[20] These were some of the most desirable and best-paying jobs available to African American women in Harlem. Contrast their wage with the $8 and lodging that Day received for a full week's work (probably more than seventy hours) as an elevator operator. The truncated work hours in the numbers bank particularly suited housewives with domestic responsibilities. Good conditions and pay compensated for the job's major drawback—numbers' illegality meant there was an ever-present threat of arrest.[21]

Why was the business of numbers—unlike, say, betting on horse races—illegal? And why did the authorities end up getting so fixated on it? The reason goes back to the success of the lottery abolition movement, which ended up forcing the banning of lotteries in New York State from January 1, 1834. Strangely, the laws used to prosecute numbers players were about lotteries—and numbers manifestly was not a lottery. There was always something dubious about the legal underpinnings of the periodic crusades against numbers, which probably explains why the authorities' most successful incursions into the world of the kings and queens of Harlem were when they secured convictions for income tax evasion, not running the numbers racket.[22]

It was not only those who were arrested and convicted who knew the absurdity of the legal situation. Many of the police and lawyers working for the district attorney found what duty compelled them to do distasteful. In April 1935, Assistant District Attorney James J. Wilson, after he had successfully prosecuted a Norma Johnson for possession of a numbers slip, paid the $28 fee for her appeal out of his own pocket. That appeal, opposed by District Attorney William C. Dodge, was successful and made it more difficult to prosecute small-fry gamblers.[23]

Nine months later, Wilson gave a speech to an American Legion branch at the West 135th Street YMCA. It made the front page of the *Amsterdam News*. Wilson urged "equality in gambling privileges": "You may go to the race course and bet on a horse. You may go down on Wall street and bet on a number down there—margins, they call it. You may go to a swanky nightclub and play poker all you want to. But just get caught trying to place a 2-cent bet on a policy number and the whole force of the law is on you." He then pointed out that the law was "the only gambling legislation which penalizes the player." Wilson wanted "to place the policy player on a plane of equality with the player in Wall street." As far as he was concerned, "there should be no special privileges for the rich gambler."[24]

It was an informed and devastating speech. Assigned to prosecute policy cases in the Court of Special Sessions, Wilson knew from experience the folly of the then current situation. As he explained, it cost $700 to prosecute an individual placing a nickel bet on a number. In 1935, there had been 6,549 policy cases tried. There were 5,700 convictions, 90 percent of which came from Harlem. "And I can tell you most of these are honest, hard-working people, innocent of any real offense." He then added that "Negroes do not get a fair break in minor cases."

But, by this time, Wilson's thoughtful commentary on race and class inequalities was irrelevant—numbers made too much money for too many people. Unfortunately for the black numbers kings and queens, white gangsters running alcohol to clubs in Harlem had a front row seat on their success. Although there was more than one attempt to take over the business, the crucial incursion into Harlem was made by Dutch Schultz, beginning in 1931. It was strictly a business decision. With Prohibition about to end, the Beer Baron of the Bronx needed a new income stream to fund his organization. He and his henchmen realized that if he could take over all of the numbers banks, he could organize them more efficiently. He could pay off not just the police but also politicians. As a result of minimizing interference in the running of numbers, he would be able to pay wages to operatives currently on percentages, and reduce wages everywhere because there was much less risk of arrest. It was a classic business strategy—his aim was to put together one huge combination running numbers, expand the game from Harlem to all five boroughs, and then reduce the costs of the operation. All that stood in his way, as far as he could see, was a few African Americans.

If Schultz had his way, the profits from numbers would no longer stay in Harlem—and in the middle of the Depression, that was of some moment. Schultz's move into Harlem prompted many to realize that if they had to have numbers, then they preferred having it run as a black and not a white business. Even the usually stiff *New York Age* managed to find some positive things to say about the black kings and queens—although the point of comparison was always Dutch Schultz, a dangerously pathological gangster.

The violent struggle for control of numbers would last for several years, with the final result being a compromise of sorts, negotiated by Lucky Luciano and Harlem's Bumpy Johnson. White gangsters would control most of the numbers in Harlem and would siphon off most of the profits elsewhere, but much of the day-to-day running of the game would be left in black hands. In the end, what was most remarkable about the struggle for control of numbers in the mid-1930s was the determination of African Americans not to lose their business to white outsiders. They may have lost in the end, but there was something magnificent about Stephanie St. Clair, the most prominent and notorious numbers queen, and others defying the white gangsters, spitting in their faces, and telling them to do their damnedest.

At the height of the bitter dispute, a black banker, or policy king, spoke to an *Amsterdam News* reporter. It was a remarkable interview. The *News* highlighted its source's words by putting them under a caption printed in bold typeface: "Calls Policy Negro Game." According to the banker, who was president of the Harlem union of numbers bankers, "You know this is a Negro game in a Negro neighborhood and it has been carried on by Negroes for twelve years without outside groups." In their attempts to reorganize the business, Schultz and the racketeers were trying to shift numbers gambling away from the black-dominated system of runners into white-run storefronts. The banker deplored this in terms with which anyone sympathetic to Garveyite arguments could only agree: "Many collectors who before now earned a few dollars are now walking the streets destitute because the money is continually being played in stores and then carried out of the community by undesirable elements."[25] While black economic nationalism would so often entail efforts to influence the practices of businesses owned and operated by whites, Harlem's indigenous numbers trade—while it lasted—was that rare thing, a major black financial asset, one well worth defending.

Equally, many of the tactics later used in the struggle for economic rights in Harlem—the forming of collective associations, the use of boycotts of white businesses—were employed by the black kings and queens. As the banker told the *News*: "We intend to appeal directly to the people not to play in the stores, and if the storekeepers refuse to stop writing 'numbers' we are going to have their places boycotted." And he prophesied with some accuracy what would happen if they lost. "If the white racketeers succeed in forcing us out of the game, they will institute their own fake system and rob all the people without giving them a chance to win."[26] Black kings and queens may have defaulted occasionally and not paid off when black gamblers hit; however, they never engaged in the wholesale rigging and fixing of the numbers that Dutch Schultz and his heirs perpetrated in Harlem.

● ● ●

Perhaps I paint myself into some corner as a romantic, but, for me, the creation of numbers and the valiant attempts to retain it as "a Negro game in a Negro neighborhood" were signal achievements. It is surely time to recognize that business and everyday life—not just politics, arts, and literature—contributed mightily to the "New Negro" phenomenon and were part of what made Harlem that phenomenon's epicenter. Numbers was a key manifestation of the New Negro mentality of communal empowerment, and the fight to exclude white control was one of Harlem's heroic struggles. To be sure, not everyone has seen it this way. Too many persist in trivializing numbers, dismissing it as a minor criminal enterprise or a passing splash of local color. Indeed, one of the fascinating developments, starting back in the 1940s, has been the way that almost everyone has forgotten the African American role in inventing numbers and creating an industry.

One of the more striking illustrations of this erasure of the black role in numbers occurred in the literary field. In 1943, the Pulitzer Prize–winning author Ira Wolfert published *Tucker's People*. The lengthy and painfully didactic novel is revealing of various aspects of numbers in the 1930s. According to the book's blurb, "It tells the story of Tucker who became Boss of the Harlem rackets by making crime pay off like Big Business." And, as one would expect from someone on the left, he emphasized the business side of numbers: "Everything about the business was a regular business, standardized inside and out. Players, collectors, controllers, office workers and bankers were standardized. The arrests of collectors were standardized. Lawyers' fees on policy cases, bail bonds, fines handed down by magistrates, even the police were standardized."[27]

The novel's main character, Leo Minch, was happy, or at least as happy as he was ever likely to be, running a numbers bank in Harlem. Everyone benefited. "The bulk of the money it made circulate remained in the community where everybody had a chance to get a piece of it." As he told his wife, "People need the numbers to have a little hope in their lives." But Minch was unlucky, for "he had been born in the time of Rockefeller."[28]

Joe Minch, Leo's estranged brother, worked for Ben Tucker, a gangster who had become rich selling beer during Prohibition. Tucker knew that during Thanksgiving week there was a superstition that meant many gamblers would bet on any combination of 2, 5, and 7 (in other words, 257, 275, 527, 572, 725, and 752). He had paid a man $25,000 to rig the number and ensure that one of those numbers hit. Every bank would go bust and the bankers would be forced to come, cap in hand, to Tucker, who would lend them the money in return for a two-thirds interest in their business. Joe, trying to save Leo from bankruptcy, explained, "They're going to merge all you banks together, buy you out and make you all one combination to be run economical, big time, on a big time business basis." On the Wednesday evening of Thanksgiving week, "an enormous event was set in motion. The number 527 hit. A monopolist had made his first move. The consequences were incalculable."[29] For the rest of the novel, Wolfert details how those consequences played out in the lives of his characters.

Clearly, Wolfert was familiar with numbers. He recognized that numbers was not just some gambling fad but a business and that the gangster takeover was the inevitable outcome of the application of American business principles to an illegal activity. Much of what occurs in *Tucker's People* embellished or reworked recognizable Harlem people or events. Tucker himself was based on Dutch Schultz, who had made his fortune out of beer and sought to force all the numbers bankers into one big combination. What occurred on Thanksgiving in 1934 in the novel replayed some of the historic events from Thanksgiving in 1931. Even the number that bankrupted the numbers banks—527—was the same.

Yet, for all the verisimilitude of parts of *Tucker's People*, what is absent is any sense of Harlem as a place. Indeed, there were hardly any African Americans in the book. There were a few mentions of Edgecombe Avenue—although as far as any readers relying only on the novel were concerned, this famous thoroughfare could be located in the Meatpacking District. The novel has a strangely disembodied feel. It is as though Wolfert wanted to write about monopoly power, figured that for the full dimensions of the moral struggle to be apparent his protagonists had to be white, and pretty much expunged African Americans from their considerable role in the story of numbers.

Today, *Tucker's People* is forgotten. Rather better known is *Force of Evil* (1948), a film Martin Scorsese has championed as "a classic of the American cinema."

According to the film critic David Thomson, Abraham Polonsky was responsible for the script (although Wolfert is credited as coauthor). If so, he did a truly impressive job of converting the 496 pages of Wolfert's sprawling *Tucker's People* into a taut, eighty-minute noir film. This is one of those not very frequent occasions where the adaptation of a novel to the screen takes the original material to a completely new and higher level of artistry. Polonsky's film is about more than his few involved individuals; in his hands, the numbers racket stands in for the entire rotten capitalist system. Thomson aptly summed up the film: "It's a black fable out of Karl Marx, but shot as if Fritz Lang had made it in Germany."[30]

When Thomson used the word "black," however, he was not referring to African Americans. Indeed, if *Tucker's People* began to erase blacks from the story of numbers, Polonsky's film version of the material completed the process. *Force of Evil* is very much located in a place, but that place is not Harlem. The opening shots of Trinity Church and the haunting black-and-white images of Wall Street, filmed from above and accompanied by John Garfield's voice-over, are memorable. So, too, are the final scenes under the George Washington Bridge. By my count, however, just seven African American faces are projected on the screen—fleetingly. One is in a crowd of people in court, and the other six are in a band playing in a club. The number 527 was embedded in African American culture. In the film, though, the banks were broken not at Thanksgiving but on July 4, and the number that broke them was not 527 but what Polonsky called the "liberty number," or 776.

The director had appropriated the story of numbers and made it his own. In his desire to make a fable for all Americans, he cut his subject free from its black roots in Harlem. From his point of view, perhaps this was understandable. Yet, once again, the tantalizing chimera of equality, promised in the rhetoric of the American Revolution but never delivered to African Americans, was used to mask black achievement, this time, unusually, in the economic sphere. And that is why, for all the admitted power of Polonsky's *Force of Evil*, I prefer to look at things differently.

Numbers was a signal contribution to the New Negro phenomenon. It grew out of, marked the rhythms of, and altered the course of daily life in Harlem. It was a great business achievement that was, for a time, owned and operated by African Americans, providing employment opportunities, enhancing wages, and even creating black millionaires. Indeed, much of the profusion of associational life and artistic activity that gave interwar Harlem its renown had this illicit form of "race capital" flowing through it, in one way or another. Casper Holstein, patron of worthy causes, both in Harlem and his native Virgin Islands, bankrolled the famous literary prizes awarded by *Opportunity* magazine that garlanded the stars of the Harlem Renaissance—all with the money that poured in from numbers.[31] Numbers exemplified the New Negro values of assertion, race pride, autonomy, and building black businesses. That simple statement by the *New York Times* reporter summed it up best: numbers was "a brilliant Harlem success story." It is about time we acknowledged that.

NOTES

I would like to thank the Australian Research Council for its generous funding of my research, and my collaborators in researching Harlem's history, Stephen Robertson and Stephen Garton. I would also like to thank Daniel Matlin and Andrew Fearnley for their shrewd and sharp commentary on this piece.

1. Paul Buhle and Dave Wagner, *A Very Dangerous Citizen: Abraham Lincoln Polonsky and the Hollywood Left* (Berkeley: University of California Press, 2001), 236–37.
2. Jonathan Gill, *Harlem: The Four Hundred Year History from Dutch Village to Capital of Black America* (New York: Grove, 2011), 273.
3. The few scholarly works that pay attention to numbers in Harlem include Shane White, Stephen Garton, Stephen Robertson, and Graham White, *Playing the Numbers: Gambling in Harlem Between the Wars* (Cambridge, MA: Harvard University Press, 2010); Adrian Burgos Jr., *Cuban Star: How One Negro-League Owner Changed the Face of Baseball* (New York: Hill and Wang, 2011); LaShawn Harris, *Sex Workers, Psychics, and Numbers Runners: Black Women in New York City's Underground Economy* (Urbana: University of Illinois Press, 2016).
4. See, most obviously, Davarian L. Baldwin and Minkah Makalini, eds., *Escape From New York: The New Negro Renaissance Beyond Harlem* (Minneapolis: University of Minnesota Press, 2013).
5. Winthrop D. Lane, "Ambushed in the City: The Grim Side of Harlem," *Survey Graphic* 6 (March 1925): 692; Daniel Matlin, "Harlem: The Making of a Ghetto Discourse," present volume.
6. Langston Hughes, quoted in *New York Times*, March 1, 1971. As is well known, W. E. B. Du Bois also attempted to control the depiction of black urban life, perhaps most famously in his review of Claude McKay's novel *Home to Harlem* (1928). See Shane Vogel, *The Scene of Harlem Cabaret: Race, Sexuality, Performance* (Chicago: University of Chicago Press, 2009), 132–66.
7. Of late there have been some very good studies of some facets of Harlem business life. See, for example, an account of Black Swan Records, in David Suisman, *Selling Sounds: The Commercial Revolution in American Music* (Cambridge: Harvard University Press, 2009), 204–39; of Negro league baseball and the New York Cubans, in Burgos, *Cuban Star*; and of real estate, in Kevin McGruder, *Race and Real Estate: Conflict and Cooperation in Harlem, 1890–1920* (New York: Columbia University Press, 2015).
8. *New York Herald*, January 25, 1861.
9. James Weldon Johnson, *Black Manhattan* (New York: Alfred A. Knopf, 1930); Abram L. Harris, *The Negro as Capitalist: A Study of Banking and Business Among American Negroes* (Philadelphia, PA: American Academy of Political and Social Science, 1936); Juliet E. K. Walker, *The History of Black Business in America: Capitalism, Race, Entrepreneurship* (New York: Macmillan Library Reference, 1998) (also published in a two-volume second edition by University of North Carolina Press, in 2009).
10. More and more of these successful African Americans turn up in the historiography. Some left America. See Vladmir Alexandrov, *The Black Russian* (New York: Atlantic Monthly Press, 2013). I am particularly taken with the career of "Back Number Budd,"

an African American who, at the end of the nineteenth century, kept huge files of old newspapers and sold individual papers, particularly to lawyers searching for material needed in their court cases. See Ellen Gruber Garvey, "Back Number Budd: An African American Pioneer in the Old Newspaper and Information Management Business," in *Capitalism by Gaslight: Illuminating the Economy of Nineteenth-Century America*, ed. Brian P. Luskey and Wendy A. Woloson (Philadelphia: University of Pennsylvania Press, 2015), 215–32.

11. On this point, see the excellent article by David Suisman, "Co-workers in the Kingdom of Culture: Black Swan Records and the Political Economy of African American Music," *Journal of American History* 90 (March 2004): 1295–1324.
12. *New York Times* (August 20, 1938), 7.
13. Buhle and Wagner, *A Very Dangerous Citizen*, 236–37.
14. For a fuller account of the operations of numbers, see White et al., *Playing the Numbers*.
15. *New York Age* (February 21, 1925), 1.
16. *New York Age* (March 10, 1928), 1.
17. Wallace Thurman, "Odd Jobs in Harlem," in *The Collected Writings of Wallace Thurman: A Harlem Renaissance Reader*, ed. Amritjit Singh and Daniel M. Scott III (New Brunswick, NJ: Rutgers University Press, 2003), 75; *New York Age* (June 12, 1926), 2; *New York Age* (March 9, 1935), 6; *New York Age* (December 6, 1931), 1.
18. *New York Age* (June 2, 1923), 1. On dreams in Harlem, see White et al., *Playing the Numbers*, 86–95.
19. Edward Day is not his name; I have masked it in accordance with the wishes of the Municipal Archives. Parole Case Files #26014 (1935), Municipal Archives of the City of New York.
20. *Sidney Cusberth Against Herman McTootle et al.* (1935) #205931, District Attorney's Closed Case Files, Municipal Archives.
21. For a similar point about the importance of numbers to African American women in Harlem, see Harris, *Sex Workers, Psychics, and Numbers Runners*, 54–93.
22. For a more detailed consideration of the legal situation, see White et al., *Playing the Numbers*, 126–30.
23. *New York Amsterdam News* (April 20, 1935), 1.
24. *New York Amsterdam News* (January 18, 1936), 1, 4.
25. *New York Amsterdam News* (June 21, 1933), 1, 4. This sense of rightful black ownership of numbers resonates with the idea of "community rights" explored in Shannon King, *Whose Harlem is This, Anyway?: Community Politics and Grassroots Activism During the New Negro Era* (New York: New York University Press, 2015).
26. *New York Amsterdam News* (June 21, 1933), 1, 4. On "Don't Buy Where You Can't Work," see Cheryl Lynn Greenberg, *"Or Does It Explode?": Black Harlem in the Great Depression* (New York: Oxford University Press, 1991), 114–39.
27. Ira Wolfert, *Tucker's People* (New York: L. B. Fischer, 1943), 58–59.
28. Wolfert, *Tucker's People*, 65–71.
29. Wolfert, *Tucker's People*, 80, 118.
30. David Thomson, "Was This the Most Dangerous Film in American History?," *New Republic*, July 29, 2012, https://newrepublic.com/article/105544/david-thomson-force-of-evil.
31. On Casper Holstein, see White et al., *Playing the Numbers*, 153–56.

9.

HARLEM, USA

Capital of the Black Freedom Movement

BRIAN PURNELL

In June 2016, Adriano D. Espaillat, who describes himself as "Latino of African descent," won a historic election.[1] For seventy-two years, an African American represented the black sections of northern Manhattan, including Harlem, in the United States Congress—first, Adam Clayton Powell Jr., from 1945 to 1971, and then, until 2017, Charles B. Rangel. Over the decades, Harlem's congressmen had served as national power brokers and senior leaders of the Democratic Party. Now, however, without an African American representing Harlem in Congress, many black Harlemites believed their political power was disappearing. Rudy Williams, age sixty-three, a substance abuse counselor and Harlem resident, said that Espaillat's win marked "the end of a culture." "We have no more face," said Reginald Jones, age fifty-one. "It's a perpetual loss of ground, a loss of the black community having identity." Espaillat offered his opponents an olive branch. "To those who voted for one of my worthy opponents, I pledge to work my heart out to represent you, knowing that our district is not a Latino or black or Asian district," Espaillat said. "It's a district that belongs to all of us, and we simply cannot succeed unless all of us are moving forward together." On the heels of twenty years of gentrification in the historic "capital of black America," the *New York Times* opined that Espaillat's victory "draw[s] the curtain on an era—already a long time in passing—in which Harlem was the center of black political power in New York City and beyond."[2]

But for all Harlem's renown as a historic "race capital" and an African American political power base, there has been little recognition of the sustained role the neighborhood played over several generations as the capital of America's black freedom movement. This movement, one of the most significant aspects of twentieth-century U.S. history, connects rarely to popular and scholarly histories of Harlem. And despite the existence of valuable scholarship that showcases the importance of Harlem to various aspects of the long black freedom movement, most overviews of this movement have relegated Harlem's significance to a short span of years during the interwar period.[3] This has obscured the critical ways Harlem has shaped political and social history over the course of the twentieth century.

Beyond the Marcus Garvey phenomenon of the interwar years, Harlem tends to come into view in histories of the black freedom movement only when the story shifts from the "civil rights" phase of activism, usually identified with a southern setting, to the "black power" phase, when activism was promoted by groups with major organizational bases in northern, midwestern, and western cities. A truncated history of the black power movement that starts in the mid-1960s overlooks many years in which Harlem served as a vital setting—a site of both "roots and routes"—for the actions, ideas, individuals, and organizations that made the modern black freedom movement.[4]

Notwithstanding the critiques of Harlem-centrism and Harlem exceptionalism, there remains much work to do to fill in gaps in our knowledge of the neighborhood. In some respects, we have yet to grapple with the extent of Harlem's reach and influence, particularly in the second half of the twentieth century.[5] Such a reassessment accords well with the broader historiographical shifts that have occurred over the past two decades, which have begun to examine the civil rights movement outside the South, and to debate the existence of a "long civil rights movement."[6] This literature has expanded our definition of civil rights beyond citizenship rights, capturing in turn the variety of campaigns that encompassed economic justice, electoral political power, black cultural expression, community organizing, and criminal justice, and recovering the diverse and formidable array of men *and* women who made the movement. It is through such lenses that it now becomes possible to recognize "Harlem, USA," as the neighborhood was designated in the 1960s, not merely as the somewhat nebulous "capital of black America" but also more concretely as the capital of the black freedom movement throughout much of the twentieth century.

The draw Harlem exerted on a variety of black activists and intellectuals from across the United States and beyond, from the 1910s to the 1960s, made it in effect the "address" of the long black freedom struggle—a known location where people, organizations, and ideas important to the movement could be reached and a place from which a great array of black political actions and ideas emanated. A formulation of Harlem as the movement's address suggests that the neighborhood's importance often lay in its multitude of *connections to*, and *two-way communications with*, other places, rather than in its separation from them. Harlem served as an incubator of black political ideas. It provided a training ground for a variety of activists, women and men whose actions and ideas made the history of the black freedom movement.

Harlem also was a hub, a point of disembarkation for black freedom movement activists and ideas and a terminal to which they returned. It was these multidirectional lines of connection, rather than any divergence from the broader patterns of black urban life and politics, that made Harlem the capital of the black freedom movement. Historians can avoid the temptation of creating new varieties of exceptionalism—whether of the Harlem or the southern varieties—while attending to the importance of place within the movement in general, and its northern (or "Freedom North") variants in particular.[7]

Capitals serve many purposes for a nation. They focus political power—or the quest for it. They produce representative cultural expressions and propel national economies. They cultivate intellectual debate and artistic creation. They attract people, change them, and send them back out into the wider world. In truth, no capital exerts a monopoly over the political, cultural, or intellectual life of a nation. During the twentieth century, numerous other places generated or molded vital elements of the African American freedom struggle. Oakland, from the 1940s through the late 1960s, was a key site where southern migrants engendered specific brands of black power radicalism. Detroit became a leading center of electoral and trade union power and radicalism. Twentieth-century Chicago was a rich seedbed of black literature, electoral politics, business development, consumerism, and activism. And Atlanta's influential black elite, university powerhouses, churches, and businesses set the stage for the Southern Christian Leadership Conference and the Student Nonviolent Coordinating Committee campaigns of the 1950s and 1960s.[8]

But if "black is a country," and if a long black freedom movement helps define this country, then Harlem is indeed its historic capital.[9] More (and more consistently) than any other location, it was Harlem that harbored connections and confluences of people from across the African diaspora, who found themselves thrown together into an urban crucible and who involved themselves in every type of political, intellectual, and cultural activism that constituted the black struggle. Harlem served as a clearinghouse and conduit, a place where people congregated, generated, and debated ideas; launched significant organizations, publications, and social movements; and worked to turn a century of freedom dreams into a world anew. Historians can connect the disparate dots of the black freedom movement through the history that flowed through, and from, Harlem.

Harlem's sustained significance to the black freedom struggle stemmed from histories of ideas and actions. First, Harlem emerged in the early decades of the twentieth century as an organizational base and intellectual hub for many influential black activists and political thinkers. Next, from the 1940s through to the 1960s, when Harlem typically recedes from survey narratives of the black freedom movement, the neighborhood became a pivotal center of black organizing and strategizing. Finally, in the late twentieth and early twenty-first centuries, Harlem incrementally lost its status as a movement capital, instead coming to symbolize for many the threatened loss of black urban places to gentrification and its attendant forms of demographic, structural, and physical change. Tracing Harlem's evolving significance over this century-long period highlights the neighborhood's contribution to the theory and practice of black politics. It also illuminates the nature of the black freedom struggle as, in the words of Vincent Harding, a "long continuous movement, flowing like a river."[10]

HARLEM STATE OF MIND

At first, Harlem confused Harry Haywood. When he arrived in New York after his discharge from the U.S. Army when World War I ended, this future leading intellectual of international communism called it "a strange city" and felt that "Harlem was different from what I had known on Chicago's South Side." Many black men and women, Haywood observed, worked in the city as domestics, cooks, and janitors. How, he wondered, could a black population so excluded from manufacturing jobs, and so socially separated from working-class whites, ever organize radical political movements? Slowly, though, the black metropolis that had so confounded Haywood emerged in his mind as "a powerful center of the Black liberation movement."[11]

As Harlem was transformed from the 1910s onward by streams of black migrants from the South and the Caribbean, the neighborhood became an environment that inspired black "freedom dreams."[12] The people who came to Harlem from the 1910s through the 1940s, the institutions they founded, the ideas they spread, and the intellectual and activist work they did made Harlem the capital of the modern black freedom movement. Multiple strains of "New Negro" militancy and leftist radicalism in the interwar years ensured that Harlem was symbolically identified with modern forms of black citizenship that reverberated around the world.[13]

During this early period, Hubert Harrison was one of Harlem's chief freedom dreamers. Alongside others, he established a mode of activist-intellectual work, oriented toward the masses, which made Harlem a center of black radical politics. From his arrival in New York from the Danish Caribbean island of Saint Croix, in 1900, to his death, in 1927, at the age of forty-four, Harrison wrote and lectured extensively—in halls and on the streets—on almost every major topic related to modern black activism in the United States: labor rights, women's rights, black empowerment, socialism, African and diaspora independence, the dangers of class hierarchy in black communities, and the importance of art and literature created by, and for, black people. W. A.

Domingo, the first editor of Marcus Garvey's newspaper, *Negro World*, said that Garvey, A. Philip Randolph, and the leading black activists of their generation "all followed Hubert Harrison."[14]

The story of how Garvey arrived in Harlem in 1916 and made the neighborhood the headquarters of his Universal Negro Improvement Association (UNIA) is well known.[15] He and his first wife, Amy Jacques, spread ideas about Pan-Africanism around the world, from Harlem, where the UNIA published *Negro World*, which Harrison edited for a time. The organization's Liberty Hall was located on 138th Street. By 1921, at least one million people followed Garvey as UNIA members.[16] Garveyites paraded through Harlem's streets, and thousands flocked to see their militaristic displays of black manhood. A famous photograph features a car driving through Harlem with a placard announcing, "The New Negro Has No Fear."[17] Harlem was a place that made it possible for black people to believe in a world where that slogan was true.

Radical socialists like Harrison, and Pan-Africanist nationalists like the Garveys, were joined by black civic nationalists in constructing Harlem as a symbolic place that represented manly black citizenship. Nothing exemplifies this aspect of the early history of the long black freedom movement more than the exploits of the U.S. 369th Infantry Regiment, one of the most successful combat units to fight in the French theater during World War I. During the 1910s, this all-black military unit fought at least two massive civil rights campaigns. The first involved its very right to exist during an age of Jim Crow segregation. The second occurred when American racism forced the soldiers of the 15th New York Guard (which became the U.S. 369th Regiment) to become attached to the French forces in order to fight in combat. Due to its exploits on the battlefield and the popularity throughout France of its famous jazz orchestra, the 369th became an internationally recognized symbol of black freedom, firmly associated with Harlem. Whether its members, who called themselves "Harlem's Rattlers" (though the regiment became known popularly as the "Harlem Hellfighters"), were traveling through liberated France or were parading up Fifth Avenue, they displayed tangible signs of black citizenship and equality that evoked an image of Harlem as unlike any other location in the United States.[18]

Harlem during the 1910s and 1920s became the black freedom movement's capital through the multiple ways its intellectuals and activists imagined black people's political possibilities. Alongside the Garvey movement, Harlem's ideological diversity was exemplified by the "race first" socialists of the African Blood Brotherhood, based in Harlem;[19] the black socialists and trade unionists around A. Philip Randolph and his publication, the *Messenger*;[20] and the Harlem branch of the Communist Party of the United States of America, which elevated a cadre of black women activists and which also made inroads into electoral politics through Vito Marcantonio and Benjamin Davis.[21] The interracial National Association for the Advancement of Colored People (NAACP), which had its national headquarters in Lower Manhattan, played a pivotal role in Harlem's identification with the long black freedom movement through the work of Sugar Hill resident W. E. B. Du Bois, who served as editor of its monthly magazine, *The Crisis*, from 1910 to 1933.[22]

Far from being dampened by the onset of the Great Depression, Harlem's New Negro militancy intensified during the 1930s. A broad array of organizations, from the Communist Party to the Harlem Housewives League, mounted economic boycotts of local merchants who refused to hire black workers. Violent convulsions in Harlem in March 1935 also established a new template for the American "race riot" as a minority community's assault against businesses, buildings, and policing practices that perpetuated racism.[23]

Harlem would also become the home base for twentieth-century black trade unionism's most important leader, A. Philip Randolph. A migrant from Florida, Randolph burst onto Harlem's stepladder-speaker stage in the 1910s, and he emerged in the 1940s at the head of the next phase of the black freedom movement. At the peak of Randolph's influence, Harlem had evolved from a place where diverse activist-intellectuals imagined black freedom and created institutions and organs that trumpeted radical ideas into an actual political power base for black freedom activists. Harlem became not just a state of mind but also the address of the modern black freedom movement.

ADDRESS OF THE LONG BLACK FREEDOM MOVEMENT

While interwar Harlem's political and cultural vibrancy has been a mainstay of histories of twentieth-century African American life, only a handful of scholars have explored Harlem's remarkable role from the 1940s through the 1960s as, in Martha Biondi's words, a "launching pad for the U.S. civil rights movement."[24] There is much that our understanding of the long black freedom struggle can gain by recognizing this role, and much remains to be said about Harlem's connections to civil rights campaigns elsewhere. Consider the standard recounting of the 1955–1956 bus boycott in Montgomery, Alabama. No other event is so widely considered to mark a turning point in the history of the black freedom movement. Rosa Parks and Martin Luther King Jr. emerged as national figures. The Southern Christian Leadership Conference blossomed. Nonviolent direct action became the national movement's primary protest tactic. A year of protest revealed a unified black community. Activist lawyers won a victory against racial segregation in the United States Supreme Court. Through black southerners' endeavors, American equality triumphed.[25] On the basis of this sketch, the Montgomery Bus Boycott has nothing to do with Harlem. A different picture appears, though, when we consider connections among people and organizations from around the country.

We find E. D. Nixon, Montgomery's activist lion, strategizing for decades, along with Rosa Parks, through the NAACP, to defeat Jim Crow. More than twenty-five years before the boycott, Nixon, a Pullman porter, had organized the Montgomery chapter of the all-black Brotherhood of Sleeping Car Porters union. As a Pullman porter, Nixon traveled the country. He knew about the union's strongholds in Harlem, where the union's dynamic leader, A. Philip Randolph—who also led the radical unionist National Negro Congress (NNC)—was based. Nixon knew of Harlem's brash congressman Adam Clayton Powell Jr. and of the successful protest that Powell, with support from the NNC, led against Jim Crow private bus companies in New York City. Nixon read black newspapers. Perhaps he read, in the May 3, 1941, edition of the *Pittsburgh Courier*, that "Militant Harlem Negroes have won their fight against the two big bus companies that monopolize bus traffic in their section of the metropolis, and have exacted an agreement to hire 170 colored drivers and maintenance men." Perhaps, fourteen years later, when Montgomery police arrested Rosa Parks, Nixon remembered that the same newspaper article stated, "If this can be done in New York, it can be done in other places, and should be done."[26]

Randolph's activism from the 1940s through the 1960s shows how Harlem functioned as an address of the black freedom movement. Randolph spent his entire public life (1911–1968) in Harlem. Beginning in the 1920s, Randolph organized the Brotherhood of Sleeping Car Porters, the nation's largest black trade union. For a time, he served as president of the NNC, a diverse national mass movement of radical and liberal black trade unionists that pushed to eliminate racism from America's labor movement. In 1940, Randolph's deep disagreements with communists ended his connection with the NNC, but he continued his leadership of the black freedom movement as the head of the all-black March on Washington Movement, a national effort to end racial discrimination in federally contracted industries and in the U.S. armed forces. Randolph's threat to bring 10,000 black people to march on Washington, DC, caused President Franklin D. Roosevelt to issue an executive order barring racial discrimination in employment at federally contracted firms and to create the Fair Employment Practices Commission. This represented unprecedented influence in national politics for a black social movement. The March on Washington Movement had national reach, but its leadership, and its organizational support from the NAACP and the National Urban League, was centered on New York City and, above all, on Harlem.[27]

Just as Garvey in the 1920s and Malcolm X in the 1960s were figureheads who gave Harlem both symbolic recognition and clout as the black freedom movement's capital, so too did Randolph, with his national role and platform, serve this function, especially during the 1940s. Yet most histories of the black freedom movement fail to recognize the extent of either Randolph's or Harlem's significance during this period. During and after World War II, the neighborhood incubated powerful grassroots struggles by black New Yorkers that yielded unprecedented municipal and state antidiscrimination laws targeting housing, employment, and education, which became models for federal civil rights laws.[28] Some of Harlem's mainstays during this time, like the actor, singer, and activist Paul Robeson, became victims of the Cold War purges against communists, but Randolph, along with another of the civil rights movement's most important, and least appreciated, figures, Ella Baker, carried the activism of the 1920s and 1930s into later decades and extended black Harlem's political importance through midcentury.

Depression-era Harlem served as a significant training ground for black freedom movement activists who would shape black activism on a national scale. It was from Harlem that Baker entered the world, armed with knowledge and experiences about radical politics. As a masterful facilitator, Baker had a profound influence on the most significant southern organizations and individuals in the black freedom movement. Compared with Harlem, no other black metropolis nurtured as many individuals who played significant roles in the black freedom movement from the 1940s through the 1960s. Whereas the male succession of Garvey, Randolph, and Malcolm X attained status as figureheads based in and associated with Harlem, Baker—along with Grace Campbell, Audley "Queen Mother" Moore, Esther Cooper Jackson, and others—never received this level of renown. These women were nonetheless vital in entrenching Harlem's capital status through the work they did in launching, building, and engineering political activism.[29]

Baker migrated to Harlem from North Carolina in 1927. Immediately, she became involved in radical activism and intellectual debate. She attended education programs at Harlem's 135th Street Library. Down the block, she "drank of the 'nectar divine' " from the stepladder orators on the corner of 135th Street and Seventh Avenue. She participated in political and cultural events at the Harlem YMCA. Barbara Ransby recounts that Baker joined other activist intellectuals, like Pauli Murray, and "represented a new model of black womanhood in this era. Untrammeled by attachments to either birth families or husbands, these women were adventuresome, educated, and ambitious." The Depression catalyzed the radicalism of Baker, Murray, the novelist Ann Petry, and other women in Harlem. Baker participated in Harlem's cooperative leagues. She worked with the journalist Marvel Cooke and wrote investigative reports on the exploitative labor conditions black domestics experienced. With Harlem as her base, Baker expanded her knowledge of workers' rights, community organizing, and political strategies.[30]

Baker credited her time in Harlem during the 1930s with turning her mind to all the radical possibilities of democratic activism. "New York was the hotbed of, let's call it radical thinking," Baker would remember. "You had every spectrum of radical thinking.... The ignorant ones, like me, we had lots of opportunity to hear and to evaluate whether or not this was the kind of thing you wanted to get into. Boy it was good, stimulating!"[31] She became the lead field organizer for the NAACP in the 1940s and journeyed south to support local leaders who formed branches and registered voters. She pushed the NAACP's national office to be more attentive to its members, especially those who faced persecution for their membership.[32] In the 1950s, she helped lead the Southern Christian Leadership Conference and eventually advised the student activists who formed the Student Nonviolent Coordinating Committee, in 1960.

Harlem between the 1920s and 1940s possessed a unique and unprecedented milieu that taught and trained black freedom activists like Baker. Despite a reorientation within recent historiography toward Freedom North studies, the significance of Harlem and New York to the post–World War II civil rights movement still does not receive the broad recognition it warrants. Imagine, however, what the civil rights movement of the 1950s and 1960s would have lost, had Baker not come to Harlem or had countless movement foot soldiers, such as Peggy Trotter Dammond Preacely, not learned how to become activists there.

Preacely was a Harlem resident who traveled south to work with the Student Nonviolent Coordinating Committee in Mississippi during the early 1960s. She remembered Harlem as "an incredible training ground for black activism. There were so many black organizations and institutions. . . . We heard Malcolm X speak at the local Muslim mosque, and we hung out late into the night at Micheaux's [sic] famous black bookstore on 125th Street." On Saturdays in the early 1960s, she and other young people picketed the local Woolworth's to show support for the southern students leading the sit-ins. "The people I picketed with in those days," Preacely remembered, "were both black and white, from my own Harlem community and from the whole of New York City."[33]

Many activists and intellectuals who shaped the black freedom movement came of age in Harlem. Could dynamic theories of black political movements in the latter half of the twentieth century have flourished without the lives and writings of the radical lesbian feminist poet Audre Lorde or the gay novelist, essayist, and orator James Baldwin, both Harlem born, who came of age in black Manhattan during the 1930s and 1940s?[34] Their lives make Harlem an essential place in any history of the black freedom movement.

As the modern black freedom movement's primary address, Harlem was not only a location that sent trained activists out into the world but also a place of arrival and return. The public life of Adam Clayton Powell Jr., the preacher turned politician, demonstrates how Harlem served as a kind of "return address" for the movement.[35] For twenty-five years, Harlem gave Powell a national bully pulpit. Through Powell, Harlem solidified its status as a national and international fulcrum of black political power.

In 1944, Powell's election made Harlem the second black metropolis (after Chicago) to send a black man to Congress. Powell's father was pastor of one of Harlem's largest black churches, Abyssinian Baptist. Powell Jr. became pastor in the late 1930s. At the same time, he also assumed a central role in Harlem's protests against job discrimination. This work connected him to Harlem's leftist black "united front" as well as to A. Philip Randolph and to Randolph's associate Bayard Rustin.[36]

During the mid-1930s, Powell organized Harlem's "Don't Buy Where You Can't Work" boycotts. By 1937, those efforts had created the Greater New York Coordinating Committee for Employment—207 groups with roughly 170,000 members. Powell used this base to launch more boycotts of Harlem's businesses that refused to hire or promote black workers. In 1941, Powell led the successful boycott of two private bus companies. This secured the promotion of some blacks from janitors to drivers, and it even instituted what would later be called "affirmative action" hiring goals, when the bus companies agreed to hire more black workers in the future to compensate for past discrimination.[37] From his position as one of Harlem's power brokers, Powell pushed for equality in jobs, black economic power, more black elected officials, and the importance of militant protest and black political and cultural solidarity. "The white man only respects two things," Powell told an audience in 1967, "your vote and your dollar." It was a message he had been promoting for thirty years.[38]

Like Garvey, Powell possessed international stature. In 1955, he was the only African American to attend the major Third World forum on decolonization, the Asian-African Conference for International Order, held in Bandung, Indonesia.[39] When two Indonesian delegates from Bandung visited the United States, they arrived first in Harlem. Powell gave them a tour and introduced them to another internationally known Harlem political figure, Malcolm X.[40] On a world stage, Powell and Malcolm X were treated as ambassadors, and Harlem was their capital.

The way the neighborhood itself served as a barometer of black political protest also made Harlem the capital city of the black freedom movement. Before Powell took office, another violent uprising had shaken the community, in 1943. Like the uprising of 1935, this communal discontent exploded after false rumors spread that police had killed an African American. Relations between blacks in Harlem and the city's police force were so strained that it was not outside Harlemites' imaginations that a police officer could unjustly murder a black citizen.

Harlem's uprisings in 1935, 1943, and 1964 all placed the neighborhood at the forefront of new forms of political dissent that rained violence upon those institutions that represented the worst forms of social alienation in the urban North: police, businesses, and housing. These "race riots" were unlike previous waves of racial violence in American cities, in which pitched battles had erupted between white and black citizens. During the mid-twentieth-century urban uprisings, police and National Guard troops unleashed the full power of state violence. They killed scores of black people. Black discontent manifested in rage that razed huge tracts of ghetto neighborhoods. Harlem, ground zero for so many of the campaigns and strategies that shaped twentieth-century black politics, had become a capital of the most radical forms of black protest, too.[41]

In 1937, not long after the first of these uprisings, Bayard Rustin arrived in New York. Rustin was a gay man who, during his early activist years, never freely expressed his sexuality. From the time he arrived, and throughout his decades of work with the national civil rights and labor organizing movements, New York City remained Rustin's home, "the place to which he would always return."[42] Harlem served as his political headquarters for roughly twenty-five years. He was Randolph's right-hand man during the March on Washington Movement. From Harlem, he carried the ethos of the economic and civil rights campaigns into the Fellowship of Reconciliation's Committee on Racial Equality, which became the Congress of Racial Equality, and, later, into the Southern Christian Leadership Conference's direct action campaigns.[43]

Randolph, Baker, Preacely, Powell, Rustin, Malcolm X, and many others represented links in chains that connected different eras of black protest to one another and rooted the long black freedom movement to its capital, Harlem. The continuities between the mid-twentieth-century phase of the long civil rights movement and the prior black civic radicalism of the earlier decades come into focus when we connect the dots between the influential figures of both periods. Martin Luther King Jr. became a national civil rights spokesman. The wing of the black freedom movement most associated with King had deep ties to the American labor movement. In 1963, King's leadership fulfilled A. Philip Randolph's vision of twenty years earlier, of a march on Washington to demand economic and civic justice.

That day, Randolph was at King's side. So was Rustin, the chief tactician of the march.[44] So, too, was Anna Arnold Hedgeman, an important organizer of the march and another under-recognized figure. Hedgeman was instrumental in mobilizing thousands of white people to join the march. She was one of a few black women seated on the dais at the Lincoln Memorial. She, too, embodied Harlem's role in this watershed moment. From the 1930s to the 1950s, Hedgeman had received a great deal of her political education in Harlem. She attained influence within New York City Mayor Robert Wagner's cabinet during the 1950s, although the racism and sexism of Democratic leaders often stifled her voice.[45]

From Randolph and Rustin and Hedgeman to King; from the Harlem activism of the 1930s, 1940s, and 1950s to August 28, 1963; from King's "I Have a Dream" speech to the decades of intellectual and political vibrancy that swirled around the streets of Harlem and impelled generations to keep alive a black movement for jobs and freedom—Harlem, seemingly absent from the history that made the March on Washington for Jobs and Freedom, assumes an integral place in the genesis of that important event. The editors of the New York–based movement periodical, *Freedomways*, recognized how the tumult of protest activity during the summer of 1963 connected black people around the country into a broad, national movement for black power. "This revolution of long-deferred equal rights," they wrote, "has linked the Negroes of Birmingham to those of Philadelphia, of Boston, of Saint Louis, of Cambridge, Maryland, of Harlem, New York, in one irrepressible marching column that is determined to secure a birth of freedom *here* and *now*."[46]

The international dimensions of Harlem's role as the American black freedom movement's capital become apparent through Malcolm X. A national minister of the Nation of Islam, Malcolm X's initial attraction to that organization's black nationalism had been due to its resemblance to the Garveyite teachings he had absorbed from his parents. Malcolm X was, in many ways, the heir of Harlem's lineage of black radical street intellectuals, stretching back to Hubert Harrison in the 1910s.[47] In Harlem during the 1940s, Malcolm X met the Communist organizer Vicki Garvin, who tried to recruit the young "Detroit Red" into the Communist Party of the United States of America. Garvin mentored Malcolm X. Later, she welcomed him into a community of African American activist expatriates in Ghana.[48]

Audley "Queen Mother" Moore, the sometime Garveyite, sometime communist, herself an institution in Harlem's black radicalism, inevitably crossed paths with Malcolm X. Moore lived for nearly a century and spent decades leading a global black movement that centered on black political power, reparations for slavery, and cultural identity rooted in African ancestry.[49] Through individuals such as Moore and Malcolm X, Harlem's radical milieu shaped, and was shaped by, circuits of black activism that extended across the world. For a time, globe-trotting leaders of emerging black and Third World nations would be drawn inexorably to the African American movement's capital, Harlem, USA.

HARLEM IS EVERYWHERE

The black freedom movement's historic capital has moved in two different directions in the decades since the 1960s. For a time, Harlem retained its character as a unique "setting and symbol" of black political activism, but in its politics, as in its environment and daily life, Harlem gradually became more generic, one of many places where urban black Americans experienced the late twentieth- and early twenty-first-century struggles with crime and drugs, mass incarceration, urban redevelopment, and gentrification. By the early 2000s, Harlem was everywhere—still a symbol of black identity in the United States, still recognizable around the world as an iconic black metropolis, but no longer a capital city of black political activism.

In the peak years of the black power movement and of Third World liberation struggles, Harlem remained a hub of political radicalism. A short distance from the United Nations headquarters, the neighborhood was a meeting place for anticolonial revolutionaries and visiting heads of state from newly independent African countries. In the late 1950s, Ghana's Kwame Nkrumah and the Guinean political leader Sékou Touré both visited the neighborhood. Harlem's black nationalist community was left electrified by the speech the Congo's independence leader, Patrice Lumumba, gave at the Henry Lincoln Johnson Lodge on 126th Street. When, in September 1960, Cuba's revolutionary leader, Fidel Castro, relocated to the iconic Hotel Theresa on Seventh Avenue during his visit to the United Nations, he confirmed Harlem's global importance to revolutionary politics. Both Touré and Castro met with Malcolm X during their visits. The speeches that all of these leaders gave in Harlem coupled the struggle against American racism with global decolonization movements. Moreover, their presence in Harlem underscored the area's importance as a site of black radical global politics.[50]

Such qualities were certainly evident to Malcolm X, who regarded Harlemites as "the most wide-awake, race-conscious black people in America":

> With the United Nations here in New York City, and the many delegates from Africa & Asia constantly mingling with the people of Harlem, the thinking of our people is automatically in tune with current events at an international level. And with New York's 9 daily newspapers, 7 television channels, and an innumerable number of radio stations constantly showering him with "up to the minute news reports from all over the world"—its [sic] just impossible for the black man in Harlem to remain asleep.[51]

Harlemites continued to be at the forefront of mass expressions of black discontent when, during the summer of 1964, Harlem's uprising (which quickly spread to Brooklyn's Bedford–Stuyvesant) set the pattern for the "long, hot summers" of violence that engulfed hundreds of U.S. cities in the mid- to late 1960s. As in 1935 and 1943, the violence Harlemites initiated unleashed their pent-up frustrations with limited civil rights gains that had little or no effect on the everyday lives of black people in Harlem.[52]

The 1964 Harlem uprising also fired the black nationalist imaginations of writers and artists who made Harlem—and particularly Amiri Baraka's Black Arts Repertory Theatre/School, on 135th Street—the most important incubator of the black arts movement, which spread rapidly across U.S. cities. As James de Jongh has shown, Harlem's uprising became a symbol of "apocalypse and revelation" and of a resurgence of militant race pride, in the poems of Lucia Martin, Bob Allen, Calvin Hernton, and David Henderson.[53]

Harlem's importance as a base for black political organizing persisted through the mid-1970s. The long-standing Pan-African character of its political activism was extended with the formation of nationally important groups such as Blacks in Solidarity with South African Liberation and the Patrice Lumumba Coalition. Both of these organizations were at the forefront of U.S.-based campaigns for African liberation in the mid-1970s, organizing boycotts against companies that conducted business with apartheid and colonial regimes and petitioning the United Nations against seating the South African delegation.[54]

By the mid-1980s, though, Harlem no longer drew in an array of dynamic black political activists from across, and beyond, the United States. While the Harlem Tenants Council and other activist groups made the community a notable battleground in resistance to gentrification, and while the neighborhood's streets still host protests and rallies with regularity, Harlem no longer serves as a training ground for black activists who fan out across the country, spreading the ideas and strategies that propel a black freedom movement.[55] Rather, Harlem's history since the 1980s is characterized more by commonplace connections with black urban communities across the nation that have struggled against the effects of poverty, drugs, police brutality, and displacement.

Several factors account for Harlem's loss of status as capital of the black freedom movement. Four decades of economic and social policies tied to globalization, neoliberalism, and mass incarceration fundamentally disrupted Harlem's ability to serve as a hub, or a clearing house, of radical black social movement politics. Gentrification fundamentally transformed Harlem's ability to house masses of diverse black people committed to radical political change.[56] Mass incarceration policies decimated Harlem's already tenuous social and political capital. For a while, the Harlem activists whom the sociologist Michael Javen Fortner has called the "black silent majority" led a political movement that advocated tougher prosecution of illegal drug users and sellers. The punitive policies and increased policing for which they advocated became laws, and eventually metastasized into the mass incarceration crisis that afflicts contemporary black metropolises. Harlem became, in the words of Leith Mullings, "a community whipsawed by the drug epidemic and the so-called war on drugs." As in black urban centers throughout the country, these policies did inestimable damage to Harlemites' abilities to build broad, radical social movements.[57]

The concomitant erosion of the labor movement (which had made possible the rise of a person like Randolph) and of the urban liberal ethos of the Democratic Party (which had made possible the rise of a radical like Powell) knocked Harlem off the power axes that had made it such a dynamic place for radical politics.[58] Relatedly, the primary political ideologies—socialism, communism, black internationalism, Pan-Africanism, radical black nationalism, and liberal civic nationalism—that had developed in Harlem over the course of fifty years, promoted the growth of numerous institutions and organizations (the UNIA, African Blood Brotherhood, NAACP, Congress of Racial Equality, Communist Party of the United States of America, March on Washington Movement, NNC,

Organization of Afro-American Unity, and so many others), inspired and trained a bevy of intellectuals and leaders, and connected Harlem to black movement centers around the world lost their powerful influence over black mass movements. Remnants of various forms of black radicalism remain, but in the absence of liberation ideologies that globally inspired so many dynamic African diasporic movements and thinkers—that made Harlem's Malcolm X into a major international theorist of Pan-African liberation—Harlem's position as a capital of black freedom intellectualism and activism no longer exists.

Such a state of affairs makes contemporary Harlem's politics generic but does not diminish Harlem's historical position as capital of the modern black freedom movement. Harlem was the principal place from which black freedom ideas and actions originated and spread, and the place with which leaders from around the world identified modern black power. In the midst of the community's many struggles over its identity as a black metropolis, Harlem's history as the capital of the black freedom movement deserves recognition and analysis.[59]

The Black Lives Matter movement that has arisen over the past few years indicates that, in the age of social media, ideas and tactics circulate with such rapidity through activist networks linking multiple locations that a movement capital might now be an anachronism. But for historians seeking to reckon with the nature of the black freedom movement in the twentieth century, the many pathways that brought generations of activists to and from New York should underscore the words of Harold Cruse, writing in 1967: "The truth of the matter is that Harlem has, in this century, become the most strategically important community of black America. . . . The trouble is that Harlem has never been adequately analyzed in such terms."[60]

NOTES

1. Cameron Joseph, "New York's Newest Congressman Adriano Espaillat to Make History," *New York Daily News*, January 3, 2017, http://www.nydailynews.com/news/politics/new-york-newest-congressman-adriano-espaillat-history-article-1.2932252.
2. William Neuman and Samantha Schmidt, "After Congressional Primary, Harlem's Reign as a Power Base May be Over," *New York Times*, June 29, 2016.
3. For important works that address Harlem's significance during particular phases of the long black freedom struggle, see Mark Naison, *Communists in Harlem During the Great Depression* (Urbana: University of Illinois Press, 1983); Martha Biondi, *To Stand and Fight: The Struggle for Civil Rights in Postwar New York City* (Cambridge, MA: Harvard University Press, 2003); Stefan M. Bradley, *Harlem vs. Columbia University: Black Student Power in the Late 1960s* (Urbana: University of Illinois Press, 2009); Adina Back, "Exposing the 'Whole Segregation Myth': The Harlem Nine and New York City's School Desegregation Battles," in *Freedom North: Black Freedom Struggles Outside the South, 1940–1980*, ed. Jeanne Theoharis and Komozi Woodward (New York: Palgrave Macmillan,

2003), 65-91; Thomas J. Sugrue, *Sweet Land of Liberty: The Forgotten Struggle for Civil Rights in the North* (New York: Random House, 2008), esp. chaps. 3, 6-10, 12; Peniel E. Joseph, *Waiting 'Til The Midnight Hour: A Narrative History of Black Power in America* (New York: Henry Holt, 2006), esp. chaps. 1, 2, 6; Mandi Jackson, "Harlem's Rent Strike and Rat War: Representation, Housing Access and Tenant Resistance in New York, 1958-1964," *American Studies* 47 (Spring 2006): 53-79; Shannon King, *Whose Harlem Is This, Anyway?: Community Politics and Grassroots Activism During the New Negro Era* (New York: New York University Press, 2015).

4. Martha Biondi reveals how black New Yorkers during and after World War II pioneered struggles over housing, education, employment, and police brutality that laid groundwork for the northern mobilizations of the 1960s and 1970s. See Biondi, *To Stand and Fight*. The roles of Malcolm X and Harlem in the earlier phases of black power politics are explored in Peniel E. Joseph, "Malcolm X's Harlem and Black Power Activism," in *Neighborhood Rebels: Black Power at the Local Level*, ed. Peniel E. Joseph (New York: Palgrave Macmillan, 2010), 21-44; Manning Marable, *Malcolm X: A Life of Reinvention* (New York: Viking, 2011), esp. chaps. 2, 4, 7, 9-10, 12. On the significance of "roots and routes," see Paul Gilroy, "Roots and Routes: Black Identity as an Outernational Project," in *Racial and Ethnic Identity: Psychological Development and Creative Expression*, ed. Herbert W. Harris et al. (New York: Routledge, 1995), 15-30; Rhonda Y. Williams, *Concrete Demands: The Search for Black Power in the 20th Century* (New York: Routledge, 2015), esp. quote at 3.

5. A key work that addresses this exceptionalism is King, *Whose Harlem Is This, Anyway?*, 1-12. See also Davarian L. Baldwin and Minkah Makalani, eds., *Escape from New York: The New Negro Renaissance Beyond Harlem* (Minneapolis: University of Minnesota Press, 2013). *Escape from New York* limits Harlem's significance to the interwar years, a restriction that the present essay seeks to address.

6. On the benefits of a "long civil rights movement" frame, see especially Jacqueline Dowd Hall, "The Long Civil Rights Movement and the Political Uses of the Past," *Journal of American History* 91 (March 2005): 1233-63. See also Brian Purnell, "Freedom North Studies, the Long Civil Rights Movement, and Twentieth-Century Liberalism in American Cities," *Journal of Urban History* 42 (May 2016): 634-40.

7. Brian Purnell, "The Civil Rights Era and Southern History," *Reviews in American History* 42 (December 2014): 718-29. See also Alex Lichtenstein, "The Other Civil Rights Movement and the Problem of Southern Exceptionalism," *Journal of the Historical Society* 11 (September 2011): 351-76; Clarence Lang, "Locating the Civil Rights Movement: An Essay on the Deep South, Midwest, and Border South in Black Freedom Studies," *Journal of Social History* 47 (Winter 2013): 371-400.

8. On Oakland, see, for example, Donna Murch, *Living for the City: Migration, Education, and the Rise of the Black Panther Party in Oakland, California* (Chapel Hill: University of North Carolina Press, 2010). On Detroit, Dan Georgakas and Marvin Surkin, *Detroit: I Do Mind Dying—A Study in Urban Revolution*, 3rd ed. (Chicago: Haymarket, 2012). On Chicago, Adam Green, *Selling the Race: Culture, Community, and Black Chicago, 1940-1955* (Chicago: University of Chicago Press, 2007). On Atlanta, Maurice J. Hobson, *The Legend of the Black Mecca: Politics and Class in the Making of Modern Atlanta* (Chapel Hill: University of North Carolina Press, 2017).

9. LeRoi Jones (Amiri Baraka), "Black Is a Country" (1962), reprinted in LeRoi Jones, *Home: Social Essays* (1966; Hopewell, NJ: Ecco, 1998), 82-86. On the currency the "black belt thesis" held in Harlem's political circles in the 1920s, see Gerald Horne, *Black Liberation/Red Scare: Ben Davis and the Communist Party* (Newark: University of Delaware, 1994), 68-69.

10. Vincent Harding, *There Is a River: The Black Struggle for Freedom in America* (New York: Harcourt Brace, 1981), xix.
11. Harry Haywood, *Black Bolshevik: Autobiography of an Afro-American Communist* (Chicago: Liberator, 1978), 349–50.
12. Robin D. G. Kelley, *Freedom Dreams: The Black Radical Imagination* (Boston: Beacon Press, 2002). On Harlem's status as a cosmopolitan "black contact zone," see Winston James, "Harlem's Difference," present volume.
13. On the late nineteenth and early twentieth centuries, see Gilbert Osofsky, *Harlem: The Making of a Ghetto—Negro New York, 1890–1930* (New York: Harper and Row, 1966); Nathan Irvin Huggins, *Harlem Renaissance* (New York: Oxford University Press, 1971); David Levering Lewis, *When Harlem Was in Vogue* (New York: Alfred A. Knopf, 1981); George Chauncey, *Gay New York: Gender, Urban Culture, and the Making of the Gay Male World, 1890–1940* (New York: Basic Books, 1994); Irma Watkins-Owens, *Blood Relations: Caribbean Immigrants and the Harlem Community, 1900–1930* (Bloomington: Indiana University Press, 1996); Kevin McGruder, *Race and Real Estate: Conflict and Cooperation in Harlem, 1890–1920* (New York: Columbia University Press, 2015); King, *Whose Harlem Is This, Anyway?*
14. Jeffrey B. Perry, ed., *A Hubert Harrison Reader* (Middletown, CT: Wesleyan University Press, 2001), 1–2; Hubert Harrison, "Prejudice Growing Less and Cooperation More," *Pittsburgh Courier*, January 29, 1927, reprinted in Perry, *Hubert Harrison Reader*, 252. See also Jeffrey B. Perry, *Hubert Harrison: The Voice of Harlem Radicalism, 1883–1918* (New York: Columbia University Press, 2009); Winston James, *Holding Aloft the Banner of Ethiopia: Caribbean Radicalism in Early Twentieth-Century America* (New York: Verso, 1998), 122–231.
15. Robert A. Hill and Barbara Blair, eds., *Marcus Garvey: Life and Lessons* (Berkeley: University of California Press, 1987), xv–lxiii, 33–110; Ula Taylor, *The Veiled Garvey: The Life and Times of Amy Jacques Garvey* (Chapel Hill: University of North Carolina Press, 2002), 1–40; Colin Grant, *Negro with a Hat: The Rise and Fall of Marcus Garvey* (New York: Oxford University Press, 2008), esp. 73–94; James, *Holding Aloft the Banner of Ethiopia*, 134–56.
16. Rod Bush, *We Are Not What We Seem: Black Nationalism and Class Struggle in the American Century* (New York: New York University Press, 1999), 96.
17. Reproduced in Davarian L. Baldwin, "Introduction: New Negroes Forging a New World," in Baldwin and Makalani, *Escape from New York*, 14–15.
18. Jeffrey T. Sammons and John H. Morrow Jr., *Harlem's Rattlers and the Great War: The Undaunted 369th Regiment and the African American Quest for Equality* (Lawrence: University Press of Kansas, 2014). See also R. Reid Badger, "James Reese Europe and the Prehistory of Jazz," *American Music* 7 (Spring 1989): 48–67.
19. Minkah Makalani, *In the Cause of Freedom: Radical Black Internationalism from Harlem to London, 1917–1939* (Chapel Hill: University of North Carolina Press, 2011); James, *Holding Aloft the Banner of Ethiopia*, 155–84.
20. Jervis Anderson, *A. Philip Randolph: A Biographical Portrait* (New York: Harcourt Brace, 1972); Theodore Kornweibel Jr., *No Crystal Stair: Black Life and the Messenger, 1917–1928* (Westport, CT: Greenwood, 1975); Paula F. Pfeffer, *A. Philip Randolph: Pioneer of the Civil Rights Movement* (Baton Rouge: Louisiana State University Press, 1990); Andrew E. Kersten and Clarence Lang, eds., *Reframing Randolph: Labor, Black Freedom, and the Legacies of A. Philip Randolph* (New York: New York University Press, 2015).
21. Erik McDuffie, *Sojourning for Freedom: Black Women, American Communism, and the Making of Black Left Feminism* (Durham, NC: Duke University Press, 2011). On Vito Marcantonio, see Gerald Meyer, *Vito Marcantonio: Radical Politician, 1902–1954* (Albany: State

University of New York Press, 1989). On Benjamin Davis, see Horne, *Black Liberation/Red Scare*. An excellent general history is Naison, *Communists in Harlem*.

22. David Levering Lewis, *W. E. B. Du Bois: Biography of a Race, 1868–1919* (New York: Henry Holt, 1993), esp. chaps. 14–15, 17; David Levering Lewis, *W. E. B. Du Bois: The Fight for Equality and the American Century, 1919–1963* (New York: Henry Holt, 2000), esp. chaps. 1–9. See also Patricia Sullivan, *Lift Every Voice: The NAACP and the Making of the Civil Rights Movement* (New York: New Press, 2009), 25–60.
23. Cheryl Greenberg, "The Politics of Disorder: Reexamining Harlem's Riots of 1935 and 1943," *Journal of Urban History* 18 (August 1992): 395–441. See also Elliot Rudwick and August Meier, "Black Violence in the Twentieth Century: A Study in Rhetoric and Retaliation," in August Meier and Elliot Rudwick, *Along the Color Line: Explorations in the Black Experience* (Urbana: University of Illinois Press, 1976), 224–37.
24. Biondi, *To Stand and Fight*, 1.
25. See, for example, the account in David J. Garrow, *Bearing the Cross: Martin Luther King, Jr., and the Southern Christian Leadership Conference* (New York: Quill, 1986), 11–82.
26. "Harlem's Bus Victory," *Pittsburgh Courier*, May 3, 1941.
27. Erik S. Gellman, " 'The Spirit and Strategy of the United Front': Randolph and the National Negro Congress, 1936–1940," in Kersten and Lang, *Reframing Randolph*, 129–62; Sugrue, *Sweet Land of Liberty*, 59–86; Pfeffer, *A. Philip Randolph*, 45–88. The March on Washington Movement gathered 18,000 to 20,000 people at Madison Square Garden on June 16, 1942. Historian Glenda Gilmore has called this event "the largest black rally to date" to occur up to and including the New Deal and World War II period. In addition to Randolph, in attendance were Mary McLeod Bethune, leader of the National Council of Negro Women and member of President Roosevelt's "Black Cabinet"; Walter White, head of the National Association for the Advancement of Colored People; and Pauli Murray and Adam Clayton Powell Jr., both at the start of their long careers as black freedom movement activists. See Glenda Elizabeth Gilmore, *Defying Dixie: The Radical Roots of Civil Rights, 1919–1950* (New York: W. W. Norton, 2009), 366–67.
28. Biondi, *To Stand and Fight*.
29. See Minkah Makalani, "Black Women's Intellectual Labor and the Social Spaces of Black Radical Thought in Harlem," present volume.
30. Barbara Ransby, *Ella Baker and the Black Freedom Movement: A Radical Democratic Vision* (Chapel Hill: University of North Carolina Press, 2003), 67, 71. On Pauli Murray, see Rosalind Rosenberg, *Jane Crow: The Life of Pauli Murray* (New York: Oxford University Press, 2017). On Marvel Cooke, see LaShawn Harris, "Marvel Cooke: Investigative Journalist, Communist, and Black Radical Subject," *Journal of the Study of Radicalism* 6 (Fall 2012): 91–126. On Ann Petry, see Farah Jasmine Griffin, *Harlem Nocturne: Women Artists and Progressive Politics During World War II* (New York: Basic Civitas, 2013), 79–131.
31. Ella Baker, quoted in Ellen Cantarow with Susan G. O'Malley and Sharon Hartman Strom, *Moving the Mountain: Women Working for Social Change* (Old Westbury, NY: Feminist Press, 1980), 64.
32. Charles M. Payne, *I've Got the Light of Freedom: The Organizing Tradition and the Mississippi Freedom Struggle* (Berkeley: University of California Press, 1996), 67–102.
33. Peggy Trotter Dammond Preacely, "It Was Simply in My Blood," in *Hands on the Freedom Plow: Personal Accounts by Women in SNCC*, ed. Faith S. Holsaert et al. (Urbana: University of Illinois Press, 2010), 166. See also David Emblidge, "Rallying Point: Lewis Michaux's National Memorial African Bookstore," *Publishing Research Quarterly* 24 (December 2008): 267–76.

34. See Audre Lorde, *Zami: A New Spelling of My Name* (1982; Freedom, CA: Crossing Press, 1997); James Baldwin, *The Price of the Ticket: Collected Nonfiction, 1948–1985* (New York: St. Martin's/Marek, 1985).
35. On how Marcus Garvey's newspaper, *Negro World*, "gave black internationalism, for the first time, a return address," see Michael O. West and William G. Martin, "Introduction: Contours of the Black International—From Toussaint to Tupac," in *From Toussaint to Tupac: The Black International Since the Age of Revolution*, ed. Michael O. West, William G. Martin, and Fanon Che Wilkins (Chapel Hill: University of North Carolina Press, 2009), 10.
36. Adam Clayton Powell Jr., *Adam by Adam: The Autobiography of Adam Clayton Powell, Jr.* (New York: Dafina, 1971), 1–21, 46–54, 77–84. See also Biondi, *To Stand and Fight*, 1–66.
37. On "Don't Buy Where You Can't Work" campaigns, see Cheryl Lynn Greenberg, *"Or Does It Explode?": Black Harlem in the Great Depression* (New York: Oxford University Press, 1991), 114–39, esp. 131–36. On the 1941 Harlem bus boycott campaign, see Dominic J. Capeci Jr., "From Harlem to Montgomery: The Bus Boycotts and Leadership of Adam Clayton Powell Jr. and Martin Luther King Jr.," *Historian* 41 (August 1979): 721–37.
38. On Powell's philosophy of black protest, see Adam Clayton Powell Jr., *"Keep the Faith, Baby!,"* LP record (Jubilee Records, 1967), https://www.youtube.com/watch?v=9GgVXvNpDEk (side 1) and https://www.youtube.com/watch?v=9gmy6pEO1io (side 2). See also Adam Clayton Powell Jr., *Keep the Faith, Baby!* (New York: Trident, 1967).
39. Powell, *Adam by Adam*, 102–17; Brenda Gayle Plummer, *Rising Wind: Black Americans and U.S. Foreign Affairs, 1935–1960* (Chapel Hill: University of North Carolina Press, 1996), 249–54.
40. Louis A. DeCaro Jr., *On the Side of My People: A Religious Life of Malcolm X* (New York: New York University Press, 1996), 123–24.
41. Greenberg, "Politics of Disorder." See also Dominic J. Capeci Jr., *The Harlem Riot of 1943* (Philadelphia, PA: Temple University Press, 1977); Themis Chronopoulos, "Police Misconduct, Community Opposition, and Urban Governance in New York City, 1945–1965," *Journal of Urban History* 44 (July 2018): 643–68.
42. Jerald Podair, *Bayard Rustin: American Dreamer* (New York: Rowman and Littlefield, 2009), 14.
43. John D'Emilio, *Lost Prophet: The Life and Times of Bayard Rustin* (Chicago: University of Chicago Press, 2004); *Brother Outsider: The Life of Bayard Rustin*, directed by Nancy Kates and Bennett Singer (Passion River Studio, 2010).
44. On Rustin and the March on Washington, see Podair, *Bayard Rustin*, 49–66.
45. Jennifer Scanlon, *Until There Is Justice: The Life of Anna Arnold Hedgeman* (New York: Oxford University Press, 2016), esp. 151–71.
46. "Harlem—A Community in Transition," *Freedomways* 3 (Summer 1963): 261–62 (emphasis in original).
47. Perry, *Hubert Harrison Reader*, 2.
48. Dayo F. Gore, "From Communist Politics to Black Power: The Visionary Politics and Transnational Solidarities of Victoria "Vicki" Ama Garvin," in *Want to Start a Revolution?: Radical Women in the Black Freedom Struggle*, ed. Dayo F. Gore, Jeanne Theoharris, and Komozi Woodard (New York: New York University Press, 2009), 72–94.
49. Erik S. McDuffie, " 'I Wanted a Communist Philosophy, but I Wanted Us to Have a Chance to Organize Our People': The Diasporic Radicalism of Queen Mother Audley Moore and the Origins of Black Power," *African and Black Diaspora: An International Journal* 3 (July 2010): 181–95.

50. Brenda Gayle Plummer, "Castro in Harlem: A Cold War Watershed," in *Rethinking the Cold War*, ed. Allen Hunter (Philadelphia, PA: Temple University Press, 1998), 133–56; Joseph, "Malcolm X's Harlem"; Jason Parker " 'Capital of the Caribbean': The African American–West Indian Harlem Nexus and the Transnational Drive for Black Freedom, 1940–1948," *Journal of African American History* 89 (Spring 2004): 98–117; Garrett Felber, " 'Harlem Is the Black World': The Organization of Afro-American Unity at the Grassroots," *Journal of African American History* 100 (Spring 2015): 199–225.
51. Malcolm X, untitled script of radio broadcast for the Mr. Muhammad Speaks series, script no. 33, n.d. [early 1960s], 5–6, folder 6, box 6, reel 6, Malcolm X Collection, Schomburg Center for Research in Black Culture, New York City. I thank Daniel Matlin for sharing this quotation with me.
52. Michael W. Flamm, *In the Heat of the Summer: The New York Riots of 1964 and the War on Crime* (Philadelphia: University of Pennsylvania Press, 2017). See also *The Kerner Report: The National Advisory Commission on Civil Disorders* (Princeton, NJ: Princeton University Press, 2016).
53. James de Jongh, *Vicious Modernism: Black Harlem and the Literary Imagination* (Cambridge: Cambridge University Press, 1990), 146–77. On Harlem's role in the black arts movement, see James Smethurst, *The Black Arts Movement: Literary Nationalism in the 1960s and 1970s* (Chapel Hill: University of North Carolina Press, 2005), 100–178.
54. Francis Njubi Nesbitt, *Race for Sanctions: African Americans Against Apartheid, 1946–1994* (Bloomington: Indiana University Press, 2004); Robin D. G. Kelley and Betsy Esch, "Black Like Mao: Red China and Black Revolution," *Souls* 1 (Fall 1999): 6–41.
55. Kelly Bit, "Harlem Residents: Clinton Is Symbol of Gentrification," *New York Sun*, July 20, 2006, http://www.nysun.com/new-york/harlem-residents-clinton-is-symbol/36435.
56. Johanna Fernandez, "The Fire This Time: Harlem and Its Discontents at the Turn of the Century," in *Dispatches from the Ebony Tower: Intellectuals Confront the African American Experience*, ed. Manning Marable (New York: Columbia University Press, 2000), 108–20. See also Michael Henry Adams, "The End of Black Harlem," *New York Times*, May 27, 2016, http://www.nytimes.com/2016/05/29/opinion/sunday/the-end-of-black-harlem.html; John Del Signore, "Harlem Rents are 90 Damn Percent Higher than in 2002," June 8, 2015, http://gothamist.com/2015/06/08/rents_in_harlem_are_90_damn_percent.php; Robert Kolker, "Whose Harlem Is It?," *New York Magazine*, July 6, 2008, http://nymag.com/realestate/features/48328.
57. Michael Javen Fortner, *Black Silent Majority: The Rockefeller Drug Laws and the Politics of Punishment* (Cambridge, MA: Harvard University Press, 2015). See also Donna Murch, "Who's to Blame for Mass Incarceration?," *Boston Review*, October 16, 2015, http://bostonreview.net/books-ideas/donna-murch-michael-javen-fortner-black-silent-majority; Michael Javen Fortner, "Historical Method and the Nobel Lie: A Reply to Donna Murch," *Boston Review*, October 23, 2015, http://bostonreview.net/books-ideas/response-michael-javen-fortner-donna-murch-black-silent-majority; Leith Mullings, "Losing Ground," *Souls* 5 (June 2003): 1–21.
58. On the ways in which mass incarceration and the "war on crime" facilitated the decline of the labor movement and Democratic liberalism, see Heather Ann Thompson, "Why Mass Incarceration Matters: Rethinking Crisis, Decline, and Transformation in Postwar American History," *Journal of American History* 97 (December 2010): 703–34, esp. 716–34.
59. Sam Roberts, "No Longer Majority Black, Harlem Is in Transition," *New York Times*, January 5, 2010, http://www.nytimes.com/2010/01/06/nyregion/06harlem.html.
60. Harold Cruse, *The Crisis of the Negro Intellectual: A Historical Analysis of the Failure of Black Leadership* (New York: William Morrow, 1967), 11–12.

10.

RICHARD BRUCE NUGENT AND THE QUEER MEMORY OF HARLEM

DOROTHEA LÖBBERMANN

In one of the founding narratives of Queer Harlem, the aspiring artist and writer Paul Arbian is found dead in a bathtub, flamboyantly dressed, wrists slit with an ornamented dagger. Arranged on the floor, and made unreadable by the bloodied waters spilling from the tub, lies the manuscript of his novel, which had been destined to become the masterpiece of the Harlem Renaissance. It is dedicated to J. K. Huysmans's decadent character Jean Des Esseintes and to Oscar Wilde, "whose golden spores of decadent pollen / I shall broadcast and fertilize / It is written."[1]

Arbian's suicide is the final scene of Wallace Thurman's novel *Infants of the Spring* (1932), the roman à clef of the younger generation of Harlem artists who protested the confines that the burden of representation had imposed on African American writers, painters, and other artists. A decadent gesture of "renunciation and repudiation," Arbian's suicide symbolizes the end of the Harlem Renaissance, an era that, in the eyes of Thurman, had failed to produce the art it had promised.[2] Arbian's death also symbolizes the turn from experience to memory, ringing in the myriad retrospective attempts to interpret the Harlem Renaissance, of which *Infants of the Spring* was among the first.

But the founding narrative of Queer Harlem continues beyond the novel; the man on whom the character Paul Arbian is based refused to die young. Richard Bruce Nugent (1906–1987), whose initials, RBN, resound in the character's last name, was one of the few artists of the Harlem Renaissance to live until the 1980s. Although proficient in many arts, Nugent stopped publishing and dropped from the limelight in the 1930s, before resurfacing in the 1980s, when scholarly interest in the Harlem Renaissance burgeoned and he was identified as an important witness to the period. Consequently, his small published oeuvre was rediscovered. His lyrical short story "Smoke, Lilies and Jade" (1926) became known as the first piece of black gay/queer literature; his scattered writings, some of which found posthumous publication, were archived at Yale; and two films—Isaac Julien's *Looking for Langston* (1989) and Rodney Evans's *Brother to Brother* (2004)—established him as one of the key ancestors of contemporary black gay/queer consciousness and art.[3]

While Queer Harlem's founding myth begins in the realm of fiction, it continues as a real-world narrative of survival. It embraces death, the imminent presence of which has characterized gay culture since the onslaught of HIV/AIDS in the 1980s, but it also transcends death to celebrate gay/queer life and creativity. It moves back and forth between fiction and history, the past and the present.

It is no surprise that Bruce Nugent became a kind of patron saint for a Queer Harlem. An accomplished actor and dancer, illustrator and painter, and writer of prose, poetry, and memoir, Nugent represents Harlem's manifold forms of creativity. His known literary work ranges from the few poems, stories, and short essays published during his lifetime to his posthumously published writings, among them the novel *Gentleman Jigger* (2008), which was begun during the 1920s, in parallel with Thurman's *Infants of the Spring*. His publication history, therefore, necessitates jumps in time, as do the many interviews he gave in later years, on which much of the canonical scholarship on the Harlem Renaissance is based.

Through his close connections to Greenwich Village and Washington, DC, his European travels, and his later residence in Hoboken, New Jersey, Nugent symbolizes the porousness of Harlem, its openness to other boroughs, cities, and countries, even its transnationality. As a "Black Dandy," both product of and rebel against capitalist modernity, he traverses various social classes, exploiting the social capital of having been born into Washington's black elite but refusing to be tied to its norms.[4] As a bon vivant, he emphasizes the sensual and affective that, in earlier assessments of the Harlem Renaissance, had been understood as something the African American experience could contribute to American modernism and that, in contemporary approaches, has had an important theoretical impact, not least on the construction of memory. Most of all, Nugent—whose own light complexion, and whose work's themes of bisexuality and desire for white men allowed him to oscillate between black and white, gay and straight—has invited discussion about race, gender, and sexuality from a queer perspective. In many respects, then, for a variety of scholars and commentators, Bruce Nugent *is* Harlem, and Harlem *is* queer.[5]

In this chapter, I inquire into this narrative's construction, discussing the cultural mechanisms that have enabled this equation—the appropriation, the misunderstanding, the forgetting. I am interested in the visions, as well as the disruptions and challenges, that the memory of Nugent provides for a black queer historiography of Harlem. I am particularly interested in the anachronisms of this narrative, which construct queer moments of "touch" between the early and late twentieth century: moments of affective identification and appropriation in the concepts of same-sex desire, of black homosexuality, and of black–white erotic relationships.[6] These queer temporalities translate, for a queer memory, the temporal vectors of the "promise" and "wasness" of Harlem that Andrew M. Fearnley develops in the first chapter of the present volume. In their affective dynamics, they make up what I call Queer Harlem: a palimpsest of voices; a utopian place across time and space; a necessarily flawed, unreliable, and faulty narrative of sexualities and desires that queers dominant narratives of time, space, and racial and sexual identity.

Nugent is a queer object of a queer memory particularly because of the ephemeral nature of his work. It is telling that he was also a dancer, whose performance cannot be anything but fleeting.[7] The smallness of his written output, which is repeatedly explained as his "laziness," extricates Nugent from the ideals of productiveness and efficiency in a market economy—and from his "purpose" as a "New Negro" to "uplift" the race.[8] It also opens a window onto the lived experience that takes place outside representation—its contingencies, pleasures, pains, and reality.

Nugent's legacy lies not only in his aesthetic impulses, which were taken up by future generations of artists, but also in his active role in shaping the historiography of the Harlem Renaissance. Described as early as 1930 as a fascinating conversationalist, Nugent came to be viewed, in his later years, as an authoritative source on what became known as the Harlem Renaissance.[9] Already in 1971, Nugent spoke "brilliantly" into the tape recorder of Zora Neale Hurston's biographer Robert Hemenway, who complimented him for "never once lapsing into clichés."[10] And while the historian David Levering Lewis's primary interest was not in gay/queer history, the acknowledgements for his landmark work *When Harlem Was in Vogue* (1981) show how important Nugent's testimony was to him in the mid- to late 1970s: "Somewhere in Hoboken, New Jersey, Richard Bruce Nugent lives. To him, above all, this book owes whatever quality it may have of being written from the inside of its subject, for many portraits of personality and unravelings of complex relationships were possible largely because of his astonishingly accurate memory and the objective perceptions of the past which he helped to create."[11]

These venerating words not only suggest the charming authority with which Nugent made his listener believe his memories to be "accurate" and "objective" but also posit Nugent as the double creator of a past—through his participation in the Harlem Renaissance and through his retrospective testimony about that moment.

If Nugent embraces many qualities of Harlem's history, his racial and sexual ambiguity also presents a challenge for the politics of cultural memory. Although Nugent's writing, visual art, and oral statements confirm his commitment to black culture, he stretches the received boundaries of both blackness and homosexuality. Some of his protagonists can and do pass for white (as did Nugent, occasionally), they desire white men (as did Nugent), and they proclaim their bisexuality (which Nugent did, at least to the extent that he married). A focus on these characteristics can function to divert attention away from the precarious position of black homosexuality, especially in light of contemporary discussions of white, gay, middle-class hegemony and a "down-low" discourse in black culture that excludes nonconformant sexualities from the concept of blackness.[12]

How does this politics of identity and memory relate to Harlem's contemporary development, whereby a corporate takeover endangers a very specific black community and commodifies its rich history? Does the resistive spirit of Nugent linger in Harlem through institutions like Jazzmobile, which he cofounded in the mid-1960s and which to this day invites Harlemites and others to enjoy African American music uptown? Might Nugent usefully encapsulate the ephemerality of black Harlem, on the one hand, and a rethinking of Harlem's centrality to the New Negro experience, on the other?

These questions assume particular importance in the context of recent black and queer studies scholarship that challenges the centrality of Harlem, New York, and even cities in general, to black and/or queer formations. Key texts in African American studies that advocate a departure from Harlem-centrism and Harlem exceptionalism have, in practice, left behind consideration of queer lives, literature, and culture, for which Harlem was a dominant "setting and symbol."[13] Within queer studies, meanwhile, J. Halberstam's critique of the "metronormative" mainstreaming of queer experience into an urban lifestyle and Scott Herring's complementary study of queer rural experience show that the city cannot be taken as the only telos and topos of queer practice, reminding us of the need to denaturalize urban gay narratives such as Queer Harlem.[14] With these interventions in mind, it becomes both possible and necessary to reassess the significance of the city, and Harlem, to the study of queer black fiction and culture.

This chapter reasserts the need for black and queer studies to attend to place, to Harlem's place, and to Harlem *as* place—not only for recovering the historical shape and variety of sexual possibilities but also as a helpful framework for contemplating the complex interplay between past and memory, fiction and history. Yet it also takes into account the ephemerality of place itself. My interrogation of Nugent's position in the memory of Queer Harlem exposes the need to look at place's symbolic power and historical malleability; at the same time, it argues for the importance of resisting the streamlining of a pre-Stonewall black/queer subjectivity into an urban gay liberation narrative.[15]

QUEERING THE RACE CAPITAL: NUGENT'S BLACK DANDY

As Harlem is suspended between its "promise" and its "wasness," so Queer Harlem is caught between various queer(ing) temporalities of racialized and sexualized time: the progress narratives produced by white histories of "civilization" and those of the gay and lesbian mainstream; the utopian and dystopian concepts of queer futurity and antifuturity; the hedonistic embrace of the "now" or the affective idea of nostalgia.[16] But rather than identifying Nugent or his reception with any of these positions, I want to highlight how he represents what Heather Love calls "the resistance of queer historical figures to our advances toward them." One way in which Nugent enacts this resistance is through the figure of the Black Dandy, a point I develop from Elisa Glick's inspiring essay.[17]

It is not difficult to recognize the figure of the dandy in Thurman's Nugent character Paul Arbian. Like Nugent's own protagonists—Alex in "Smoke, Lilies and Jade" and Stuartt in *Gentleman Jigger*—Arbian admires the decadent fin de siècle art, fiction, and posture and is himself cultured, stylish, provocative, and of ambiguous sexuality. It is through this figure, as Glick has demonstrated, that the younger generation of Harlem Renaissance writers—above all, Thurman and Nugent—intervened in the dominant discourse of the Harlem Renaissance.

As a dandy, Nugent is difficult to incorporate into a mainstream black gay narrative that moves dependably toward black and gay liberation. It is telling that, instead of distancing himself from a character in Carl Van Vechten's widely denounced novel *Nigger Heaven* (1926), a dandy nicknamed the Scarlet Creeper, Nugent remarks, in an interview from 1989, "That sounds like me in my monkey suit." Looking back, Nugent embraces the figure of the Black Dandy despite its roots in nineteenth-century minstrel characters, whose racist construction, as Eric Lott has shown, is steeped in homoerotic anxiety. On the one hand, Nugent thereby proves loyal to another dandy of the 1920s, Van Vechten, willfully ignoring the color line that separates them, and the history of black representation. On the other hand, he recognizes his own earlier self-construction as a Black Dandy who rejects the figure's minstrel roots and replaces them with European decadence (Huysmans, Wilde), thereby appropriating a white tradition and translating it into a black, modernist, queer context.[18]

The Black Dandy effectively queers the race capital and the Harlem Renaissance's figurehead, the New Negro. Both the New Negro and the Black Dandy claim and rewrite history, yet they embrace different temporalities. Alain

Locke's New Negro is modern, on time, and at the right place, namely the Black Metropolis, whence he looks into the future; Nugent's Black Dandy is a modernist, yet he has fallen out of time and place, originating in a white European tradition of the late nineteenth century that clatters against the black American 1920s. He is concerned with the presence of an urban diversity rather than the future of a sanitized, regularized race capital. He is more easily lost to history because the New Negro's vision is advanced through prodigious and influential *written* projects, which were preserved, whereas the Black Dandy expresses himself largely in ephemeral modes—sociability, dance, music, and the like.[19]

Locke's essay "The New Negro," one of the most prodigious of these written projects, has been regarded as the principal manifesto for the Harlem Renaissance—it was written with that intention and has been read as such ever since. The exclusion of any reckoning with sexuality from this text, which famously envisions Harlem as a "race capital," is particularly intriguing, as Locke had organized his wing of the Harlem Renaissance through a male homoerotic network, a "fraternity of friends" sustained though correspondence and congregation.[20] (Nugent, though not a member of this fraternity, maintained a complicated relationship with Locke, which he discussed in later interviews.)[21]

Their queer sexualities, however, did not shape the idea of the New Negro, and neither Locke nor anyone else wrote a manifesto for Queer Harlem in the 1920s. The infamous and thrilling reputation of Harlem's drag balls, rent parties, and cross-dressers notwithstanding, none of the queer intellectuals in Harlem would describe the neighborhood as the "queer capital," or even as the promise thereof.[22] The concept of racial uplift excluded (queer) sexuality from its discourse and from the self-construction of a black middle class, as evidenced by the heteronormativity and homophobia displayed by leaders such as W. E. B. Du Bois and Adam Clayton Powell Jr.[23]

While homosexuality was more visible within working-class Harlem, which could less easily command alternative spaces than middle-class Harlem, the dandy moved between and played with class positions. His hypervisibility and stylistic performance, and especially his ironic detachment, made the idea of writing in the definitive, immobilizing genre of the manifesto counterproductive. The Black Dandy was found in performance rather than in text.

Nugent's lyrical short story "Smoke, Lilies and Jade," which, ironically, critics have treated as something akin to a Queer Harlem manifesto, makes visible the differences between the New Negro's modernity and the Black Dandy's modernism.[24] It shows its protagonist, Alex, ruminating on writers past and present (from Wilde to Langston Hughes), on sophistication and beauty, and on the possibility of loving "two at the same time" (that is, a white man and a black woman) as it follows him turning life into art. As a leitmotif, the smoke—materialized in the ellipses that structure the text—is a visualization of the train of thought that takes the protagonist's mind in many directions, giving a rhythmic element of retardation to the narrative (the sharing of a light for a cigarette, furthermore, turns the motif into a cruising device). Eventually, Alex's thoughts take him on a walking tour (imagined? remembered? actual?) during which the ellipses also visualize the echo of the clicking footsteps of Beauty, his future lover:

> The street was so long and narrow ... so long and narrow [...] ... Alex walked music ... the click of his heels kept time with a tune in his mind ... [...] Alex walked and the click of his heels sounded ... and had an echo ... sound being tossed back and forth ... back and forth ... somebody was approaching ... and their echoes mingled ... and gave the sound of castanets ... Alex liked the sound of the approaching man's footsteps ... he walked music also ...[25]

The hesitancy in this writing, the pleasure in making a moment last and watching it go by, the emphasis on the aesthetic as a means of pleasure rather than of politics—all of these characteristics show the Black Dandy to be both more nearsighted and more farsighted than the New Negro, indulging in literary and nonliterary forms unsuited to the New Negro's project of racial vindication.

Elisa Glick has uncovered the rebellious power of the Black Dandy and his disruptive, queering potential by demonstrating that his artificiality serves as a critique of the authenticity and primitivism that governed the discourse of blackness during the Harlem Renaissance. Likewise, the Black Dandy "queers the New Negro's quest for origins"—the consuming search for African roots—and complicates notions of "whiteness" and "blackness" equally essential for the New Negro. Such complication can be seen in the racial ambiguity of *Gentleman Jigger*'s protagonist, Stuartt, who spends a third of the novel in white company without exposing his blackness.[26] This artificiality, multi-rootedness (if rootedness at all), and racial ambiguity reveals the constructed nature of the "authentic blackness" that has so often been attributed to Harlem—in part as a consequence of Lockean "race capital" discourse.

The Black Dandy's ability to turn life into art enables him to deal with racial fetishization in ways that are unthinkable for the New Negro. Cognizant of his dependence on white patronage, the New Negro was critical of the "fad" that blackness had become and of the racialized exploitation and exoticization it entailed. While Thurman is explicitly critical of the power relations that inform this interracial exchange, Nugent differentiates more complexly between fetishization as a sexual practice and as cultural politics.[27] When white slummers fetishize black bodies, Nugent (like his characters) fetishizes white bodies. In "Smoke," for example, Alex fetishizes his white male lover, whose beautiful lips make him think of "that passage from Wilde's Salome [sic]."[28] Nugent has disconnected racial fetishization as such from the wholesale cultural exoticization of blackness, with its immediate social and economic consequences. But as many of the dialogues in *Gentleman Jigger* show, the Black Dandy's license to reverse exoticization fully acknowledges the power of racism.

As a final point, the Black Dandy opposes capitalism's efficiency. His work is not dedicated to a purpose, be it racial or sexual "uplift." "Smoke," for instance, is the story of a dandy's indolence, his lying in bed thinking of the things he could do ("to write or draw ... or something").[29] Through his refusal to be a productive member of society, the Black Dandy exposes the New Negro's complicity in a logic of profit. It is significant, then, that Nugent himself left such a small body of work behind—that he was "lazy," that he did not insist on ownership, and that he did not carefully preserve his work.[30] (Perhaps it is equally true to type that what remained of his work was eventually found by people with the desire to publish and archive it, most notably the scholar and activist Thomas A. Wirth.)

The ephemerality that characterizes Nugent's work emerges not only in the motifs of smoke and walking that, like those of driving and moving, permeate his oeuvre, but also in the motif of dancing. Dancing, realizes Stuartt, the protagonist of *Jigger*, is his "perfect medium."[31] It is also an important motif in Nugent's illustrations and other artwork, though interestingly, and true to medium, there are no records of Nugent himself as a dancer. The ephemerality of dance helps queer subjects to simultaneously be visible and get lost from history, "lost from the evidentiary logic of heterosexuality." But dance, as José E. Muñoz states, "like energy, never disappears; it is simply transformed."[32]

Nugent's fascination with dance can be traced throughout his life. In 1964, long after he ceased publishing, he was cofounder, with the renowned artist Romare Bearden and others, of the Harlem Cultural Council, and he served as board member and vice president for a number of years. While Nugent's activities on the council have yet to be researched, it is well known that the council created Dancemobile and Jazzmobile, the latter of which still organizes open-air concerts in Harlem today. Some of the energy of Nugent's actual and fictional dancing has, perhaps, flowed into these institutions.

Nugent's written work was always close to lived experience; much of it is based on autobiography. Thus, if Nugent's life came to be known as the stuff of Thurman's fiction (a fiction in which he commits suicide, leaving behind a soaked manuscript bearing a dedication that ends with a pompous "it is written"), it seems important that he would emerge from the written text to continue living, whether "it"—the dedication, the masterpiece itself, or the experience of a queer life in Harlem and elsewhere—be "written" or not.

TOUCH: AN UNRELIABLE BRIDGE TO THE PAST

The Black Dandy is a figure of pleasure. As such, he critiques the conventionally aspirational gestures of the New Negro and complicates the memory of the Harlem Renaissance. His happy unrestraint disrupts the teleology, from past suffering to future freedom, that is characteristic of gay liberation narratives. In Nugent's *Gentleman Jigger*, for instance, Stuartt is a kind of queer superman whose decadent lifestyle; expert handling of party guests, conversation partners, and lovers; and manipulation of people and their possessions for his own good (but also theirs) make him emerge victorious from every situation. A wishful-satirical autobiographical text, the novel elevates its protagonist to the status of one of the most successful modern artists, a social "sensation," the "rare phenomenon [of] a beautiful man," and, finally, a dancing star of the stage and screen.[33]

Both sexual orientation and racial identity are important topics of the novel, but their seriousness (which, in Nugent, is profound) is undermined by quips and a cheerful aloofness. Ultimately, these topics are taken up to prove the elegance with which Stuartt handles them. In one scene, for instance, friends wish Stuartt to define his sexual orientation.

> "Or," Leslie continued, "are you attracted to men?"
>
> "Yes again." It was Stuartt's delight to play with words. Leslie was so serious.
>
> "Then are you queer?" It was almost an assertion.
>
> "Queer?" Stuartt thought for a moment, lit a cigarette, and inhaled a puff before answering. "I don't think I'm very different from Rusty or Bill. But maybe I don't understand you. What do you mean by 'queer'?"
>
> "I mean: do you like men?"
>
> "Yes, don't you? And women, too. And I'm very fond of eats. Does that make me queer?"[34]

Refusing to be pinned down to one sexual identity, Stuartt points to a continuum of pleasures that extends from smoking to sexuality to food. As Nugent's fictionalized alter ego, Paul Arbian, says in the same context, "The primary function of the sex act is enjoyment. Therefore I enjoyed one experience as much as the other."[35]

The same nonchalance Stuartt displays about his sexual orientation he also displays about his racial identity. Having become part of the white society of Chicago and a successful dancer on stage and screen, he discloses his blackness at a crucial moment—in support of the "Scottsboro Boys"—which causes a public sensation. But it changes little for Stuartt, to whom the uproar is "amusing" and means "less than nothing."[36] Instead of becoming a hero for the black cause who sacrifices his career, Stuartt maintains an elegant equilibrium between racial solidarity and the satisfaction of creating a sensation.

The lightness with which Stuartt plays with questions of identity, and his refusal to suffer from the intersections of a gay/black identity, should make it difficult for scholars to find a place for Nugent in teleological narratives of gay progress. Yet the ephemerality and ambiguities that accompany Nugent's posture of cheerfulness have made it easy to claim him for a variety of queer/gay narratives. The creative confusion between Thurman's and Nugent's own fictionalizations, Nugent's biography and oral testimonies, and all the other versions of Nugent from the 1920s through the 1980s have helped establish a Queer Harlem continuum that stretches across genres and times. Bruce Nugent has become a bridge to the past at the same time that he has involuntarily helped speed up a fuzzy temporality. Satisfying the queer desire of "touch," Nugent has enabled scholars, writers, and filmmakers to find in him an ancestor figure. The result has been a variety of anachronisms.

One kind of anachronism involves a confusion of discourses. To his interviewers, Nugent repeatedly tried to explain the difference between the 1920s and the 1980s. "Homosexuality has always been a dirty *word*," he said in the 1980s. "But . . . homosexuality, the *practice* of it, was not a dirty thing."[37] This differentiation between language and practice informs the homosexual discourse in the 1920s, a discourse that pathologizes same-sex practices and desires. Before Stonewall, homosexuality was a practice: "We didn't call it . . . we did it," as Nugent said in one interview. Yet, in a gesture typical of 1980s criticism, Eric Garber calls "Smoke, Lilies and Jade" a "defense of homosexual love."[38] This imposes a gay rights consciousness on a text that was written at a time when gay rights were not part of the ideological realm. "Smoke" is not a defense of, nor does it propagate, homosexual love. This appropriation ignores the ambivalence and sexual fluidity of a text that refuses to defend or be a manifesto for gay black love.

The historiography of Queer Harlem abounds in such anachronisms. I assess them in two diverging ways. On the one hand, I understand them to be part of a specific queer temporality that diverges from linear, progressive narratives and is fueled by the desire to write the history of homosexuality in (black) America, not only in order to legitimize political claims in the present but also to complicate the national grand historical narratives of race and gender. On the other hand, I see these anachronisms as the result of an attempt by later generations to streamline Queer Harlem into a gay liberation narrative, thereby forcing it into a new hegemonic, identity-driven discourse that effectively "dequeers" the past, to use Elisabeth Windle's phrase.[39]

Garber's anachronism—and he is by no means alone—is part of the dynamics of historiography, especially that of nonhegemonic subjects who are forced to have a history to justify their claims.[40] But the teleology and linearity these histories demand are complicit in the hegemonic streamlining of history, thereby inverting their nonhegemonic claims. So while these anachronisms are creative and affective, their sub- and reversions of history run the danger of reinforcing received historiography. They can easily reduce the complicated intersections of lived experience, desire, sexual activities, and sexual and racial identities to a common denominator, "gay."[41]

Clearly, Nugent's own vocabulary complicates this, as he sometimes followed his interlocutors' use of language. The writer Samuel R. Delany, who knew Nugent personally, remembers that, during the 1960s, Nugent critiqued the labeling that words like "homosexual" and "gay" perform. Yet, in 1983, Nugent would accept such language and declare, in an interview with Thomas A. Wirth, "You see, I'm a homosexual."[42] Then again, when asked how he had been able to write anything as "gay" as "Smoke, Lilies and Jade," his answer, in 1986, was, "I didn't know *it was gay* when I wrote it." And as Charles Michael Smith reports, Nugent did not even frequent "gay" bars and "gay" places: "I was not fond of the company of gay people. I still don't enjoy their company very much [because those I meet] don't have anything to talk about." Yet scholars such as Henry Louis Gates Jr., writing in a foreword to a collection of Nugent's work, describe him as "boldly and proudly gay," the "most openly homosexual of the Harlem Renaissance writers."[43]

Concepts of pride and openness, as Gates uses them here, translate Nugent's queerness into the coming-out narrative that depends on the ideology of the closet. This narrative was not used before the 1960s and suggests a form of "gay men's isolation" that does not fit with 1920s categories. Moreover, as Marlon B. Ross argues, the narrative of the closet is inherently white and implies the uncloseted sexuality of nonwhite subjects. A "doorway marking the threshold between the up-to-date fashions of sexuality and the outmoded, anachronistic others," the closet supports a (racialized) "evolutionary logic" that is furthermore complicated by its allegiance to a neoliberal discourse.[44]

The rediscovery of Queer Harlem in the 1980s was, in part, a project to "out" black writers like Locke, Hughes, Claude McKay, Countee Cullen, Thurman, Nella Larsen, and others and to establish the memory of a homosexual "underworld" of gay and lesbian performers that confirms the claim of a tradition to undergird contemporary gay identity. In their (supposedly) necessary creations of a "usable past," these anachronisms colonize the past. Elizabeth Freeman points to the complicity of the idea of a usable past with ideologies of "productiveness" that are dependent on normative concepts of biological reproduction and economic efficiency. While queer temporality in many respects depends on anachronisms in order to combat what Freeman calls "chrononormativity," these colonizing strategies ultimately thwart the queer impulse.[45]

LOOKING FOR/FINDING BRUCE

Bruce Nugent's decadent pollen has fertilized not only cultural history and literary criticism but also the work of creative artists, particularly filmmakers. His refusal of smooth absorption into a narrative of progress has found its way into the films he has inspired, if to varying degrees and effects. But both *Looking for Langston* (1989), directed by Isaac Julien, and *Brother to Brother* (2004), directed by Rodney Evans, address the concept of time and the creative confusion between documentation and fiction that have featured in my discussion of Nugent's place in cultural memory. More specifically, both films have engendered analyses around their uses of queer temporality.[46]

As an experimental film and audiovisual collage, *Looking for Langston* circles around the motifs of desire, race, and the enigma of queer black sexuality symbolized by Langston Hughes. Meanwhile, as a coming-of-age drama, *Brother to Brother* has a clear narrative arc in which a gay black student and artist, Perry, finds a voice through his friendship with an aged Nugent. In their different genres, both films use Nugent's artistic, aesthetic, erotic, and political heritage to develop their own aesthetics and stories. Both films also play with time: in *Looking*, various time zones coexist, from the Harlem Renaissance through to the death of James Baldwin, in 1987, and the club scene of 1980s London; in *Brother*, old Bruce escorts young Perry back to the Harlem of the 1920s, where young Bruce and the renaissance's insurgent younger generation interact at "Niggeratti Manor." While the continuous black-and-white aesthetics in *Looking* create a uniformity of time, the aesthetics of *Brother* construct two different time zones, the borders of which are overcome at a certain point (when Perry leaves the colorful present and enters the black-and-white renaissance world) but are otherwise not questioned.

Both films function as archives, summoning the history of homosexuality within black culture. In Julien's case, this is done through the collage-like insertion of film footage, images, music, and texts from the 1920s through the 1980s; in Evans's case, it happens through reconstructions of the Harlem Renaissance, footage from the civil rights movement, and an imagined scene between Eldridge Cleaver and James Baldwin. Harlem plays a crucial role in both films. In Julien's work, the neighborhood is manifested through the setting of a 1920s black nightclub, references to Hughes and Nugent, and plentiful footage from earlier documentary and narrative films. In Evans's film, Harlem is more straightforwardly a destination the characters visit. In both films, the neighborhood radiates to places and times beyond itself—to Julien's 1980s London and to Evans's contemporary Brooklyn and other New York neighborhoods. (The present tense in *Brother* is tellingly vague. Shot in the early 2000s, the film could just as well take place in the 1980s.)

Although Nugent's presence in *Brother* is larger than in *Looking*, both films place him as one (possible) black gay artist/predecessor of many and as a central figure for the memory of Queer Harlem. Julien focuses on a politicized aesthetics whereas Evans is interested in creating a more directly usable past.[47] Thus, *Looking* is indebted and pays tribute to Nugent's modernism. Conversely, in *Brother*, Nugent appears as a character, namely as the benevolent ancestor who teaches a young, troubled artist how to cope with the intersection of blackness and homosexuality. If in *Looking* Nugent is a vehicle (not) to arrive at Langston, in *Brother* he is the vehicle for the protagonist to arrive at himself. While Julien acknowledges Nugent as an aesthetic predecessor and fellow artist, Evans sees Nugent largely as a historical subject whose life as a gay black artist is beneficial for the self-understanding of contemporary gay black men.

The gay community's desire to pinpoint Hughes's sexuality and claim him for a gay/queer memory, as expressed in the title *Looking for Langston*, is diverted through a reading and visualization of Nugent's story "Smoke, Lilies and Jade." In this way, the film resurrects Nugent for a gay black memory and emphasizes the importance of his queer aesthetics. But the point of the film is the absence of Langston (the uncertainty about his homosexuality)—or rather, the "looking," the search, the desire, the cruising—for which Nugent delivers a language, or an aesthetics. Julien visualizes the dream section of Nugent's "Smoke" in a surreal marsh landscape, while the text is read offscreen. Text and image, in this sequence, do not mirror but complement each other. Julien uses the text as a stepping stone for his own visual art. This creates a deferential distance between Nugent's and Julien's work and acknowledges the gap between their respective media and times. This distancing gesture, however, is undermined by the ubiquity of smoke that serves as a leitmotif and thus lets Nugent's spirit permeate the whole film.

Smoke is a powerful symbol in *Looking for Langston*. Julien picks up Nugent's meanings of smoke as ambiguity, pleasure, possibility, and ephemerality and adds to them the unpredictability of memory. The smoke that billows through the frames adds motion to scenes that otherwise depend on stillness, thereby bridging moving and still images, film and photography, memory and history. The most important scene, in this respect, occurs in the nightclub, where male couples are dancing but their movement is arrested. They stand motionless in dancing postures, cheek-to-cheek, mirror images of each other, as if seen through a kaleidoscope. The only thing moving (besides the camera) is the smoke—produced by a smoke machine and a cigarette. When movement starts, it is as if a photograph is brought to life.[48] The smoke is thus a kinetic and life-giving force that, like Nugent, bridges past and present. Like Nugent's appeal in other appropriations, it allows for queer moments to touch each other across the historical divide.

The touch across a historical divide is also the subject of *Brother to Brother*. Old Bruce enables Perry to touch a past that he can make use of. At the same time, Perry serves as the device through which the audience touches and understands Bruce Nugent.[49] "Smoke" here appears on the diegetic level, as Perry finds what has become Nugent's masterpiece in an anthology. He and (later) Bruce cite the text, focusing on its emphasis on the power of imagination. While *Looking* departs from Nugent's writing, exclusively, *Brother* also shows Nugent as a painter. Moreover, Nugent's role as a witness plays an important part in the film, with every scene from the 1920s based on his writing or interview comments.

When Perry meets him, Bruce lives in a homeless shelter.[50] "[Evicted] from his own history," he shows Perry how much Harlem was a home to the young artists of the 1920s. The nostalgia of the movie is not primarily sentimental; rather, it is "driven by a queer relationship to temporality, an insistence on the pleasures of the past." In this past, young Bruce is a clown in the company of friends (possibly in consequence of Nugent's description of Stuartt as a "court jester") and, as such, a strong contrast to Perry, who is a serious and rather lonely person. As Windle points out, "Nostalgia for the gay Harlem Renaissance is one way out of the problem of an intersectional identity that feels impossible."[51]

A stepping stone into the past is the ruined building of 267 West 136th Street in Harlem; when Perry and old Bruce enter it, they are transported back to the 1920s, when this was Niggeratti Manor, the site of the founding of *Fire!!* by a young Nugent, Thurman, Hughes, Hurston, Aaron Douglas, and others, and the site of hilarious parties involving other luminaries such as Van Vechten. A literary history book come alive, "267" will eventually be the place where the filmic (but not the historical) Nugent dies.

Both films address the attraction between black and white men. Much has been written about the only major white character in *Looking*, and the film's examination of racialized desire and its representation in light of the Robert Mapplethorpe controversy.[52] The indefinite position of the white man as a menace, controller of the gaze, and object of desire leaves an ambiguity that both acknowledges and questions racialized power. *Looking* portrays the attraction between black and white men as politically charged but nonetheless existent and potentially successful in bringing pleasure.

In *Brother*, Perry is confronted, less ambiguously, with racial fetishization through his white lover. His refusal to be fetishized is politically laudable but leaves him without sex and romance. A relationship that was possible during the 1920s—we see the Thurman character with his white lover—is no longer possible in the film's present day. In leaving out Nugent's own reverse fetishization of white men, *Brother* simplifies him for a less ambiguous construction of black male homosexuality. As Windle points out, Evans is reacting to a context of the down-low—the suppression of homosexuality by the black middle class since the late 1990s—which, together with the film's didactic impulse, may explain its decision to handle black homosexuality in a less complex manner.[53]

Clearly, the gay black memory for which Evans appropriates Nugent is more narrowly defined than it is for Julien.[54] Even though Julien streamlines Nugent—most importantly, he leaves out the female object of desire from Nugent's dream passage—*Looking* explores Nugent not only as a symbol of the presence of black homosexual desire but also as a symbol of the search for that desire across time. The openness of this construction is closer to a queer imaginary than Evans's film, which culminates in Perry's college essay on the Harlem Renaissance. Through Nugent, this young, black, gay artist has found a tradition and a voice and will succeed in his Black History class. Thus, even though *Brother* rejects the gay narrative of progress in turning to nostalgia, this nostalgia stands in the service of a productiveness that ultimately de-queers the film. Still, like *Looking*, *Brother* combats "chrononormativity" for a narrative of touch.

CONCLUSION

How does Bruce Nugent figure in the Queer Harlem of today? Nugent is a reminder of the ephemerality of queer lives and the malleability of their places and memory. In my analysis of his work and its afterlife, Nugent's resistance to the commodification of his particular queerness into a coherent narrative has been countered by attempts to include him in gay and gay/black narratives of progress, while also inspiring their critique. In addition, Nugent's position as a shaper of the (queer) memory of Harlem extends the role he plays for Queer Harlem, from the confines of the 1920s through to the 1990s. At the same time, the centrality of his position in that memory is antithetical to his peripatetic and ephemeral stance. But what sustains Nugent as an important entry point to a reading of Queer Harlem is his insistence on the diverse, intersectional character of "identities," performances, and (sexual) acts, as well as pleasure, as guiding principles for understanding raced and gendered, eroticized and sexualized human encounters.

Nugent also offers an important lens onto the conjuncture between the contemporary, neoliberal mainstreaming of homosexuality in U.S. society and the gentrification of Harlem. The resulting "metronormativity" that identifies gay "lifestyle" with urban consumerism effaces queer lives outside the white, heteronormative, city-dwelling middle class. Metronormativity has become such an important paradigm that, as Michael Henry Adams remarks, "gay" increasingly "becomes code for white, for rich, for 'gentrifier.'"[55]

The gentrification of Harlem, which is discussed in more detail in the next two chapters of the present volume, has led both to the mainstreaming of homosexuality as an asset in the entertainment economy and to the simultaneous disappearance of queer places, like the Mount Morris Baths on Lenox Avenue, whose existence had preceded the Harlem Renaissance. The closing of the baths in 2003 echoes the "cleaning up" of Times Square that, as Samuel R. Delany has shown, put an end to a male same-sex culture of cross-racial and interclass "contact." Their disappearance parallels the strict policing and gradual disappearance of queer-of-color clubs in other parts of New York City, as described by José Muñoz.[56] In a world made "safe" for the white heterosexual middle-class family, places of "contact" such as the bathhouse are increasingly replaced by dating websites and digital transnational networks, while the rules for being "out" have become more constricted. These developments, then, have amplified and narrowed Harlem's queer symbolism while also recomposing (and sanitizing) its setting.

Even as Harlem loses its specific queer subcultures, gay and lesbian culture is celebrated as a hallmark of New York City. From October 2016 to February 2017, the Museum of the City of New York staged an exhibition called *Gay Gotham: Art and Underground Culture in New York*. Bruce Nugent—via paintings, drawings, and texts—was highlighted as one of the city's ten important gay and lesbian writers, artists, musicians, dancers, models, and the like, whose peer networks the exhibition visualized through lines painted onto the floor. (The other artists were Mercedes de Acosta, Leonard Bernstein, Harmony Hammond, Bill T. Jones, Greer Lankton, George Platt Lynes, Robert Mapplethorpe, Andy Warhol, and Arnie Zane.)

Not surprisingly, for a show at the Museum of the City of New York, it retells the migration narrative of the big city as a place of queer fulfillment and describes the queer artists as contributors to New York's cultural landscape. However, as the list of names indicates, it is a "celebration of upper-class gay white male creativity," effacing queers of color and the lesbian and feminist movements.[57] So, while Nugent's eventual canonization is as gratifying as it is astonishing—and while the show's attention to networks is in line with Nugent's own understanding of creativity—this is probably not the network he would have liked to find himself within, particularly given his vocal opposition to the exclusion of African American artists from the Metropolitan Museum of Art's 1969 exhibition *Harlem on My Mind*.[58]

If Bruce Nugent's Harlem Renaissance project was to queer the New Negro, the imperative today is to write blackness into queerness. While Harlem-centrism and Harlem exceptionalism are presently being challenged, and for good reason, the fact that Harlem itself is experiencing major changes that are pushing black queer culture to the fringes of the contemporary neighborhood suggests not a need to step away from Harlem's queer past and queer memory but a need to comprehend them anew. In this regard, the narrative forms employed in a film currently in production may prove telling. According to its director, Jeff L. Lieberman, *My Harlem* will tell the story of the relationship between two gay men who bond over a protest against the homophobia of the ATLAH World Missionary Church on Lenox Avenue. One black, one white, they explore their respective worlds while the film explores Harlem's history and the sexual and racial politics of gentrifying Harlem today.[59] It is doubtful that this story will call up the posture of the Black Dandy, nor should it; the queerness Nugent embodies clearly effaces many other black queer practices and concerns. Yet Nugent's openness to contact across the "color line" and his questioning of categories of race and sexuality may remain important, if controversial, matters for Harlem today.

NOTES

1. Wallace Thurman, *Infants of the Spring* (1932; Boston: Northeastern University Press, 1992), 284.
2. Elisa F. Glick, "Harlem's Queer Dandy: African-American Modernism and the Artifice of Blackness," *Modern Fiction Studies* 49 (Fall 2003): 435.
3. *Smoke, Lilies and Jade* is also the title of Carl Hancock Rux's play, which combined the short story with Bruce Nugent's biography. It was commissioned by the Public Theater in New York and was later performed by the CalArts Center for New Performance. The story also influenced Steven Corbin's novel *No Easy Place to Be* (New York: Simon and Schuster, 1989).
4. Glick, "Harlem's Queer Dandy," 422.
5. See for instance Eric Garber, "A Spectacle in Color: The Lesbian and Gay Subculture of Jazz Age Harlem," in *Hidden in History: Reclaiming the Gay and Lesbian Past*, ed. Martin Duberman et al. (New York: New American Library, 1989), 318–33; Simon Dickel, *Black/Gay: The Harlem Renaissance, the Protest Era, and Constructions of Black Gay Identity in the 1980s and '90s* (East Lansing: Michigan State University Press, 2011); Seth Clark Silberman, "Lighting the Harlem Renaissance a *Fire!!*: Embodying Richard Bruce Nugent's Bohemian Politic," in *The Greatest Taboo: Homosexuality in Black Communities*, ed. Delroy Constantine-Simms (Los Angeles: Alyson, 2001), 211–30.
6. On "touch," see especially Carolyn Dinshaw, *Getting Medieval: Sexualities and Communities, Pre- and Postmodern* (Durham, NC: Duke University Press, 1999). See also J. Halberstam, *In a Queer Time and Place: Transgender Bodies, Subcultural Lives* (New York: New York University Press, 2005), 3.
7. Thomas A. Wirth, introduction to *Gay Rebel of the Harlem Renaissance: Selections from the Work of Richard Bruce Nugent*, ed. Thomas A. Wirth (Durham, NC: Duke University Press, 2002), 31.
8. Laziness was a posture Nugent cultivated; see his portrayal in Wallace Thurman, *The Blacker the Berry* (1929; New York: Collier, 1970), 164. In 1982, Nugent told Jean Blackwell Hutson that Alain Locke had not helped him find a patron because Locke thought him too lazy. See "Oral History Interview with Richard Bruce Nugent, 1982," Schomburg Center for Research in Black Culture, New York Public Library.
9. Edward Perry, "Richard Bruce Nugent," *Interstate Tattler* (July 18, 1930), quoted in Wirth, *Gay Rebel*, 19.
10. Robert Hemenway, *Zora Neale Hurston: A Literary Biography* (1977; Urbana: University of Illinois Press, 1980).
11. David Levering Lewis, *When Harlem Was in Vogue* (New York: Oxford University Press, 1981), xii. The Schomburg Center for Research in Black Culture holds three and a half

hours of digitized audiotapes of Lewis's interviews with Nugent, recorded from 1974 to 1977, as well as Hutson's videotaped recording. Another interview with him appears in *Before Stonewall: The Making of a Gay and Lesbian Community*, directed by Greta Schiller (First Run Features, 1984). Printed interviews include *You Must Remember This: An Oral History of Manhattan from the 1890s to World War II*, ed. Jeff Kisseloff (San Diego, CA: Harcourt, Brace, Jovanovich, 1989), 252–333; "You See, I Am a Homosexual," in Wirth, *Gay Rebel*, 268–72; Charles Michael Smith, "Bruce Nugent: Bohemian of the Harlem Renaissance," in *In the Life: A Black Gay Anthology*, ed. Joseph Beam (1986; Washington, DC: Red Bone, 2008), 162–72.

12. See C. Riley Snorton, *Nobody Is Supposed to Know: Black Sexuality on the Down Low* (Minneapolis: University of Minnesota Press, 2014).

13. See, especially, Davarian L. Baldwin and Minkah Makalani, eds., *Escape from New York: The New Negro Renaissance Beyond Harlem* (Minneapolis: University of Minnesota Press, 2013). The editors of a special issue, "The Harlem Renaissance and the New Modernist Studies," concede their neglect of "queer politics." Adam McKible and Suzanne W. Churchill, "Introduction: In Conversation—The Harlem Renaissance and the New Modernist Studies," *Modernism/Modernity* 20 (September 2013): 429.

14. Halberstam, *In a Queer Time and Place*; Scott Herring, *Another Country: Queer Anti-Urbanism* (New York: New York University Press, 2010).

15. Typical of the streamlining of deviant nonwhite sexualities into the neat contours of contemporary gay identity discourse, as I will discuss further, is A. B. Christa Schwarz, *Gay Voices of the Harlem Renaissance* (Bloomington: Indiana University Press, 2003). For a critique, see Mason Stokes, "Say My Name," *American Literary History* 17 (March 2005): 171–82.

16. Halberstam, *In a Queer Time and Place*; Heather Love, *Feeling Backward: Loss and the Politics of Queer History* (Cambridge, MA: Harvard University Press, 2007); Lee Edelman, *No Future: Queer Theory and the Death Drive* (Durham, NC: Duke University Press, 2004); José Esteban Muñoz, *Cruising Utopia: The Then and There of Queer Futurity* (New York: New York University Press, 2009).

17. Love, *Feeling Backward*, 34; Glick, "Harlem's Queer Dandy."

18. Kisseloff, *You Must Remember This*, 282; Glick, "Harlem's Queer Dandy," 417; Eric Lott, *Love and Theft: Blackface Minstrelsy and the American Working Class* (New York: Oxford University Press, 1993).

19. The performative character of the Black Dandy challenges the prescriptive character of the New Negro in the same way that, as Shane Vogel has shown, Harlem's cabaret culture challenges the discourse of uplift. See Shane Vogel, *The Scene of Harlem Cabaret: Race, Sexuality, Performance* (Chicago: University of Chicago Press, 2009).

20. On the misogynist nature of this circle, see Lewis, *When Harlem Was in Vogue*, 96. See also George Chauncey, *Gay New York: Gender, Urban Culture, and the Making of the Gay Male World, 1890–1940* (New York: Basic Books, 1994), 264.

21. Wirth, *Gay Rebel*, 22–25.

22. On Harlem's multisexual nightlife, see Chauncey, *Gay New York*, esp. 244, 246, 257, 259.

23. Wirth, *Gay Rebel*, 22; Chauncey, *Gay New York*, 198, 254. See also Kevin K. Gaines, *Uplifting the Race: Black Leadership, Politics, and Culture in the Twentieth Century* (Chapel Hill: University of North Carolina Press, 1996).

24. See Garber, "A Spectacle in Color."

25. Bruce Nugent, "Smoke, Lilies and Jade," first published in *Fire!! A Quarterly Devoted to the Younger Negro Artists* 1 (November 1926), reprinted in Wirth, *Gay Rebel*, 75–87; see esp. 77, 87, 81.

26. Glick, "Harlem's Queer Dandy," 415, 423, 428. In contrast to other "passing" novels from this period, Nugent's never focuses on the act of passing as a problem for its protagonist. See Richard Bruce Nugent, *Gentleman Jigger: A Novel of the Harlem Renaissance*, ed. Thomas A. Wirth (Philadelphia, PA: Da Capo, 2008).
27. On Thurman's criticisms, see Glick, "Harlem's Queer Dandy," 421.
28. Nugent, "Smoke," 83.
29. Nugent, "Smoke," 75.
30. According to the Lewis interviews archived at the Schomburg Center, Nugent appears to have been generous in sharing his material with Thurman. The destruction by fire of almost all copies of the magazine *Fire!!* in which "Smoke, Lilies and Jade" was first published suggests that fate conspired to stress the Black Dandy's ephemerality, too.
31. Nugent, *Gentleman Jigger*, 318. For walking and driving, see, for example, Richard Bruce Nugent, "Geisha Man," in Wirth, *Gay Rebel*, 110; Nugent, *Gentleman Jigger*, 164. On dancing, see David A. Gerstner, *Queer Pollen: White Seduction, Black Male Homosexuality, and the Cinematic* (Urbana: University of Illinois Press, 2011), 52–58.
32. Muñoz, *Cruising Utopia*, 81.
33. Nugent, *Gentleman Jigger*, 190, 211.
34. Nugent, *Gentleman Jigger*, 113.
35. Thurman, *Infants of the Spring*, 47. While this is the Nugent fictionalized by Thurman (as Paul), his tone is similar to the Nugent fictionalized by Nugent (as Stuartt).
36. Nugent, *Gentleman Jigger*, 319, 325–26.
37. Wirth, *Gay Rebel*, 21 (emphasis added).
38. Schiller, *Before Stonewall*; Garber, "Spectacle in Color," 330.
39. Elisabeth Windle, " 'It Never Really Was the Same': *Brother to Brother*'s Black and White and Queer Nostalgia," *MELUS: Multi-Ethnic Literature of the U.S.* 41 (December 2016): 20. For a detailed discussion of the historiography of Queer Harlem from the perspective of the 1980s and 1990s, see Dickel, *Black/Gay*, 83–168.
40. For instance, Gregory Woods assumed that "the kind of openness we now reasonably demand" is the only possible representation of homosexuality. Even though "Harlem writers may have had to remain closeted," he argues, "they were no less gay for that." Woods, "Gay Re-Readings of the Harlem Renaissance Poets," *Journal of Homosexuality* 26, no. 2/3 (1993): 127–42, esp. 140. According to Silberman, this "follows a spectacular logic that offers a qualitative scale placed on 'gayness,' one that locks the history of (re)presentation of 'homosexual desire' within an illusionary narrative of progress but makes the search for the 'most' gay paramount in any historical gay research." Silberman, "Lighting," 227.
41. As Dickel notes, it is worth differentiating between an earlier group of scholars who wrote of a relatively new gay consciousness, and a more self-conscious approach to the history of sexuality. Dickel, *Black/Gay*, 89–90. I use "gay" to describe homosexuality as an identity informed by the coming-out discourse of the post-Stonewall era, which connotes a centrism and a normativity in the neoliberal gay movement. By contrast, "queer" denotes a variety of erotic, sexual, and gender practices that challenge a variety of norms and presents an "open mesh of possibilities, gaps, overlaps, dissonances and resonances, lapses and excesses of meaning." See Eve Sedgwick, *Tendencies* (Durham, NC: Duke University Press, 1993), 8.
42. Samuel R. Delany remembered that Nugent observed, "I just don't see why everyone has to be labeled. I just don't think words like homosexual—or gay—*do* anything for anybody" (quoted in Joseph Beam, "Samuel R. Delany: The Possibility of Possibilities," in Beam, *In the Life*, 157; emphasis in original); Wirth, *Gay Rebel*, 268.

43. Smith, "Bruce Nugent," 167–68 (emphasis in original); Henry Louis Gates Jr., foreword to Wirth, *Gay Rebel*, xi.
44. Chauncey, *Gay New York*, 6; Marlon B. Ross, "Beyond the Closet as Raceless Paradigm," *Black Queer Studies: A Critical Anthology*, ed. E. Patrick Johnson and Mae G. Henderson (Durham, NC: Duke University Press, 2005), 165.
45. Elizabeth Freeman, *Time Binds: Queer Temporalities, Queer Histories* (Durham, NC: Duke University Press, 2010), 5, 10. The concept of a "usable past" is deployed, but not explicated, in Shawn Anthony Christian, "Enacting 'Smoke, Lilies and Jade' as Black Gay Print Culture," *Ethnic Studies Review* 36, no. 1 and 2 (2013): 33.
46. *Looking for Langston*, directed by Isaac Julien (Strand, 1989); *Brother to Brother*, directed by Rodney Evans (Wolfe, 2004). My readings of these films are indebted to Manthia Diawara, "The Absent One: The Avant-Garde and the Black Imaginary in *Looking for Langston*," in *Representing Black Men*, ed. Marcellus Blount and George P. Cunningham (New York: Routledge, 1996), 205–24; José Esteban Muñoz, *Disidentifications: Queers of Color and the Performance of Politics* (Minneapolis: University of Minnesota Press, 1999), 57–74; Kobena Mercer, *Welcome to the Jungle: New Positions in Black Cultural Studies* (New York: Routledge, 1994), 221–32; Kara Keeling, "Looking for M—: Queer Temporality, Black Political Possibility, and Poetry from the Future," *GLQ* 15, no. 4 (2009): 565–82; Windle, "It Never Really Was the Same."
47. Christian, "Enacting," 33.
48. This is an intentional effect, according to Julien's audio commentary on the DVD.
49. Evans explains that he invented Perry to create a contemporary frame for what would otherwise have been a biopic about Nugent. See Rodney Evans, "Fading Into Memory: *Brother To Brother* and the Love Between Generations," https://web.archive.org/web/20060308030914/http://www.movienet.com/brothertobrother.html (accessed April 9, 2018).
50. Here the film diverts from historical fact. See Thomas A. Wirth, introduction to Nugent, *Gentleman Jigger*, xvii.
51. John Leonard, "Birth of the Cool," *New York Magazine* (June 20, 2005), 78; Nugent, *Gentleman Jigger*, 46, 172; Windle, "It Never Really Was the Same," 10, 18.
52. See Mercer, *Welcome to the Jungle*, 171–220.
53. Windle, "It Never Really Was the Same," 10–13.
54. Here I depart from Dickel's argument that *Looking* constructs a gay black memory at the expense of a more nuanced queer memory. See Dickel, *Black/Gay*, 130.
55. Michael Henry Adams, "Homo Harlem," unpublished manuscript. I thank Adams for sharing his manuscript with me. It is astonishing that he has not yet found a publisher for the work. Is this part of the (selective) mainstreaming of Harlem?
56. Samuel R. Delany, *Times Square Red/Times Square Blue* (New York: New York University Press, 1999); Muñoz, *Cruising Utopia*.
57. Eugene Patron, "A New York Century on Exhibit," *Gay & Lesbian Review*, December 12, 2016, http://www.glreview.org/a-new-york-century-on-exhibit; Cassandra Langer, "Unmet Promises: Gay Gotham at the Museum of the City of New York," *Hyperallergic*, February 11, 2017, https://hyperallergic.com/356721/unmet-promises-gay-gotham-at-the-museum-of-the-city-of-new-york.
58. Wirth, *Gay Rebel*, 37.
59. Victor Hoff, "My Harlem," *LGBTQ Weekly* (November 10, 2016).

PART III
BLACK NO MORE?

11.

RACE, CLASS, AND GENTRIFICATION IN HARLEM SINCE 1980

THEMIS CHRONOPOULOS

In recent years, meetings, rallies, pickets, and demonstrations against gentrification have become commonplace in Harlem, with residents protesting landlord practices and city government policies that are contributing to the unaffordability of the neighborhood for low-income people. Demonstrators resent the fact that the new tenants are often middle- and upper-income whites, and this adds a racial dimension to a gentrification conflict that scholars have traditionally framed in terms of class.[1] Many longtime residents fear that Harlem will no longer be the "most iconic African American neighborhood" and the political and cultural "capital of black America." To be sure, these designations are socially constructed and subject to debate. However, it is undeniable that, for almost a century, Central Harlem has been an important black neighborhood with a majority black population. Moreover, during the challenging years of disinvestment, it was long-term residents who formed community organizations that took care of the neighborhood and advanced inclusive visions of revitalization that eventually influenced the ways that the city government rebuilt Harlem.[2]

In this chapter, I seek to determine the nature and causes of the demographic changes that have led to a flurry of commentary predicting the end of Harlem's status as the "capital of black America." I examine neighborhood change in Central Harlem since 1980, with an emphasis on race, class, housing, education, employment, and government policy.[3] The chapter is based on ethnographic, historical, and quantitative research conducted since the late 1990s.

Most social scientists have identified the displacement of low-income residents as one of the most important characteristics of gentrification. In what follows, I argue that displacement needs to be understood more specifically as one of three processes—displacement, replacement, and exclusion—through which gentrification is manifested. In Harlem, some existing residents are forcibly displaced by landlords; others are replaced because they move voluntarily, though when one interrogates this movement, the gentrification of the area becomes one of its most salient causes; and still others are excluded from living in the neighborhood because they cannot afford to move there or because landlords and real estate companies are seeking more affluent individuals or people who fit a certain demographic group. The city government has also been active in promoting gentrification in Harlem in its efforts to transform low-income neighborhoods into more affluent ones. Neighborhoods always change, but the ways in which they change tell us about the social and political forces contributing to such transformations, while the political mobilizations aroused by such trends reveal a great deal about how particular communities conceive of and identify with place.[4]

An important concept that helps explain the attachment of existing residents to Harlem and their insistence that the neighborhood should remain black is the "spatial imaginary" described by George Lipsitz. Lipsitz argues that "the white spatial imaginary views space primarily as a locus for the generation of exchange value."[5] In that sense, houses are investments whose value appreciates with the passage of time, while the tax code benefits homeowners, contributing to higher home prices. Lipsitz contends that embracing the white spatial imaginary has not served blacks well, because racial segregation and other factors have compromised their free movement to many areas. Instead, alternative conceptions of space have taken root in black communities, which treasure such neighborhoods, partly out of necessity and partly because of an attachment to place that goes beyond exchange value. Although Lipsitz emphasizes the expressive cultural elements of the black spatial imaginary, the concept also manifests itself socially and politically. Through the formation of community and social movement organizations, black people have mobilized for the improvement of their neighborhoods and have made claims for affordable housing, accessible public health, efficient transportation systems, decent schools, and equitable municipal services.[6]

Part of the history of Harlem is an evolving spatial imaginary that was born during the Marcus Garvey era, intensified during the Great Depression, fragmented in the immediate post–World War II period, and underwent a resurgence from the late 1950s onward. It insisted on the community control of urban space, through which Harlem's predominantly low-income residents, by mutual cooperation, would create an independent and self-sufficient urban world.[7] This spatial imaginary rejected top-down, government-led urban development and Harlem's exploitation by private and outside forces. The stance of community control persisted despite the fact that, throughout the postwar period, Harlem's population continued to decline (figure 11.1), housing units continued to be lost (figure 11.2), and corporations continued their practice of disinvestment.

Moreover, what makes the case of Harlem unique is that attachment to the area went even beyond the strong sense of community ownership, which has been common in many black urban neighborhoods. In the eyes of many of its own residents, as well as outside commentators, Harlem was and continues to function as the preeminent site of black America, and even of the black diaspora. For example, in 1977, the International Key Women of America formed a Harlem branch, with the goal of rebuilding the neighborhood and restoring its status as "the proud capital of black America." The organization, which had become one of the largest entities in housing construction and rehabilitation in the nation, planned to involve federal housing officials and local residents in an effort to rebuild Harlem from the bottom up.[8]

From the late 1970s onward, this black spatial imaginary began to shift because of the neoliberalization of the economy and the changing nature of urban governance. Neoliberalism is a theory of political-economic practices that promotes the deregulation of markets, the reduction of international trade barriers, the privatization of state companies, the growth of private investment, and the withdrawal of the state. When it comes to cities and urban neighborhoods, neoliberalism is an important conceptual variable. Since the 1980s, the

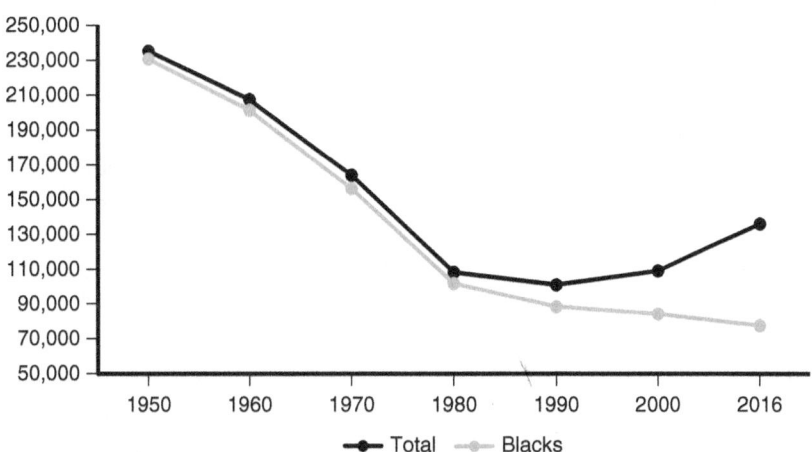

11.1 Total population and black population in Central Harlem, 1950–2016.

United States Census surveys (1950–2000) and the Five-Year American Community Survey (2016), which represents the average of the 2012–2016 period.

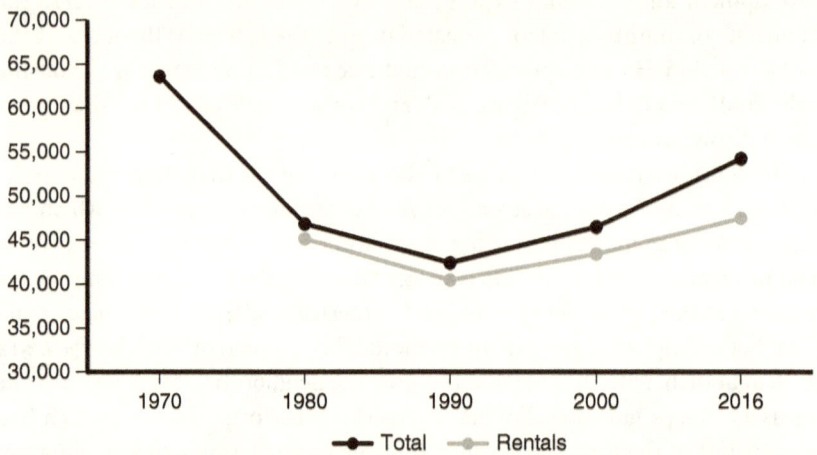

11.2 Total number of occupied housing units in Central Harlem, and rentals, 1970–2016.
United States Census surveys (1970–2000) and the Five-Year American Community Survey (2016), which represents the average of the 2012–2016 period. The 1970 survey of rentals was incomplete and is not included.

private sector has viewed the development, finance, and marketing of real estate as one of the most lucrative arenas for capital investment. Urban governments have responded with the provision of developmental subsidies to global corporations and regulatory flexibility in real estate projects. The result is the remaking of large portions of cities with luxury housing, high-end commerce, and corporate offices, an infrastructure that mostly serves middle- and upper-class people. In the United States, this means that cities are being steadily revitalized after a long period of decline, but in a manner that raises questions about the ability of ordinary people to continue being part of these cities.[9]

This new political-economic structure has altered the black spatial imaginary in Harlem. While aspects of the radical politics of community control remained, the old vision of low-income residents collectively controlling and developing neighborhood land was replaced by the idea that local organizations could facilitate urban development projects that involved outsiders. Although hostile political forces in city hall did not help the situation, wider, structural forces would probably have facilitated this change regardless of local politics. In the 1980s, a more moderate vision of urban development came to the fore. This vision contributed to the rebuilding of Central Harlem with affordable housing mostly designated for local residents. Such rebuilding continued in the twenty-first century, although the neoliberalization of urban space also encouraged the more intense gentrification of Central Harlem.[10]

RETURN OF THE BLACK MIDDLE CLASS: INCIPIENT GENTRIFICATION IN THE 1980S

The June 1981 issue of *Black Enterprise* carried an article by Elliott D. Lee entitled "Will We Lose Harlem? The Symbolic Capital of Black America Is Threatened by Gentrification." Lee reported that, after many years of abandonment and decline, the middle class was returning to Harlem and buying up its famous (and famously deteriorated) brownstones, and he predicted that although almost all of these newcomers were black, whites were going to follow. Lee viewed gentrification as a process through which middle-income people move from the suburbs and more expensive parts of the city to urban neighborhoods populated by low-income renters. "Delicatessens replace corner stores," he wrote, "fancy restaurants replace 'greasy spoons,' whites replace people of color."[11] Indeed, a number of Lee's interviewees were certain that heavy gentrification was going to occur, with affluent whites buying properties, and that existing Harlem residents needed to mobilize in order to hold on to the neighborhood. This was one of the first major articles to define gentrification as a process that threatened Harlem's African American identity.

At the time Lee's article was written, Mayor Edward I. Koch (1978–1989) had developed an antagonistic relationship with New York City's African Americans. Koch was elected mayor in 1977, campaigning as the most conservative mayoral candidate in order to distinguish himself from his Democratic opponents. Once elected, Koch used elements of neoliberalism and neoconservatism to run the government, manage the economy, and gain the electoral support of white ethnics. He reformed the city government into a business-friendly entity that subsidized corporate and real estate expansion while cultivating a culture of racial intolerance by rhetorically attacking the city's black and Latinx populations. Given this prevailing climate, Harlem residents viewed Koch's urban development initiatives with suspicion.[12]

In 1981, the Koch administration decided to auction thirteen of the numerous Harlem brownstones, some located in East and West Harlem, that the city government had claimed after their owners abandoned them. Homesteaders, who used their own money and labor to repair the buildings, had been occupying many of these brownstones, a practice that epitomized Harlem's spatial imaginary with its ideals of community ownership, self-help, and grassroots urban development. Nonprofit organizations formed to support homesteaders and provide technical assistance, the Urban Homesteading Assistance Board being among the most prominent. As building abandonment worsened during the 1970s, the city and federal governments came to the aid of some homesteaders, collaborating with the likes of the board and helping to fund the rehabilitation of buildings. Such assistance worked to undermine radical conceptions of self-help by making homesteaders increasingly reliant on government agencies. In the early 1980s, the Koch administration decided to use lotteries to sell some city-owned buildings, moving away from the policy of cooperating with homesteaders and further weakening grassroots tenant mobilizations.[13]

In auctioning off the brownstones, the Koch administration hoped to encourage middle-class resettlement of Harlem, a move that provoked widespread opposition. Local residents formed the Anti-lottery Committee of Harlemites to prevent the takeover of neighborhood buildings by outsiders, and Central Harlem's Community Board 10 voted overwhelmingly against the lottery. In the end, a compromise gave Harlem residents three times the chance of nonresidents to buy the buildings. After the final vote, Koch expressed his outlook plainly: "They're naturals [middle-class people] for buying brownstones. . . . That's called gentrification."[14] In 1985, the city sold 149 additional brownstones, 98 of them allocated to existing Harlem residents, a move opposed by one Harlem community group, the National Reclamation Project.[15] Nevertheless, the brownstones represented a small fraction of owner-occupied housing, which in turn represented a negligible proportion of occupied housing in Central Harlem. The overwhelming majority of Harlem's housing units were rentals, and any revival of Harlem would have to involve this kind of housing.

Koch's hopes for a revitalization of Harlem by middle-class newcomers did not work out as anticipated. In the 1980s, Harlem lost 9.4 percent of its occupied housing units and 6.7 percent of its population (see figures 11.1 and 11.2). Middle-class people did move to Harlem, most of them black, but not in the sizable numbers anticipated. Furthermore, although the number of people employed in managerial and professional specialisms increased from 4,205 to 6,312 in the 1980s (figure 11.3), this was not a substantial change among a total population of 101,026 in 1990. To be sure, there were more than 10,000 individuals living in Harlem who worked in offices and stores performing secretarial and sales tasks, many of whom were lower middle class. Still, the total numbers were not large enough to denote a middle-class revival, though the rise in the numbers of professionals and managers appeared to be promising.

Despite the proliferation of narratives about the revival of Harlem, the 1980s was not an easy decade for the area. Housing and population continued to be lost, and the crack epidemic that began in the mid-1980s worsened the situation. Harlem, which for many years had been the second-largest drug market in New York City, after the Lower East Side, suffered immensely once crack was popularized and marketed. Abandoned buildings became crack houses and large groups of nomadic populations roamed Harlem's streets to purchase and consume drugs. The police department, still suffering from the results of the fiscal crisis, and whose methods and professionalism had always been problematic in Harlem, could not change the situation. Moreover, in the late 1980s the city's economy faltered and gentrification slowed. The idea of moving to

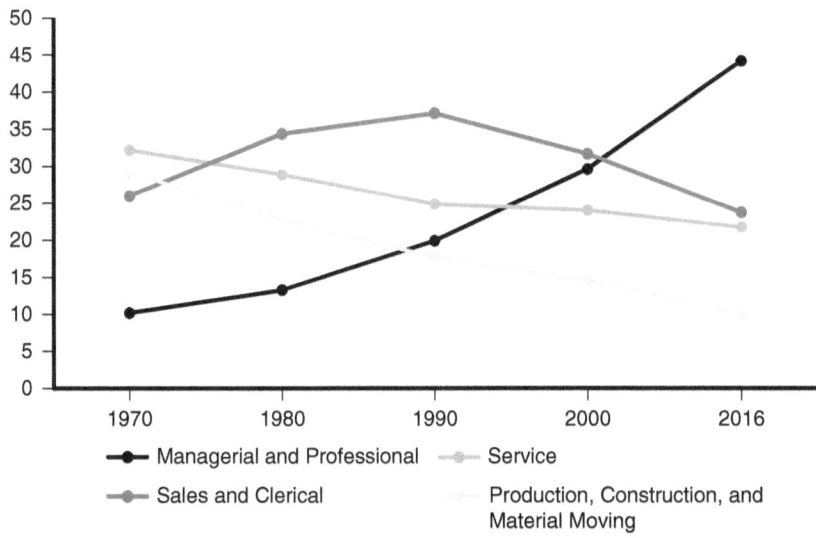

11.3 Occupations of Central Harlem residents, in percentages, 1970–2016.
United States Census surveys (1970–2000) and the One-Year American Community Survey (2016).

Harlem to take advantage of remarkable real estate opportunities was one thing; the reality of a drug epidemic along with an economic recession, and a city government unable to hold its own, was something else.[16]

BEYOND COMMUNITY CONTROL: PARTNERSHIPS AND THE REBUILDING OF HARLEM, 1986–2001

In July 1989, William M. James, chairman of the Harlem Urban Development Corporation (HUDC), wrote an editorial in the *New York Amsterdam News*, asking, "Is community control slipping away?" James argued that the city government and private sector had thwarted efforts by Harlem community organizations to generate affordable housing and jobs and had undermined efforts to "develop the community in its own terms." The HUDC was established in 1971 by Governor Nelson A. Rockefeller as a subsidiary of the state's Urban Development Corporation (UDC), in an effort to weaken radical notions of community control in Harlem. But James claimed that the city administration was now failing to recognize the HUDC as the legitimate redevelopment arm of the community: "Time and time again the city's Department of Housing Preservation and Development has ignored HUDC, using the Community Preservation Corporation and the New York Partnership to do an end run around the very agency that was put here to develop Harlem."[17]

James was referring to Koch's ten-year housing plan, which aimed to rebuild low-income neighborhoods with low- and moderate-income housing. This ambitious plan was implemented by the city's Department of Housing Preservation and Development (HPD), which used capital expenditures totaling more than $5.1 billion to rehabilitate existing structures and build new ones. The ten-year housing plan's design completed a shift from community development to public–private partnerships. Community development had relied on a number of community development corporations (CDCs) to revive small parts of their neighborhoods by spending funds that frequently came from the federal government. Public–private partnerships, by contrast, relied on powerful nonprofit umbrella intermediaries, such as the Community Preservation Corporation and the New York City Partnership, which James criticized, which managed housing programs by facilitating complicated relationships among government agencies, foundations, CDCs, community organizations, faith-based organizations, private owners, developers, builders, financial institutions, insurance companies, and investors. Given that the Koch administration viewed the HUDC with disdain, the agency was not included in most city housing plans.[18]

Although James's editorial made many valid points about redevelopment in New York City, the HUDC's vision of community control was actually a moderate one. Indeed, from the beginning, the HUDC's board of directors comprised moderate community members enjoying the support of major Harlem politicians, not champions of Harlem's low-income black spatial imaginary. In 1974, the HUDC announced a ten-year master plan to build or rehabilitate more than fifty thousand apartments. This plan never materialized, because Rockefeller resigned his governorship in 1973, the UDC almost went bankrupt in 1975, and the state did not prioritize urban development after the city's bailout and the restructuring of the UDC. The HUDC itself became a modestly funded state organization making development proposals that usually went nowhere. In general, as J. Phillip Thompson argues, "Political loyalty often took precedence over community need and policy effectiveness at HUDC, and many community activists viewed HUDC as little more than a patronage mill."[19] In 1981, the HUDC became independent from the UDC, but this did not translate into increased state attention or effectiveness. In fact, when the city government and the UDC announced a major revitalization plan for Central Harlem, in 1982, the HUDC was not included. That the HUDC was described, by the late 1980s, as an agency that advocated community control reflects the extent to which the agency had been ignored by the state and city governments.[20]

Facing the prospect of local interests being completely sidestepped by the Koch administration, Harlem leaders became more active in the realm of housing development. Until 1987, the city government excluded Harlem from most of its housing plans because the administration was feuding with neighborhood entities. That year, David N. Dinkins, a Harlem politician who was elected

Manhattan borough president in 1985, struck an agreement with Koch that addressed various community concerns about the ten-year housing plan. Under this agreement, 40 percent of housing built or renovated in Harlem would be allocated to local residents and 20 percent of the construction subcontracts would go to Harlem businesses. In return, Harlem interests would not attempt to completely control the projects. During the same period, Harlem churches established their own CDCs in order to participate in the ten-year housing plan. In 1986, an interfaith coalition of 109 congregations established Harlem Congregations for Community Improvement (HCCI). In 1989, the Abyssinian Baptist Church founded the Abyssinian Development Corporation.[21]

Despite the 1987 agreement, most of the redevelopment in Harlem occurred after Koch left office. In 1987, the HCCI published the Bradhurst Plan, a proposal to create at least two thousand low- and moderate-income housing units in more than thirty square blocks in Central Harlem. The HPD dismissed the HCCI's capability to complete the project and allowed the development of only fifty-eight apartments, which religious leaders in Harlem considered an insult. In 1989, Dinkins defeated Koch in the Democratic primary and went on to be elected mayor, prevailing over Rudolph Giuliani in the general election. During its remaining months in city hall, the Koch administration made peace with the HCCI and the Bradhurst Plan began to take shape.

Once in office, Dinkins expanded the ten-year housing plan by spending more in HPD capital funds than the Koch administration and making thousands of units more affordable. The Dinkins administration (1990–1993) also incorporated many of the CDCs that had been marginalized by Koch in the rebuilding process. The Bradhurst Development Project was initiated in 1992 and represented the largest redevelopment effort in Harlem.

Giuliani, who became mayor in 1993 after defeating Dinkins, did not see housing creation as a government priority and reduced capital expenditures for it. Yet the city continued to rehabilitate or construct housing throughout his mayoralty, making the ten-year housing plan permanent. Moreover, most of the affordability formulas restructured by Dinkins remained in effect until 2001. The affordability policies of Dinkins, and his hard bargaining with Koch even when he was borough president, acted as a crucial check on gentrification. This was a successful use of public policy to secure affordable housing and priority for local people, and it demonstrates the falseness of the neoliberal "there is no alternative" view of urban gentrification.[22]

Between 1986 and 2001, portions of Central Harlem were rebuilt because of city government initiatives. In the 1980s, the area lost 4,415 housing units, mostly because housing is always lost and the city programs began too late to compensate. In the 1990s, Central Harlem gained 4,082 housing units (see figure 11.2). Almost all of this housing went to low- and moderate-income people. While these housing numbers did not make up for the losses of the 1970s and

1980s, by the late 1990s Harlem looked like a recovering neighborhood. Mostly due to the Dinkins administration's efforts, this comeback incorporated existing Harlem residents, who gained access to new and repaired affordable housing. In that sense, many of the negative effects of gentrification were mitigated when it came to housing provision.

"PART OF THE COMMUNITY": GENTRIFICATION IN HARLEM IN THE 1990S

In May 1999, an article by the journalist Michael Grunwald appeared in the *Washington Post* under the title "Harlem Finally Rides the Economy's 'A' Train: As Crime Falls, a Retail Boom Arrives." Grunwald pointed out that, on 125th Street, Harlem's major commercial thoroughfare, one could see the development of a shopping mall featuring the Disney Store, HMV Records, and a nine-screen movie theater. Starbucks was also opening a branch on 125th Street, and so was Pathmark, a major supermarket. Grunwald summarized what he reluctantly called a "second Harlem Renaissance" as follows: "Crime is plummeting. Rents are skyrocketing. Upscale families are restoring elegant brownstones, and not just in the black-bourgeois district called 'Strivers' Row.' A government 'empowerment zone' is pumping $550 million into the area. Officials say Harlem has even surpassed the Empire State Building as New York's No. 1 destination for foreign tourists."[23] While Grunwald focused on commercial development in Harlem, his analysis touched on the dynamics of a more general government-influenced gentrification.

Four main factors lay behind the gentrification of neighborhoods in New York City during the 1990s. First, the city's economy grew again after 1994 and the real estate sector overheated, driving a larger number of existing and new residents to low-income neighborhoods. Second, crime rates declined substantially and the city government mounted initiatives against social disorder, encouraging many middle- and upper-class individuals to locate to neighborhoods they had previously avoided. Third, after extensive capital campaigns that began in 1982, subway service continued to recover, with some gentrifying neighborhoods benefiting from service improvements and expansion. Fourth, the city government had been rebuilding housing in low-income neighborhoods since 1986, making those built environments more hospitable to outsiders and more attractive to real estate investors.

During the 1990s, Central Harlem's population and housing units increased for the first time in the postwar period (see figures 11.1 and 11.2). The number of professionals and managers rose from 6,312 to 10,156 people. By 2000, this highly paid group represented 29.6 percent of employed individuals in Central Harlem (see figure 11.3), and the great majority of these people were black. Despite fears of a white invasion that dated back at least to the 1970s, the number of whites in Central Harlem increased only from 672 to 1,519 during the 1980s, and from 1,519 to 2,255 during the 1990s (figure 11.4). Whites represented a mere 2.1 percent of the 109,091 people who lived in Central Harlem in 2000.

During this period, the fastest-growing population group in Central Harlem was in fact Latinx. Throughout the postwar period, large proportions of the residents of East Harlem, the South Bronx, Washington Heights, and West Harlem had been people of Latin Caribbean and Latin American origin or descent. This had not been the case in Central Harlem, however, where Latinxs comprised only 4.3 percent of the population in 1980. By 1990, the number of Latinxs in Central Harlem had more than doubled, to 10.1 percent of the total population, and by 2000, that figure had reached 16.8 percent. By citywide standards, this was moderate, and in fact Latinx movement to Central Harlem slowed because of housing loss in the 1980s and increased gentrification in the 1990s.

The relationship of race, class, place, and belonging has been very intricate in Harlem during the age of gentrification. According to Monique M. Taylor, the "invasion" of Harlem by gentrifiers has traditionally been seen as a "white-versus-black issue," with whites assigned the role of neighborhood outsiders and blacks the role of insiders. In research conducted in the 1990s, Taylor found that many newly arriving middle-class blacks viewed themselves as belonging in Harlem but that existing working-class residents did not always agree.[24] John L. Jackson agrees with Taylor, though he views what he terms "Harlemworld" as

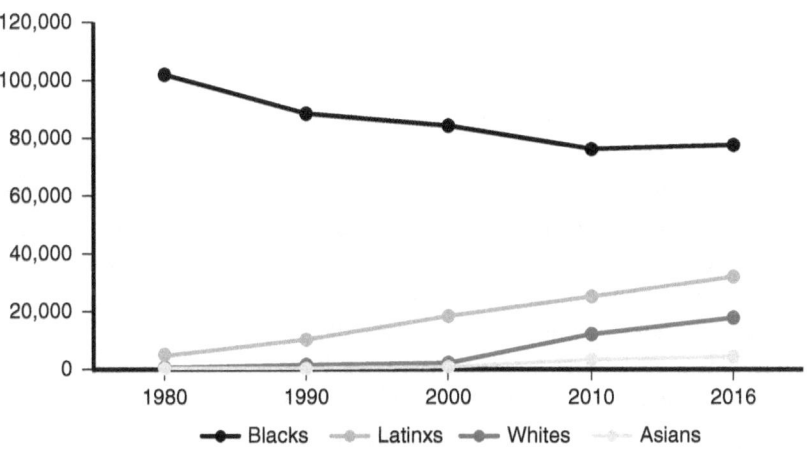

11.4 Race and ethnicity in Central Harlem, 1980–2016.
United States Census surveys (1980–2000) and the Five-Year American Community Survey (2016), which represents the average of the 2012–2016 period.

a concept that goes beyond the actual geography of the place. Jackson problematizes the concept of class by arguing that "Harlem residents not only have life histories that transcend the discrete categories of 'black underclass' and 'black middle-class,' they not only live in close proximity to other residents with markedly different socioeconomic realities, they also have social interactions that cut across many class lines."[25]

This idea of class becomes even more complicated given that the cost of living in New York City is high and that middle-class wages throughout the United States have stagnated in recent decades. In the end, the degree of acceptance that middle-class newcomers to Harlem achieve depends on various factors, including but not restricted to their race. These include the class character of the block into which they move, the way that the public space of the block is used by existing residents, and the degree to which newcomers are able to create networks and friendships in the community. In my own observations and ethnographic research in the late 1990s, I found that middle- and upper-class blacks who had lived in the neighborhood for a while were usually viewed as part of the community. This included people who were not especially community-minded and did not develop close ties with their neighbors.[26]

Something similar appeared to be happening with whites who had moved into Central Harlem. While articulating their fear of white gentrification, many existing residents told me that they viewed the whites whom they knew as "part of the community." This was the standard response of black residents who lived in buildings with white tenants or who had made friends with some of their white neighbors. Residents who did not have many interactions with whites, especially people living in northern Harlem or in public housing, tended to see things differently; they viewed whites who lived in Central Harlem with suspicion.

Knowing that the numbers of whites living in Central Harlem were negligible, I did not interrogate these responses at first. However, as time went on, I realized that the majority of whites living in Harlem did not fit the profile of the affluent gentrifier. I found bartenders, waiters and waitresses, booksellers, store attendants, graduate students, cooks, office workers, and temporary workers. I also encountered some professionals, though it was obvious that their numbers were significantly smaller. In general, class, occupation, and income appeared to be influencing how white newcomers were viewed. In 2000, the median household income of white householders in Central Harlem was $36,145 (adjusted to 2016 dollars); this contrasted to $28,730 for black householders (figure 11.5). Although many whites earned more money than other racial and ethnic groups, the difference was not large. In general, whites appeared to be accepted because their numbers were small and their incomes were close to those of the rest of the community. However, the late 1990s was exactly the period when these patterns slowly began to change.

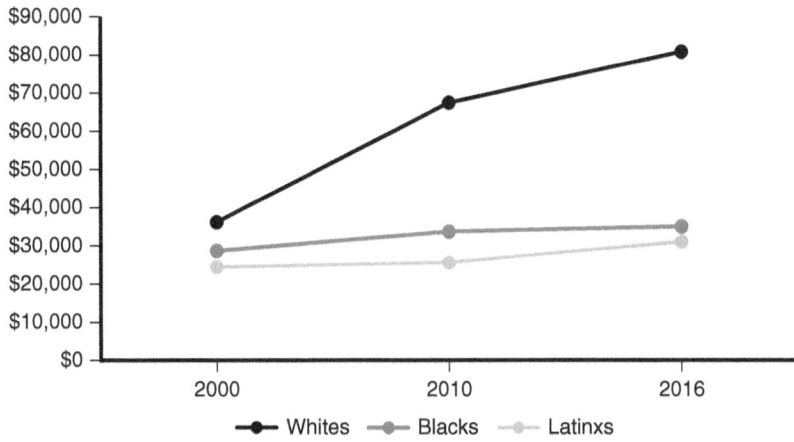

11.5 Median household income by race and ethnicity in Central Harlem, 2000–2016.
United States Census survey (2000) and the Five-Year American Community Surveys (2010, 2016), which represent averages of the 2006–2010 and the 2012–2016 periods. Figures are adjusted to 2016 constant dollars.

During the 1990s, gentrification of New York City neighborhoods by whites occurred mostly in Lower Manhattan and western Brooklyn. By this period, many of these neighborhoods had developed a cultural infrastructure that appealed to new residents. Despite articles in popular publications about the gentrification of Harlem by whites, Harlem functioned more as a symbol of gentrification than as an actual setting for gentrification. Northern Manhattan, with its Latinx and black cultural infrastructures, was not as attractive, especially for younger whites. Besides, the kind of gentrification that occurred in the 1990s followed existing networks and patterns of relocation. In that sense, Harlem was largely spared white gentrification during these years. Neil Smith's contention that "heavily black neighborhoods have been perceived as harder to gentrify" appeared to apply well to Harlem, though much of northern Manhattan was actually Latinx.[27]

TAKEOFF: GENTRIFICATION IN HARLEM IN THE TWENTY-FIRST CENTURY

"Have We Lost Harlem?" was the title of Sonia Alleyne and Kim Renay Anderson's article in the June 2003 issue of *Black Enterprise*, revisiting the prospect Elliott Lee had raised in the same magazine, twenty-two years earlier. Beneath the title of Alleyne and Anderson's article appeared the question "Harlem is renewing its reputation and its landscape, and is currently the hottest piece of real estate in New York City, but at what cost?" In the article, Matthew King II, founder and managing director of MK Capital Resources LLC, claimed, "If you want to live in Manhattan, and you can't afford the downtown rents, you're going to start to move into areas you wouldn't have normally considered." Russell Shuler, executive director of Youth Education Through Sports, expressed his mixed feelings about recent changes in Harlem, calling newcomers "foreigners" and arguing that they "will never have the same sentiment as old-school Harlemites, the same feeling of community."[28]

The *Black Enterprise* article discussed an acceleration of gentrification in Harlem, though in terms of the neighborhood's real demographic trends, this was premature. Gentrification in New York City paused for about a year and a half after the September 11, 2001, attack on the World Trade Center, which adversely affected the city's economy. Gentrification pressures resumed in 2003 and continued until the Great Recession, which commenced in 2007, when incomes stagnated and gentrification in Harlem slowed. Its intensity picked up again in the 2010s.

During this period, urban development in New York City was facilitated by the Bloomberg administration (2002–2013), which sought to transform the landscape of the city in profound ways. Unlike his predecessors, Bloomberg was a multibillionaire businessman with little political experience, and he used his personal wealth to outspend his opponents by tens of millions of dollars. New York City had taken a neoliberal political-economic path since the Koch administration, but under Bloomberg this neoliberal vision reached new heights, with the corporate world having more direct influence on municipal government. Bloomberg filled many of the crucial positions that dealt with economic development, large projects, and overall policy with affluent members of the corporate world. These appointees favored big businesses and developers and sought to attract more large corporations and affluent people to the city from around the world.[29]

The Bloomberg administration pursued three urban development strategies geared toward housing. The first sought to encourage the private development of market-rate housing. Private developers who agreed to build luxury condominiums received generous incentives and tax breaks from the municipal government. The Bloomberg administration tried to harness these entities to include affordable housing in their developments, but this was largely voluntary, and most developers chose not to include such housing in their luxury condominiums. In Central Harlem, this type of development was not widespread, as private developers usually preferred to build in other parts of Manhattan, in western Brooklyn, and in western Queens.[30]

The second strategy involved the rezoning of large portions of the city. Such policies were complex but usually resulted in low-income minority areas undergoing gentrification being "upzoned," so that taller buildings could be developed, while more affluent white areas were "downzoned," to preserve these neighborhoods' character. In Harlem, forty-four blocks around Frederick Douglass Boulevard were upzoned in 2003, allowing higher buildings with higher densities to be constructed. This area in southwestern Central Harlem became one of the epicenters of private development. In 2008, 125th Street was also upzoned, to remake Harlem's central artery as a mainstream business center with office towers, hotels, and thousands of new market-rate condominiums. Opposition by city council members tempered the plan, reducing the height limit of new buildings, providing assistance to more than seventy small businesses facing displacement, and allocating money for improvements to Marcus Garvey Park. Still, these policies, which empower a capital class that takes advantage of inequality, will fundamentally accelerate changes in the neighborhood and further compromise the vision of the black spatial imaginary.[31]

The third urban development strategy, under the New Housing Marketplace Plan, pledged to preserve or create 165,000 units of affordable housing by 2013. Much of the plan focused on the preservation of existing affordable housing units whose subsidies were due to expire. Besides the construction of rental housing for low- and moderate-income people, this plan included a major homeownership component for moderate-, middle-, and even upper-middle-income people. The plan used the remainder of city-owned land to build housing and even pursued strategies to find new land through rezoning, land banking, and public–private partnerships. Harlem benefited handsomely from these aspects of the plan, since the subsidies for thousands of low- and moderate-income housing units were renewed, while new subsidized housing was constructed. Yet the housing built for homeowners contributed to the gentrification of the area because, even though 50 percent of the units were set aside for Community District 10 residents, many middle- and upper-middle-income families from other parts of the city were accommodated.[32]

More generally, the rebuilding of Harlem continued in the twenty-first century, and gentrification sharply intensified during these years. Between 2000 and 2016, Central Harlem gained 7,787 housing units and 26,876 residents (see figures 11.1 and 11.2). Professionals and managers, who had represented 29.6 percent of the population in 2000, increased to 44.2 percent of Central Harlem's population by 2016 (see figure 11.3). All other occupation categories declined. The steep decline in the number of people performing sales and clerical occupations, which began in the 1990s, represents an important indicator of gentrification; many were lower-middle-income people priced out of Harlem, and possibly out of New York City. Median household income increased by a dramatic 41.2 percent between 2000 and 2016, defying a citywide median household income decline (figure 11.6). However, because of the high proportion of low-income households, the median household income of Central Harlem remained around $40,000.

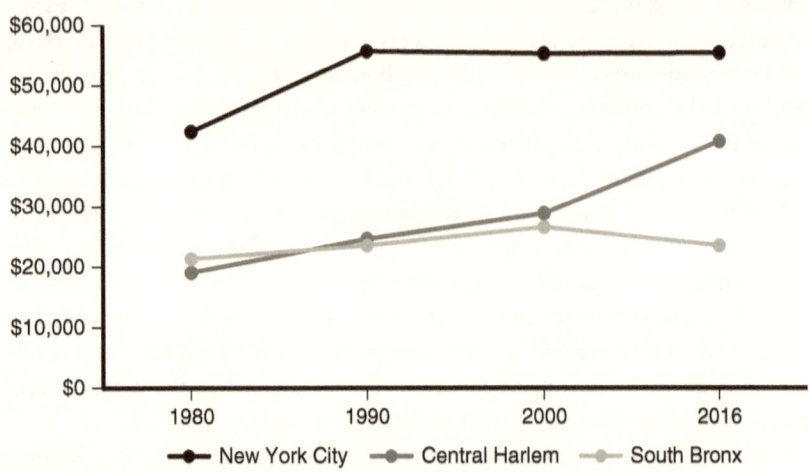

11.6 Median household income in Central Harlem, 1980–2016.
United States Census survey (1980–2000) and the Five-Year American Community Survey (2016), which represents the average of the 2012–2016 period. Figures are adjusted to 2016 constant dollars.

In terms of race and ethnicity, Central Harlem began to change markedly during these years. The number of whites increased from 2,255 in 2000 to 17,744 in 2016 (see figure 11.4). By 2016, they represented 13.1 percent of the total population, a sharp increase from the 2.1 percent they had represented as recently as 2000. Only after the Great Recession hit did their numbers stabilize. Meanwhile, the number of Latinxs also increased substantially, from 18,531 to 32,104, and by 2016 they represented 23.6 percent of Central Harlem's population. By citywide standards, the proportion of Latinxs remains low, partly because Central Harlem is becoming less affordable, partly because the influx of Latinxs to the United States declined during the Great Recession, and partly because many low- and moderate-income African Americans are staying put.

The movement of larger numbers of whites into Harlem revived discussions about the black character of the area being compromised. In the *New York Times*, the journalist Sam Roberts claimed that blacks were no longer a majority in Harlem. Of course, Roberts reached this conclusion by looking at Greater Harlem, which includes areas that had never contained a majority black population, such as parts of the Upper West Side, Morningside Heights, and East Harlem. This idea of "blackness" becomes even more complicated when one introduces Latinxs into the picture.[33]

During the 2000s, discontent with gentrification increased in Central Harlem and was manifested in terms of both race and class. Though whites remained a small proportion of the population, the increase in their numbers (see figure 11.4) and, most importantly, the change in their class characteristics made many existing residents uncomfortable. By 2016, the median household income of whites had reached $80,790 (adjusted to 2016 dollars). This was more than double the figure for blacks, which stood at $35,091 (see figure 11.5). Many of the new white arrivals were pushed to Central Harlem by high prices in other parts of New York and were attracted by homeownership opportunities in the new luxury condominiums. In interviews with long-term black residents of Harlem after 2004, I observed a condition that Filip Stabrowski defines as "everyday displacement":

> Everyday displacement is experienced by low-income and working-class residents who remain physically a part of the neighborhood, even as their living conditions, sense of security, and access to local resources are all being eroded. This understanding of displacement as ongoing and lived highlights the temporally extended and quotidian aspects of gentrification. Gentrification is a process of accumulation—of capital and profit on the one hand, and dispossession and insecurity on the other—and not merely a discrete, isolated moment of physical dislocation.[34]

In Central Harlem, everyday displacement takes two main forms. The first concerns insecurity about the ability to live in the neighborhood because of pressures applied by landlords and the market. Many households living from paycheck to paycheck are especially afraid, because a single unfortunate occurrence, such as a sudden illness or layoff, can quickly translate into eviction. The second involves the transformation of the neighborhood's cultural infrastructure. Focused until recently on 125th Street, this transformation has expanded to many other parts of the area, contributing to the displacement of existing businesses and the opening of new ones that cater to a different socioeconomic clientele. Even activities in noncommercial spaces such as parks are affected, as new residents often disapprove of cultural practices that have been occurring for many decades. They call the police to intervene in disputes that could easily be resolved with goodwill. For such reasons, many who can still afford to stay in the neighborhood nonetheless feel less inclined to do so, as their everyday existence becomes increasingly difficult because their customs, manners, preferences, and income are not in tune with contemporary market forces and the new profile of the neighborhood.[35]

For many long-standing Harlemites, though, the cost of housing is indeed becoming a significant pressure. In 2016, there were 8,968 public housing units and 18,064 affordable units in Central Harlem. This meant that low- and moderate-income people lived in at least 49.8 percent of the area's housing.

Many rent-stabilized apartments remain affordable, especially if the household has continuously occupied an apartment for many years. In 2011, as many as 54.5 percent of Central Harlem's apartments were rent-stabilized.

Yet the situation is far more precarious than this figure would suggest. Increasingly, landlords and real estate entities are attempting to force or incentivize turnovers in rent-stabilized apartments so that they can increase the rents considerably. Meanwhile, subsidies for affordable housing units expire after a period of time. The New Housing Marketplace Plan preserved the subsidies for most of those apartments, but this has not reduced the insecurity of the people living in them. At the same time, rents are increasing, even if modestly, in all kinds of apartments, contributing to a high proportion of people's income being spent on housing (figure 11.7). The proportion of residents spending more than 30 percent of their income on housing, considered to be a high threshold, is approximating the 50 percent mark in Central Harlem (figure 11.8). Almost 25 percent of Central Harlem households are spending more than half of their income on rent. While this is a trend that characterizes most of New York, its effects are especially threatening in low-income neighborhoods.

Anti-gentrification activism has been strong and in many cases has helped existing tenants to avoid eviction. The Harlem Tenants Council, led by Nellie Bailey, has staged numerous protest actions and informational meetings about gentrification and displacement. Women are in the forefront of this organization, assisting and organizing people whose housing situation is becoming precarious. Under additional pressure from local politicians, city agencies have

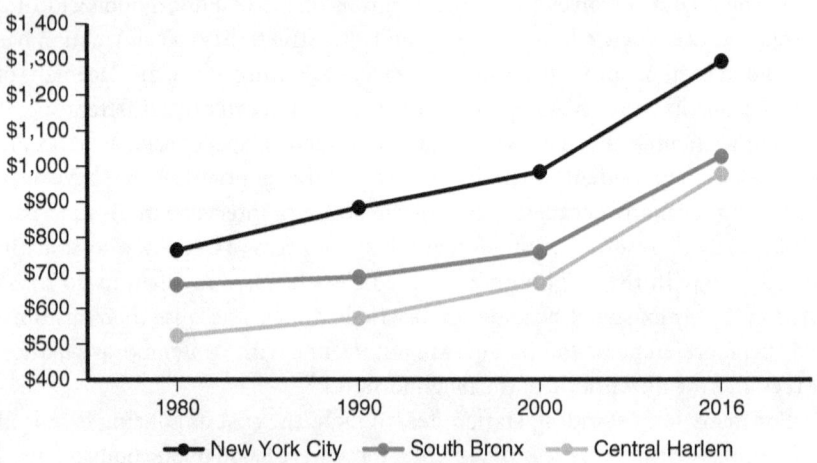

11.7 Median gross rent in Central Harlem, 1980–2016.

United States Census (1980–2000) and the Five-Year American Community Survey (2016), which represents the average of the 2012–2016 period. Figures are adjusted to 2016 constant dollars.

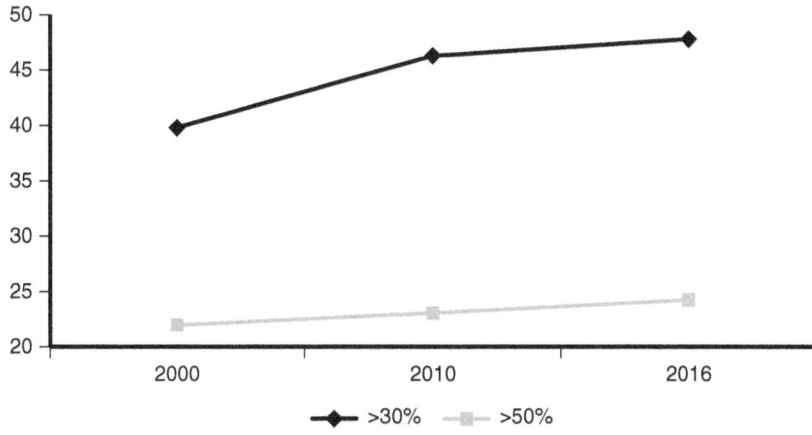

11.8 Percentage of household income spent on housing in Central Harlem, 2000–2016.
United States Census survey (2000) and the Five-Year American Community Surveys (2010, 2016), which represent averages of the 2006–2010 and the 2012–2016 periods.

also stepped up their inquiries into housing practices by companies that have a history of tenant mistreatment.[36]

The southern and western parts of Central Harlem are experiencing the most intense gentrification, though this requires some qualification. While the streets near Central Park and Morningside Heights—a neighborhood where Columbia University and other prestigious educational, medical, and religious institutions are located—are considered especially desirable, the high proportion of public and subsidized housing means developers and real estate interests operate anywhere they can. Still, northern Central Harlem has experienced less gentrification, though this also varies by building and by block. As of 2018, most of the commercial infrastructure serving the more affluent residents and visitors was still located in the southern parts of Central Harlem. But if the present rate of demographic change continues, Harlem will, within a generation, be a community and landscape fundamentally transformed.

CONCLUSION

Harlem now finds itself in a paradoxical and precarious position. Although Central Harlem has one of the largest proportions of subsidized and public housing of any urban neighborhood in the world, the area is also gentrifying at a rate that is visually arresting and profoundly disorienting for long-term residents. Many of the affluent newcomers who have made their homes in the neighborhood have little involvement with Harlem's community or culture. Everyday displacement now characterizes the experience of many of Harlem's low-income black residents, whose housing security is eroding and whose cultural infrastructure is contracting. Neighborhoods always change, but there is nothing natural, neutral, or inevitable about the ways in which they do so. Neighborhood change is, in large measure, planned, with some people's livelihoods and desires accommodated and others' considered expendable.

In 2016, Michael Henry Adams, an author, local historian, and longtime Harlem resident, wrote an op-ed for the *New York Times* entitled "The End of Black Harlem." One could view this article as simply the latest in a long succession of pieces stretching back to the early 1980s—several of which I have quoted from in the course of this chapter—that have lamented the impending end of Harlem as the cultural and social "capital of black America," without this moment ever having arrived. This time, however, things are different. Harlem is now experiencing extreme gentrification pressures as, for the first time in almost a century, large numbers of middle- and upper-class whites have moved into the neighborhood. Adams described a recent protest outside a fundraiser for a politician who supported the Bloomberg administration's plan to rezone 125th Street into a denser, mixed-use area. A few boys passing by were bewildered by the gathering:

> As we chanted, "Save Harlem now!" one of them inquired, "Why are y'all yelling that?" We explained that the city was encouraging housing on the historic, retail-centered 125th Street, as well as taller buildings. Housing's good, in theory, but because the median income in Harlem is less than $37,000 a year, many of these new apartments would be too expensive for those of us who already live here.
>
> Hearing this, making a quick calculation, one boy in glasses shot back at his companions, "You see, I told you they didn't plant those trees for us."
>
> It was painful to realize how even a kid could see in every new building, every historic renovation, every boutique clothing shop—indeed in every tree and every flower in every park improvement—not a life-enhancing benefit, but a harbinger of his own displacement.[37]

As Adams's vignette suggests, it is difficult to convince long-term residents of Harlem that the city's infrastructural improvements are being undertaken for their benefit. Infrastructural maintenance seldom occurred during most of the postwar period, when the city government repaired essential infrastructure only when it reached the breaking point. Suddenly, as affluent whites move to the neighborhood, the city government appears to care about Harlem. Trees are planted, parks landscaped, playgrounds retrofitted, and sidewalks rebuilt.

Given the neglect that Harlem has experienced, there are still many sites that reveal the disrepair of the past. But that, too, is changing.

While there are many specificities that apply to Central Harlem, developments at the local level are influenced from elsewhere as various layers of power—transnational, national, regional, and local—operate simultaneously. While Harlem as a location may matter, it is a growing economy, a citywide housing scarcity, and a city government unable to formulate meaningful housing policy that are most affecting Harlem's fortunes. The global desire to invest in urban real estate and the city's aspiration to accommodate this desire are not helping, either, because even if such transnational entities are not investing as much in Harlem, their involvement in other parts of the city pushes people to neighborhoods such as Harlem.

Crucially, subsidized and public housing have been acting as a brake on the rate of displacement, replacement, and exclusion of low- and moderate-income people in Central Harlem. However, because the city government no longer owns any land in Harlem, the creation of new subsidized housing will have to follow more creative, and probably more expensive, strategies. More than half of Harlem's housing is also rent-stabilized, meaning that rents increase by a small to moderate percentage. Rent stabilization is not the best way of keeping housing units inexpensive, however. Increases in the rents of such apartments frequently outpace inflation rates, while real estate entrepreneurs seek vacancies so that they can increase rents more rapidly. It is the low-income residents of rent-stabilized apartments who are the most vulnerable in Harlem today.

Governments have policy options, and they can choose to prioritize affordability and opportunities for local people or give free rein to capital, land speculation, and neoliberal urban development. The Dinkins episode shows that neighborhood change in the form of overwhelming gentrification is not inevitable, that there is a political choice that can be made—to adopt public policies that prioritize the lives and aspirations of low- and moderate-income people already resident in an area. Maintaining public housing, limiting rent increases, and insisting that new developments include significant amounts of affordable housing are the choices that stand between our moment and what we are told is the inevitable loss of black Harlem.

NOTES

1. Without denying the racial dimension, most scholars of gentrification focus on class. See Rowland Atkinson, "Measuring Gentrification and Displacement in Greater London," *Urban Studies* 37 (January 2000): 149–65; Matthias Bernt and Andrej Holm, "Is It, or Is Not?: The Conceptualisation of Gentrification and Displacement and Its Political Implications in the Case of Berlin-Prenzlauer Berg," *City* 13 (September 2009): 312–24; Tom

Slater, "Missing Marcuse: On Gentrification and Displacement," *City* 13 (September 2009): 292–311; Neil Smith, *The New Urban Frontier: Gentrification and the Revanchist City* (New York: Routledge, 1996).

2. David J. Maurrasse, *Listening to Harlem: Gentrification, Community, and Business* (New York: Routledge, 2006); Brian D. Goldstein, *The Roots of Urban Renaissance: Gentrification and the Struggle over Harlem* (Cambridge, MA: Harvard University Press, 2017).

3. The boundaries of Central Harlem are identical to those of Manhattan Community District 10. Unless otherwise noted, East Harlem and West Harlem are not included in this study, as their dynamics of gentrification are not the same as those of Central Harlem, the area viewed as the epicenter of black Harlem.

4. Many gentrification scholars also acknowledge processes of replacement and exclusion, though much of the focus has been on displacement, because of its more detrimental effects. Recently, some urban studies scholars have claimed that displacement is minimal and therefore that gentrification is not harmful to existing low-income residents. I disagree with this premise. For the debate, see Lance Freeman and Frank Braconi, "Gentrification and Displacement," *Journal of the American Planning Association* 70 (Winter 2004): 39–52; Kathe Newman and Elvin K. Wyly, "The Right to Stay Put, Revisited: Gentrification and Resistance to Displacement in New York City," *Urban Studies* 43 (January 2006): 23–57.

5. George Lipsitz, *How Racism Takes Place* (Philadelphia, PA: Temple University Press, 2011), 30.

6. George Lipsitz, *The Possessive Investment in Whiteness: How White People Profit from Identity Politics* (Philadelphia, PA: Temple University Press, 2006); Lipsitz, *How Racism Takes Place*, 51–70.

7. Shannon King, *Whose Harlem Is This, Anyway?: Community Politics and Grassroots Activism During the New Negro Era* (New York: New York University Press, 2015).

8. Simon Anekwe, "Key Women to Restore 'Proud Black Capital,'" *New York Amsterdam News*, February 12, 1977; Monique M. Taylor, *Harlem Between Heaven and Hell* (Minneapolis: University of Minnesota Press, 2002); John L. Jackson Jr., *Harlemworld: Doing Race and Class in Contemporary Black America* (Chicago: University of Chicago Press, 2001).

9. Themis Chronopoulos, *Spatial Regulation in New York City: From Urban Renewal to Zero Tolerance* (New York: Routledge, 2011); Neil Brenner and Nik Theodore, *Spaces of Neoliberalism: Urban Restructuring in North America and Western Europe* (Oxford: Blackwell, 2002); Jason Hackworth, *The Neoliberal City: Governance, Ideology, and Development in American Urbanism* (Ithaca, NY: Cornell University Press, 2006).

10. Brian D. Goldstein, "'The Search for New Forms': Black Power and the Making of the Postmodern City," *Journal of American History* 103 (September 2016): 375–99.

11. Elliott D. Lee, "Will We Lose Harlem?: The Symbolic Capital of Black America Is Threatened by Gentrification," *Black Enterprise* (June 1981): 192.

12. John H. Mollenkopf, *A Phoenix in the Ashes: The Rise and Fall of the Koch Coalition in New York City Politics* (Princeton, NJ: Princeton University Press, 1994); Chronopoulos, *Spatial Regulation*; Jonathan Soffer, *Ed Koch and the Rebuilding of New York City* (New York: Columbia University Press, 2010).

13. Charles Laven, "Self Help in Neighborhood Development," in *The Scope of Social Architecture*, ed. C. Richard Hatch (New York: Van Nostrand Reinhold, 1984), 104–17; Jacqueline Leavitt and Susan Saegert, *From Abandonment to Hope: Community-Households in Harlem* (New York: Columbia University Press, 1990); Ronald Lawson, "Owners of Last Resort: The Track Record of New York City's Early Low-Income Housing Cooperatives

14. Lee A. Daniels, "City to Sell Harlem Brownstones by Lottery," *New York Times*, July 24, 1981.
15. Lloyd Williams, "The Harlem Brownstone Dilemma," *New York Amsterdam News*, May 9, 1981; Anti-lottery Committee, "Harlem Brownstones," *New York Amsterdam News*, May 30, 1981; Carlyle C. Douglas, "City Taking Bids for 149 Vacant Harlem Buildings," *New York Times*, May 11, 1985.
16. Eric C. Schneider, *Smack: Heroin and the American City* (Philadelphia: University of Pennsylvania Press, 2008), 182–95; Themis Chronopoulos, "Police Misconduct, Community Opposition, and Urban Governance in New York City, 1945–1965," *Journal of Urban History* 44 (July 2018): 643–68; Charles Baillou, "Drugs, AIDS Killing off Harlem Youths," *New York Amsterdam News*, July 30, 1988.
17. Rev. Dr. William M. James, "Is Community Control Slipping Away?," *New York Amsterdam News*, July 1, 1989.
18. See Alex F. Schwartz, *Housing Policy in the United States* (New York: Routledge, 2015); Kathryn Wylde, "The Contribution of Public–Private Partnerships to New York's Assisted Housing Industry," in *Housing and Community Development in New York City: Facing the Future*, ed. Michael H. Schill (Albany: State University of New York Press, 1999), 73–91; Themis Chronopoulos, "The Rebuilding of the South Bronx after the Fiscal Crisis," in "After the Urban Crisis: New York and the Rise of Inequality," ed. Themis Chronopoulos and Jonathan Soffer, *Journal of Urban History* 43 (special issue, November 2017): 855–959.
19. J. Phillip Thompson, *Double Trouble: Black Mayors, Black Communities, and the Call for a Deep Democracy* (New York: Oxford University Press, 2005), 213.
20. Simon Anekwe, " 'New Look' for Harlem," *New York Amsterdam News*, July 17, 1971; "HUDC Gets Autonomy from UDC," *New York Amsterdam News*, September 26, 1981; Simon Anekwe, "Harlemites Gird to Mull Area's Revival Scheme," *New York Amsterdam News*, September 25, 1982; Kimberley Johnson, "Community Development Corporations, Participation, and Accountability: The Harlem Urban Development Corporation and the Bedford–Stuyvesant Restoration Corporation," *Annals of the American Academy of Political and Social Science* 594 (July 2004): 109–24.
21. Vera Titunik, "Residents Hail Plans to Develop Harlem," *New York Amsterdam News*, September 16, 1987; Alexander Von Hoffman, *House by House, Block by Block: The Rebirth of America's Urban Neighborhoods* (New York: Oxford University Press, 2003), 61; Derek S. Hyra, *The New Urban Renewal: The Economic Transformation of Harlem and Bronzeville* (Chicago: University of Chicago Press, 2008), 142–43; Michael Leo Owens, *God and Government in the Ghetto: The Politics of Church–State Collaboration in Black America* (Chicago: University of Chicago Press, 2007), 94–98.
22. Owens, *God and Government*, 133–72; Chronopoulos, "Rebuilding of the South Bronx."
23. Michael Grunwald, "Harlem Finally Rides the Economy's 'A' Train: As Crime Falls, a Retail Boom Arrives," *Washington Post*, May 5, 1999.
24. Taylor, *Harlem*, 60.
25. Jackson, *Harlemworld*, 90.
26. See also Taylor, *Harlem*, 29–58.
27. Smith, *New Urban Frontier*, 139. See also Christopher Mele, *Selling the Lower East Side: Culture, Real Estate, and Resistance in New York City* (Minneapolis: University of Minnesota Press, 2000); Sharon Zukin, *Naked City: The Death and Life of Authentic Urban Places* (New York: Oxford University Press, 2010); Themis Chronopoulos, "The Politics of Race and Class and the Changing Spatial Fortunes of the McCarren Pool in Brooklyn,

New York, 1936–2010," *Space and Culture* 16 (February 2013): 104–22; Filip Stabrowski, "New-Build Gentrification and the Everyday Displacement of Polish Immigrant Tenants in Greenpoint, Brooklyn," *Antipode* 46 (June 2014): 794–815.

28. Sonia Alleyne and Kim Renay Anderson, "Have We Lost Harlem?," *Black Enterprise* 33 (June 2003): 76–77, 80, 84. Shuler's comments were paraphrased by Alleyne and Anderson.

29. Scott Larson, *"Building Like Moses with Jacobs in Mind": Contemporary Planning in New York City* (Philadelphia, PA: Temple University Press, 2013); Themis Chronopoulos, "African Americans, Gentrification, and Neoliberal Urbanization: The Case of Fort Greene, Brooklyn," *Journal of African American Studies* 20 (December 2016): 294–322.

30. New York City Department of Housing Preservation and Development (HPD), *The New Housing Marketplace: Creating Housing for the Next Generation* (New York: HPD, 2005); Susan S. Fainstein, "Mega-Projects in New York, London and Amsterdam," *International Journal of Urban and Regional Research* 32 (December 2008): 768–85.

31. Department of City Planning, *Frederick Douglass Boulevard Rezoning Proposal* (New York: Department of City Planning, 2003); Amy Armstrong et al., *Policy Brief: How Have Recent Rezonings Affected the City's Ability to Grow?* (New York: Furman Center for Real Estate and Urban Policy, 2010); Alessandro Busà, "After the 125th Street Rezoning: The Gentrification of Harlem's Main Street in the Bloomberg Years," *Urbanities* 4 (November 2014): 51–68.

32. HPD, *New Housing Marketplace*; HPD, *Progress Report 2005* (New York: HPD, 2005); HPD, *New Housing Marketplace Plan: Creating A More Affordable, Viable, and Sustainable City for All New Yorkers* (New York: HPD, 2010); Larson, "Building Like Moses," 77–96, 133–53; New York City Housing Development Corporation annual reports (2002–2013); New York City Independent Budget Office, *Agency Capital Expenditures, 2002–2013* (New York: Independent Budget Office, 2015); Chronopoulos, "Rebuilding of the South Bronx."

33. Sam Roberts, "In Harlem, Blacks Are No Longer a Majority," *New York Times*, January 6, 2010.

34. Stabrowski, "New-Build Gentrification," 808.

35. Camilo José Vergara, *Harlem: The Unmaking of a Ghetto* (Chicago: University of Chicago Press, 2013); Khadijah White, "Belongingness and the Harlem Drummers," *Urban Geography* 36 (2015): 340–58; Melissa Checker, "Wiped out by the 'Greenwave': Environmental Gentrification and the Paradoxical Politics of Urban Sustainability," *City & Society* 23 (December 2011): 210–29.

36. Nellie Hester Bailey, "Women, Gentrification, and Harlem," in *Feminism and War: Confronting U.S. Imperialism*, ed. Robin L. Riley, Chandra Talpade Mohanty, and Minnie Bruce Pratt (London: Zed, 2008), 232–37.

37. Michael Henry Adams, "The End of Black Harlem," *New York Times*, May 27, 2016, http://www.nytimes.com/2016/05/29/opinion/sunday/the-end-of-black-harlem.html.

12.

WHEN HARLEM WAS IN *VOGUE* MAGAZINE

JOHN L. JACKSON JR.

Imagine Harlem *not* hip and happening, not coveted or cool. It seems like an eternity ago that this most famous neighborhood was marked as irredeemable by many of New York's power brokers. Yet for decades, and well into the closing years of the twentieth century, this neighborhood that had once been renowned as a promised land for aspiring blacks and a pleasure zone for "slumming" whites was widely feared and mostly written off, a place name mobilized to evoke pathology and urban danger.

It was in the early 1990s that I first started paying attention to an assortment of experts and interested pundits who were describing Harlem as a community so tragic, so shunned and scorned, that it could never be gentrified. And these prognosticators were quite confident that such a claim was self-evident. A few months into my first year in the doctoral anthropology program at Columbia University (an institution long characterized by some as *in* but not *of* Harlem), the current governor of New York, Andrew Cuomo, who was then assistant secretary for community planning and development at the federal Department of Housing and Urban Development, provided a pithy proclamation to a *New Yorker* reporter about the absolute impossibility of gentrification occurring in that notorious neighborhood: "If you expect to see Harlem as gentrified and mixed-income," he proffered, "it's not going to happen."[1] That was 1994. And the honorable governor was spectacularly wrong.

Harlem may be a special place, long perceived as the symbolic "capital of black America," but it is hardly the only locale that has been declared, falsely, to be beyond the reach and interest of would-be gentry and posited as immune to the pressures of urban change sparked by middle-class in-migration. In the same *New Yorker* article, the journalist Natalie Y. Moore is offered up as a black would-be gentrifier who learned the hard way that "black Chicago neighborhoods don't gentrify," after a South Side home she bought lost 75 percent of its market value within a few years of her purchase.[2] Moore makes the very reasonable point that there are particular attributes of neighborhoods (such as size, housing stock, and subjective cultural narratives of risk) that make some more prime for gentrification than others. She goes further, arguing that certain communities do not really need to worry about the phantom of "Negro removal," which has long been the unvarnished term detractors have used to expose "urban renewal" as a euphemism for the logic of displacement undergirding gentrification's relentless processes.[3]

During a 2017 lecture that I delivered at Brooklyn College, I engaged in a public debate with a student who had completed a meticulously researched final paper contending that the neighborhood I happened to have grown up in, Brooklyn's Canarsie, would never be gentrified, no matter how much the rest of that borough's landscape had already been radically transformed over the previous ten years.[4] Some areas continue to be characterized as outside gentrification's orbit because of the ways that race and poverty converge to dissuade wealthier white residents from relocating there. Of course, these poor and disparaged spaces are always only gentrification-proof until they are not, until the pendulum swings and the developer's hammer drops. Then, suddenly, demographic shifts that were once labeled impossible are rewritten as inevitable, from nonstarter to foregone conclusion in the blink of an eye—in Harlem and Brooklyn and even "black Chicago," but also in Detroit, Baltimore, Oakland, and West Philadelphia. It is a common enough pivot.

In the case of Harlem, Columbia University's presence has always been an indication, in part, of how and why adamant dismissals of gentrification should have sounded too self-assured all along. That institutional anchor kept Central Harlem at bay, on the other end of a large, boundary-defining Morningside Park, the other side of the proverbial tracks, while also reminding everyone of just how vulnerable Harlemites have long felt in the shadow of that powerful northern Manhattan landowner.[5] Or, put another way, since at least the 1960s a tense mutual precariousness has defined the town–gown dynamics wherein the financial prowess of a billion-dollar academic institution bumps up against the organizing skills and social capital of committed local activists (and the imagined hazard of an overly close-quartered relationship to urban danger). Again, this is not a dynamic confined to Harlem but one that can just as readily be observed in the complex relationship between, for instance, the University of Chicago and that city's South Side.[6]

The Harlem landscape's recent transformations typify, in many respects, how effectively gentrification has devoured neighborhoods once declared immune to its multipronged machinations. Through most of the second half of the twentieth century, in the eyes of many, Harlem possessed, like many inner-city areas, a threatening blackness that served as a proxy for fears about violent crime, social chaos, and interpersonal hostility. And, as with many urban communities, these discourses of threat and danger have proven not to be the insurmountable obstacle to gentrification that many commentators predicted.

However, Harlem's gentrification has also had a certain atypicality, born of Harlem being—well, "Harlem." By dint of the neighborhood's extraordinarily overdetermined iconicity as the former seat of the Harlem Renaissance, an alternative imagery of Harlem as the epitome of a sophisticated black modernity—urbane black couples in fur coats, photographed in front of elegant brownstones; echoes of Duke Ellington and Ella Fitzgerald at the Apollo Theater—has lingered and has been enthusiastically assimilated into the marketing of a "new Harlem Renaissance" that indicates, authenticates, and domesticates gentrification. To an unusual degree, Harlem's urban renewal has been facilitated by the complex, layered nature of the locale's perceived blackness.[7]

Notwithstanding this, in Harlem and other supposedly gentrification-resistant places, there is a common logic afoot, generated by forces that conspire to create a kind of bifurcated and even socially schizophrenic portrait of America's racialized and largely impoverished urban environments. Recasting what I have previously called a "two-world model" of black life in the United States, I would emphasize that gentrification in places like Harlem helps to produce a distinctly dualistic, "two-world" rendering of existence in contemporary urban America.[8] In a sense, gentrification works to promote two divergent versions of metropolitan experiential possibility, two seemingly distinctive interpretations of what the inner city is, and these opposing interpretations can be difficult to reconcile.

This is, of course, another "tale of two cities." We are talking about the self-same physical places recalibrated via public discourse in big and small ways—and for rich versus poor onlookers. How do metropolitan areas spatialize material vulnerability and economic disadvantage? The pattern that dominates in the context of cities in the United States has been a geographic polarization predicated on ideologies of race, racism, and specifically racial markets, an iteration of the ways in which advertisers sell distinctive narratives to niche audiences via symbols that resonate with classic and irrational tropes of racialization. This long-standing polarization—entrenched during the decades after World War II in the separation between white suburbs and black/Latinx inner cities—continues to haunt the American psyche, even as inner cities become the racially mixed frontiers of a transnational "urban renaissance."[9] It animates recent coverage of Harlem by producing a range of modalities through which that neighborhood can lend itself to seemingly irreconcilable accounts that both extend traditional representations of Harlem's exotic and threatening difference *and* cultivate emergent extensions of those possibilities in the wake of a gentrifying landscape that shifts beneath residents' feet—from impossible to possible to seemingly unstoppable. Moreover, questions of racial and urban authenticity continue to be the engine both for gentrification's multifaceted machinery and for its opponents' most powerful pushbacks against the ghosts haunting that machine.

The idea of Harlem as the essential "ghetto" domain of an impoverished, inner-city black community continues to mark some sections of the neighborhood, in the eyes of realtors and would-be gentrifiers, as beyond the frontiers of the "new Harlem"—just as the idea of the neighborhood as rightfully belonging to the black poor underlies much of the local activism in opposition to gentrification.[10] Meanwhile, a newer vision fetishizes inner-city locations as the principal terrain of what is novel, exciting, and fashionable in multicultural city life. Importantly, this second vision occupies a complex relationship to the first, as the "ghetto" image both impedes and, in some ways, nurtures the sense of urban revival. That is to say that no small part of the much-hyped "excitement" of these neighborhoods derives from the faint tinge of danger that lingers as a reminder of their recent "no-go" past and that filters into mainstream consciousness through the "ghettocentricity" of hip-hop and other popular cultural commentary.[11] But in Harlem's case, this type of fetishization is both intensified and modulated by the distinctive imagery of black bourgeois grandeur imprinted on sites such as Strivers' Row, Sugar Hill, and the Hotel Theresa. In short, the agglomeration of images that constitute a notion of Harlem as the historic "race capital" of black America has clear implications for how *financial* resources are supposed to flow through its thoroughfares, and it governs many of the images that make up variously pitched portraits of its people.

In what follows, I call attention to two competing conceptions of what we might call "racial capital," in an economic or quasi-economic sense, both of which circulate in and around black inner-city areas in general and Harlem, the mythologized "race capital," in particular. The first of these conceptions is indigenous to black urban communities and, in successive forms, has long fueled the determination of local people to make these urban neighborhoods sites of black autonomy and economic flourishing. The second sense of racial capital, though, is the one in which gentrification trades. It is the valuable currency that is carefully derived, or selectively extracted, from the accreted imagery of black urban areas within the American racial mindscape and that moves with particular liquidity through Harlem. The story of Harlem over the past two decades is, in part, the story of these two forms of racial capital—the depletion (or at least continued absence) of one; the accumulation (and reappropriation) of the other.

■ ■ ■

When the historian David Levering Lewis wrote his magisterial book *When Harlem Was in Vogue* (1981), his aim was to capture the neighborhood in its pre-Depression heyday, a slice of time retrospectively labeled the "Harlem Renaissance," when the community's reputation as the "Mecca of the New Negro" was cemented.[12] Carl Van Vechten was not a native Harlemite, and he was not African American, but some of his most famous photographs from the early twentieth century—of the likes of Nella Larsen, Claude McKay, and Countee Cullen—appear in Lewis's book as iconic reflections of that bygone period, a time when Harlem was understood to be home to the most celebrated African Americans and diasporic Africans in the world.[13] Reading Lewis's scrupulous history prompts the unavoidable realization that Harlem has always held its "race capital" status in the context of substantial class diversity, one of the modalities through which racial belonging is undeniably reckoned.[14]

It is, possibly, too easy for critics to interpret Lewis's classic late twentieth-century text as predicated on an unabashedly prelapsarian supposition: Harlem was in vogue at one time, not too many decades ago, but it no longer is—the once mighty neighborhood has been felled by decay and neglect. And it can be argued, of course, that Lewis's narrative ends precisely when it does—with the 1929 stock market crash and the Great Depression that the crash helped to cause—so as to craft a simple origin story for the beginning of the end of Harlem's greatness, a definitive moment when a poverty-stricken version of the neighborhood became all the more difficult to ignore, let alone survive. The diagnosis of Harlem as a segregated and exploited "ghetto" had, in fact, begun to emerge even as the renaissance was at its height.[15] But "when America catches a cold," as the vernacular saying goes, "black America gets pneumonia." In 1929, it was America that got pneumonia, which meant the certain death of any rose-colored portrait of black life anywhere in the nation, including, and especially, in the vaunted "race capital."

In 1982, Jervis Anderson, then a staff writer for the *New Yorker*, published *This Was Harlem: A Cultural Portrait, 1900–1950*, chronicling the demographic shifts, cultural particularities, economic realities, and celebrity sightings in Harlem that unfurled over the entire first half of the twentieth century.[16] Again, the title of this work implies that the Harlem rendered between its covers is no more. There is a decided past-tenseness to Anderson's evocation of the place's glory. And to make the transition from storied past to spoiled present all the more explicit, the book does not close with the Depression. Instead, it covers almost as much of Harlem's post-1929 existence at the time of its writing as it does the "renaissance" that had crested in the preceding years. And "renaissance," we should remember, implies that even this prior canonical moment was already understood as a kind of "take two," a historic rebound.

Writing, unsuspectingly, on the eve of changes that would soon excite talk of a "new renaissance" in Harlem, Anderson amplified a discourse of "*wasness*" that had coalesced around Harlem's image for decades.[17] But even as this sense of decline had deepened among residents and onlookers alike, Harlem had continued to be a focus for dreams of black accomplishment and flourishing—sometimes couched as revival—not least among its own residents. Even when the Harlem-based writer George Schuyler disparaged any black middle-class power broker or would-be leader in a neighborhood such as Harlem by calling that person "a lampblacked Anglo-Saxon," there was still a clear version of social success that such a figure in any black neighborhood, especially this one, represented.[18] But the question has always been: Success on whose terms? What is success supposed to look like in Harlem?

One of the debates that undergirds these questions *and* propels discussions of gentrification and urban change turns on interpretations of assimilation's ultimate implications. Is this putative direction good for African Americans or not? Does the professional or material advancement of individual black people constitute "black success" if that advancement takes assimilationist paths? Or is "black success" intrinsically communal, such that assimilation constitutes a major threat to collective success or even survival?[19] For scholars such as E. Franklin Frazier and Nathan Hare, assimilation meant little more than pathetic black wannabes, "eunuch leaders," mimicking white behaviors and "aping white fetishisms" at the expense of their communities' own political and existential interests.[20] What counts as "interests" in this context, of course, is up for grabs, and there has long been an investment in material well-being within segregated black communities—in Harlem and elsewhere—that was more complicatedly tabulated than many traditional economic models might allow for or statistically capture. Integration might come at a price, and that price would have to paid, some maintained, both in the hard currency of black business owners and also in a more intangible, identity-based currency, or racial capital—a dynamic only further pronounced in the purported geographic "race capital," a designation grounded in certain presumptions about what "black success" entails.

More explicitly than many of their colleagues, the economists George A. Akerlof and Rachel E. Kranton have tried to popularize a new subfield of economic theorizing, a way of thinking about economic actors as beholden to conceptualizations of the kinds of subjects/persons they imagine themselves to be. They label this recasting of what might be considered quintessentially anthropological contentions or assumptions "identity economics," which they describe as an analysis of economic life that demonstrates an appreciation for the measurable extent to which "individuals' behavior depends on who they think they are."[21] And these economists proffer a triumvirate of factors at play in their formulation: social categories (such as race and ethnicity), social norms (assumptions about how said categories of people are supposed, assumed, or expected to behave), and "identity utility" (a notion they deploy to highlight the fact that actors gain some sense of pride, satisfaction, or symbolic reward from their identities, and the ways in which those identities presuppose certain behavioral propensities).

This disciplinary recalibration of economic variables is also (in some ways) only a relatively minor tweak of classical assumptions about utility-maximizing *Homo economicus*. Such identity-predicated economic decisions are not necessarily at odds, then, with "rational choice theory." That is, they can be less irrational noise or distraction (introduced into a normally "rational" system) than an argument for a kind of mutation at the kernel of utility-spurred rationality in the first place. Notions of utility need not be reducible, then, to conventional measures of material gain. Utility can derive from merely doing the kinds of things that members of one's race, gender, occupation, or religion are supposed to do.

This logic would ostensibly work for a social category such as "class," too—and in ways that potentially could be shorn of strict adherence to Marxian understandings of class-based material self-interest and rewired to discussions about how and why people might, say, vote against their ostensible economic self-interest—because that vote becomes a behavioral technique for increasing an identity-based utility that is distinct from traditional models of class-based agency and interest. Identity's utility is sui generis in this depiction of things—and sometimes hard for outsiders to square with their own assumptions of what utility-maximization should objectively mean for members of a given social group.

Akerlof and Kranton make a point of talking about more than racial or ethnic identities. Indeed, they maintain that their model accommodates any number of identities, whether sociopolitically salient, fraught, or seemingly innocuous. However, it is important to think about the extent to which they are arguing for a theorizing of links between subjecthood and economic agency that serves as an interesting foil for any discussion about how identities are conceived and performed in urban spaces like Harlem, spaces that have long been test cases for ideologies linking politicized identities to specific forms of economic activity—everything from the economic boycotts mounted by civil rights campaigners against discriminatory businesses to the restrictive covenants drafted by real estate agents committed to delimiting a housing market by race for reasons that are not, strictly speaking, straightforwardly financial.[22]

One iteration of the thinking that Akerlof and Kranton have called "identity economics" has long operated as a vernacular belief among certain champions of black urban economic achievement, who are advocates for clearly articulated sociopolitical coordinates grounding economic actions in the context of a larger racialist/racist society. Some of these theories have been codified into particular models of race-based economics that make a specific case for how racial identity and economic activity should co-relate, providing explicit mandates for how a version of "identity economics" should translate into Harlemites' spending, investing, and using their money.

For example, PowerNomics, a concept and company developed by social entrepreneur Claud Anderson, articulates its project as being specifically geared toward building the wealth of black America. It aims to teach, as a kind of racial project, a form of capitalism that is not quite capitalism by stricter Marxist or neoliberal definitions. Its approach to racial and economic intersectionality might be characterized as a kind of group-based self-help project that boasts an unabashed commitment to racialist logics of socioeconomic behavior. "Power-Nomics is factual and based on an analysis of history," one online advertisement for this program reads. It continues, "In PowerNomics, Dr. Anderson teaches how to practice capitalism in our society that is based on capitalism. He offers Black America specific principles, strategies and activities to use to own and control resources, to produce group wealth, become more self-sufficient and economically competitive, to change behavior and to establish systems of accountability. PowerNomics can build a productive and healthy Black America that strengthens the country as a whole."[23]

Anderson's PowerNomics represents, in many ways, an updated rendition of the Chicago-based Afrocentric scholar and author Jawanza Kunjufu's book *Black Economics: Solutions for Economic and Community Empowerment* (1991), which placed the late twentieth-century black economic condition within historical and global contexts meant to prove the neocolonial character of the black community's relationship to white America. This neocolonialism, Kunjufu argued, explains how and why black people only "spend three percent of our $600 billion in our communities."[24] In versions of what might be called the "black counterpublic," where texts such as PowerNomics and *Black Economics* circulate far and wide—in the open-air book stalls that appear on the sidewalks of Harlem's 125th Street and Lenox Avenue, for instance, and their virtual equivalents online—this kind of analysis is sometimes glossed as increasing the number of times a dollar "turns over" in a black neighborhood before leaving town with the assets and investments of "outsiders" (read as Asian and white storeowners), who purportedly set up businesses in black communities without otherwise investing in their black neighbors' well-being.

An alternative contemporary formulation of this notion of racial capital, *Blackonomic$*, produced by the entrepreneur and author James Clingman, is characterized quite succinctly and confrontationally: "Black empowerment with an attitude: You got a problem with that?"[25] The combative tone itself is doubtless meant to signify the no-nonsense behavioral penchant that black identity embodies, a distillation of the rhetorical performance expected of black identity within popular culture. The claim seems to be that this is what black economics, if it were truly *black*, would sound like.

The question remains, though, what does black empowerment actually entail? And the answers proffered by Anderson, Kunjufu, and Clingman all pivot on the straightforward contention that such empowerment requires acting in service to the corporate integrity of a decidedly racialized community. It requires an "identity economics" without which, in a racist nation, they avow, a black race capital like Harlem must surely fall (at the hands of gentrification). Empowerment is understood, here, through the prism of a black economic nationalism that is itself deeply imprinted by Harlem's own history, from interwar "Don't Buy Where You Can't Work" campaigns to Malcolm X's self-help speeches from the 1950s and 1960s.[26]

From this vantage point, Harlem's gentrification both stems from and exacerbates black people's inability to own and control their places—to accumulate and safeguard racial capital—and the loss of black America's race capital is felt as a heavy blow. Many of the demographic shifts wrought by gentrification are only further manifestations of what these authors might label black *dis*empowerment, an extension of the marginalization and exploitation that have long trapped blacks in their accepted roles as renters not homeowners, employees not employers—and that would also find them to be the first group to lose out on the possibility of neighborhood prosperity in a revanchist city.[27]

And so, in some ways, the trajectory looks clear, maybe even preordained. From hip to slum to up-and-coming (again). But is it at the cost of black enfranchisement and in service to racio-financial lopsidedness?[28] Moreover, whereas a notion of Harlem's desirability was once posited as what *was*—decidedly past tense—it is clear that Harlem is now, in the current moment, recalibrating, attracting new businesses and residents, which often reads as *white* businesses and residents, even though what some would call "the new black middle class" got there first.[29]

But it is not just that. The current changes quite explicitly traffic in lucrative stories of Harlem's former glory, and in some cases have even contributed to the material restoration of certain iconic buildings and sites to satisfy this wish to experience the community's past attractions. Gentrification feeds voraciously on these reclaimed tales. There is a nonmagical alchemy at work that turns what was deemed a deficiency (Harlem's distinctive black history) into its most valuable possession. What once placed this neighborhood off-limits for many now turns it into a hypnotic beacon drawing people in. Harlem's racial past is precisely what sells its multiracial present. In a version of gentrification that is enhanced, not thwarted, by a sense of its black history, the place's "race capital" bona fides translate into a gentrifying impulse spurred on by both when the place was—and was not—in vogue.

● ● ●

To illustrate some of the ways in which race now gets mobilized for popular consumption in a gentrifying context, I want to briefly explore one of the senses of "racial capital" discussed above—the version that turns Harlem into a kind of "quotation-marked-off place" that stands in for the whims and wishes of various interlocutors, including and especially those most invested in the changes linked to this neighborhood's current demographic shifts.[30] Of course, these are the very motifs or tropes that gentrification discourse trades on. A weighty, highly consequential symbolic value is effectively culled from codified stereotypes of black urban difference within the American racial psyche, stereotypes that have quite a bit of mobility in and beyond the geographic borders of contemporary Harlem—or better still, in and beyond the borders of the "new Harlem" spied in recent magazine fashion spreads that exemplify how notions of Harlem's black past are packaged for consumption in ways that, at minimum, produce some of the same assumptions about race and place that also fuel processes of gentrification.

"Harlem Fashion Week 2017," for example, provided *Vogue Italia* magazine with an opportunity to explain some of the history behind that relatively new fashion event, while also showcasing the unique contemporary look that ostensibly defines it.[31] From the magazine's coverage, one gets the sense of a classic runway setting without the typical runway. Instead, we have the staging of fashion runways in spaces clearly repurposed for the temporary display of strutting black and brown models, this being the interior space of the Museum of the City of New York at Fifth Avenue and 103rd Street. These models, male and female, help to embody, literally, the significance of invoking "Harlem" in discussions of current fashion trends. Debuting three years earlier, Harlem Fashion Week was pitched as a way to offer Harlem up as an important new node for the fashion industry. *Vogue Italia*'s 2017 photo spread highlights the neighborhood's distinctiveness—specifically, a racial distinctiveness marked by the place's complex and transnationally organized racial capital—an approach that suits *Vogue*'s recent embrace of such diversity.[32]

Vogue Italia's Harlem Fashion Week photographs proffer an aesthetics of radicality that links African prints and militarized army fatigues with breezy tank tops and haute couture. Ensembles include black power fists and beaded dresses, extended braids, and what could reasonably be read as ethnic face paint. There are black women of various epidermal hues and even an Afrocentric flourish or two, including the Eye of Horus (an Afrocentric favorite) on one black male model's bare chest. Oliver Bencosme's photographs try to take advantage of the white walls and staircases of the museum space that the models occupy as a color-clarifying backdrop for the varieties of dark flesh and multicolored outfits that constitute the object of onlookers' gazes. Harlem's particularity is cobbled together from the sartorial assemblages and also is constituted by the very skin of the models themselves—all models of color, without even a token nod to the fashion industry's general acceptance of a kind of white normativity in its fashion displays. Since this is coverage of a specific indoor event, it dispenses with one of the central features of most magazine renderings of the neighborhood, namely, visual representations of the actual Harlem landscape, though hip-hop artists had also shown that it was possible to evoke a mythologized "Harlemworld" without the details of the actual urbanscape.[33] Still, Harlem is reckoned explicitly enough in the exclusive blackness of the models themselves and via their outfits, which represent a kind of sartorial mash-up of black power iconography, African-inspired prints and cuts, and the powerful recasting of black figures as exemplifications, par excellence, of the difference that a fashion show staged in Harlem represents.

Unlike *Vogue*'s Harlem Fashion Week spread, most of the high-fashion industry's explicit invocations of Harlem quite emphatically mobilize contemporary urban landscapes as opposed to more sanitized and relatively nondescript interiors. "Fall's Brightest, Boldest Prints Take a Trip to Harlem," published in *Vogue* in November 2014, is a fascinating example of how representations of the neighborhood pivot on, and further entrench, gentrification-based presuppositions.[34] This spread implies, arguably, a mixed-race Harlem of the post-gentrification present through the two models' similar look and the peopleless urban spaces in which they are posed (figure 12.1). Taking a "trip to Harlem," in this instance, evacuates the everyday bustle and historic congestion of the relatively dense urban enclave and replaces it with an aestheticized and color-rich cipher of urbanity sans any urban residents to speak of.

Leaning against lampposts and the gates of urban parks is our principal sartorial tour guide through the neighborhood, a young woman who narrates the community's tale mostly alone (except when joined by a similarly hued male model in a couple of the shots), and whose ensembles are selected to suit a week of clubbing, churchgoing, commuting, voting, and excursions to Brooklyn and Hell's Kitchen. The grates over residential windows and the security grilles on local stores do most of the work of invoking the sense of urban threat that is otherwise bracketed out of these arguably dystopic renderings of Harlem.

The entire spread feels almost sepia-toned (a common device in such renditions of Harlem) in its depiction of bricks and locks, of tattered storefronts and foyers with conspicuously peeling paint. Of course, there are also historic churches and classic brownstones on display, and the contrast between these differently classed signifiers of Harlem is key to the neighborhood's lore and legacy, not least to its lucrative contemporary housing market. The distinction between these settings helps to demarcate the borders of the "new Harlem" as well as to frame Harlem's varied allures, its storied past, and its "slum fashion." All of this seems to be another version of a Harlem that is only viewable in the present through the lens of a particular version of its faded past.

Another short (and admittedly, in certain respects, atypical) recent *Vogue* spread on Harlem that merits attention here is Chioma Nnadi's May 2014 article "Calvin Klein's Next Chapter: The Legendary Designer Teams Up with

12.1 Harlem's return to *Vogue* magazine pictures models within an otherwise peopleless postgentrification landscape that accentuates the neighborhood's historic brownstones.

"Fall's Brightest, Boldest Prints Take a Trip to Harlem," *Vogue* (November 2014). Alessio Boni/Vogue © Condé Nast. Reprinted with permission.

Harlem Village Academies," which showcases new school uniforms designed for Harlem Village Academies (HVA), a group of charter schools in the area, by none other than the celebrity designer Calvin Klein.[35] The young people in these six images, three boys and three girls posed in matching seasonal uniforms, are seemingly offered up as gentrification's preppy progeny of mixed-racial hope and intellectual possibility. The photographs and article represent an interesting attempt to signal a model for what educational achievement might or should look like in a seemingly remade black urban oasis.

"With a network of five charter schools from elementary through high school level, the academies are pioneering a new and progressive model for public education against all odds," Nnadi writes. "While students from the local community often enter the system behind grade level, HVA consistently ranks number one of all public, nonselective high schools in New York for college enrollment." This glimpse of HVA and its fun new school outfits is also, at the same time, an articulation of the long-standing debate about public education in contemporary America. Of course, there are no classrooms or textbooks featured in the photographs (or mentioned in the article), but issues of class sizes and school resources hover just beyond the piece's discursive horizon. "The Harlem Village Academies has a 91 percent graduation rate," Klein himself enthuses, "which far exceeds the New York City high school average, and they needed imaging that would reflect their achievements." And, explains Nnadi,

> When Deborah Kenny, the school's trailblazing founder, approached him [Klein] for help reimagine [sic] the visual identity of the academies for the tenth anniversary—from the uniforms, to the website—the legendary designer's answer was a resounding yes....
>
> The minimalist crisp white polos, sporty crew-neck shirts, and tailored jumpers speak to his legacy as one of the founding fathers of American sportswear and a distinctly New York state of mind. "Many live in Harlem, and the culture of style, music, and sports is very familiar to them. It's instinctive," he says. "For me, it was important that the uniforms were cool, as well as being appropriate and affordable."

Harlem represents a "cool" and "instinctive" cultural milieu, according to Klein, and his uniforms are inspired by such attributes. The story moves quickly from graduation rates to "style, music, and sports" in ways that proffer a concrete calculus for black schoolchildren's success and failure, especially when operating "against all odds."

What is not explicitly invoked in this short piece is clear: the teachers of young Harlem students, the very people most often blamed for public school underachievement. In the context of "value-added assessments" of teacher quality that center on debates about the impact of teaching (good or bad) on the lives and future prospects of young black children, one now-hegemonic assumption among school reformers is that "a run of ineffective teachers will ruin students' lives forever," while "three effective teachers in a row could close the achievement gap."[36]

Of course, the argument can be made that *Vogue* is hardly the most appropriate venue for a detailed discussion of the many issues that organize current debates about public education (privatization, merit pay, class size, the role of poverty, standardized testing, and so on). But the telescoped link offered up between sartorial stylings and graduation rates posits a version of cultural analysis rooted in one of the key notions animating those aforementioned public debates: the role of broader cultural factors in determining the plight of young, poor, and racialized school children in urban America.

In *Elle* magazine's February 2017 "Elle Editorial: Take the A Train," canonical neighborhood spaces—the Apollo Theater, Sylvia's restaurant, Dapper Dan's boutique—are aestheticized in ways that are meant to place the present quite decidedly within the past.[37] Photographs of models positioned on Harlem streets, in local businesses, and even on the 125th Street subway platform alternate between oversaturated and hypercolorful imagery and black-and-white shots that, with a less-than-careful examination, could pass as historical photographs. Indeed, the oscillation in this particular spread, between theatrical colorfulness and its measured and muted opposite, captures the foundational tensions between present and past, now and then, that provide Harlem with its own brand of nonlinearity, short-circuiting more straightforward trajectories joining past to future. As the photographer Camilo José Vergara has admitted with regard to the well-known stock of images of this neighborhood, when in the field, a photographer always has a "Harlem in my head in addition to the one in front of my eyes."[38]

The efflorescent colors of now are constituted in and through the *Elle* shoot's concomitant simulation of Harlems gone by. The contrast with, say, *Vogue*'s more monochromatic rendering of Harlem in "Fall's Brightest, Boldest Prints Take a Trip to Harlem" is therefore striking. Whereas each of the *Vogue* shots seems to represent the past–present tensions within the self-same frame, the *Elle* spread parses that distinction into separate images, shuffling back and forth between them in ways that demonstrate a Harlem vibrant with new life and possibility but still beholden to the kinds of iconic and racialized histories that prop up the neighborhood's present-day realities. In fact, something significant happens as one scrolls through the *Elle* images, first to last. While black-and-white photographs start out as an easy proxy for the past (leaving color to the present), one sees a slow morphing of the dynamic, such that the color photographs present as the more purposeful re-creations of the past while the few grayscale images instead simulate the gritty realism of a decidedly contemporary (and precarious) urban life. That subtle change does a useful job of thematizing the fungibility of temporality and its signifiers in a place like Harlem.

Finally, "Harlem Reshuffled," published in *GQ* in July 2014, is another explicit past-tensing of Harlem in a sepia-toned aesthetic.[39] It also offers up an even more eclectic version of local street life, replete with grand pianos sited under the Twelfth Avenue elevated train tracks and a multiracial assortment of community representatives. More tightly cropped than the *Vogue* spreads, these images give viewers less of the peopleless landscape to negotiate. The frame is filled, instead, with the camera's main subjects, important emissaries from Harlem's various social sectors, from philanthropists to hip-hop artists, musicians to butchers, Instagram all-stars to entrepreneurs. The opening to the spread reads:

> Ever since Duke Ellington first tickled the ivories north of 110th Street, Harlem has been one of the liveliest neighborhoods in New York. And now it's on

a whole new creative streak: Artists are setting up shop, restaurants are popping up faster than you can do the Harlem Shake, and bands—hip-hop, jazz, rock—play at more than just the Apollo (which, for the record, is still booking epic shows). Here, our favorite locals suit up and take us on a tour of the new uptown.

The unabashed context for all of these media commentaries on Harlem is, of course, gentrification, but this particular spread most clearly invokes the "reshuffled" nature of gentrification's impact on the neighborhood. In the other pieces described here, gentrification might be said to serve more silently as the understated backdrop, the presumed context that clarifies, say, how and why some local schools succeed while others fail—or that explains why certain things readily constitute what Afrocentric militancy in a Harlem-based fashion world would necessarily entail.

This *GQ* spread's images showcase some of the lore that makes Harlem's racial symbolism so rich (in a variety of contexts, from music to merchandising), dramatizing quite pointedly the ongoing debate about who controls Harlem's capital, who really owns and runs that town. The local black business owners featured in the spread are conspicuously outnumbered by other Harlemites who, at the very least, do not read as phenotypically "black"—though it merits noting that the ability to "pass" for white would have characterized a good portion of local black business owners during the height of the Harlem Renaissance. Moreover, attending to the arguably patriarchal (or at least paternalistic) articulations of racial empowerment that sometimes inform vernacular definitions of black economic success (such as, for example, privileging a model of traditional male-headed households wherein fathers have to earn enough money for mothers to stay home with the children), it seems less than trivial to redeploy decidedly gendered fashion ads to speak to questions of urban living that are constituted, through and through, by assumptions about more than just the sparks that fly from the intersection of race and class.

Ultimately, all of these magazine spreads demonstrate—in other than hyperpolitical ways—some of the fault lines that animate debates about gentrification and what it implies for Harlem's possible future. And they serve as interesting reminders of the versions of "racial capital" discussed in this chapter, including the sense that Harlem's racialization has explicit commercial implications that can be differently capitalized upon and rendered visually intelligible and conspicuous. Furthermore, they underscore the value of looking to popular culture for assistance in comprehending how the meanings of places are produced and contested in the context of urban gentrification, and how these contestations become marked and modulated by the particularity of Harlem's wasness.

Invoking Harlem's storied past and invisibilizing versions of its palimpsest-filled (and sometimes conspicuously peopleless) present, these fashion spreads help to underscore some of the stakes in ongoing debates about how Harlem holds its capital—defined both in terms of its status as the "capital of black America" and with respect to the performance of individual and/or collective versions of black material success and socioeconomic empowerment. If "identity economics" privileges a determination of how and why "identity politics" might be more than just noise and irrational excess vis-à-vis the economic decisions local actors make, the discussion of "racial capital" as a way of rewiring race and class to the past, present, and future of black America helps to demonstrate how important it is to place Harlem's gentrification dilemmas into a larger conversation about the multifarious ways in which racial identities continue to be mapped onto disputed and demographically changing urban geographies.

NOTES

1. Andrew Cuomo, quoted in Kelefa Sanneh, "Is Gentrification Really a Problem?," *New Yorker*, July 11 and 18, 2016, http://www.newyorker.com/magazine/2016/07/11/is-gentrification-really-a-problem.
2. Natalie Y. Moore, quoted in Sanneh, "Is Gentrification Really a Problem?." See also Natalie Y. Moore, "Gentrification Might Be Real, But It's the Least of Chicago's Problems," *Grist*, February 19, 2015, http://grist.org/cities/gentrification-might-be-real-but-its-the-least-of-chicagos-worries.
3. Moore, "Gentrification Might Be Real." See also, for example, James Baldwin's comments in Kenneth B. Clark, "A Conversation with James Baldwin" (1963), in *Conversations with James Baldwin*, ed. Fred L. Stanley and Louis H. Pratt (Jackson: University Press of Mississippi, 1989), 42. For an article that correlates the probability of an area's gentrification with its proportion of black and Latinx residents in 1980, see Jeffrey M. Timberlake and Elaina Johns-Wolfe, "Neighborhood Ethnoracial Composition and Gentrification in Chicago and New York, 1980 to 2010," *Urban Affairs Review* 53 (March 2017): 236–72.
4. This lecture was part of my weeklong residency at Brooklyn College as the 2017 Hess Scholar-in-Residence. On Brooklyn's gentrification, see Suleiman Osman, *The Invention of Brownstone Brooklyn: Gentrification and the Search for Authenticity in Postwar New York* (New York: Oxford University Press, 2011).
5. Stefan M. Bradley, *Harlem vs. Columbia University: Black Student Power in the Late 1960s* (Urbana: University of Illinois Press, 2009); Themis Chronopoulos, *Spatial Regulation in New York City: From Urban Renewal to Zero Tolerance* (New York: Routledge, 2011), 5–32.
6. For the wider context of town–gown relations in urban America, see Davarian L. Baldwin, "When Universities Swallow Cities," *Chronicle of Higher Education*, July 30, 2017, http://www.chronicle.com/article/When-Universities-Swallow/240739.
7. On James VanDerZee's photograph *Couple in Raccoon Coats* (1932), and on Barron Claiborne's twenty-first-century restaging of that photograph for the fashion spread in "Harlem Renaissance: Vintage Uptown Cool," *Vibe* (September 2002), see Paula J. Massood, *Making a Promised Land: Harlem in Twentieth-Century Photography and Film* (New Brunswick, NJ: Rutgers University Press, 2013), 160.
8. John L. Jackson Jr., *Harlemworld: Doing Race and Class in Contemporary Black America* (Chicago: University of Chicago Press, 2001).

9. On this transnational phenomenon, see Libby Porter and Kate Shaw, eds., *Whose Urban Renaissance?: An International Comparison of Urban Regeneration Strategies* (New York: Routledge, 2009).
10. A key organization staging local resistance to gentrification has been the Harlem Tenants Council, founded in 1995 and led by Nellie Hester Bailey. See Bailey, "Women, Gentrification, and Harlem," in *Feminism and War: Confronting U.S. Imperialism*, ed. Robin Riley, Chandra Talpade Mohanty, and Minnie Bruce Pratt (London: Zed, 2008), 232–37. For a historical treatment of the idea and practice of "community rights" with respect to Harlem, see Shannon King, *Whose Harlem Is This, Anyway?: Community Politics and Grassroots Activism During the New Negro Era* (New York: New York University Press, 2015).
11. Robin D. G. Kelley, *Yo' Mama's Disfunktional!: Fighting the Culture Wars in Urban America* (Boston: Beacon, 1997).
12. On the retrospective naming of the Harlem Renaissance, see Andrew M. Fearnley, "When the Harlem Renaissance Became Vogue: Periodization and the Organization of Postwar American Historiography," *Modern Intellectual History* 11 (April 2014): 59–87. The words "Harlem: Mecca of the New Negro" appeared on the cover of the famous *Survey Graphic* 6 (March 1925), a special issue edited by Alain Locke.
13. David Levering Lewis, *When Harlem Was in Vogue* (New York: Alfred A. Knopf, 1981).
14. This passage is riffing off Stuart Hall's famous articulation of race as "the modality in which class is lived." See Hall et al., *Policing the Crisis: Mugging, the State, and Law and Order* (London: Macmillan, 1978), 394.
15. See Daniel Matlin, "Harlem: The Making of a Ghetto Discourse," present volume,
16. Jervis Anderson, *This Was Harlem: A Cultural Portrait, 1900–1950* (New York: Farrar, Straus and Giroux, 1982).
17. I have explored this phenomenon of "wasness" in Jackson, *Harlemworld*.
18. Nathan Hare, *The Black Anglo-Saxons* (New York: Marzani and Munsell, 1965), 192.
19. Debates about Harlem's future have historically functioned as a resonant means of contemplating the future of "black peoplehood." See Daniel Matlin, " 'A New Reality of Harlem': Imagining the African American Urban Future during the 1960s," *Journal of American Studies* (2017), doi:10.1017/S0021875817000949.
20. Hare, *Black Anglo-Saxons*, 75.
21. George A. Akerlof and Rachel E. Kranton, *Identity Economics: How Our Identities Shape Our Work, Wages, and Well-Being* (Princeton, NJ: Princeton University Press, 2011), 28.
22. On the interwar economic boycotts waged by the Harlem community, see King, *Whose Harlem Is This, Anyway?*; Cheryl Lynn Greenberg, *"Or Does It Explode?": Black Harlem in the Great Depression* (New York: Oxford University Press, 1991). On restrictive covenants, see Martha Biondi, *To Stand and Fight: The Struggle for Civil Rights in Postwar New York City* (Cambridge, MA: Harvard University Press, 2003), esp. 112–36.
23. PowerNomics Corporation of America, http://www.powernomics.com.
24. Jawanza Kunjufu, *Black Economics: Solutions for Economic and Community Empowerment* (Chicago: African-American Images, 1991), back cover.
25. James Clingman, *Blackonomics*, http://www.blackonomics.com, accessed December 8, 2017.
26. On the history of political organizing and social movements in Harlem, see Brian Purnell, "Harlem, USA: Capital of the Black Freedom Movement," present volume.
27. For a discussion of such defenses/reclamations, see Neil Smith, *The New Urban Frontier: Gentrification and the Revanchist City* (New York: Routledge, 1996).
28. See Lance Freeman, *There Goes the 'Hood: Views of Gentrification from the Ground Up* (Philadelphia, PA: Temple University Press, 2006).

29. By the term "new black middle class," I mean the group described in Bart Landry, *The New Black Middle Class* (Berkeley: University of California Press, 1987). On black middle-class gentrifiers in Harlem, see Monique M. Taylor, *Harlem Between Heaven and Hell* (Minneapolis: University of Minnesota Press, 2002).
30. For a discussion of Harlem as a "quotation-marked-off place," see Jackson, *Harlemworld*.
31. "Harlem Fashion Week 2017," *Vogue Italia*, February 17, 2017, http://www.vogue.it/en/fashion/news/2017/02/17/harlem-fashion-week-2017.
32. On the way in which diversity has been incorporated into new forms of urban privilege, see Sylvie Tissot, *Good Neighbors: Gentrifying Diversity in Boston's South End* (New York: Verso, 2015).
33. On hip-hop's symbolic deployment of Harlem, see Jackson, *Harlemworld*, esp. 218–20.
34. "Fall's Brightest, Boldest Prints Take a Trip to Harlem," *Vogue*, November 1–10, 2014, http://www.vogue.com/slideshow/fall-prints-patterns#1.
35. Chioma Nnadi, "Calvin Klein's Next Chapter: The Legendary Designer Teams Up with Harlem Village Academies," *Vogue*, May 14, 2014, http://www.vogue.com/article/calvin-klein-teams-up-with-harlem-village-academies.
36. Diane Ravitch, *Reign of Error: The Hoax of the Privatization Movement and the Danger to America's Public Schools* (New York: Vintage, 2013), 100–101.
37. "Elle Editorial: Take the A Train," *Elle*, February 24, 2017, http://www.elle.com/fashion/a43304/elle-editorial-harlem-take-the-a-train-march-2017.
38. Camilo José Vergara, *Harlem: The Unmaking of a Ghetto* (Chicago: University of Chicago Press, 2013), 19.
39. Sebastian Kim, "Harlem Reshuffled," *GQ*, July 1, 2014, https://www.gq.com/gallery/harlem-reshuffled.

HARLEM: AN AFTERWORD

On January 1, 2018, Harlemites gathered in brownstones and apartments of varying sizes to celebrate the New Year. The tradition of daylong open houses, where friends, family, and neighbors stop by for black-eyed peas and collard greens, perhaps a little soup joumou in commemoration of Haiti's independence, is an annual rite. These delicacies of the African diaspora are served in rituals of remembrance and new beginnings, reminders of shared histories—culinary, cultural, and political. They are also affirmations of an ongoing project of black creativity and freedom. Food is always accompanied by music and conversation.

These days, much of the talk revolves around a changing Harlem, shared observations about the "newcomers" (who, although they are of various races, are most often imagined as white), and about what change means for black Harlem. There is some nostalgia, but not a lot of sentimentality. There is a sense of mourning and loss, a little anger, and a lot of "what comes next?"

The Harlem of myth and lore, muse to artists and musicians, poets and orators, incubator of freedom dreams, is a Harlem of black and brown people. Others have called it home, have built structures of brick and mortar, but its black and brown citizens have given Harlem her life, breath, blood, and flavor. Without them, Harlem would be just another New York neighborhood, few of which have as distinct an identity. And, like other unique neighborhoods, such as Greenwich Village, the East Village, and Hell's Kitchen, the one constant is change. That Harlem has maintained its identity for as long as it has may be because of our ongoing need for it, our need for a place where black humanity and possibility are cherished and nurtured.

Such a demand is an indication of the deeply entrenched economic, social, and political forces arrayed against black people. Harlem has always offered a respite from the harshest and most violent forms of white supremacy, even though its very existence as a black enclave is the result of residential segregation. Harlem contested notions of blackness as dreadful, ugly, and incompetent. It challenged Harlemites to think of themselves as larger than life itself, as a world-historical people who spoke European and African languages and worshipped a God too expansive to be contained by any one name in any one language. Together, Harlem's children dared to create something beautiful and profound. From northern Manhattan they launched this thing of beauty, worldwide.

Harlem has given us Baldwin and Bambara, Billie and Bearden, Hughes and Malcolm. Each of them, in turn, chronicled Harlem's struggle and despair, but they also bequeathed us a setting that symbolizes black aspiration, a setting that bore the burden of representation of achievement and failure. Though recognized as the birthplace of the Harlem Renaissance, it is also widely understood to have been the site of drug epidemics and ensuing violence, housing projects, and once-stately brownstones divided into cramped, single-room apartments.

The irony is that these two Harlems have always existed side by side, intersecting, interacting, informing, and influencing each other. Recall that Ann Petry published *The Street* (1946), her searing novel about black working-class Harlem, whose inhabitants are walled in, unable to escape the processes and systems that contain them. And yet, at the same time, she also experienced the Harlem of the American Negro Theater, where her fellow actors included the young Harry Belafonte, Sidney Poitier, Ruby Dee, and Ossie Davis and their promise of a new black activist theater. As heroin took over the neighborhood, so did the sounds of bebop and rhythm and blues, and the early organizing work of Ella Baker and Pauli Murray. Harlem has always been both/and. Therein lay the sense of possibility, the sense of struggle infused with, dare I say, hope (not optimism)?

These days, the same old-timers who regale with tales of Harlem's past tragedies and triumphs do so as survivors. Some of them are the unprotected elderly, waging fights with unscrupulous landlords who want them out of suddenly valuable properties. They talk of the cognitive disconnection of walking past cafés and coffee shops that seem unwelcoming to black and brown faces, and though they are pleased with the bright, shiny produce of the new Whole Foods, they remain suspicious of it and wonder what will happen to the bodegas and smaller markets that serviced the community when no major supermarket chains would. And a refrain echoes through the community: "Where will they go, the people who cannot afford to stay?" The irony of Harlem icons becoming

Harlem brands that market the neighborhood's history and culture to those who have little investment in their real histories is not lost on these older residents.

One night a few years ago, during a "polar vortex," I roamed the soul food restaurants of Harlem in search of pork neck bones. I'd promised an older friend, who was recovering from surgery, that I would try to get some for her as a treat. I didn't bother to go into any of the new restaurants that dot Frederick Douglass Boulevard. I didn't go to the nouveau soul food spots, where glamorous clientele, black and white, sip on overpriced cocktails. I went to the buffets and the smaller establishments. No neck bones to be found.

Finally, I went to Sylvia's, long a required stop for tourists in search of "authentic" Harlem cuisine. The waitress there told me they didn't have neck bones on the menu. I asked if I could speak to the ladies in the kitchen, who might know where I could find them. They graciously obliged me. These lovely ladies, busy and lovingly gruff, told me, "You not gon' find neck bones in these places. This is the *new* Harlem. You gon' have to cook them yourself."

They followed with instructions on how this novice cook should prepare the neck bones, and directions on where I might find the meat—in one of those tightly packed "supermarkets" where many average Harlemites still shop. There, I found a package of neck bones, next to the smoked ham hocks. In the new Harlem, you can find food marketed as "soul food" along with a wide and welcome array of restaurant choices. But much of the food of the migrants from the South and the Caribbean, the food that followed them and sustained them in this unfamiliar terrain, is difficult to find outside of home kitchens.

On August 5, 2008, as Barack Obama prepared to accept his party's nomination, the *New York Times* writer Timothy Williams published an article titled "In Changing Harlem, Soul Food Struggles." It opened with a description of Louise's Family Restaurant, where "The white Formica counter . . . is the original, and is more than 40 years old. Southern dishes like pig's feet with black-eyed peas and candied yams cost $8. Sweet lemonade is still served in a plastic foam cup."

Louise was Sylvia's sister, and she opened her restaurant in 1964, just two years after her more famous sibling. By the time Williams published his article, Louise had passed away and her daughter ran the business. That frigid night in 2014, when I went in search of neck bones, comfort food for a dear friend, Louise's was no more; it closed shortly after Williams's article appeared. Failing grades from the health inspector and a declining demand for foods considered unhealthy and old-fashioned had helped to bring about its demise.

The ever-so-gifted songwriter and musician Bernard Ighner tells us, "Everything must change." So too must Harlem. What does this inevitability mean for her black and brown progeny and for the gifts of history, culture, and political vision that they have given the world?

Street names and institutions like the Schomburg Center for Research in Black Culture archive and keep alive the legacy of black Harlem. Recent programs at the Schomburg have celebrated the newly acquired James Baldwin and Sonny Rollins collections as homecomings for these native sons. They join the likes of Phillis Wheatley, Malcolm X, and others in the Schomburg's august stacks. But the center does not only house the relics of Harlem's past. It is a living, breathing site, welcoming contemporary scholars, community members, young people, offering vibrant programming in the arts and stimulating dialogues about urgent intellectual and political matters. In this way, it aspires to stake a claim, to guarantee that whatever comes does not lose sight of what has come before, that black and brown Harlem continues to have a venue and voice.

While the Schomburg preserves Harlem's past, The Brotherhood/Sister Sol, a youth development organization in Central Harlem, attends to its present and seeks to ensure its future as a multiracial, democratic space of possibility. Bro/Sis services Harlem's black and Latinx young people, ages eight to twenty-two, and focuses on "issues such as leadership development and educational achievement, sexual responsibility, sexism and misogyny, political education and social justice, Pan-African and Latino history, and global awareness." These children of Harlem are thus emboldened, by their understanding of history, their community activism, and their cultural work, to claim this place. They do so with a sense of pride and devotion to progressive social change for their community and for the world.

Along with expensive restaurants and unaffordable housing, they, too, are contemporary Harlem, and they do not sing their neighborhood's death knell. Instead, they address its concerns and needs. Quotes from Audre Lorde, Angela Davis, James Baldwin, and Junot Díaz adorn murals painted by young people and provide stimulating visuals for the community garden that they maintain. They were actively engaged in helping to overturn policies such as stop-and-frisk, which victimized far too many of their members. For several weeks throughout the spring, summer, and fall, they manage a local farmers' market that provides fresh, local produce to the surrounding community at affordable prices. Just as restaurants such as Louise's nourished one generation of Harlemites, the farmers' market helps to nourish another. And, following in the tradition of those who came before, these young people claim the past, while building upon and transforming it for the future. They, too, are stakeholders in Harlem's new day.

Farah Jasmine Griffin
Harlem, USA

CONTRIBUTORS

EDITORS

ANDREW M. FEARNLEY is Lecturer in Twentieth-Century U.S. History at the University of Manchester. He completed his PhD at the University of Cambridge and has held fellowships at the Max Planck Institute in Berlin as well as lectureships at the University of Leeds and the University of Groningen, before starting at Manchester in 2013. His essays have appeared in *Modern Intellectual History*, *Historical Journal*, and in edited volumes published by Yale University Press, University of Toronto Press, and University of Arkansas Press.

DANIEL MATLIN is Senior Lecturer in the History of the United States of America Since 1865 at King's College London. After completing his PhD in American History at the University of Cambridge, he was A. H. Lloyd Research Fellow at Christ's College, Cambridge, and a Leverhulme Early Career Fellow at Queen Mary University of London, before arriving at King's in 2012. His monograph *On the Corner: African American Intellectuals and the Urban Crisis* (Harvard University Press, 2013) was co-winner of the Benjamin Hooks National Book Award for Outstanding Scholarly Work on the American Civil Rights Movement and its Legacy and co-winner of the Arthur Miller Centre First Book Prize for American Studies. His published work also includes articles in *Journal of American History* and *Journal of American Studies*. He is working on a book about the history of ideas of Harlem.

OTHER CONTRIBUTORS

THEMIS CHRONOPOULOS is Associate Professor of Political and Cultural Studies at Swansea University. He is the author of *Spatial Regulation in New York City: From Urban Renewal to Zero Tolerance* (Routledge, 2011). A number of his current research projects concern dynamics of race and class in urban neighborhoods, and he is working on a second book, which will examine the crisis in municipal services in New York City from 1945 to 1985.

CLARE CORBOULD is Associate Professor of History in the Faculty of Arts and Education at Deakin University. She is the author of *Becoming African Americans: Black Public Life in Harlem, 1919–1939* (Harvard University Press, 2009) and coeditor of *Remembering the Revolution: Memory, History, and Nation Making from Independence to the Civil War* (University of Massachusetts Press, 2013).

FARAH JASMINE GRIFFIN is William B. Ransford Professor of English and Comparative Literature and African-American Studies at Columbia University and Director of Columbia's Institute for Research in African-American Studies. Among her major publications are *Harlem Nocturne: Women Artists and Progressive Politics During World War II* (Basic Civitas, 2013), *If You Can't Be Free, Be a Mystery: In Search of Billie Holiday* (Free Press, 2001), and *Who Set You Flowin'? The African American Migration Narrative* (Oxford University Press, 1995). She is a board member of The Brotherhood/Sister Sol, a youth support organization in Harlem.

JOHN L. JACKSON JR. is Richard Perry University Professor and Dean of the School of Social Policy and Practice at the University of Pennsylvania. As of January 2019, he will be Walter H. Annenberg Dean of the Annenberg School for Communication at the University of Pennsylvania. He is a cultural anthropologist, and his books include *Harlemworld: Doing Race and Class in Contemporary Black America* (University of Chicago Press, 2001), *Real Black: Adventures in Racial Sincerity* (University of Chicago Press, 2005), *Thin Description: Ethnography and the African Hebrew Israelites of Jerusalem* (Harvard University Press, 2013), and, with Carolyn Moxley Rouse and Marla F. Frederick, *Televised Redemption: Black Religious Media and Racial Empowerment* (New York University Press, 2016). He has produced numerous films about African American and Afro-Caribbean life and history.

WINSTON JAMES is Professor of History at the University of California, Irvine. His publications include *Inside Babylon: The Caribbean Diaspora in Britain* (Verso, 1993), which he coedited with Clive Harris; *Holding Aloft the Banner of*

Ethiopia: Caribbean Radicalism in Early Twentieth-Century America (Verso, 1998), which won the Gordon K. Lewis Memorial Award for Caribbean Scholarship from the Caribbean Studies Association; *A Fierce Hatred of Injustice: Claude McKay's Jamaica and His Poetry of Rebellion* (Verso, 2000); and *The Struggles of John Brown Russwurm: The Life and Writings of a Pan-Africanist Pioneer, 1799–1851* (New York University Press, 2010). His current project is the completion of a two-volume study of Claude McKay's political evolution.

DOROTHEA LÖBBERMANN teaches in the Department of English and American Studies at the Humboldt-Universität zu Berlin. She is the author of *Memories of Harlem: Literarische (Re)Konstruktionen eines Mythos der zwanziger Jahre* (Campus, 2002) and many essays exploring Harlem in relation to memory, place, tourism, and sexuality.

MINKAH MAKALANI is Associate Professor of African and African Diaspora Studies at the University of Texas at Austin. He is the author of *In the Cause of Freedom: Radical Black Internationalism from Harlem to London, 1917–1939* (University of North Carolina Press, 2011) and coeditor, with Davarian Baldwin, of *Escape from New York: The New Negro Renaissance Beyond Harlem* (University of Minnesota Press, 2013). He is currently at work on a history of C. L. R. James's return to Trinidad in 1958–1962, titled *Calypso Conquered the World: C. L. R. James and the Politically Unimaginable in Trinidad*.

PAULA J. MASSOOD is Professor of Film Studies at Brooklyn College, CUNY, and is on the doctoral faculty in the Program in Theatre at the Graduate Center, CUNY. She is the author of *Black City Cinema: African American Urban Experiences in Film* (Temple University Press, 2003) and *Making a Promised Land: Harlem in Twentieth-Century Photography and Film* (Rutgers University Press, 2013). She is also the editor of *The Spike Lee Reader* (Temple University Press, 2007). She is currently President-Elect of the Society for Cinema and Media Studies.

BRIAN PURNELL is Geoffrey Canada Associate Professor of Africana Studies and History and Director of the Africana Studies Program at Bowdoin College. His first book, *Fighting Jim Crow in the County of Kings: The Congress of Racial Equality in Brooklyn* (University Press of Kentucky, 2013), won the New York State Historical Association's Dixon Ryan Fox Manuscript Prize. He has published numerous essays on the history of African American freedom struggles and is currently writing a history of African Americans in New York City.

CHERYL A. WALL is Board of Governors Zora Neale Hurston Distinguished Professor of English at Rutgers University. Her books include *Women of the Harlem Renaissance* (Indiana University Press, 1995), *Worrying the Line: Black*

Women Writers, Lineage, and Literary Tradition (University of North Carolina Press, 2005), and *The Harlem Renaissance: A Very Short Introduction* (Oxford University Press, 2016). She has also edited two volumes of Zora Neale Hurston's writings and two volumes of critical essays on Hurston.

SHANE WHITE is Challis Professor of History at the University of Sydney. His six books include, with Graham White, *Stylin': African American Expressive Culture, from its Beginnings to the Zoot Suit* (Cornell University Press, 1999) and, with Stephen Garton, Stephen Robertson, and Graham White, *Playing the Numbers: Gambling in Harlem Between the Wars* (Harvard University Press, 2010), as well as *Prince of Darkness: The Untold Story of Jeremiah G. Hamilton, Wall Street's First Black Millionaire* (Picador, 2016). He is a cofounder and coeditor of the website *Digital Harlem: Everyday Life, 1915–1930*.

INDEX

Abbot, Robert S., 51
Abrahams, Peter, 5
Abyssinia, 56, 127, 159
Abyssinian Baptist Church, 209, 251
Abyssinian Development Corporation (ADC), 251
Across 110th Street (Shear), 86
Adams, Michael Henry, 235, 240n55, 262
Africa, 1, 2–3, 4, 27, 32, 41, 49, 92, 111, 113, 121, 127, 130, 133, 167, 212–14
African Blood Brotherhood (ABB): in Harlem, 124, 125, 130, 151, 205, 214, *figure* 6.1; women, 118, 147–48, 149, 150–51
Afropolitanism, 133–34, 141n100
Akerlof, George A., 272–73
Allen, Bob, 213
"Ambushed in the City" (Lane), 74, 75, 78, 81, 82, 185
American Negro Labor Congress (ANLC), 151, 154, 157
American Negro Theater, 286
American West Indian Association, 151, *figure* 6.1
American West Indian Ladies Aid Society (AWILAS), 155–56
Amos 'n' Andy, 59
Anderson, Claud, 274
Anderson, Jervis, 28, 271
Anti-lottery Committee of Harlemites, 248
Apollo Theater, 38, 96, 269, 279, 281
Appardurai, Arjun, 11
Asian-African Conference for International Order (Bandung Conference), 210
Aspects of Negro Life (Douglas), 40
Autobiography of an Ex-Colored Man (Johnson), 167

Baby Sister (Himes), 91–93; depiction of Harlem, 94, 96, 99, 101; opposition to, 94–98, 100–101, 104–5
Bailey, Nellie, 260, 283n10

Baker, Ella, 15, 145, 208–9, 211, 286
Baker, Houston A., Jr., 7, 28
Baldwin, James, 5, 84, 85, 92, 209, 232, 286, 288
Bambara, Toni Cade, 286
Bandung Conference. *See* Asian-African Conference for International Order
Banjo (McKay), 120–21, 139n76
Baraka, Amiri (LeRoi Jones), 29, 34–35, 213
Beale Street (Memphis), 48
Bearden, Romare, 117, 228, 286
Bedford-Stuyvesant (New York), 213
Belafonte, Harry, 95, 118, 286
Bencosme, Oliver, 276
Benjamin, Walter, 11
Bentley, Gladys, 121
Bercovici, Konrad, 74–75, 81, 82
Bethune, Mary McLeod, 218n27
Biggs, Lodie, 145
black arts movement, 35, 38, 85, 213
Black Atlantic (Gilroy), 7
black business, 81, 120, 192, 197–98, 251, 272–75, 281, 287; scholarship on, 15, 184, 186–87, 198n10
black church, 56, 96, 112, 125, 126, 144, 150, 161, 203, 209, 237, 251, 277
"black contact zones" (James), 9, 112–14, 126, 132, 134nn3–4, 142n100
Black Economics (Kunjufu), 274
Black Elks, 53
Blacker the Berry (Thurman), 123
Black Lives Matter, 215
Black Manhattan (Johnson), 4, 32–33, 43n30, 167
black middle class: departure from Harlem, 16; formation of Harlem, 3, 59–60, 131; moralizing of, 95–96, 97, 98, 224, 226; tensions with working class, 174, 179; as urban gentry, 39,

black middle class (*cont.*)
  63–65, 131, 247–52, 253–54, 267–68, 270, 272, 275, *figure 2.5*. *See also* Harlem: social structure
Black Mecca (Thurman and Rapp), 182n21
black nationalism, 112, 126, 205, 210, 212, 213, 214; critiques of, 55–58, *figure 2.3*; and economic campaigns, 194–95, 272–75
Blackonomics (Clingman), 274
black press: circulation, 11–12, 49; role in community formation, 11–12, 49–50, 65–66, 205–6; gentrification, 247, 249, 252, 255–56; use of "ghetto" term, 84–85, 88n30; in New York, 124–25; numbers (gambling), 54, 183–84, 194; society pages, 48–49, 65. *See also specific newspapers*
Blacks in Solidarity with South African Liberation, 214
black soldiers, 56, 65–66, 130, 141n90, 204–5
Blake, Eubie, 180
blaxploitation films, 86, 108n55
Bloomberg, Michael, 256, 262
the blues (musical genre), 14, 83, 121, 143, 173, 175, 180, 181n18, 188, 286
Boas, Franz, 150
Bojangles (Bill Robinson), 76
bolito (gambling), 183–84. *See also* numbers (gambling)
Bond, J. Max, Jr., 38
Boni, Albert, 80–81
Bontemps, Arna, 34, 72
Book of American Negro Poetry (Johnson), 167–68
Bradhurst Plan, 251
"Breaking Through" (Hunton), 71, 73, 74–75, 76, 80, 81, 82
Briggs, Cyril, 112, 124, 125, 144, 148, 150, 151, 157
Bronzeville (Chicago), 48. *See also* South Side (Chicago)
Brooklyn (New York): Bedford-Stuyvesant, 213; black population in, 5, 114, 131; cultural depictions of, 182n20, 232, 277; gentrification, 255, 256, 268, 277; Jewish "ghettos," 88n30
Brotherhood of Sleeping Car Porters, 120, 156, 207
The Brotherhood/Sister Sol, 288
Brother to Brother (Evans), 222, 232–35
Brown, Egbert Ethelred, 126, 150
Brown, Sterling A., 6, 128, 140n85
Bunche, Ralph, 97
Burroughs, Williana Jones, 13, 147, 153–55, 156, 159, 161

Cadogan, Edith, 118
Calloway, Cab, 52
Calverton, V. F., 29
Campbell, E. Simms: background, 51, 68n20; idea of black modernity, 12, 48–55, 56, 58, *figure 2.5*; cartoon series, 11–12, 47, 60, 65–66; on class divisions, 63–65; knowledge of New York City, 51–53, 60, 63; and political movements, 55–58, *figure 2.3*; depiction of women, 57, 60–63, *figure 2.4*. *See also* "Harlem Sketches" (Campbell)
Campbell, Grace, 4, 13, 112, 118, 147, 148–53, 154, 155, 159, 161, 208; Harlem Tenants League

(HTL), 155, 156, 157; residence, 148, 162n14, *figure 6.1*
Cane (Toomer), 176
Caribbean (region), 49, 111, 113, 139–40n78, 167
Caribbean migrants: 4, 48, 114, 115–16, 147, 151, 155–56, 168, 170; settlement in Harlem, 116, 171; tensions with African Americans, 82, 122, 170, 177
Castro, Fidel, 213
Cayton, Horace, 72
Central Park, 261
Césaire, Aimé, 127, 139n76
Chestnut, J. L., Jr., 10
Chicago: black community, 144, 203, 209; black population of, 6–7, 114, 119, 123, 127, 135n11; gentrification, 44n44, 268; compared to Harlem, 10, 13, 28, 48, 112, 114–15, 118, 130, 135n11, 136n31, 146, 158, 165, 204, 209; housing in, 119, 136n31; migration, and, 115, 121, 148; numbers (gambling), 54, 188; print media, 35, 48, 124; riot (1919), 28; writers, 92, 94, 130. *See also* South Side (Chicago)
Chicago Defender, 33, 49, 51, 65, 125. *See also* black press
Chocolate Dandies (Blake and Sissle), 180
Citizens Committee for the Schomburg, 36
"City of Refuge" (Fisher), 82, 111, 165, 169–70
civil rights movement: footage, 232; Harlem as organizational hub, 15, 201–3, 209, 212–13, 215; historiography on, 202, 206, 209, 211, 215; across New York City, 207–12; and other U.S. cities, 203. *See also specific organizations and leaders*
Clark, Kenneth B., 36, 76, 102
Clark, Mamie, 36
Clarke, John Henrik, 19n32
Clarke, Shirley, 91, 98–101, 104, 107n39
Clayton, Buck, 14
Clingman, James, 274–75
Cohn, Arthur, 92–94, 95, 98, 104
Columbia University, 99, 261, 267, 268
Communist Party of the United States of America (CPUSA): and African Blood Brotherhood, 151; black women members, 147, 148, 153, 154, 155, 156, 157; in Harlem, 151, 158, 205, 206, 214
community development corporations (CDCs), 249–50. *See also* Harlem Urban Development Corporation (HUDC) and Urban Development Corporation (UDC)
"community rights" (King), 4, 156–57, 199n25
"congregation," 12, 73–74, 76, 78, 80–83, 87n9
Congress of Racial Equality (CORE), 101, 211, 214
Connie's Inn (New York), 51, *figure 2.1*
Cooke, Marvel, 208
Coolidge, Calvin, 77
Cool World (Clarke), 91, 98–101, 102, 104, 107n39
Cool World (Miller), 98
"Cordelia, the Crude" (Thurman), 176–77, 178
Cotton Comes to Harlem (Himes), 103–4
Cotton Comes to Harlem (Davis), 103–4, 108n55
Couple in Raccoon Coats (VanDerZee), 60
Crisis, 124, 206
Crusader, 124, 125, 148, 150
Cruse, Harold, 215
Cullen, Countee, 76, 231, 271

"culture capital," idea of (Johnson), 166–69, 180
Cunard, Nancy, 116
Cuomo, Andrew, 267

Damas, Léon-Gontran, 139n76
Dancemobile, 228
Dapper Dan, 279
Dark Ghetto (Clark), 76
Dark Princess (Du Bois), 6
Davis, Angela, 288
Davis, Benjamin, 112, 205
Davis, Ossie, 103–4, 286
DeCarava, Roy, 92
Dee, Ruby, 286
Delany, Samuel R., 231, 236, 239n42
Díaz, Junot, 288
Dinkins, David N., 16, 250–52, 263
Domingo, W. A., 119; business, and, 120, 137n36; newspaper editor, 124, 155, 204–5; radicalism, 151
"Don't Buy Where You Can't Work," 210, 275. *See also* economic boycotts
Douglas, Aaron, 40–41, 130, 234
Douglass, Frederick, 30
Drake, St. Clair, 72
dream books, 190. *See also* numbers (gambling)
Du Bois, W. E. B., 41, 118, 182n19; *Dark Princess*, 6; in Harlem, 112, 144, 150, 206; view of black urban life, 124, 182n19, 185, 198n6, 226. *See also* National Association for the Advancement of Colored People (NAACP)
Duhamel, Marcel, 101
Dunbar, Paul Laurence, 167
"Durham" (Frazier), 81

East Village (New York), 285
economic boycotts, 206, 210, 273, 275. *See also* "Don't Buy Where You Can't Work"
Edgecombe Avenue, 196
Elle, 279–80
Ellington, Duke, 37, 40–41, 76, 112, 269, 280
Ellison, Ralph: on Harlem, 5, 28, 30, 41; idea of ghetto, 85, 90n63; relationship with Chester Himes, 97, 107n32
Emancipator, 124, 125, 155
Emperor Jones (O'Neill), 179
Empire Friendly Shelter, 148, 150, 154, 162n14, figure 6.1
"End to the Neglect of the Problem of the Negro Woman!" (Jones), 159–60, 162n7
Engels, Friedrich, 150
English, Daylanne K., 29, 82–83
"Enter the New Negro" (Locke), 75, 78, 81
Escape from New York (Baldwin and Makalani), 2, 66n3, 216n5
Espaillat, Adriano D., 16, 201
Esquire, 47, 51, 60, 64–65
Ethiopia. *See* Abyssinia
Europe, James Reese, 167
Evans, Rodney, 222, 232–33, 234–35
exceptionalism, 9, 140n82. *See also* Harlem exceptionalism

Fauset, Jessie, 3
Federal Bureau of Investigation (FBI), 183

Ferris, William H., 150
"Few Know Real Harlem" (Rapp and Thurman), 179
"Fifth Avenue, Uptown" (Baldwin), 84
Fire!! (magazine), 123, 176, 234, 239n30
Fisher, Rudolph: compared to other writers, 171, 176, 178; literary fiction about Harlem, 14, 82, 112, 131, 166, 169–70, 180; observations on Harlem, 118–19
Fitzgerald, Ella, 37, 269
Florence Mills Social Parlour and Afro-Restaurant (London), 146
"Foolish Man Blues" (Smith), 181n18
Force of Evil (Polonsky), 183, 187, 196–97
For Love of Imabelle (Himes), 91, 93, 94, 99
Foster, William, 158
Frazier, E. Franklin, 81, 272
Frederick Douglass Bookstore, 146

Gaisseau, Pierre-Dominique, 92–93, 105n6, 106n10
Garvey, Amy Ashwood, 123, 145, 146
Garvey, Amy Jacques, 112, 205
Garvey, Marcus: cultural depictions of, 55, 56, 177, 182n27; ideology of, 4, 133, 168, 194, 205, 244; in Harlem, 4, 15, 32, 56, 73, 112, 120, 121, 122, 123, 126, 127, 130, 144, 187, 202, 205, 207, 208, 210; influence on later leaders, 210, 212; *Negro World*, and, 49, 125, 168, 205, 219n35. *See also* Universal Negro Improvement Association (UNIA)
"Garvey Must Go," 122, 127
Garvin, Vicki, 212
Gates, Henry Louis, Jr., 30, 88n32, 89n49, 231
Gay Gotham (exhibition), 236
Gentleman Jigger (Nugent), 222, 225, 227, 228, 229–30
gentrification: in New York City, 248, 252, 255–56, 263; in U.S. cities, 268
gentrification, Harlem: role of city government, 244, 246–47, 252, 256, 263; cultural industries, 276–82; demographic change, and, 17n1, 258–59, 275, 285, figure 11.4; "new Harlem Renaissance," 1, 17, 252, 269; opposition to, 214, 243, 257, 258–59, 260; press coverage, 247, 249, 252, 255–56, 275–76, 281–82; and queer space, 235–36; symbol of, 1–3, 16–17, 201, 243, 247, 255, 262–63
ghetto: disease imagery, 89n58, 94; Harlem as symbol of, 5, 12, 71–72, 85, 99, 269, 270, 271; and "race capital" idea, 5, 72–74, 78, 83, 84, 85–86, 90n63; and "slum," 77; use of term, 5, 72, 84–85, 105n3
Gill, Jonathan, 183
Gilroy, Paul, 7, 28, 30
Giovanni, Nikki, 34
Giuliani, Rudolph, 251
Gone Are the Days (Davis), 104, 108n58
GQ, 280–81
Great Depression, 5, 34, 48, 72, 91–92, 206, 208, 271
Greater Fisk Herald, 6
Greater New York Coordinating Committee for Employment, 210
Great Migration: black press, and, 49; cultural depictions of, 14, 167, 169, 171, 176–77, 178, 236; migrants, relations with Caribbean immigrants, 48, 117–18; and "race capital" idea, 76, 116, 204; second phase of, 85, 203; U.S. states as origins of, 114–16; 190–91, 206, 208. *See also* immigration

Greenwich Village (New York), 132, 222, 285
Grimké, Angelina, 76
Grunwald, Michael, 252

Haldeman-Julius Quarterly, 84
"Hampton-Tuskegee" (Moton), 81
Hansberry, Lorraine, 92
Hare, Nathan, 272
Harlem: boundaries of, 83, 264n3, 268, 270, 276, 277; compared to, Central American cities, 7, 139n78; compared to, Chicago, 10, 13, 28, 48, 112, 114–15, 118, 130, 135n11, 136n31, 146, 158, 165, 204; compared to, London, 7, 112, 114, 126–29, 232; compared to, Paris, 7, 112, 114, 126–29; compared to, Washington, DC, 3, 28, 131; cultural exchange in, 113, 118–22, 133, 137n44, 166–68, 172, 180; dense public sphere, 4, 13–14, 48, 53, 112, 121, 125–26, 144–46, 205–6; drugs, and, 35, 212, 214, 248–49, 286; gentrification (*see* gentrification, Harlem); ghetto (*see* ghetto: Harlem as symbol of); housing (*see* housing, in Harlem); international interest in, 5, 14, 34, 39, 49, 92–93, 276–77; and political power, 4, 114, 121–22, 201–3, 205–6, 209, 212–14; population of, 1, 3, 5, 16, 17n1, 33, 48 114–17, 118–19, 122–23, 135n11, 146, 166, 179, 245, 248, 252–53, 257–61, 270–71, *figures* 11.1, 11.4–11.8; as race capital (*see* race capital); segregation, and, 6, 18n12, 166, 273, 286; setting and symbol, 3, 5, 7, 10, 15, 17, 19n28, 40, 75, 169, 176, 212, 224; social structure, 63–65, 85, 97, 131–32, 248, 252–54, 257, 259, 262, *figures* 2.5, 11.3; sociological accounts of, 10, 51, 74, 94, 100, 102, 185; symbol of black modernity, 3, 9–10, 12, 30–32, 41, 48, 50–53, 59, 65–66, 74, 76, 112, 165–66, 176, 182n20, 204–5, 222, 225–26, 269; tourists, 39–40, 51, 252, 287; visual representations of, 9–10, 12–13, 48, 53, 56, 59, 65, 91–92, 99, 105n3, 196–97, 232–35, 269–70, 276–77, 279–82, *figures* 2.1–2.5, 12.1; women, and, 60–63, 95–98, 117, 144–47, 208–9, 245
Harlem (Gill), 183–84
Harlem (magazine), 165
Harlem: A Melodrama (Thurman and Rapp), 165, 169, 182n24, 182n27
"Harlem: An American Cancer" (Himes), 94
"Harlem: A Vivid Word Picture" (Thurman), 84
Harlem Congregations for Community Improvement (HCCI), 251
Harlem Cultural Council (HCC), 36, 228
"Harlem Drape," 14, 70n72
Harlem Educational Forum (HEF), 126, 150–51, 152–53, 154, *figure* 6.1
Harlemese (idiom), 14, 23n75, 166, 170, 172, 176, 180
Harlem exceptionalism: critiques of, 7–9, 13, 18n5, 140n85, 146, 224–25, 236; idea of, 2–8, 11, 12, 13–14, 18n12, 27–29, 31–32, 81, 111, 128–29, 184, 202–3
"Harlem Facets" (Thurman and Rapp), 85, 118
Harlem Fashion Week, 276, 277
"Harlem Gang Leader" (Parks), 99
"Harlem Hellfighters" (369th Infantry Regiment), 53, 167, 205
Harlem Hospital, 120
Harlem Housewives League, 206
"Harlem: Mecca of the New Negro" (special issue), 2–3, 27, 144, 185, 283n12. *See also Survey Graphic*
Harlem: Negro Metropolis (McKay), 165
Harlem on My Mind (exhibition), 36, 236
Harlem Renaissance, 281, 286; criticism of, 2, 6, 89n49, 128, 221; cultural memory of, 1, 17, 28, 37, 92, 221–23, 229, 232–36, 252, 269, 270–71, 282n7; numbers (gambling), and, 185, 190, 197; scholarship on, 2, 6–7, 71–72, 82–83, 221–23, 225–26, 227, 236; use of term, 1, 3, 6–7, 17, 34, 37, 71, 90n63, 232, 236; writers associated with, 71, 92, 127, 130, 165–66, 185, 197, 221, 225–26, 231. *See also* "new Harlem Renaissance"
Harlem riots (1935, 1943, 1964), 56, 86n1, 213: effects on Harlem's symbolism, 34, 71–72, 85, 213; template for urban rebellions, 206, 210. *See also* urban uprisings
Harlem Shadows (McKay), 4, 165
"Harlem Sketches" (Campbell): aesthetics, 50, 55, 56, 59; demise, 65–66; "Harlem" as symbol of black urban modernity, 50, 52–55, 63, *figure* 2.2; humor, 49–50, 58, *figure* 2.3; title, 47, 65; women, depictions of, 60–63
"Harlem's Rattlers," 205. *See also* "Harlem Hellfighters" (369th Infantry Regiment)
Harlem Tenants Council (HTC), 214, 260, 283n10
Harlem Tenants League (HTL), 155, 156–58, *figure* 6.1
"Harlem: The Culture Capital" (Johnson), 80, 81, 166–67, 168
Harlem Urban Development Corporation (HUDC), 35–36, 37, 249–50
Harlem USA (radio program), 65
Harlem Village Academies (HVA), 277–79
Harlem Week, 37
Harrington, Michael, 5, 35
Harrington, Ollie, 51
Harris, Joel Chandler, 30
Harrison, Hubert: Harlem radicals, 112, 144, 149, 153, 154, 204, 205, 212; Liberty League, 124; public speaker, 121, 125, 148, 149, 153, 154, 204; role as editor, 125, 205; Socialist Party of America, 153
Haywood, Harry, 204
Hedgeman, Anna Arnold, 211
Hell's Kitchen (New York), 277, 285
Henderson, David, 213
Hendrickson, Elizabeth, 13, 147, 155–58, 159, 161
Hendrix, Jimi, 28
Hernton, Calvin, 213
Heyward, DuBose, 29, 179
Hill District (Pittsburgh), 48
Himes, Chester: early career, 92, 105n2, 107n28; depiction of Harlem, 5, 90n63, 92–94, 103–4; literary style, 12–13, 93, 99, 102, 104; and National Association for the Advancement of Colored People (NAACP), 95–98; relations with Ralph Ellison, 107n32
Himes, Chester, works by: *Baby Sister* 91–102, 104–5; *Cotton Comes to Harlem*, 103–4; *For Love of Imabelle*, 91, 93, 94, 99; "Harlem: An American Cancer," 94; *If He Hollers Let Him Go*, 91, 101; *Mamie Mason*, 97–98, 107n33
Hill, Herbert, 98, 102, 107n35
hip-hop, 270, 277, 280, 281

Holiday, Billie, 112, 286
Hollywood, 92, 96–97, 105n2, 108n55, 183; "message movies," 95; and National Association for the Advancement of Colored People (NAACP), 95, 107n35. *See also specific films and directors*
Holstein, Casper, 183–84, 187, 197
Home to Harlem (McKay), 4, 83, 165, 169, 173–76, 182n20, 198n6
Hotel Theresa, 213, 270
housing, in Harlem, *figure* 11.2; architecture, 38–39, 48, 79, 247, 269, 277, 286; condition of, 35, 74, 94, 99, 126, 248, 251, 252, *figure* 12.1; cost of, 48, 74, 79, 85, 119, 126, 136n31, 141n96, 157, 166, 254, 259–60, 263, *figures* 11.5, 11.7; historic preservation, 37, 39; overcrowding, 13, 48, 74, 79, 99, 118–19; policies, 1–2, 16, 245–52, 256, 257, 263, 273; protests about, 150, 156–57, 161, 210, 260–61
Housing Question (Engels), 150
"Howard" (Miller), 81
Howard University, 3, 31, 148, 155
Hughes, Langston: in Harlem, 112, 132, 185, 232, 234, 286; literary fiction, 50, 65, 123, 131, 132, 143, 173, 180, 182n32, 226; New Negroes, and, 75, 76, 123, 226; queer studies, and, 231, 232, 233, 234; views of Harlem, 5, 85, 90n63, 92, 112, 130, 131, 185. *See also Looking for Langston* (Julien)
Huggins, Nathan Irvin, 7, 72
Huiswoud, Hermina Dumont, 157
Huiswoud, Otto, 118, 158
Hunton, Eunice Roberta: career, 71, 86n1; "Breaking Through," 71, 73, 74–75, 76, 80, 81, 82; omission from *New Negro*, 71, 81; on segregation, 74, 76, 82; and ghetto, 72, 73, 75, 77, 80, 81, 82, 84
Hurston, Zora Neale, 14, 165, 170–73, 182n32
Hutson, Jean Blackwell, 36, 145, 237n8

"identity economics" (Akerlof and Kranton), 272–73, 274–75, 281–82
If He Hollers Let Him Go (Himes), 91, 101
Ighner, Bernard, 278
immigration: Caribbean, 4, 147, 155; demographics of, 117, 136n25; and immigrants, relations with African Americans, 117–18, 122; Italian, 137n44; restrictions on, 5, 122. *See also* Great Migration; Johnson-Reed Act
Infants of the Spring (Thurman), 221, 222, 225, 229
International Key Women of America, 245

Jackson, Esther Cooper, 208
Jackson, Louise, 150
Jamaica, Queens (New York), 5, 153
James, Kathleen, 118
James, William, M., 249–50
jazz: and Harlem, 121, 143, 281; as literary inspiration, 131, 143, 168, 169, 173, 175, 178, 179, 180; musicians, 118, 205
Jazzmobile, 224, 228
Jeremiah, the Magnificent (Thurman and Rapp), 182n21, 182n27
Jim Crow: ideology of, 29–30; protests against, 124, 160, 205, 206–7; urban conditions, and, 41, 73–74, 82, 94, 160. *See also* Harlem: segregation

Johnson, Charles S., 3
Johnson, James Weldon, 63; and Claude McKay, 173; "culture capital" idea, 14, 166–67; disavowal of "ghetto" term, 77, 79–80; futurity, 17, 29, 32–33; Harlem exceptionalism, 3, 4, 27–28, 50, 73, 74, 78–79, 121, 174, 178; and Hubert Harrison, 148; parents, 118; uplift, 181n10
Johnson, James Weldon, works by: *Autobiography of an Ex-Colored Man*, 167; *Black Manhattan*, 4, 32–33, 43n30, 167; *Book of American Negro Poetry*, 167–68; "Making of Harlem," 78, 84; "Harlem: The Culture Capital," 80, 81, 168
Johnson, Bumpy, 194
Johnson-Reed Act, 5, 77, 122, 168
Jones, Claudia, 146, 147, 158–61
Julian, Hubert, 53
Julien, Isaac, 222, 232–33, 235

Kallen, Horace, 77, 88n24
Kamoinge Workshop, 9
Kaufman, Bob, 40
Kelley, Robin D. G., 39, 87n9, 158
Kellogg, Paul, 9, 74, 76, 81
King, Martin Luther, Jr., 206, 211
King, Shannon, 157. *See also* "community rights" (King)
Klein, Calvin, 278–79
Knight, Gwendolyn, 117
Koch, Edward I., 247–48, 250–51
Kranton, Rachel E., 272–73
Ku Klux Klan, 75, 76
Kunjufu, Jawanza, 274

Lafayette Hall, 150
Lafayette Theatre, 51, 126, *figures* 2.1, 6.1
Lane, Winthrop D., 74, 78, 81, 82, 185
La Revue de Paris, 5
Larsen, Nella, 83, 271
Lawrence, Jacob, 117
Le Ciel et la Boue (Gaisseau), 92–93, 107n38
Lee, Canada, 118
Lee, Carl, 98, 100, 107n39
Lee, Elliott D., 247, 255
Levine, Joseph E., 98, 107n38
Lewis, David Levering, 7, 40, 223, 270–71
Lewis, Earl, 73
Lewis, Mollie, 97
Liberty Hall, 126, 205, *figure* 6.1. *See also* Universal Negro Improvement Association (UNIA)
Liberty League, 124
Lieberman, Jeff L., 236
Locke, Alain: critiques of, 14, 72, 76, 167–68, 169, 182n19; "cultural pluralism," 74, 76, 88n24; futurity, 11, 23n74, 27, 29, 30–32; ghetto imagery, 73, 75, 77–78, 82, 83, 85, 88n41, 89n58; "race capital" idea, 2–4, 10, 14, 33, 35, 50, 73, 77–81, 83, 116, 129, 133, 134, 166, 170, 172, 178, 227; role as editor, 19n28, 43n31, 71, 73, 74–75, 80–81, 82, 144, 185, 225–26, 237n8; sexuality, and, 225–26, 231
Locke, Alain, works by: "Enter the New Negro," 75, 78, 81; "Harlem: Mecca of the New Negro," 2–3, 27, 144, 185, 283n12; "New Negro," 81, 166, 226; *New Negro*, 29, 32, 33, 71, 74, 80–83, 144, 167, 169, 170, 185

298 Index

London: black internationalism, 7, 13, 113, 146; Claude McKay, and, 119, 129; compared to Harlem, 7, 112, 114, 126–29, 232
Long Way from Home (McKay), 143
Looking for Langston (Julien), 222, 232–33
Lorde, Audre, 126, 209, 288
Louise's Family Restaurant, 287, 288
Louis, Joe, 122
L'Ouverture, Toussaint, 36, 175
Luciano, Charles "Lucky," 71, 194
Lumumba, Patrice, 214

"Making of Harlem" (Johnson), 78, 84
Malcolm X: parents, 118; and Harlem radicals, 15, 209; ideas of, 212, 275; international status, 6, 210, 212–13, 215; symbolic association with Harlem, 37, 112, 206, 207, 208, 209, 211, 288
Mamie Mason (Himes), 97–98, 107n33
Manchester Guardian, 5
Marcantonio, Vito, 205
March on Washington (1963), 15, 103
March on Washington Movement (1940s), 15, 207, 211, 214, 218n27
Marcus Garvey Park, 257. *See also* Mount Morris Park
Marshall Hotel (New York), 167
Martin, Lucia, 213
McKay, Claude, 76, 112, 123, 151, 231, 271; and the black vernacular, 131–32, 165, 169, 173, 180, 182n19; commentator on Harlem, 114, 119, 121, 129, 130, 134, 143–44, 151; depiction of Harlem, 4, 14, 83, 120–21, 166, 169, 173–76, 182n20, 198n6; *négritude*, 127, 139n76; on intra-ethnic relations, 116, 117, 118, 119, 122, 137n50, 180
McKay, Claude, works by: *Banjo*, 120–21, 139n76; *Harlem: Negro Metropolis*, 165; *Harlem Shadows*, 4, 165; *Home to Harlem*, 4, 83, 165, 169, 173–176, 182n20, 198n6; "If We Must Die," 123
"Mecca" (Brown), 6
Messenger, 75, 124, 125, 130, 138n56, 141n90, 205
Michaux, Lewis H., 209
Miller, Kelly, 6, 81, 126
Miller, Warren, 9, 98–99, 107n39
Montgomery Bus Boycott, 15, 206–7
Moon, Henry Lee, 97, 107n30
Moore, Audley "Queen Mother," 126, 208, 212
Moore, Natalie Y., 268
Moore, Richard B.: editor, 124, 125, 155; in Harlem, 112, 118; Harlem Educational Forum, 150, 151; Harlem Tenants League, 156, 157; radical organizer, 144, 146, 151, 153
Morningside Park, 261
Moton, Robert, 81, 124
Mount Morris Baths, 236
Mount Morris Park, 38. *See also* Marcus Garvey Park
Moynihan Report, 19n28
Mule Bone (Hughes and Hurston), 180, 182n32
Murray, Albert, 37, 102
Murray, Pauli, 208, 218n27, 286
Museum of the City of New York, 236, 276
My Harlem (Lieberman), 236–37

Nail, John E., 78
Nardal, Jane, 146
Nardal, Paulette, 146
National Association for the Advancement of Colored People (NAACP): film industry, and, 95, 103, 107n35; members of, 78, 86n1, 97, 98, 153, 208, 218n27; New Negroes, and, 124; in New York, 4, 53, 130, 205–6, 207, 208–9; opposition to *Baby Sister*, 91, 92, 95–98, 104, 105; opposition to sensationalism, 13, 93
National Negro Congress (NNC), 207, 214
National Urban League (NUL), 4, 97, 101, 130, 207
Nation of Islam, 212
Neal, Larry, 35
négritude, 127, 139n76
Negro Ghetto (Weaver), 34
"Negro Life in New York's Harlem" (Thurman), 84, 168
Negro World, 49, 124, 125, 141n90, 150, 205, 219n35
"new Harlem Renaissance," 1, 17, 252, 269
New Housing Marketplace Plan, 257
"New Negro" (Locke), 81, 166, 226
New Negro (Locke), 144; contents, 71, 74, 169, 185; depiction of Harlem, 32, 33, 81, 82, 83, 167, 170; ghetto imagery in, 80, 81–82; reviews, 29. *See also Survey Graphic*
New Negroes: beyond New York, 6, 66n3, 81, 127–28, 144–45; demographics of, 122–23; as Harlem promoters, 3, 12, 30, 32, 50, 73, 75–76, 77, 88n32; numbers (gambling), 15, 194–95, 197–98; queering of, 223–24, 225–28, 229, 236, 238n19; radicalism of, 123–26, 149–50, 154, 204, 205, 206; use of term, 75, 165, 205; women, 144, 147, 149–50. *See also* race capital
New York Age, 32–33, 49, 124, 149, 189–190, 194
New York Amsterdam News, 124; gentrification, 249–50; "Harlem Sketches" (Campbell) printed in, 47, 49, 51, 52, 58, 75n69, *figure* 2.2; numbers (gambling), 193, 194. *See also* black press
New York City, 3, 112, 118, 130; antidiscrimination laws, 207–8; boroughs of, 5; fashion capital, 63, 171; population, general, 16, 114, 115, 135n11, *figure* 11.4; population, Latinx, 253, 255, 258; queer artists, 236
New York Times: use of "ghetto" term, 84–85, 88n30; on Harlem's transformation, 17n1, 201, 258, 262, 287; literary reviews, 179; numbers (gambling), 187, 198
"Niggeratti Manor," 232, 234
Nigger Heaven (Van Vechten), 225
Night-Club Map of Harlem (Campbell), 51, *figure* 2.1
Nixon, E. D., 206–7
Nkrumah, Kwame, 213
Nnadi, Chioma, 277–79
Not Without Laughter (Hughes), 173
Nugent, Richard Bruce: as Black Dandy, 222, 225–26, 238n19; and film, 222, 232–35; *Gentleman Jigger*, 222, 225, 227, 228, 229–30; as historiographer, 16, 222–23, 230–31, 239n30; literary fiction, 221, 226–31; queer Harlem, 132, 222–25, 230; "Smoke, Lilies and Jade," 222, 225, 226–28, 230, 231, 233, 237n3, 239n30
numbers (gambling): beyond New York City, 54, 189; and business history, 184, 186–87, 192;

cultural depictions of, 183–84, 185, 187, 195–97; game of, 184, 187–90; in Harlem, 54, 60, 184–85, 194–95, *figure* 2.1; police, and, 190–93. *See also* race capital: economic meanings

135th Street Library. *See* Schomburg Center for Research in Black Culture
O'Neill, Eugene, 179
Only One New York (Gaisseau), 106n10
Opportunity, 171, 197
Organization of Afro-American Unity, 215
Ormes, Jackie, 51
Ortiz, Fernando, 113
Osman Pasha (Rapp), 176
Osofsky, Gilbert, 7, 72
Ottley, Roi, 4, 12, 116, 118
Owen, Chandler, 4, 124, 125, 173

Padmore, George, 127
Pan-Africanism, 113, 125; Alain Locke, and, 23n74; cultural depictions of, 56, 58, 175; in Harlem, 112, 117, 120, 134, 205, 213–14, 215, 288; Marcus Garvey, and, 125
Paris: black internationalism, 7, 13, 92, 113, 114, 146, 165; as capital, 11; compared to Harlem, 7, 112, 114, 126–29
Parks, Gordon, 64, 99
Parks, Rosa, 206, 207
Passing (Larsen), 83
Patrice Lumumba Coalition, 214
Patterson, Louise Thompson, 147, 158
People's Educational Forum (PEF). *See* Harlem Educational Forum (HEF)
Perl, Arnold, 104
Petry, Ann, 5, 41, 65, 208, 286
"Photographic Report on Harlem" (Kamoinge Workshop), 10
Pickens, William, 153
Pinktoes (Himes), 97–98, 101, 107n33
Pittsburgh Courier: black fiction in, 169, 171, 172–73; circulation, 49, 67n11; use of "ghetto" term, 84; "Harlem Sketches" (Campbell), printed in, 47, 52–53, 65, *figures* 2.3–2.5; New York coverage, 27, 47, 49, 65, 207. *See also* black press
place-making, concepts of, 22n57, 50: "black spatial imaginary" (Lipsitz), 244–46; "community rights" (King), 4, 199n25; "congregation," 73–74, 76; "Harlemworld" (Jackson), 253–54, 275–77; "provincializing" (Putnam), 2, 7, 139n78; queer studies, and, 224–25; "return address" (Purnell), 15, 202–3, 209, 219n35; social spaces, 9, 13, 146, 147, 153–54, 158
place-making, Harlem as site of: 2–4, 5, 8–12, 15–16, 17, 50–51, 73–74, 75–77, 83, 96–97, 270, 272–77; "unplaceability," 102–3, 196–97
Plan for New York City, 1969 (New York City Planning Commission), 34, 85
Poitier, Sidney, 95, 286
Polonsky, Abraham, 183, 187, 197
Porgy (Heyward), 179
Powell, Adam Clayton, Jr., 182n24, 226; political leader, 15, 112, 201, 207, 209–10, 214, 218n27;

symbolic association with Harlem, 37, 209–10, 211
Powell, Adam Clayton, Sr., 132, 209
PowerNomics, 274
Preacely, Peggy Trotter Dammond, 209, 211
Purlie Victorius (Davis), 103–4
Putnam, Lara, 139–40n78

Queens (New York), 5, 256
Queer Harlem, 16, 132, 166, 182n19, 221, 222–24, 226, 230, 231, 235
Quicksand (Larsen), 83

race capital, 2–6, 48, 50, 53, 76, 80–81, 129, 134, 166–67, 180, 201–2, 262, 282; class, and, 3, 91–92, 271, 277; economic meanings, 14–15, 185, 197, 270–75, 281–82; gender, and, 13–14, 144, 208; gentrification, and, 6, 243, 247, 262, 270, 275–76, 281; ghetto, and, 5, 72–74, 76, 78, 83, 84, 85–86, 90n63; international perceptions of, 5, 34, 44n35, 210, 212–13; sexuality, and, 225–26, 227; temporality, and, 11, 28–29, 31–32, 35, 38, 40–41, 270–71. *See also* Harlem exceptionalism; New Negroes; Renaissance (European)
race film industry, 106n19
Rage in Harlem (Himes), 93
Raisin in the Sun (Hansberry), 92, 93
Randolph, A. Philip, 116; as editor, 124, 125, 173; and Harlem's radicals, 15, 124, 205, 206, 207–8, 210, 214, 218n26; symbolic association with Harlem, 4, 112, 126, 208, 211
Randolph, Lucille, 116
Rangel, Charles B., 201
Rapp, William Jourdan, 169, 176, 178, 179, 180, 182n21, 182n27
Razaf, Andy, 118
Reid, Ira De A., 120
Renaissance (European), 4, 31
Renaissance Complex, 38
Riverside Church, 99
Robeson, Paul, 208
Robinson, Sugar Ray, 37
Rockefeller, Nelson A., 249, 250
Rohan, Nanette, 117
Rollins, Sonny, 288
Roosevelt, Franklin D., 97, 207, 218n27
Rose, Ernestine, 145
Rustin, Bayard, 210, 211

San Juan Hill (New York), 48, 187
Schoell, Franck L., 5
Schomburg, Arturo, 33, 35, 117, 126, 145
Schomburg Center for Research in Black Culture (135th Street Library), 11, 29, 35–39, 126, 145, 208, 288
Schultz, Dutch, 185–86, 193–94, 195, 196
Schuyler, George S., 72, 272
Scottsboro case, 159, 229
"Second Harlem Renaissance." *See* "new Harlem Renaissance"
Selasi, Taiye, 141n100
Senghor, Léopold, 127, 139n76
Seventh Ward (Philadelphia), 48
Shaler, Nathaniel, 30

Shamberger, Eulace, 6
Shuffle Along (Blake and Sissle), 182n32
Shuffle Along (Wolfe), 182n32
Siege of Harlem (Miller), 9
Silent Protest Parade, 53
Sissle, Noble, 180
"Sketches." *See* "Harlem Sketches" (Campbell)
slavery: contrasted with later black progress, 48, 50, 65–66, 96; in New York City, 186; as temporal marker, 27
Smith, Bessie, 89n49, 143, 181n18, 182n24
"Smoke, Lilies and Jade" (Nugent), 222, 225, 226–28, 230, 231, 233, 237n3, 239n30
soapbox speakers, 4, 13, 58, 125–26, 145, 149, 206, 208
Socialist Party of America, 148, 149, 150, 151, 153, 155
Society of American-Soviet Friendship, 159
Southern Christian Leadership Conference (SCLC), 203, 206, 209, 211
Southern Road (Brown), 6
South Side (Chicago), 10, 48, 119, 165, 204, 268
St. Clair, Stephanie, 194
St. Nicholas Historic District. *See* Strivers' Row
St. Nicholas Park, 112
Stokes, Rose Pastor, 151
"Story in Harlem Slang" (Hurston), 171, 172
The Street (Petry), 286
street vendors, 79, 274
Strivers' Row, 38, 39, 59, 119, 174, 252, 270
Student Nonviolent Coordinating Committee (SNCC), 203, 209
The Studio Museum in Harlem, 35, 36, 39
suburbs, 16, 85, 94, 247, 269
Sugar Hill (New York), 59, 119, 206, 270
superexploitation, 158, 159–60
Survey Graphic, 9, 31; advertisements in, 78; contents, 71, 73, 74–77, 185; depictions of Harlem, 2–3, 9, 27, 30, 72, 77–78, 80, 81, 83, 144; Harlem riot (1935), 85; reviews, 5. *See also* "Harlem: Mecca of the New Negro" (special issue)
Sweet Flypaper of Life (Hughes and DeCarava), 92
Sylvia's (restaurant), 279, 287

Taylor, Edward K., Jr., 36
Tenderloin Riot (1900), 4
Their Eyes Were Watching God (Hurston), 172
This Was Harlem (Anderson), 28, 271
Thurman, Wallace, 116, 123; collaborations with William Jourdan Rapp, 176–80, 182n21, 182n27; on cosmopolitanism, 111, 118, 168; depiction of Harlem, 14, 84, 85, 165, 166, 169, 189; depiction of Harlem writers, 221, 222, 225, 227, 228, 230, 234, 239n30; sexuality of, 231
Thurman, Wallace, works by: *Blacker the Berry*, 123; "Cordelia, the Crude," 176–77, 178; "Few Know Real Harlem", 179; *Harlem: A Melodrama*, 169, 176–79; "Harlem: A Vivid Word Picture," 84; "Harlem Facets," 85, 118; *Infants of the Spring*, 221, 222, 225, 229; "Negro Life in New York's Harlem," 84, 168
Tillie's Chicken Shack (restaurant), 52, *figure* 2.1
Tin Pan Alley, 48

Tolson, Melvin, 34
Toomer, Jean, 176
Touré, Sékou, 213
Tucker's People (Wolfert), 195–97

Uncle Remus, 168
Universal Negro Improvement Association (UNIA): in Harlem, 4, 15, 53, 73, 123, 125, 126, 130, 133, 205, 214, *figure* 6.1; membership, 57, 113, 130, 205; parodies of, 55, 57. *See also* Liberty Hall; *Negro World*
University of Chicago, 51, 268
uplift ideology, 12, 51, 95–97, 148, 185, 226
Uptown Chamber of Commerce, 39
urban crisis, 5, 35, 85
Urban Development Corporation (UDC), 36, 249, 250
Urban Homesteading Assistance Board, 247
Urban League. *See* National Urban League (NUL)
urban uprisings, 17, 72, 210. *See also* Harlem riots (1935, 1943, 1964)
Utopia Neighborhood House, 152

VanDerZee, James, 60
Van Vechten, Carl, 225, 234, 271
Vergara, Camilo José, 280
"Vestiges" (Fisher), 170
Virgin Islands Protective League, 155
Vogue, 276–77, 279, 280, *figure* 12.1
Vogue Italia. *See Vogue*

Wagner, Robert, 211
Walker, Juliet E. K., 186
Walker, Madam, 187
Waller, Fats, 121
Wall Street, 48, 54, 193, 197
Walrond, Eric, 118
Washington, Booker T., 75, 76, 124, 126
Washington, Isabel, 182n24
"wasness": built environment, 35–40, 275, 277; in culture industries, 17, 279–82, 282n7, 286–87, *figure* 12.1; Harlem as symbol of, 5, 11, 35–40, 275–76, 277, 279–81; queer temporality and, 223, 225, 226, 230, 231; race capital and, 28–29, 275; in scholarship, 28, 270–71
Waters, Ethel, 76
Weaver, Robert C., 34
West 135th Street YMCA, 193, 208
"What I Saw in Russia" (Pickens), 153
Wheatley, Phillis, 36, 167, 288
When Harlem Was in Vogue (Lewis), 223, 270–71
Whiteman, Paul, 89n49
White, Maude, 155, 157
White, Walter, 97, 218n27
Williams, John A., 98
Wiseman, Frederick, 100–101, 107n39
Wolfert, Ira, 183, 187, 195–97
Womack, Bobby, 86, 90n64
Wright, Richard, 10, 41, 92, 115

Yeah, Man (nightclub), 51, *figure* 2.1

zoot suit. *See* "Harlem Drape"

GPSR Authorized Representative: Easy Access System Europe, Mustamäe tee
50, 10621 Tallinn, Estonia, gpsr.requests@easproject.com

www.ingramcontent.com/pod-product-compliance
Lightning Source LLC
Chambersburg PA
CBHW021355290426
44108CB00010B/252